Automotive Electrical and Electronic Systems

Second Edition

By Chek-Chart,
a Division of
The H. M. Gousha Company

Roger Fennema, *Editor*

1817
HARPER & ROW, PUBLISHERS, New York
Cambridge, Philadelphia, San Francisco, Washington,
London, Mexico City, São Paulo, Sydney

Acknowledgments

In producing this series of textbooks for automobile mechanics and technicians, Chek-Chart has drawn extensively on the technical and editorial knowledge of the nation's carmakers and suppliers. Automotive design is a technical, fast-changing field, and we gratefully acknowledge the help of the following companies in allowing us to present the most up-to-date information and illustrations possible:

  Allen Testproducts
  American Motors Corporation
  Borg-Warner Corporation
  Caldo Automotive Supply
  Champion Spark Plug Company
  Chrysler Motors Corporation
  Coats Diagnostic (Hennessy Industries)
  Ford Motor Company
  Fram Corporation, A Bendix Company
  General Motors Corporation
  AC-Delco Division
  Delco-Remy Division
  Rochester Products Division
  Saginaw Steering Gear Division
  Buick Motor Division
  Cadillac Motor Car Division
  Chevrolet Motor Division
  Oldsmobile Division
  Pontiac Division
  Jaguar Cars, Inc.
  Marquette Mfg. Co. (Bear Mfg. Co.)
  Mazda Motor Corporation
  Nissan Motors
  The Prestolite Company, An Eltra Company
  Robert Bosch Corporation
  Sun Electric Corporation
  Toyota Motor Company
  Volkswagen of America

The authors have made every effort to ensure that the material in this book is as accurate and up-to-date as possible. However, neither Chek-Chart nor Harper & Row nor any related companies can be held responsible for mistakes or omissions, or for changes in procedures or specifications made by the carmakers or suppliers.

The comments, suggestions, and assistance of the following contributors were invaluable:
  Les Clark, Russ Suzuki, Angel Santiago, Al Bauer, and Bryan Wilson — General Motors Training Center, Burbank, Calif.
  Pete Egus — AC-Delco, Los Angeles, Calif.
  Robert Baier, Dan Rupp, Nick Backer, and Bill Takayama — Chrysler Training Center, Ontario, Calif.
  Robert Van Antwerp, Jim Milum, and Ed Moreland — Ford Training Center, La Mirada, Calif.
  Bob Kruse — Merry Oldsmobile, San Jose, Calif.

At Chek-Chart, Ray Lyons managed the production of this book. Original art and photographs were produced by Gordon Agur, Jim Geddes, C. J. Hepworth, Janet Jamieson, Kalton C. Lahue, and F. J. Zienty. The project is under the direction of Roger L. Fennema.

Library of Congress Cataloging and Publication Data:

Chek-Chart, 1987
  Automotive Electrical and Electronic Systems
  (Harper & Row/Chek-Chart Automotive Series)
v. 1. Classroom Manual.   v. 2. Shop Manual.

ISBN: 0-06-454014-6 (set)
Library of Congress Catalog Card No.: 87-8660

Contents

On the Cover:
Front—Assorted GM Computer Command Control Components, courtesy AC-Delco Division of the General Motors Corporation.
Rear—A late-model CS-series alternator and permanent magnet, planetary-drive starter, courtesy Delco Remy Division of the General Motors Corporation.

Contents

Introduction to Automotive Electrical and Electronic Systems

Automotive Electrical and Electronic Systems is part of the Harper & Row/Chek-Chart Automotive Series. The package for each course has two volumes, a *Classroom Manual* and a *Shop Manual*.

Other titles in this series include:
- Automatic Transmissions and Transaxles
- Automotive Brake Systems
- Automotive Engine Repair and Rebuilding
- Engine Performance Diagnosis and Tune-Up
- Fuel Systems and Emission Controls

Each book is written to help the instructor teach students to become excellent professional automotive mechanics. The 2-manual texts are the core of a complete learning system that leads a student from basic theories to actual hands-on experience.

The entire series is job-oriented, especially designed for students who intend to work in the car service profession. A student will be able to use the knowledge gained from these books and from the instructor to get and keep a job. Learning the material and techniques in these volumes is a giant leap toward a satisfying, rewarding career.

The books are divided into *Classroom Manuals* and *Shop Manuals* for an improved presentation of the descriptive information and study lessons, along with the practical testing, repair, and overhaul procedures. The manuals are to be used together: the descriptive chapters in the *Classroom Manual* correspond to the application chapters in the *Shop Manual*.

Each book is divided into several parts, and each of these parts is complete by itself. Instructors will find the chapters to be complete, readable, and well thought-out. Students will benefit from the many learning aids included, as well as from the thoroughness of the presentation.

The series was researched and written by the editorial staff of Chek-Chart, and was produced by Harper & Row Publishers. For over 58 years, Chek-Chart has provided car and equipment manufacturers' service specifications to the automotive service field. Chek-Chart's complete, up-to-date automotive data bank was used extensively to prepare this textbook series.

Because of the comprehensive material, the hundreds of high-quality illustrations, and the inclusion of the latest automotive technology, instructors and students alike will find that these books will keep their value over the years. In fact, they will form the core of the master mechanic's professional library.

How To Use This Book

Why Are There Two Manuals?

This two-volume text — **Automotive Electrical and Electronic Systems** — is not like any other textbook you've ever used before. It is actually two books, the *Classroom Manual* and the *Shop Manual*. They should be used together.

The *Classroom Manual* will teach you what you need to know about basic electricity and the electrical systems in a car. The *Shop Manual* will show you how to fix and adjust those systems, and how to repair the electrical parts of a car.

The *Classroom Manual* will be valuable in class and at home, for study and for reference. It has text and pictures that you can use for years to refresh your memory about the basics of automotive electrical and electronic systems.

In the *Shop Manual*, you will learn about test procedures, troubleshooting, and overhauling the systems and parts you are studying in the *Classroom Manual*. Use the two manuals together to fully understand how the parts work, and how to fix them when they don't work.

What's In These Manuals?

There are several aids in the *Classroom Manual* that will help you learn more:

1. The text is broken into short bits for easier understanding and review.

2. Each chapter is fully illustrated with drawings and photographs.

3. Key words in the text are printed in **boldface type** and are defined on the same page and in a glossary at the end of the manual.

4. Review questions are included for each chapter. Use these to test your knowledge.

5. A brief summary of every chapter will help you to review for exams.

6. Every few pages you will find short blocks of "nice to know" information, in addition to the main text.

7. At the back of the *Classroom Manual* there is a sample test, similar to those given for National Institute for Automotive Service Excellence (NIASE) certification. Use it to help you study and to prepare yourself when you are ready to be certified as an expert in one of several areas of automobile mechanics.

The *Shop Manual* has detailed instructions on overhaul, test, and service procedures. These are easy to understand, and may have step-by-step, photo-illustrated explanations that guide you through the procedures. This is what you'll find in the *Shop Manual:*

1. Helpful information tells you how to use and maintain shop tools and test equipment.
2. Safety precautions are detailed.
3. System diagrams help you locate trouble-spots while you learn to read the diagrams.
4. Tips the professionals use are presented clearly and accurately.
5. A full index will help you quickly find what you need.
6. Test procedures and troubleshooting hints will help you work better and faster.

Where Should I Begin?

If you already know something about a car's basic electrical and electronic systems, and how to repair them, you may find that parts of this book are a helpful review. If you are just starting in car repair, then the subjects covered in these manuals may be all new to you.

Your instructor will design a course to take advantage of what you already know, and what facilities and equipment are available to work with. You may be asked to take certain chapters of these manuals out of order. That's fine. The important thing is to really understand each subject before you move on to the next.

Study the vocabulary words in boldface type. Use the review questions to help you understand the material. While reading in the *Classroom Manual,* refer to your *Shop Manual* to relate the descriptive text to the service procedures. And when you are working on actual car systems and electrical parts, look back to the *Classroom Manual* to keep the basic information fresh in your mind. Working on such a complicated piece of equipment as a modern car isn't always easy. Use the information in the *Classroom Manual,* the procedures of the *Shop Manual,* and the knowledge of your instructor to help you.

The *Shop Manual* is a good book for work, not just a good workbook. Keep it on hand while you're working on equipment. It folds flat on the workbench and under the car, and can withstand quite a bit of rough handling.

When you do test procedures and overhaul equipment, you will also need a source of accurate manufacturers' specifications. Most auto shops have either the carmaker's annual shop service manuals, which lists these specifications, or an independent guide, such as the **Chek-Chart Car Care Guide.** This unique book, which is updated every year, gives you the complete service instructions, electronic ignition troubleshooting tips, and tune-up information that you need to work on specific cars.

PART ONE

Basic Electrical Test Procedures

1

Circuit Tracing, Troubleshooting, and Wiring Repair

Finding the cause of an electrical problem and then repairing that problem can be done either in a haphazard way or in a logical, organized manner. The hit-or-miss approach to electrical service is inefficient, inaccurate, and unacceptable. Time and effort can be wasted without solving the problem. An organized approach to service is often called troubleshooting. It consists of a step-by-step examination of the symptoms, isolation of the cause, and repair of the problem.

We begin by reviewing basic shop and vehicle system safety precautions, which are elementary to any automotive service situation. Then we'll review automotive wiring diagrams, which can be one of the troubleshooter's most helpful guides. Next, you will be introduced to the sources of specifications and procedures that are essential to successful troubleshooting. With this in hand, you then will be introduced to a 10-step troubleshooting checklist that can guide you through almost any electrical service job. Finally, some common wiring and connector repair procedures will be presented.

In Chapter 2, we will examine the use of common troubleshooting tools. Before troubleshooting any electrical problem, you should check the condition of the battery. Battery service is detailed in Chapter 3.

ELECTRICAL SAFETY

Most professional mechanics work for years without ever suffering a serious injury. By following a few common sense rules of safety, you can follow in their footsteps and avoid personal injury to yourself or to others in the vicinity.

Shop Service Safety

The following precautions should be observed whenever you perform any shop activity.
1. Know the location of shop first-aid supplies and the number to call for emergency medical assistance.
2. Never use gasoline as a cleaning solvent unless it is specifically recommended. If gasoline is used, have a fire extinguisher handy and exercise extreme caution.
3. All auto repair shops have flammable liquids and combustible materials. You can minimize fire hazards by not smoking within the shop area at any time.
4. Keep flames and sparks away from a charging battery. Highly explosive hydrogen gas forms during the charging process.
5. Do not arc the terminals of a battery to see if it is charged. The sparks can ignite the explosive hydrogen gas as easily as an open flame.

6. Always wear safety goggles in any area or during any job where an eye hazard could exist.

7. Remove all jewelry such as rings and watches before starting work. Remove sweaters, tuck in loose clothing, and tie back long hair.

8. If you are not sure how to use any tool, machine, or test equipment, ask your instructor about its safe operation before using it.

9. Make sure your hands, the floor, and your entire work space are dry before touching any electrical switches or plugs, or using any electrical equipment.

10. Keep floors, aisles, and your work area clear of all tools, parts, and materials. Mop up any spilled liquids immediately.

11. Do not carry sharp tools such as screwdrivers, awls, or scrapers in your pockets. Carry them in your hand with the cutting edge facing downward.

12. Make sure that any component you clamp in a vise is properly secured before you work on it.

13. Do not splash cleaning solvents when putting parts into, or removing them from, a cleaning tank.

14. If an air nozzle is used to dry the cleaned parts, make sure the airstream is directed away from yourself and anyone else in the immediate area.

15. Before starting an engine, be sure the parking brake is set, the drive wheels are blocked, and the transmission or transaxle is placed in neutral (manual) or Park (automatic).

16. Do not run the engine in a closed area or room. Connect the vehicle exhaust pipe to shop exhaust ducts or make sure there is sufficient ventilation to prevent the accumulation of poisonous exhaust gases.

17. Keep your hands and other body parts away from hot exhaust components. Catalytic converters heat up rapidly and retain their heat for a long time after the engine is shut off. If you must work around such objects when they are hot, wear safety gloves.

18. Do not drive a vehicle faster than five miles per hour in, or when entering or leaving, the shop area.

Vehicle System Safety

Observe the following precautions whenever you perform test or service procedure on a vehicle electrical system.

1. Always disconnect the negative battery cable:
   a. When working on or near the electrical system, unless a test procedure specifies otherwise.
   b. Before disconnecting any electrical wires, such as those attached to the alternator or starter.
On most batteries, the negative or ground terminal is marked with a minus ($-$) sign and the positive or insulated terminal with a plus ($+$) sign.

2. Make sure you connect the battery cables to their proper terminals. Connecting the cables backwards will reverse the polarity and can damage the alternator.

3. When charging a battery:
   a. Always connect a battery charger to the battery terminals before plugging the charger into the power outlet.
   b. Disconnect the battery cables or unplug the alternator to prevent possible damage to the electrical system from a voltage surge.

4. When jump starting a vehicle with a booster battery, always make the final ground connection on the engine or chassis instead of the battery itself. The electrical arc which can occur when this connection is made could cause an explosion if it occurs near the battery.

5. When disconnecting electrical wires:
   a. Always pull on the connector, if one is used.
   b. To remove wires from electrical components such as an HEI module, carefully pry the wires from the terminal with a small screwdriver blade. Pulling on the wire can cause internal damage.
   c. Remove a spark plug wire by twisting its boot ½ turn in both directions to break the seal, then pull upward on the boot to remove the wire from the plug terminal. Pulling on the wire can cause internal damage.

6. Always hold secondary wires with insulated pliers when doing an ignition system check.

7. Do not short circuit or ground any solid-state electronic components or electrical terminals, or apply battery voltage directly to electronic components, unless specified in a test procedure.

8. Refer to manufacturer's instructions when connecting older test equipment to breakerless ignition systems. Some older test equipment will not work properly and may even damage the system.

9. When servicing any electronic ignition or engine control system:
   a. Make sure the ignition is off before disconnecting or connecting the wiring harness connector to the control unit.

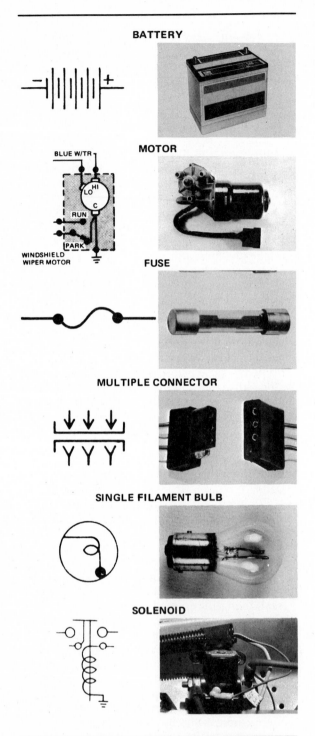

Figure 1-1. Here are some common automotive diagram symbols and the actual hardware that they represent.

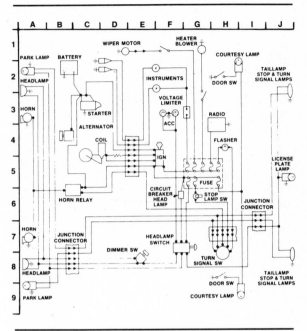

Figure 1-2. This simple system diagram has been divided into grids so that an index can be used.

b. Do not remove the grease used to prevent corrosion from the connectors.

10. When servicing any Chrysler electronic ignition or engine control system:

a. Do not touch the switching transistor on the control unit while the engine is running.

The high voltage present can produce a severe electrical shock.

b. Do not file the sharp edges of the reluctor teeth.

11. When servicing any Ford electronic ignition or engine control system:

a. Do not let the straight pin used to pierce wires for voltage checks touch ground.

b. Do not disconnect the spark plug wires directly above the pick-up coil. An arc from the wire may damage the pick-up coil.

12. When servicing the AMC-Prestolite electronic ignition, do not check continuity of the distributor sensor unit with a test lamp or connect the sensor to a 12-volt circuit.

TRACING SPECIFIC CIRCUITS

As we learned in Chapter 6 of the *Classroom Manual*, system and schematic or circuit diagrams are used to show you on paper what the electrical system of a particular car contains. These diagrams use color coding, circuit numbers, and symbols that you must be able to interpret. Figure 1-1 shows the symbols for some common automotive electrical components and photographs of the actual components.

When faced with the system diagram of an entire automobile, it may be difficult at first for you to locate and follow an individual circuit. However, once you get to know how the various automakers design their circuit diagrams, this will be easier. The first step in finding a

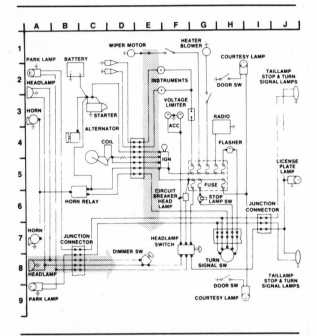

Figure 1-3. To find the dimmer switch, look in grid E8.

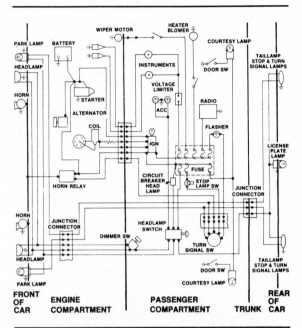

Figure 1-4. When no index is supplied, you must search the area of the diagram that corresponds to the area of the car in which the specific component is installed.

particular circuit is to check the index to the diagram, if one is provided.

Diagrams are usually indexed by grids, figure 1-2. The diagram is marked into equal sections like a street map. Each section is lettered along the top of the diagram and numbered along one side. The diagram's index will list a letter and number for each major part and many connection points, such as the fuse panel and the bulkhead connector. Figure 1-3 shows how to find a part when the letter and number of its grid are known.

If the diagram is not indexed, you must locate a major part by its location on the automobile. Most system diagrams are drawn so that the headlamps are on one side of the diagram and the taillamps are on the opposite side. The front of the car is usually on the left of the diagram, figure 1-4.

Once you have found a major part of the circuit you are looking for, the rest of the circuit can be easily traced. Sometimes it is helpful to place a blank sheet of paper on top of the system diagram and actually draw the individual circuit. Remember, the circuit must include:
- A power source
- All related loads
- A ground connection for each circuit branch.

You need to know how to interpret an electrical diagram and relate it to the automobile in order to troubleshoot an automobile. There is more to troubleshooting, however, than being able to understand the circuit that has failed.

SPECIFICATION AND SERVICE PROCEDURE SOURCES

Before you can successfully troubleshoot an automotive electrical system, you must have access to the necessary specifications or service procedures. Complete and accurate specifications are the only tool that will tell you how the system *should* operate. Without specifications, all the sophisticated test equipment in a shop is useless. Test results mean nothing until they are compared to specifications that indicate what the test results should be. Service procedures go hand-in-hand with specifications. You need to know the steps peculiar to a particular system in order to obtain the correct results. The following paragraphs describe what specifications and procedures are commonly available and where to find them.

The main sources of electrical specifications are:
- Manufacturer's service manuals
- Independent manuals.

Manufacturers usually publish a new service or factory shop manual for each model year, containing specifications for that model year only. However, the information is often divided and scattered throughout the manual, separated by the repair and overhaul information that is also included.

Independent manufacturers of replacement components, test equipment, and service man-

AMERICAN MOTORS
1978-87

UNDERHOOD SERVICE SPECIFICATIONS

AMTU1   AMTU1

CYLINDER NUMBERING SEQUENCE

4-CYL. FIRING ORDER: 1 3 4 2   6-CYL. FIRING ORDER: 1 5 3 6 2 4   8-CYL. FIRING ORDER: 1 8 4 3 6 5 7 2

1978-79 2.0L (121) eng.   1983-84 2.5L (150) AMC eng.   1980-83 2.5L (151) GM eng.   1978-79 3.8L (232), 1978-87 4.2L (258)   1978-79 304, 360 eng.

TIMING MARK

1978-79 2.0L (121) eng.   1984 2.5L (150) AMC, 1982-87 4.2L (258) eng.   1980-83 2.5L (151) GM eng.   1978-81 3.8L (232), 4.2L (258) eng.   1978-79 304, 360 eng.

BATTERY

Engine	Year	STANDARD BCI Group No.	STANDARD Crank. Perf.	OPTIONAL BCI Group No.	OPTIONAL Crank. Perf.
4-cyl.	1978	22F	305	—	—
	1979-83	55	380	56	450
	1984	55	370	—	—
6-cyl.	1978-79	22F	305	24	410
Pacer	1979	22F	305	24, 56	410, 450
Concord, AMX	1978-79	22F	305	24	410
Concord, AMX	1980-83	54	330	56	450
Eagle	1980	22F	305	56	450
Eagle	1981-82	54	305	56	450
Eagle	1983-87	54	320	56	450
8-cyl.					
304	1978	22F	305	24	440
Pacer	1978	22F	305	22F	385
304	1979	54	305	24	440
Pacer	1979	54	305	56	450
360	1978	24	385	24	440

COMPRESSION PRESSURE

At cranking speed or specified rpm, engine temperature normalized, throttle open.

Engine	Year	PSI	Maximum Variation PSI
121	1978-79	116-160	44
2.5L (151)	1980-83	140 @ 160 rpm	*
2.5L (150)	1984	155-185	30
All Others	1978-86	120-150	30

* Lowest cylinder pressure must be more than 70% of highest cylinder pressure.

IGNITION POINTS

Engine	Year	Gap (inches)	Gap (mm)	Dwell (degrees)	Spring Tension (ounces)
4-cyl.	1978-79	.018	.45	44-50	18-23

IGNITION PICKUP

Application	Resistance (ohms)	Air Gap (in./mm)
1978-79	400-800	.017 min.
1980-83 2.5L (151)	500-1500	—
1980-87 2.5L (150), 4.2L (258)	400-800	.017 min.

IGNITION COIL

Resistance (ohms at 75°F or 24°C)

1980-81 4-cyl. eng.: Primary, 0.4-0.5; Secondary, 8000-9500.

1982-83 4-cyl. eng.: Primary, 0-2; Secondary, 6000-30,000.

1984 4-cyl. eng.: Primary, 1.13-1.23; Secondary, 7700-9300.

1978-87 6-, 8-cyl. eng.: Primary, 1.13-1.23; Secondary, 7700-9300.

IGNITION RESISTOR

Engine	Type	Resistance (ohms)	Temperature (deg. F/C)
4-cyl.			
1978-79	Wire	2.0	—
1984	Wire	1.3-1.4	75/24
6-cyl.			
1978-87	Wire	1.3-1.4	75/24

Figure 1-5. A sample page from a specifications book.

uals often print books of specifications. The specifications may apply to a single model year but usually cover a span of years. Figure 1-5 shows part of a typical page from a typical specifications book.

Carmakers' shop manual order addresses
Factory shop manuals are available directly from the vehicle manufacturers or from car dealers. Most imported car dealers carry factory manuals in their parts departments or can obtain them for you. Most domestic vehicle dealers do not sell shop manuals, but they can be ordered from the manufacturer by mail.

The addresses for ordering factory shop manuals from the major domestic carmakers are provided below. A catalog of available manuals will also be sent on request.

- American Motors Corporation
  AMC-Renault
  Service Procedures & Publications
  14250 Plymouth Road
  Detroit MI 48232
- Chrysler Motors
  Service Publications
  c/o Dyment Distribution Service
  20026 Progress Drive
  Strongsville OH 44136
- Ford Motor Company
  Service Publications
  c/o Helm Incorporated
  Publications Division
  Box 07150
  Detroit MI 48207
- General Motors Corporation
  Buick Division
  Service Publications
  902 E. Hamilton Avenue
  Flint MI 48550
- Cadillac, Chevrolet, Pontiac and
  Hydra-matic Division
  c/o Helm Incorporated
  Publications Division
  Box 07130
  Detroit MI 48207
- Oldsmobile Division
  Service Publications
  920 Townsend Street
  Lansing MI 48921
- GMC Truck & Coach Division
  Service Publications
  660 South Boulevard, East
  Pontiac MI 48053

ORGANIZED TROUBLESHOOTING

Many customers bring their cars in for service when they have a specific problem. The most common electrical faults are opens, shorts, and grounds. Test meters and test lights can be used to track down these faults. The following paragraphs explain the general methods you should use to troubleshoot an electrical circuit malfunction.

The complexity of a modern automobile electrical system demands that you approach any system problem in a logical, organized manner. To help you develop this good habit, here is a 10-step checklist for electrical troubleshooting.

1. Ask The Owner or Driver
If possible, you should talk to the person who was operating the car when the problem first appeared. Questions to ask include:
- What other circuits and accessories were being used when the problem occurred?
- Were there any sparks, odors, noises, or other unusual signs?
- Has this problem occurred before? If so, what repairs were made?

Many shops have a service writer who talks to the customers and prepares a work order for the mechanic to follow. If you cannot talk to the customer, check the work order for this information.

2. Know The System
Review the appropriate chapters in the *Classroom Manual* or the manufacturer's shop manual to get a general idea of what circuits and loads are involved. This is the time to locate the car's system diagram for reference.

3. Operate The System
Now that you know what the general problem area is and what units are involved, you can begin to examine the automobile. You should make sure that the customer or service writer described the situation accurately and completely. For example, if the service order says, "Fix the headlamp high beams", you should turn on the high beams and see if they are totally out, glow dimly, or if only one side is not working. At the same time, you can look for related problems that may not have been noticed or mentioned. For example, is the high-beam indicator also completely out? These related symptoms can give you clues to the circuit problem.

4. List The Possible Causes
This can be a mental list, or you can make notes on a slip of paper. It should include any ideas you gained from steps 1 through 3. By looking at the system diagram, you may see other possible causes. For example, if the complaint is that a certain fuse frequently burns out, see what circuits share that fuse. If the fuse serves the turn signals, the backup lamps, the radio,

and the windshield washer pump, then any one of those circuits could be bad. A list of possible causes will help you to organize your thoughts when you begin to actually test the system. And don't overlook the obvious — begin with the simplest possible cause. Never condemn an alternator for a low-voltage problem until you've first checked for a loose drive belt.

5. Isolate The Problem Circuit

If your list of possible causes includes several circuits, you must narrow the list. In step 4, our sample list of possible causes included the turn signals, the backup lamps, the radio, and the windshield washer pump. To narrow this list, you can turn off all other accessories and operate the suspected circuits one at a time. If you turn one on and the fuse blows, then the trouble will be within that particular circuit.

6. Know The Problem Circuit

Now that you know which circuit is to be investigated, you can study that circuit in detail. The circuit diagram will tell you:
- Where the circuit receives battery current
- What switches control current flow
- What circuit protection is involved
- How the loads operate
- Where the circuit is grounded.

Understanding the total circuit is necessary if you are to troubleshoot efficiently.

7. Test Systematically

All d.c. automotive circuits are connected to the battery terminal at one end and to ground at the other. There may be more than one ground path through parallel circuit branches, but the basic pattern remains. Because of this pattern, the most logical way to troubleshoot an electrical circuit is to start at one end and work your way to the other.

These general guidelines will help you when the problem circuit has many components:
- If the fault is in a single unit of a multiple-unit circuit, start the test at that unit.
- If the fault affects all the units in a multiple-unit circuit, start the test at the point where the circuit gets its power.

For example, if the problem is in a lighting circuit, are all the bulbs out? If only one bulb in the circuit will not operate, start testing at the bulb. If all the lights in a circuit do not operate, start testing at the point where the current first enters the circuit.

With some systems, such as electronic ignitions or engine control systems, the best approach is to perform an area, or general, test of the overall system operation. This will let you narrow down the cause of a problem to a

specific subsystem. At that point, you can then perform pinpoint or detailed tests to isolate the faulty component.

8. Verify Your Findings

Once the exact trouble spot has been located, be sure of the failure. For example, if the fault has been traced to a switch, remove the switch and test it separately. If it works outside of the circuit, then perhaps the problem was caused by a loose connection. Checking and tightening a terminal connection takes much less time than replacing a part that was never at fault.

9. Repair

Only after you have narrowed the problem down to a specific conductor, terminal or part should you begin repairs. Much of the *Shop Manual* covers repair procedures for specific electrical components. Much of troubleshooting requires only the simple procedures for wiring repair that are discussed at the end of this chapter.

10. Test Your Repair

This should be the final step of your troubleshooting procedure. If you operate the problem circuit and the problem is gone, then you have succeeded. Sometimes, a circuit will have more than one problem in it. For example, a lighting circuit could suffer from both a corroded connector and a loose ground wire. If cleaning the connector does not solve the problem, you must return to step 7 and test the remainder of the circuit. Testing your repair work can avoid added frustration for you and the customer.

WIRING REPAIR

The primary wiring used in most automotive applications is a multistrand copper wire covered with colored plastic insulation, as we learned in Chapter 5 of the *Classroom Manual*. Solid wire generally is used inside starter motors, alternators, and other components. Repair of such wiring is generally not a part of normal automotive service but is left to rebuilders.

Some GM vehicles have aluminum wiring in their forward body harnesses. Engine control harnesses may contain shielded cables or wiring with twisted leads designed for low-current circuits. These kinds of wiring require special techniques.

Whenever wiring is replaced, it should be the same size or larger than the damaged wiring. As explained in Chapter 5 of the *Classroom Manual*, wire sizes are specified by AWG or metric specifications. Be sure to use replacement wire with the same color insulation to

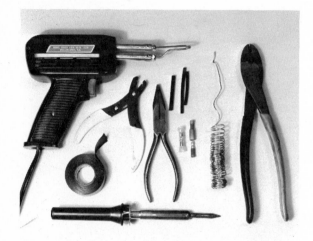

Figure 1-6. These tools will be needed during most wiring repair jobs.

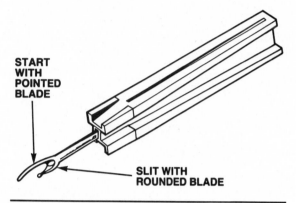

Figure 1-7. A seam splitter should be used for opening wire harnesses. (GM)

preserve the color coding for the next technician that may have to work on the circuit.

The rest of this chapter presents common procedures for automotive electrical wiring, including the repair of damaged wiring with soldered or crimped connectors and the repair of frequently used multiple connectors.

Safety

Several steps of conductor repair involve special procedures that you must understand fully before beginning. Read all instructions before attempting a repair job.

You will be using a soldering tool to heat the copper wire, then melting solder (a soft tin-lead compound) onto the hot wire strands. Soldering tools can reach 500°F (260°C), so keep them away from your skin, clothing, wiring insulation, and all flammables. The melting solder gives off dangerous fumes that you should not inhale.

Tools and Supplies

Most wiring repairs can be performed using these few tools, figure 1-6:
● Wire cutting, stripping, and crimping tool. This can be a combination tool or separate units. A knife and pliers will not do the job properly, but can be used in an emergency.
● Assorted styles and sizes of terminals.
● Soldering tool. A soldering gun heats faster than an iron and often has a smaller tip for delicate jobs.
● Pliers for holding heated metal.
● Resin-core solder. The core material eats away oxidation on metal without leaving corrosion.

Never use acid-core solder for electrical soldering, because the acid will promote corrosion.
● Electrician's tape or heat-shrink tubing and a heat source such as matches or a hot-air gun. These insulate the finished job.

Repair Methods

The most common repair methods are:
● Splicing
● Connector attachment
● Insulation repair
● Aluminum wiring repair
● Twisted/shielded cable repair (low-current wire).

Splicing

Connecting two or more wires without using a terminal is called splicing. It is commonly used to insert fusible links or to replace a section of damaged wiring. If you are going to use heat-shrink tubing for insulation, slip a piece over one of the sections of wire before soldering.

If one or more wires in a harness is damaged, it is not necessary to replace the entire harness. If the harness is enclosed in a plastic conduit, just open the conduit and pull out the damaged wire. If the harness is wrapped with tape, use a seam splitter, figure 1-7, to avoid damage to the insulation inside the harness (seam splitters are available from sewing supply stores). Proceed as follows:
1. If working with a taped harness, start a small slit in the tape away from the wires with the pointed end of a seam splitter. Slit the tape as required with the rounded blade, working carefully to avoid damaging wire insulation.
2. Use the correct opening in the wire stripping tool to remove about 1 inch (25 millimeters) of insulation from the wire ends to be joined,

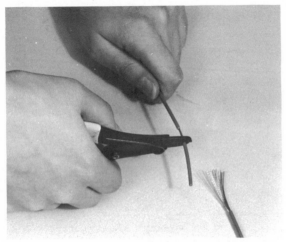

Figure 1-8. Remove insulation with a wire stripping tool.

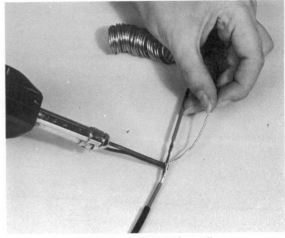

Figure 1-11. Apply the solder to the splice.

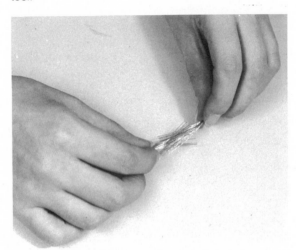

Figure 1-9. Braid the bare wire strands together.

Figure 1-12. A correctly soldered splice.

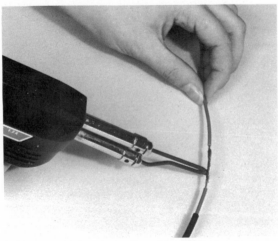

Figure 1-10. Heat the splice with a soldering tool.

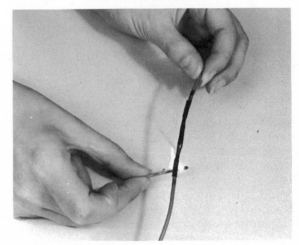

Figure 1-13. Insulate the splice with heat-shrink tubing.

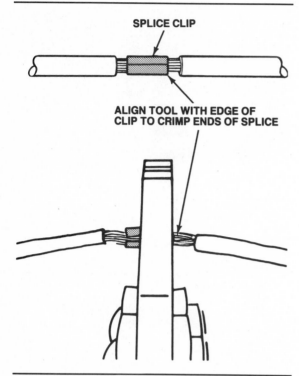

Figure 1-14. The proper installation of a splice clip. (GM)

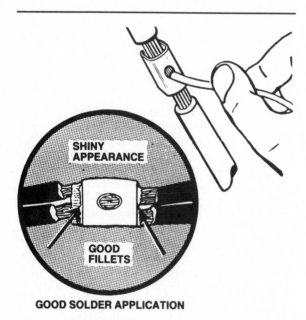

Figure 1-15. Applying solder to the splice clip joint. (GM)

figure 1-8. If you are not certain of the wire size, start with the largest stripper hole and work down until you can remove a clean strip of insulation without nicking or cutting the wire strands.

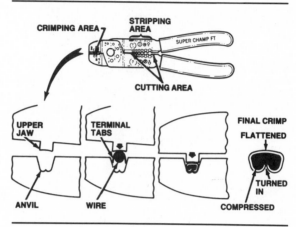

Figure 1-16. This typical crimping tool will form a properly crimped splice. (Ford)

3. Braid the bare strands together and twist them securely, figure 1-9.
4. Hold the broad side of the soldering tool to the bare wire splice, figure 1-10. Heat the wire splice with an 80 to 120 watt iron or gun. If working with 12- or 10-gauge wire, you can use up to 150 watts.
5. Touch the resin-core solder to the bare wire, not to the soldering tool, figure 1-11. Solder must melt from the heat of the wire splice and flow evenly through all the strands.
6. Use only enough solder to flow into the cracks, not a large amount, figure 1-12. Too much solder will make a weak splice and can trap contamination that will cause high resistance.
7. Cool the splice thoroughly and wrap with tape or use heat-shrink tubing to insulate. To use heat-shrink tubing, slip a length of tubing over the wire and past the splice area before soldering. After soldering, slip the tubing over the splice. Apply heat with a match or a hot-air gun, figure 1-13. The tubing will shrivel tightly over the repaired area.

Use a heat sink when soldering an electronic component or clamp the component in an alligator clip attached to a vise. This will draw heat away from the component while you are soldering the leads.

Wires can also be spliced using splice clips, a crimping tool and the procedure given in the next section, figure 1-14. When the splice is made, heat the front side of the clip with the soldering iron or gun and apply the solder to the hole in the back of the clip, figure 1-15.

Connector attachment
Connectors can be attached with solder or simply by crimping, depending upon the service conditions in which they will be used.

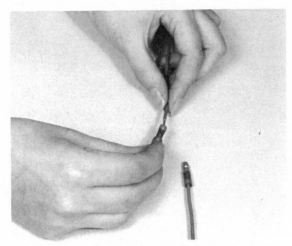

Figure 1-17. Insert the stripped wire in the terminal barrel.

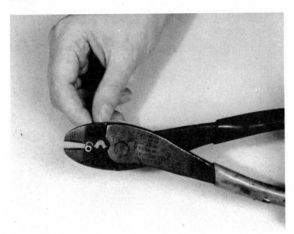

Figure 1-18. Crimp the terminal.

Attach connectors as follows:
1. Match the terminals to the wire gauge. Most terminals will fit a small range of gauges.
2. Use the correct opening in the wire stripping area of the crimping tool, figure 1-16, to remove just enough insulation from the wire so that it will fit the terminal barrel. Work carefully to avoid nicking or cutting the wire strands.
3. Insert the bare wire into the terminal barrel, figure 1-17. Use a crimping tool to squeeze the barrel. If the barrel has a seam, place the seam toward the convex side of the crimping hole, figures 1-16 and 1-18.
4. Crimp the connector in the area of the unstripped insulation, then solder and cool the barrel, if necessary.
5. Insulate the barrel with the terminal's tubing, figure 1-19. If the terminal is not insulated, cover the connection with electrical tape or heat-shrink tubing.

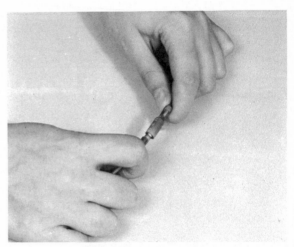

Figure 1-19. Insulate the terminal with the supplied tubing.

Figure 1-20. A properly wrapped splice using electrical tape. (GM)

Insulation repair
Insulation repair is required whenever wiring has been repaired, or when the insulation is damaged but the conductor inside is not affected. There are two ways to repair insulation: with plastic electrical tape or heat-shrink tubing.

If electrical tape is used, wrap three turns of tape over the repair area, overlapping the tape about ½ inch onto the undamaged insulation at each end of the repair, figure 1-20. If the taped wired is not protected in conduit or another harness covering, tape it a second time to entirely overlap the first piece of tape.

Heat-shrink tubing is a plastic tubing that shrinks when heated. It is available from electronic supply stores in various diameters, lengths, and colors to cover specific wire sizes. When heat-shrink tubing is used, it must be cut to size and installed on the wire before the wire is spliced or attached to a connector. After the repair has been made, slide the tubing in place and heat it with a hot-air gun or a match. This shrinks the tubing to the diameter of the wire and insulates the repaired area.

Aluminum wiring repair
Late-model GM products use a front body wiring harness made of 14- and 16-gauge solid-

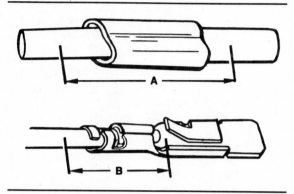

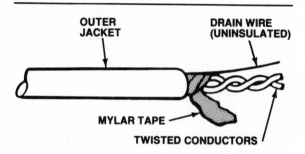

Figure 1-21. Petroleum jelly should be applied to the marked area. (GM)

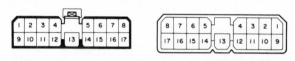

Figure 1-23. Use a splice clip on the drain wire and position as shown. (GM)

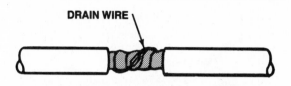

Figure 1-24. This connector diagram identifies connector sockets, pins, and circuit numbers. (American Isuzu)

OUTER JACKET

DRAIN WIRE (UNINSULATED)

MYLAR TAPE

TWISTED CONDUCTORS

Figure 1-22. This type of cable is used in systems carrying very low current. (GM)

cable aluminum wires enclosed in a plastic conduit. Special repair procedures for this harness are as follows.

GM recommends the use of a special repair kit that includes an assortment of aluminum wires in 6-inch (15-cm) lengths with terminals attached to one end, splice clips, and anticorrosion petroleum jelly. Any splice made should be at least 1½ inches (38 mm) away from other splices, connectors, or harness branches.

If a terminal in this harness fails:
1. Pull the damaged wire out of the conduit.
2. Cut off about 6 inches (15 cm) of wire connected to the defective terminal.
3. Strip about ¼ inch (6 mm) of insulation from the end of the wire being repaired and from the kit replacement wire.
4. Place wire ends in a splice clip and crimp firmly.
5. Apply petroleum jelly to the splice clip crimp area and aluminum core to prevent galvanic corrosion. See figure 1-21A.
6. Wrap the splice area with insulating tape to seal out moisture.

If a wire has been damaged and a section must be replaced:
1. Cut out the damaged section.

2. Strip ¼ inch (6 mm) of insulation from ends of wire on both sides of the damage.
3. Splice in a replacement section as described in steps 4, 5, and 6 above. Coat both the terminal crimp area and aluminum core with petroleum jelly. See figure 1-21B.

Twisted or shielded cable repair
Late-model vehicles with electronic engine control systems may use wire that carries very low current (0.1 or 0.2 ampere). Two-conductor twisted or shielded cable, figure 1-22, is used between the electronic control module and the distributor on GM vehicles. It often is used on other carmakers' vehicles to protect wiring from RFI and EMI signals. To repair this type of wiring:
1. Carefully remove and discard the outer jacket. Do not cut into the drain wire or Mylar tape, figure 1-22.
2. Unwrap but do not remove the aluminum-Mylar tape, since it is used to rewrap the conductors after splicing has been completed.
3. Untwist the conductors and strip the insulation as described under "Splicing" above. Be sure to stagger the splices to prevent the possibility of shorts.
4. Splice and tape each wire using splice clips and resin-core solder. Wrap each wire splice with tape to insulate, then rewrap the conductors (but not the drain wire) with the Mylar tape.
5. Splice the drain wire as in step 4 and wrap it around the conductors and Mylar tape, figure 1-23.
6. Tape over the spliced area with electrical tape using a winding motion. The electrical tape replaced the section of jacket cut away and discarded in step 1.

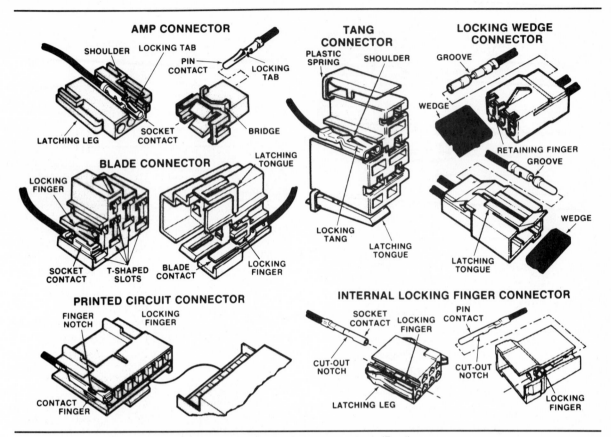

Figure 1-25. Hard-shell connectors take many forms; these are typical. (Ford)

CONNECTOR REPAIR

The electrical connectors used on late-model cars may join together 1 to 40 pairs of wires. This makes connector and terminal identification essential for efficient troubleshooting. Connectors are shown on wiring diagrams and schematics. Most carmakers also provide drawings similar to figure 1-24 as a means of identifying the terminals or cavities with their circuit numbers.

Molded or Single-Wire Connectors

Connectors used with 1 to 4 wires are generally molded units in which the individual wires and terminals cannot be separated for repair. Cut the damaged wire or wires out of both halves of the connector and splice a new connector in with pigtail leads. When a single wire in a molded multiple connector is damaged, it is often possible to splice in a new single-wire bullet connector to bypass the damaged area.

Hard-Shell Connectors

Many multiple-wire connectors are manufactured of hard plastic. They are used to hold the male and female terminals (pins and sockets) of individual connectors. Several common types are shown in figure 1-25. You can test circuit operation by probing the rear of the individual connections without separating the connector shells.

Individual terminals also can be replaced in this type of connector. After separating the connector halves or disconnecting the connector from the component to which it is attached, the damaged terminal is released from the shell with a special terminal removal tool or a small screwdriver, figure 1-26.

Once the damaged terminal has been replaced by soldering or crimping, reinstall it in the connector shell. Most terminals used in this type of connector have a locking tang of some kind. In cases where the terminal is removed from the shell but is not damaged, the locking tang must be reformed. Figure 1-27 shows one type of tang being reformed.

Weather-Pack® Connectors

Special weather-proof connectors are used in engine and body harnesses of late-model GM cars. This type of connector uses a rubber seal on the wire ends of the terminals. On small connectors, a secondary sealing cover is used

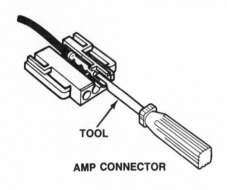

TOOL

AMP CONNECTOR

RAISING RETAINING FINGERS TO REMOVE CONTACTS

LOCKING WEDGE CONNECTOR

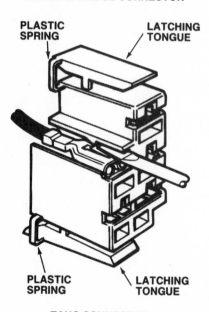

PLASTIC SPRING   **LATCHING TONGUE**

PLASTIC SPRING   **LATCHING TONGUE**

TANG CONNECTOR

Figure 1-26. A terminal removal tool or screwdriver is used to release the terminals from the connector. (Ford)

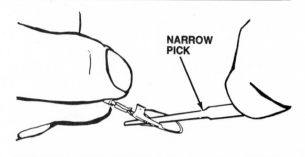

NARROW PICK

Figure 1-27. Reforming the locking tang on a wire terminal. (GM)

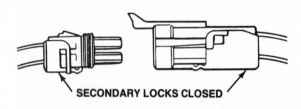

SECONDARY LOCKS CLOSED

Figure 1-28. Fully assembled Weather-Pack® connections. (GM)

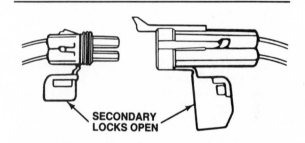

SECONDARY LOCKS OPEN

Figure 1-29. Small connectors use secondary locks. (General Motors)

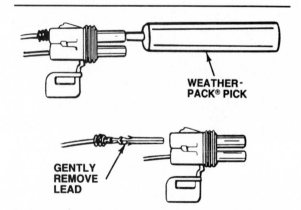

WEATHER-PACK® PICK

GENTLY REMOVE LEAD

Figure 1-30. Removing a terminal with a Weather-Pack® pick. (GM)

on the rear of each connector half. GM does not recommend replacement of a Weather-Pack® connector with a non-weatherproof type.

To service this type of connector:
1. Separate small connectors by simply pulling apart, figure 1-28. To separate large connectors, remove the bolt from the center of the connector body before pulling apart.

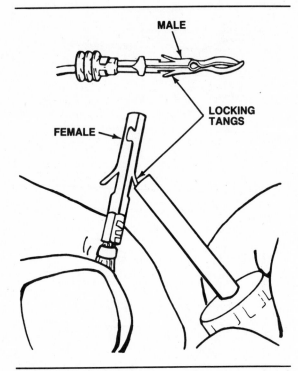

Figure 1-31. The proper way to reform Weather-Pack® locking tangs. (GM)

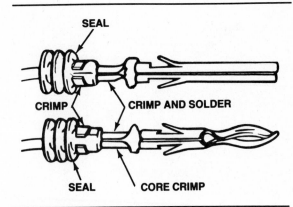

Figure 1-32. Installing a new terminal and cable seal. (GM)

2. Flip the secondary lock hinges downward on small connectors, figure 1-29. On large connectors, push the locking nib upward as far as possible with a wide pick and pull the retainer out.

3. Insert a Weather-Pack® pick in the front of the terminal cavity and push the terminal free of the connector. Pull the pick out and carefully remove the terminal, figure 1-30.
4. If the same lead and terminal are to be reinstalled, reform the locking tang as shown in figure 1-31.
5. If the lead or terminal requires replacement, splice a new terminal and cable seal on the wire, figure 1-32.

2

Electrical Faults and Basic Test Equipment

ELECTRICAL FAULTS

In the *Classroom Manual*, we saw some ways to stop current flow through a circuit, such as switches, relays and circuit protectors. Sometimes current flow stops when we do not want it to, and sometimes too much current will flow in a circuit. We will now see what can cause some electrical faults and ways to identify and find the problems. We will also learn about the use of meters and other basic test equipment.

The problems which stop or affect current flow fall into two categories:
1. High-resistance faults
2. Low-resistance faults.

High-Resistance Faults

A high-resistance connection, figure 2-1, can be caused by corrosion, a damaged wire, a defective part or a loose connection. Because of the increase in resistance, the current flow is less than what is required to properly operate the loads in the circuit.

An open circuit, figure 2-2, results from a broken wire, no contact between connectors or a defective part. The resistance across an open circuit, or simply, an "open", is infinite, so no current can flow.

Low-Resistance Faults

A shorted circuit, or "short", figure 2-3, is the result of an unwanted connection between two conductors. It allows current to bypass all or part of the normal circuit and normal resistance.

A grounded circuit, figure 2-4, is the result of an unwanted connection between a conductor and ground. All or part of the normal circuitry and normal resistance is bypassed. This is called, simply, a "ground".

A ground is really a type of short circuit. From the point where the short occurs, the current bypasses all remaining circuit conductors and loads and flows directly to ground. The short circuit path is simply a short to ground. Because automotive electrical systems are single-wire systems using a common chassis ground, most short circuits occur as shorts to ground. It is possible, however, to find a short circuit within a circuit component, such as a short across part of the windings in an alternator rotor or stator. Remember that all grounds are shorts, but that not all shorts are grounds.

SIMPLE TEST DEVICES

You can do a lot of troubleshooting using simple continuity testers. While an ohmmeter

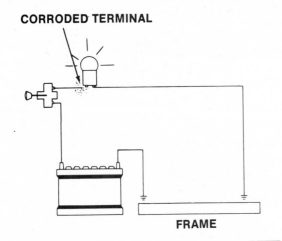

Figure 2-1. A high-resistance connection reduces current flow.

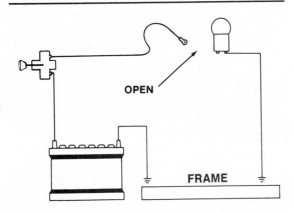

Figure 2-2. An open circuit creates infinite resistance and stops current flow.

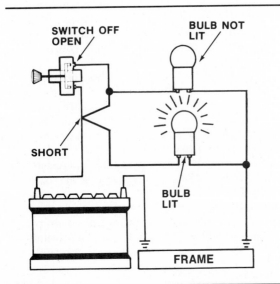

Figure 2-3. A short circuit.

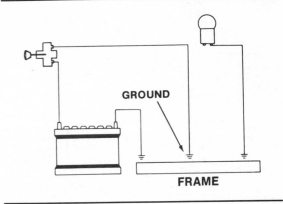

Figure 2-4. A grounded circuit.

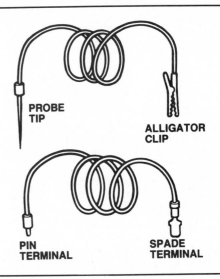

Figure 2-5. Jumper wires use various terminals. (Ford)

is the ideal continuity tester because it will show the degree of continuity, the go/no-go feature of the following devices and their quick and easy use make them ideal to locate problem areas:
- Jumper wires
- 12-volt test lamp
- Self-powered test lamp.

Jumper Wires

A jumper wire is simply a length of wire with connectors on both ends that allows you to temporarily bridge or "jump" a suspected open or gap in a circuit. This means that you can use it to bypass a switch, connector, or any other nonresistive circuit part. Figure 2-5 shows two sample jumper wires with various types of connector tips. You can make or buy jumper wires with any type of connector tips needed.

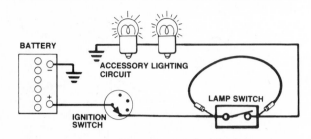

Figure 2-6. If the lamp lights only when the switch is bypassed with a jumper wire, there is a problem with the switch.

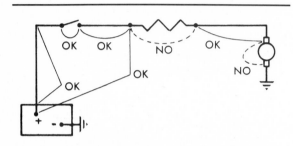

Figure 2-7. Some proper and improper connections with a jumper wire. (Chevrolet)

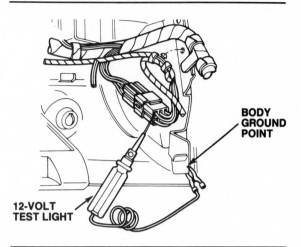

Figure 2-8. Typical 12-volt test lamp use. (Ford)

The jumper wire is technically a continuity tester, but it does not give you any electrical output. If the circuit works properly after you install the jumper wire, figure 2-6, you know that there is an open in the circuit. In this case, the switch is faulty. To make this test:
1. Turn all switches on.
2. If the lamps do not light, bypass the lamp switch with a jumper wire.
3. If the lamps then light, the switch is defective.

A jumper wire must *never* be used to bypass an item that has resistance, or in a way that would ground a hot lead. This would reduce circuit resistance, allowing excessive current flow which could damage loads and conductors, or even start an electrical fire. Many jumper wires include an inline fuse or circuit breaker to protect the circuit. Figure 2-7 illustrates some proper and improper jumper wire connections.

12-Volt Test Lamp

This device is similar to a jumper wire but it contains a bulb that glows when there is power in the circuit or to the component being checked. This type of test lamp is used to check for open circuits and relies upon the vehicle's battery to power the circuit or component being tested. It is not polarity-sensitive and can be

connected either way in a circuit. It is not a good idea, however, to use a 12-volt tester on electronic components, because the current draw added by the test lamp may damage the component.

When you become familiar with the 12-volt test lamp, you easily can recognize high-resistance circuits by the effect they have on the bulb's illumination. As current drops in a high-resistance circuit, the usual bright glow of the bulb dims.

The 12-volt test lamp usually has a sharp probe tip for insertion through wire insulation or the end of a connector for testing, figure 2-8. However, they are manufactured with a variety of different tips for different uses and you should have several different types in your troubleshooting kit. Figure 2-9 shows typical 12-volt test lamp designs.

The two checks which the 12-volt test lamp can make are called voltage-seeking and ground-seeking tests. The voltage-seeking test indicates whether or not voltage is available to the circuit at a particular point. This test could be in a lighting circuit, figure 2-10:
1. Connect one test lamp lead to a known chassis ground.
2. Touch the other test lamp lead to various parts of the circuit.
3. If the lamp lights at one test point but not at the next, the circuit is open between these two points.

The ground-seeking test indicates whether or not a conductor, switch, or load is grounded. This test could be used in a warning lamp circuit that has a grounding switch. For example, the oil pressure warning lamp in figure 2-11 should light when the ignition switch is on the

TYPICAL PROBE-TYPE TEST LIGHTS

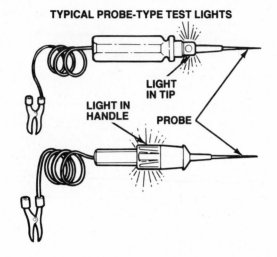

LIGHT IN TIP

LIGHT IN HANDLE

PROBE

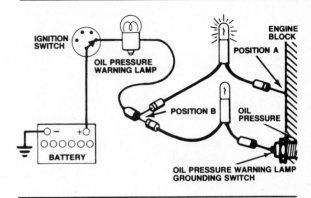

IGNITION SWITCH

OIL PRESSURE WARNING LAMP

BATTERY

ENGINE BLOCK

POSITION A

POSITION B

OIL PRESSURE

OIL PRESSURE WARNING LAMP GROUNDING SWITCH

Figure 2-11. This ground-seeking test with a 12-volt probe lamp shows that the oil pressure warning lamp grounding switch is defective.

WRAP-AROUND TEST LIGHT

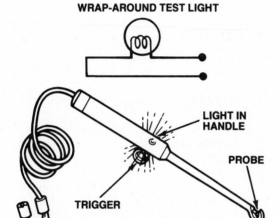

LIGHT IN HANDLE

PROBE

TRIGGER

VEE NOTCH

Figure 2-9. Typical 12-volt test lamps. (Ford)

CONTINUITY TESTER

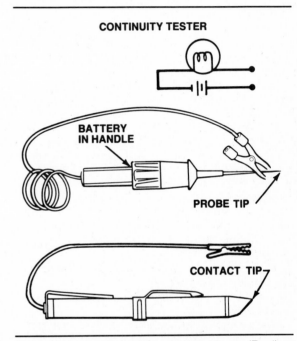

BATTERY IN HANDLE

PROBE TIP

CONTACT TIP

Figure 2-12. Typical self-powered test lamp. (Ford)

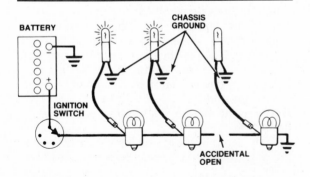

BATTERY

CHASSIS GROUND

IGNITION SWITCH

ACCIDENTAL OPEN

Figure 2-10. This voltage-seeking test with a 12-volt probe lamp is similar to a voltmeter's available voltage test.

Accessory or On position with the engine not running. If it does not:
1. Disconnect the wire from the grounding switch.
2. Connect one test lamp lead to the wire and touch the other test lamp lead to the engine block, figure 2-11A. If the test lamp and the warning lamp light, the problem may be at the grounding switch.
3. Keep one test lamp lead connected to the wire and touch the other test lamp lead to the grounding switch, figure 2-11B. If the test lamp and the warning lamp do not light, the grounding switch is defective.

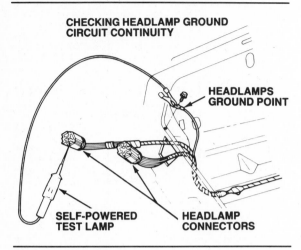

Figure 2-13. Typical self-powered test lamp use. (Ford)

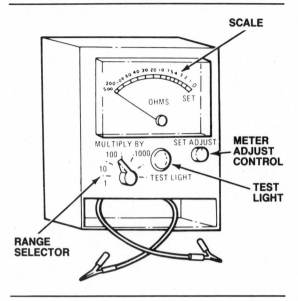

Figure 2-14. Analog meters indicate a continuous range of values across the meter scale. (Ford)

Self-Powered Test Lamp

Often called a continuity lamp, this tester is similar to the 12-volt test lamp just described. However, the tester contains its own battery to power the circuit or component, figure 2-12. Do not connect the tester to a circuit containing power from the vehicle battery; that may burn out the tester lamp. For this reason, whatever you test with a self-powered test lamp must be disconnected from the vehicle battery.

The self-powered test lamp can be used to check for either an open or a short circuit. The tester bulb will glow whenever it is connected to a complete circuit, figure 2-13.

As with a 12-volt test lamp, this tester should not be used on electronic components. It can apply too much voltage to the component from its battery, damaging the component. These test lamps cannot be used to check high-resistance components, such as suppression-type ignition cables, because the low voltage of the lamp's battery cannot overcome the resistance of the cables.

METERS AND METER DESIGN

To correct electrical problems, you must be able to find and identify the cause. Many good tools exist to help in this search. These tools range from the simple test lamps just described to complex, expensive engine analyzers. In this chapter, we will study the basic operation of these tools and see how they are used to test circuits.

Since most automotive systems and test equipment operate on the conventional theory of current flow (+) to (−), we will use that theory throughout this chapter.

Voltage, current, and resistance can be measured by three basic test meters:
- Voltmeter
- Ammeter
- Ohmmeter.

Analog Meters and D'Arsonval Movement

Analog meters use a scale and a moving needle to indicate test values. They are called analog meters because the needle indicates a continuous range of values across the scale, figure 2-14. Analog meters have a low input impedance, which is the combined opposition to current resulting from the inductance, resistance, and capacitance of the meter.

All analog meters use the same mechanism, called a D'Arsonval movement, or moving coil. The D'Arsonval movement is a small coil of fine wire mounted on bearings within the field of a permanent horseshoe magnet, figure 2-15. Fine wire springs, called hair springs, are connected to both ends of the coil wire. These hair springs act as conductors to the coil. They return the coil to a base position and are used to adjust that base position.

When the meter is in use, current flows through the coil, creating a magnetic field. This coil magnetic field interacts with the permanent field of the horseshoe magnet and causes the coil to rotate in one direction or the other, figure 2-16. The direction of rotation is controlled by the direction of current flow. A pointer or needle connected to the coil indicates the value

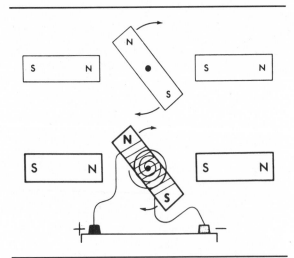

Figure 2-15. Coil motion in a D'Arsonval movement is caused by the interaction of magnetic fields. (Chevrolet)

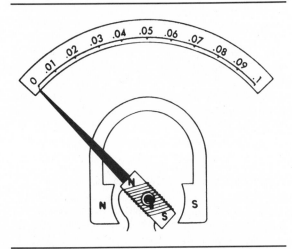

Figure 2-16. This coil movement can be used to display a value reading on a scale.

of voltage, current, or resistance on the meter dial, figure 2-16. The meter is designed so that the value it measures is proportional to current through the meter coil. The meter is calibrated (adjusted) for accuracy by the manufacturer. Some meters, however, have adjustment screws that allow you to recalibrate or "zero" them before every use, a highly recommended practice.

Test meters have two leads — long pieces of wire with connectors on the end — to make contact with the circuitry being tested. The connectors usually are either long thin shafts called probes, or small spring-loaded clips, called alligator clips. Probes are held against the test point; alligator clips require a larger contact surface for attachment. The leads may be per-

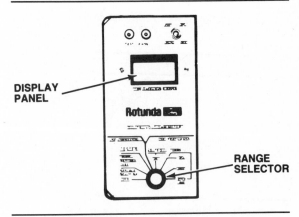

Figure 2-17. Digital test meters use an LED or LCD display panel to present the measured value numerically. (Ford)

manently connected to the meter, or they may plug into various sockets in the meter for different uses.

When measuring voltage or current in a circuit, the polarity of the test meter and the leads must correspond to the polarity of the circuit being tested. One lead is usually colored red, for positive (+), and should be used on the part of the circuit or component being tested that is nearer to the highest positive voltage. This is generally the battery positive post, except for some charging system tests when it is the alternator output terminal. The other lead is usually colored black or white, for negative (−), and should be connected to the test point nearer to the highest negative voltage. We will learn more about test lead connections shortly.

Electronic Digital Meters

In the past, all meters were analog types. Today, however, modern electronics has made available digital meters that show the values they measure in discrete digits or numbers on a display panel or screen, figure 2-17. Their readout is usually by a light-emitting diode (LED) or a liquid crystal display (LCD). Instead of a D'Arsonval movement, electronic circuitry senses current, voltage, or resistance and changes analog signals to a digital display. Digital meters do not have to be calibrated or "zeroed" before use. Not only are these meters more accurate than the older analog designs, they also eliminate the possibility of parallax error which can occur when an analog meter is viewed from an angle.

Digital meters are required when testing many of the electronic systems used on late-model cars because of their high input imped-

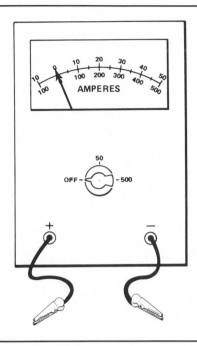

Figure 2-18. A typical analog ammeter.

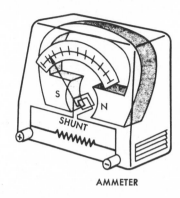

Figure 2-19. A shunt resistor is placed in parallel with the ammeter coil. (Delco-Remy)

ance. Impedance is an electrical term that refers to the amount of resistance in an alternating-current circuit. Low meter input impedance affects the accuracy of the meter reading and can damage electronic components that operate on only a few milliamperes of current.

The current draw of some low-input impedance meters can result in an inaccurate reading. Connecting a voltmeter across a circuit adds the parallel resistance of a second conductor to the circuit. This increases the current through the circuit and affects the voltage drop across the load resistance being measured. The high-impedance meter, however, will draw very little current and therefore gives more accurate readings.

Since many electronic circuits and components work with very low current, connecting a low impedance meter across the circuit can draw enough current to damage the circuit or component. For example, an exhaust gas oxygen (EGO) sensor is a generator or galvanic battery that generates a few hundred milliamperes and voltage between 0 and 1 volt. When a low-impedance meter is connected to an EGO sensor, it can draw more current than the device can deliver, creating a short circuit that destroys the sensor.

AMMETER

An ammeter, figure 2-18, measures the amount of current in a circuit. It also can be used to test

circuit continuity. This could be done simply by allowing the circuit current to flow through the D'Arsonval movement. However, the D'Arsonval coil is very small, with little current capacity. Too much current through the coil will damage the test meter.

To avoid this excessive current flow, ammeters have a resistor wired in parallel, or shunt, with the coil, figure 2-19. The resistance of the shunt resistor is very low. It actually acts as a low-resistance internal conductor in parallel with the meter movement. Therefore, the meter coil has to measure only a small part of the current flow to determine the entire current flow. Many meters have a knob or switch that moves shunt resistors of different values into parallel with the coil. This changes the proportion of current through the coil and creates different ranges of current values which the meter can safely measure.

Using An Ammeter

Ohm's Law tells us that current flow is equal at all points in a series circuit or within any single branch of a parallel circuit. An ammeter can be used to measure current flow and to test circuit continuity.

An ammeter is always connected in series with the circuit or component to be tested, figure 2-20. All of the current that normally flows through the circuit must also flow through the ammeter. If there is any other path for current flow, the ammeter reading will not be accurate. Because the internal circuitry of an analog ammeter has the large shunt resistor in parallel with the meter movement, the total resistance of the meter is very low and does not affect test measurements. This low resistance also means that if an ammeter is connected in parallel with, or across, a circuit, it will act as a jumper wire or short.

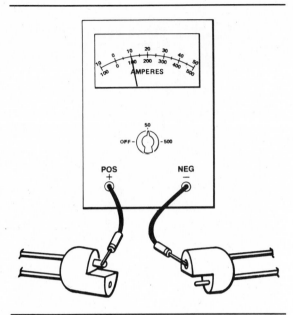

Figure 2-20. An ammeter must be connected in series with the circuit being tested.

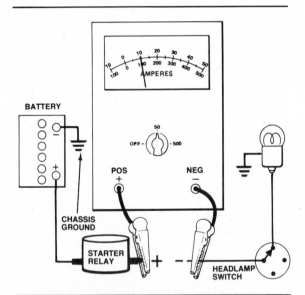

Figure 2-21. The polarity of ammeter leads must be observed, or the meter could be damaged.

Ammeter polarity

The ammeter positive (+) lead is usually colored red. This lead must be connected into the circuit at the test point nearest the positive voltage potential, figure 2-21. Current flow must *enter* this positive lead.

The ammeter negative (−) lead is usually colored black or white. This lead must be connected into the circuit at the test point nearest to the negative voltage potential. Current flow must *exit* this negative lead.

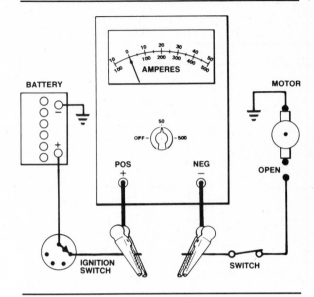

Figure 2-22. This ammeter reading of zero indicates that the circuit is open at some point.

If the ammeter's polarity is not maintained, the meter movement could be damaged. The meter would give inaccurate readings and might even be ruined.

Ammeter scales

Many ammeters have more than one current scale on the dial and a range selector switch, figure 2-18. Before starting any test, set the selector switch to the range above the maximum expected current draw. For example:
1. Set the range selector to the highest current scale.
2. Connect the ammeter in series with the circuit or component being tested.
3. If the current reading is below the full-scale reading of the next lowest range, switch to that range for a more precise reading.

If the meter is set on a scale that is below the current draw of the circuit or part, the meter may be damaged by too much current flow. Some meters are equipped with an automatic ranging feature which switches the meter to a higher or lower scale depending on the current being measured.

Some ammeters are equipped with a scale that reads in both directions from zero to measure reverse current flow. However, you should still observe system polarity when connecting the meter into the circuit.

Ammeter Tests

Compare the current flow reading given by the ammeter with the manufacturer's specifications

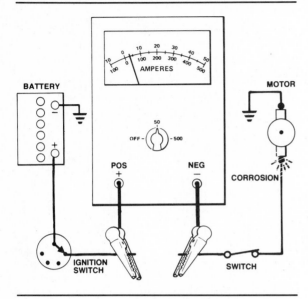

Figure 2-23. A lower than normal ammeter reading indicates a high-resistance fault in the circuit.

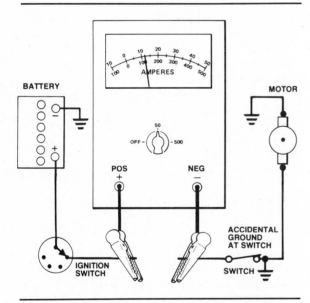

Figure 2-24. A higher than normal ammeter reading indicates a low-resistance fault in the circuit.

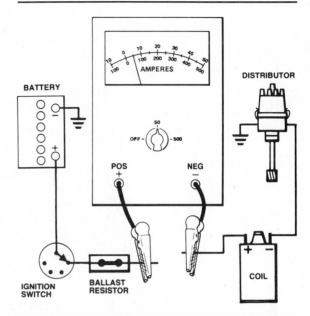

Figure 2-25. Testing an ignition coil with an ammeter.

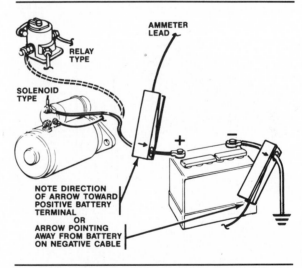

Figure 2-26. These inductive ammeter clips are measuring current flow from the battery into the starting circuit.

for the circuit being tested, or use Ohm's law to calculate the proper amount of current flow for a particular circuit.

- If the ammeter shows *no current flow*, figure 2-22, the circuit is *open* at some point. This indicates no continuity.
- If the ammeter shows *less current flow than is normal*, figure 2-23, the circuit is complete but contains *too much resistance*. This can be caused by improper or defective components or by loose or corroded connections.

- If the *current flow is greater than normal*, figure 2-24, some of the circuit's normal resistance has been bypassed by a *short* or a *ground*.

For example, many manufacturers provide current draw specifications for their ignition coil. To test the coil with an ammeter, figure 2-25:

1. With the ignition switch off, disconnect the coil primary positive wire from the coil.
2. Connect the ammeter (+) lead to the primary (+) wire.
3. Connect the ammeter (−) lead to the primary (+) terminal on the coil cap.

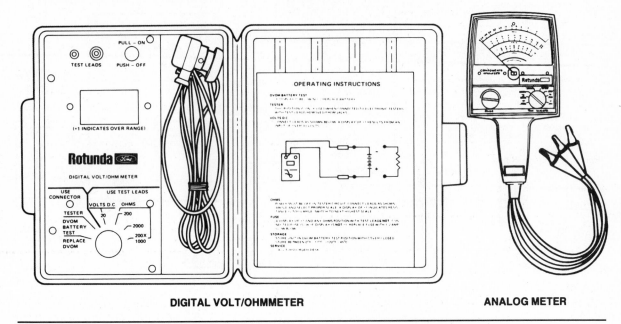

DIGITAL VOLT/OHMMETER   **ANALOG METER**

Figure 2-27. Typical voltmeters. (Ford)

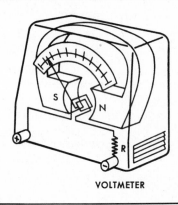

VOLTMETER

Figure 2-28. A resistor is placed in series with the voltmeter coil. (Delco-Remy)

4. Turn the ignition switch on and, depending upon the manufacturer's test instructions, either start the engine or close the ignition points.
5. Compare the ammeter reading to the coil current draw specifications.
   a. No current draw indicates an open (no continuity) primary circuit. The ignition system would not operate at all in this case.
   b. A low current reading indicates a discharged battery, high resistance in the primary wiring or the primary coil winding, or loose or corroded connections.

Inductive Ammeter

An inductive ammeter can measure current flow without being connected into the circuit. Its test lead is a clip that fits over one of the circuit's conductors, figure 2-26. Remember that current flow creates a magnetic field around the conductor. The inductive ammeter measures the strength of the conductor's magnetic field and converts it to a current reading.

Tests can be performed quickly with an inductive ammeter because you do not have to disconnect any of the circuit parts to insert test probes. However, the inductive clip must be placed over the conductor in the correct direction, figure 2-26, so that current flows through the clip in the proper direction. This maintains the correct ammeter polarity. Since most inductive ammeter clips are large enough to fit over battery cables, they may not fit into cramped test spaces.

VOLTMETER

A voltmeter, figure 2-27, can be used to:
• Measure the source voltage of a circuit
• Measure the voltage drop caused by a load
• Check for circuit continuity
• Measure the voltage at any point in the circuit.

A voltmeter is normally connected in parallel with a circuit or across (parallel with) a voltage source. For this reason, it is necessary to wire a resistor in series with the coil, figure 2-28, on

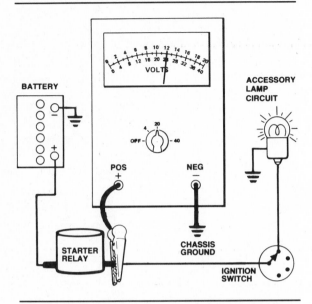

Figure 2-29. A voltmeter can be connected in parallel with a circuit to measure available voltage.

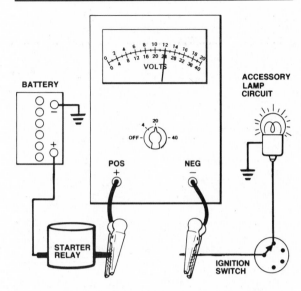

Figure 2-30. Here, the voltmeter is in series with the circuit to check circuit continuity.

analog meters to protect the D'Arsonval movement from too much current flow. Because the value of this resistor is known, the coil current flow is governed by the amount of voltage in the circuit. The high internal resistance of a voltmeter means that it will draw very little current from a circuit. This makes it safe to connect the meter in parallel or across a circuit or component. The small amount of current drawn by the voltmeter is not enough to significantly affect the circuit voltage drop.

Some voltmeters have a switch that connects resistors of various values into series with the meter movement. This creates ranges of voltage levels that the meter can safely measure.

Using a Voltmeter

We know that voltage is impressed equally on all branches of a parallel circuit. We also know that the sum of the voltage drops across all of the loads in a branch or a series equals the source voltage. To measure voltage or voltage drop, the voltmeter is connected in parallel with the circuit or part, figure 2-29. When checking for circuit continuity, the voltmeter can be connected in series with portions of the circuit, figure 2-30.

Voltmeter polarity

Like an ammeter, a voltmeter usually has a red positive (+) lead and a black or white negative (−) lead. Whether the meter is connected in series or in parallel, the polarity of the test leads must be maintained. The red positive lead

is connected to the test point nearer the positive voltage potential, and the black or white negative lead is connected to the test point nearer the negative voltage potential.

Voltmeter scales

Most voltmeters have more than one voltage scale on the dial and a range selector switch, figures 2-29 and 2-30. A typical voltmeter will have a 2- to 4-volt low-range scale, a 16- to 20-volt mid-range scale, and a 32- to 40-volt high-range scale. Before beginning any voltage test, set the selector switch to the range above the maximum system voltage. For example:
1. Set the range selector to the highest scale.
2. Connect the voltmeter in parallel with the circuit or part to be tested, figure 2-29.
3. If the voltage reading is below 20 volts, switch to the 20-volt scale for a clearer reading.
4. If the voltage is below 4 volts, switch to the 4-volt scale for a clearer reading.

If the meter is set on a 2-volt or a 4-volt scale and connected in parallel with 12 volts, the meter movement may be damaged.

Digital voltmeters

As we saw earlier, analog voltmeters should not be used to test many of the electronic systems used on late-model vehicles because of their low input impedance. Such meters may draw too much current, damaging electronic components that work with low current circuitry.

Digital voltmeters have very high impedance or resistance, often greater than ten megohms.

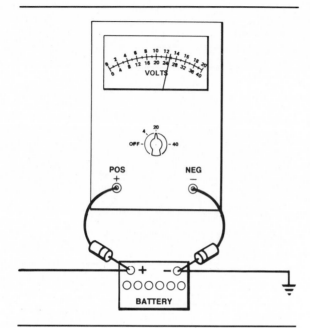

Figure 2-31. A voltmeter connected in parallel with the battery will measure actual battery voltage.

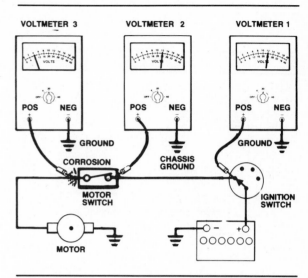

Figure 2-32. These available voltage tests will pinpoint the area of high resistance.

This is very important when testing components on computerized engine control systems. Some parts such as oxygen sensors *must* be tested using a high-impedance voltmeter; the minute amount of current conducted by a low-impedance voltmeter is enough to immediately destroy such a part. This is true of many components in computerized systems.

Unless you are familiar with a particular system and know which parts can and cannot be tested with a low impedance analog voltmeter, never begin troubleshooting until you have consulted the appropriate shop manual and obtained a high-impedance voltmeter.

Some digital voltmeters have automatic range selection, floating decimal, and automatic polarity indication. They are accurate to two decimal points. Digital voltmeters are often combined with an ohmmeter in a unit called a DVOM or digital volt-ohmmeter.

Available Voltage Tests

The voltage available within a circuit can be measured with or without current flowing through the circuit. When there is current flow, the voltmeter reading will show the voltage drop caused by circuit loads. This is because the available voltage decreases when a load comes between the test point and the battery positive terminal. When there is no current flow, the available voltage should be about 12

volts at all test points above ground in a circuit. This is usually called open-circuit or no-load voltage.

Available voltage at source
The available voltage source for all d.c. automotive circuits is the battery. Battery voltage is checked by connecting the voltmeter (+) lead to the battery (+) terminal and the (−) lead to the battery (−) terminal, figure 2-31. This measures the battery's no-load, or open-circuit, voltage.

To test available voltage under load, turn on a circuit (headlamps, starter, air conditioning, etc.) and note the voltmeter reading. The voltage will be slightly lower than open-circuit voltage, depending upon the condition of the battery and the current draw of the circuit.

Available voltage at points in a circuit
When available voltage is checked with current flowing in the circuit, high-resistance faults can be detected. The voltmeter (+) lead is connected to the test point and the (−) lead is grounded. For example, if an accessory motor is not turning fast enough to do its job, an available voltage test can pinpoint the fault. Figure 2-32 shows that the circuitry is at fault, not the motor. A corroded switch connection has reduced the voltage available to the motor so that the motor cannot run properly.

When no current is flowing, an available voltage test can pinpoint an open in the circuit. Figure 2-33 shows a circuit being tested for available voltage.
● Voltmeters 1 and 2 show that system voltage is available at those test points.

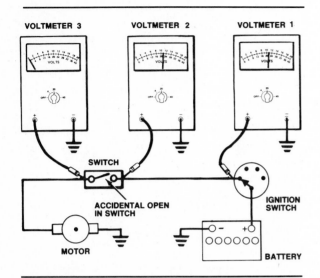

Figure 2-33. When no current is flowing in the circuit, a few no-load voltage tests will pinpoint the problem.

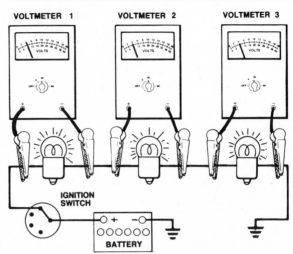

Figure 2-35. Voltage drops can be measured directly by connecting a voltmeter across the load.

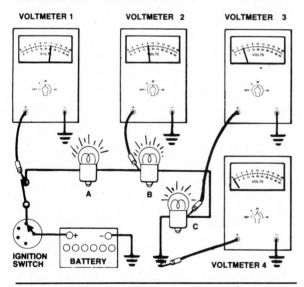

Figure 2-34. Voltage drops can be computed from a series of available voltage readings.

● Voltmeter 3 reads zero voltage, indicating that the circuit is open at some point between voltmeter 2 and voltmeter 3.

Voltage drop tests

Voltage drop is the amount of voltage that an electrical load uses to do its work. Voltage drop can also result from a high-resistance connection. Remember that *the sum of the voltage drops around a circuit equals the source voltage.*

Voltage drop tests can tell you if the load is using too much voltage to do its work. This could mean that the load's resistance is too high, or that current flow is too high. If not enough voltage is being used, then some of the

load's resistance may have been bypassed by a short or a ground. Conductors usually have no significant voltage drop, but corrosion and loose connections can create a drop and not allow enough voltage to be applied to the rest of the circuit.

Voltage drop tests are made while current is flowing through the circuit. This means that the normal operating conditions, such as heat and vibration, are affecting the circuit. Voltage drop tests are especially useful for pinpointing faults that occur during these operating conditions, but that may not occur without current flow through the circuit.

Voltage drops can be computed indirectly, or they can be measured directly.

Computed voltage drop

By doing the available voltage test described earlier, you can compute the voltage drop of any part of a circuit. Figure 2-34 shows a circuit being tested for available voltage. Voltage drops can be computed by comparing the voltage available on one side of a load to the voltage available on the other side of the load. For example:
● Voltmeter 1 reads 12 volts, while voltmeter 2 reads 8 volts. The voltage drop across bulb A is 4 volts (12 − 8 = 4).
● Voltmeter 3 reads 4 volts, so the voltage drop across bulb B is 4 volts (8 − 4 = 4).
● Voltmeter 4 reads zero volts. The voltage drop across bulb C is 4 volts (4 − 0 = 4).

By computing the voltage drop across loads while you do an average voltage test, you can detect bad conditions such as the corroded switch in figure 2-32.

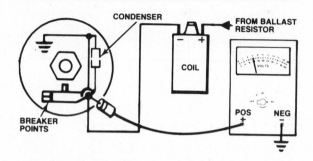

Figure 2-36. Measuring voltage drop across the ignition breaker points.

Direct voltage drop

Voltage drop does not have to be computed from two voltmeter readings. In some cases, it can be measured directly, figure 2-35. The voltmeter (+) lead is placed on the side of the load nearer the battery (+) terminal. The (−) lead is placed on the side of the load nearer to ground. The voltmeter will show the voltage drop across the load. Figure 2-35 shows the voltage drop readings for an entire circuit. You can see that the sum of the voltage drops equals the source voltage.

A single voltage drop test can be useful if you know what a normal drop should be. For example, the voltage drop across the ignition breaker points can be measured as follows:
1. Connect the (+) voltmeter lead to the primary wire connection at the breaker points, figure 2-36.
2. Be sure the breaker points are closed.
3. Turn the ignition on.
4. Turn the voltmeter to its lowest range and note the reading.
5. The normal voltage drop across the points is 0.1 volt.

If the voltage drop exceeds 0.2 volt, the points are probably burned, corroded, bent, or loose.

Whether you measure a voltage drop directly across a load, figure 2-35, or compute it by measuring between ground and both sides of a load, figure 2-34, usually depends on which way is easier to connect your voltmeter for a particular circuit.

Continuity Testing

Continuity testing is very similar to no-load voltage testing. Each will tell you if system voltage is being applied to a part of the circuit. During a no-load voltage test, the voltmeter is connected in parallel with the circuit, figure 2-33. Make a continuity test as follows, figure 2-37:

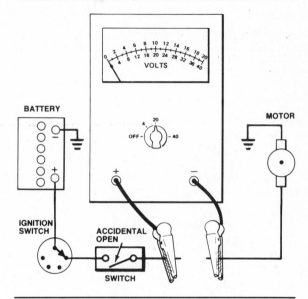

Figure 2-37. To test continuity in this motor, the voltmeter is connected in series with the circuit.

1. Disconnect the circuit leads at the test point.
2. Connect the voltmeter (+) lead to the circuit nearer to the battery (+) terminal (voltage source).
3. Connect the voltmeter (−) lead to the other side of the test point. This places the voltmeter in series.
4. Close the switch and note the voltmeter reading:
   a. If the voltmeter reads system voltage, the circuit is complete.
   b. If the voltmeter reads zero voltage, the circuit is open.

OHMMETER

An ohmmeter, figure 2-38, measures the resistance of a load or a conductor in ohms. It is constructed and used somewhat differently than an ammeter or a voltmeter. Ohmmeters are available as analog or digital meters. Analog ohmmeters use a D'Arsonval movement, but also have a resistor connected in series with the coil, figure 2-39. Analog and digital ohmmeters both have a self-contained battery to provide their own power source.

When the ohmmeter leads are connected to the device being tested, current from the meter's power source flows through the device and back to the meter. Because the source voltage and the meter's internal resistance are known, the current flow through the coil is determined by the resistance of the device being tested. Current flow through the meter coil is shown on the meter scale as a resistance measurement.

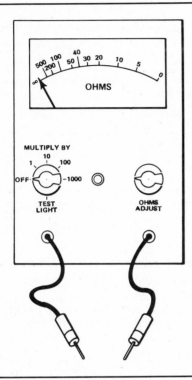

Figure 2-38. A typical ohmmeter.

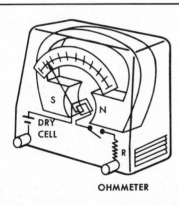

Figure 2-39. A resistor and a dry cell battery are placed in series with the ohmmeter coil. (Delco-Remy)

The ohmmeter is used to check the resistance of a load or a conductor while there is *no voltage* applied to the circuit. Ohmmeters can be battery-powered or they can plug into commercial alternating current. In either case, any current flow from an outside source will damage the meter. Before testing a component with an ohmmeter, remove the component from the circuit or be sure that the circuit is open.

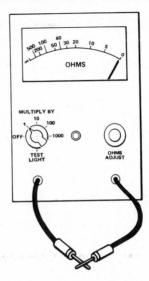

Figure 2-40. An ohmmeter is calibrated by touching the leads together and adjusting the needle to read zero.

Using An Ohmmeter

Because the ohmmeter does not use system voltage, the meter leads have no polarity. Either lead can be connected to any test point. Analog ohmmeters must be calibrated, or "zeroed", before use; digital ohmmeters do not require adjustment.

Calibrating analog ohmmeters

If there are batteries in an ohmmeter, they will weaken with age and change with temperature. The voltage applied to a.c.-powered ohmmeters also can vary. An analog ohmmeter must be calibrated, or zeroed, before each use. To zero the meter, connect the two test leads together, figure 2-40. The meter should read zero resistance. If it does not, move the calibration knob until the needle indicates zero ohms. The meter should now give accurate test measurements.

Ohmmeter scale

Just as with an ammeter and voltmeter, the analog ohmmeter internal circuitry reacts to current flow to move the needle. The ammeter and voltmeter scales show increasing values from left to right as current flow through the meter increases. The ohmmeter must show *decreasing* resistance readings in ohms as current flow through the meter increases. The ohmmeter scale is marked opposite to an ammeter or voltmeter scale, figure 2-41. The ohmmeter reads infinite resistance (no current flow) where the ammeter and voltmeter read zero.

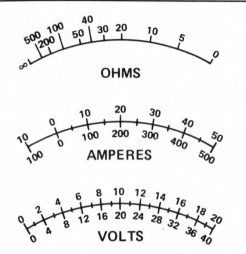

Figure 2-41. The ohmmeter scale is the reverse of the ammeter and voltmeter scales.

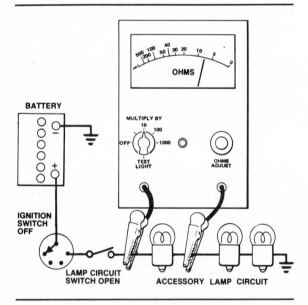

Figure 2-42. No outside current must flow through an object being tested with an ohmmeter.

Like ammeters and voltmeters, analog ohmmeters often have several scales on the dial. Digital ohmmeters also have various ranges, just like the analog ohmmeter. When using an ohmmeter, begin testing on the *lowest* scale and switch to the highest scale that gives the most precise reading.

Ohmmeter tests

The ohmmeter is connected across the component to be tested, figure 2-42. This looks similar to the parallel connection used with a voltmeter, but since there is no system voltage applied to

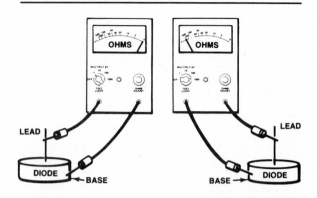

Figure 2-43. Ohmmeters are commonly used to test diodes.

the ohmmeter, it is not truly a parallel circuit branch. The ohmmeter's self-contained voltage creates current flow through a circuit consisting of the meter movement and the load being tested. That is, the ohmmeter provides a complete series circuit.

Ohmmeter measurements can pinpoint a high-resistance or a low-resistance fault.
● If a conductor or load has a high resistance or is open, the ohmmeter will measure high or infinite resistance.
● If a load has a short or ground that bypasses some of its normal resistance, the ohmmeter will indicate low resistance.

An ohmmeter is commonly used to check alternator diodes, figure 2-43:
1. Connect one ohmmeter test lead to the diode lead and the other ohmmeter test lead to the diode base. Observe the ohmmeter reading.
2. Reverse the ohmmeter test leads so that the test lead that touched the diode base in step 1 now touches the diode lead, and the test lead that touched the diode lead in step 1 now touches the diode base. Observe the ohmmeter reading.
3. Compare the two meter readings.
  a. If the diode has very high or infinite resistance in one direction and very low resistance in the other direction, the diode is good.
  b. If the diode has high resistance in both directions, it is bad.
  c. If the diode has low resistance in both directions, it is bad.
The ohmmeter also can be used to check the ignition coil primary winding. Manufacturers often provide a resistance specification for their ignition coils. To test this:
1. Either remove the two coil primary wires from their terminals on the coil cap, or make sure that the ignition switch is off.

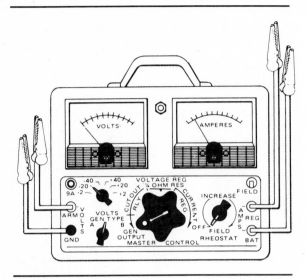

Figure 2-44. Multimeters are used for most automotive testing.

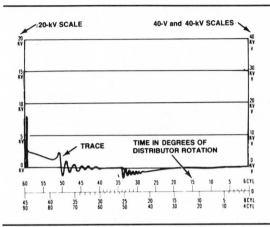

Figure 2-45. This oscilloscope screen has kilovolt scales on both sides and a low-voltage scale on the right side.

2. Connect one ohmmeter lead to each coil primary terminal on the coil cap. Observe the ohmmeter reading.

3. Compare the reading to the manufacturer's specification.

    a. If there is infinite resistance, the coil primary winding is open.

    b. If the resistance is lower than specified, the coil primary winding is shorted.

Ohmmeter and Voltmeter Comparison

Resistance can be measured directly with an ohmmeter, or it can be computed from voltage drop measurements made with a voltmeter. Resistance faults in wiring and connections often generate heat, which further increases the operating circuit resistance. In these cases, the fault may not show up readily when the circuit is shut off or the component is removed for testing. Therefore, voltage drop tests are often the best way to find a resistance problem in an operating circuit. Other advantages to voltage drop tests are:

● Meter reading is often easier and faster because small increases in wiring resistance show up as sharp increases in readable voltage drop.

● A complete circuit can be tested quickly because a voltmeter can be moved from point to point in a circuit while the circuit is operating.

An ohmmeter, however, has definite advantages for other test situations. They are particularly useful for:

● Measurement of major load parts that have specific resistance values within the usable range of the meter.

● Measurement of high-resistance items, such as spark plug cables and electronic ignition pickup coils.

● Testing the internal parts of components such as alternators, which require disassembly to reach the test points.

● Bench testing new or used parts such as switches, circuit breakers, and relays before assembly or installation.

MULTIMETERS

Various test meters can be built into a single case or console, figures 2-27 and 2-44. These are often called volt-amp testers, battery-starter testers, volt-ohm meters (VOM), or multimeters. The individual meters all operate the same, regardless of how they are constructed. These multimeters also may contain fixed-value resistors and variable-resistance carbon piles for making specific tests. We will learn more about their use in later chapters.

OSCILLOSCOPE

An oscilloscope is a sophisticated electronic test instrument that shows the changing voltage levels in an electrical system over a period of time. In this section, we will discuss the operation of the oscilloscope. Later chapters explain its use.

The oscilloscope, or scope, as it is often called, has a screen (much like a television screen) which displays a line of light called a trace. The trace indicates the voltage levels over a period of time during the electrical system's operation. The automotive oscilloscope screen is marked with various scales, figure 2-45, which show the values of different positions of

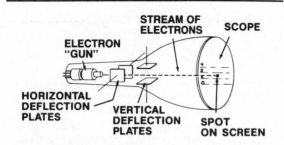

Figure 2-46. The electron gun traces a pattern of light on the inside of the cathode ray tube screen. (Marquette)

the trace. The vertical sides of the screen illustrated are marked in kilovolts (abbreviated kV, meaning thousands of volts). Just as many voltmeter scales are marked with several voltage ranges, most oscilloscope screens have a number of voltage ranges marked on each side.

Some scopes also have a low-voltage scale on one or both sides of the screen, figure 2-45. The kV scales are used to measure voltage in the secondary circuit of the ignition system. The low-voltage scales can be used to measure voltage in the ignition primary circuit and the charging system. Using a switch on the oscilloscope console, you can select the range that will give you the most legible voltage reading for the test being performed. On the screen shown in figure 2-45, the zero-voltage line is at the bottom. Some scopes have the zero line above the bottom so that both positive and negative voltage can be shown.

The distance across the screen represents time. In figure 2-45, no periods of time are shown in milliseconds or microseconds. Instead, time measurements across the bottom of the screen are given in terms of degrees of ignition distributor rotation. This is used to measure ignition dwell.

Cathode Ray Tube

The oscilloscope screen is the front of a cathode ray tube. As we said, this is the same basic device as the picture tube in your television set. Although a cathode ray tube is a complex electronic device, its operation can be explained in simple terms.

A cathode ray tube, figure 2-46, has an electron gun which shoots a high-speed stream of electrons. The inside of the oscilloscope screen is coated with phosphors so that it glows at the spot where the electron stream hits it. The stream or beam is controlled by two pairs of electrically charged plates. Depending upon the type of charge present upon the plates (+) or

(−), they will either attract or repel the negatively charged electron stream, causing it to bend or deflect.

One set of plates bends the beam up and down to change the height of the trace. These are called the vertical deflection plates. They are controlled by the voltage present in the system being tested. The higher the voltage, the more the beam is deflected, making the light appear farther up the voltage scale on the screen.

The second set of plates bends the beam from side to side so that the light travels across the screen from left to right. These are called the horizontal deflection plates. They are controlled by the speed of the engine being tested. The faster the engine runs, the faster the light will travel across the screen. Because the light travels so quickly, and the phosphors continue to glow briefly after the electron beam moves on, the trace appears as a solid line. Our eyes cannot see the single dots of light on the screen, but instead see the trace as a line of light across the entire screen. When the beam reaches the far right side of the screen, the internal circuitry of the oscilloscope quickly brings the beam back to the left side so that all we see is the left-to-right movement line of the trace. The returning right-to-left straight line, called a retrace, travels so fast that we generally do not see it at all.

SPECIAL TESTERS

A wide variety of special electronic testers has been developed over the past few years to help simplify troubleshooting procedures on computer-controlled electrical systems. While such testers make troubleshooting faster and easier, they will not think for you. To interpret the test results correctly, you must still understand the test procedures and operation of the system you are testing.

Many testers will check individual circuits and display circuit trouble codes. However, they only tell you that a circuit is functioning normally or that there is a problem somewhere in the circuit. They do not pinpoint the exact cause. To identify and correct the cause of a problem, you must still rely on traditional electrical troubleshooting methods. This section of the chapter provides general descriptions of the more common types of special electronic testers available for use.

Scanners and Data Recorders

Independent equipment manufacturers offer a special tester called a scanner, figure 2-47. The

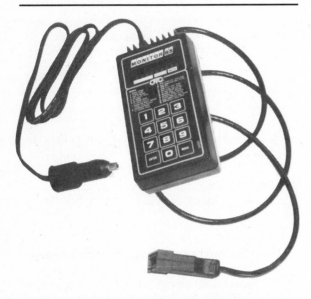

Figure 2-47. Electronic scanners plug into the test connector under the dash of GM vehicles.

scanner monitors a circuit called the serial data link that transmits a continuous stream of information concerning the status of various parts of the engine control system. The scanner relays the selected information to the technician through a digital display, and is powered by battery voltage through the cigarette lighter, the diagnostic connector under the instrument panel, or by direct connection to the battery.

Scanner test capabilities vary, depending upon the price and design of the particular unit, as well as the year of the system to which it is connected. Units containing built-in memory are restricted to use with certain specified vehicles; those designed to work with interchangeable software cartridges can be used with a wide variety of systems. A few scanners designed for 1986 and later CCC systems allow you to manually override the computer and control the engine operating conditions directly, or switch the engine into a pre-programmed test mode. This lets you determine if each control factor is operating at the optimum setting, and evaluate how a change might affect overall engine performance.

Manufacturers of such testers prepare operating instructions designed to follow the carmakers' test procedures. As system functions are changed, these instructions are revised. Generally, a system scanner will make the following tests:
- Trouble code display — the scanner retrieves trouble codes stored in the computer memory and displays them on a numerical display screen.

- Open- and closed-loop test — the scanner looks at data from the EGO and temperature sensors, then indicates whether the system is in open- or closed-loop mode.
- EGO sensor signal voltage — many scanners will display the EGO sensor voltage signal. The display may read directly in millivolts or indirectly as an index number.
- Air injection switching test — by triggering the air switching solenoid, some scanners let you test operation of the air injection system. This allows you to briefly create a lean exhaust condition, which amounts to a doublecheck of the EGO sensor.
- EGR solenoid operation — if the vehicle has an EGR vacuum solenoid, this function lets you check solenoid operation.
- Mixture control solenoid dwell — on vehicles so equipped, some scanners will display the mixture control solenoid duty cycle dwell readings.

In addition to these tests, the design of some scanners allows them to check specific sensor circuits or to activate the actuator circuits and test their operation. The following are generally included:
- MAP and barometric pressure sensors
- Throttle position sensor or switch
- Air and coolant temperature sensors
- Vehicle speed sensor
- Vapor canister purge solenoid
- Torque converter clutch solenoid
- Air conditioner switch
- Idle air control (IAC) or idle speed control (ISC) actuators.

Some manufacturers sell data recorders that allow you to plug a cassette recorder into the system's serial data terminal. You can then drive the vehicle and record up to 60 minutes of actual operating conditions. When the data recorder is later connected to a large engine analyzer, the analyzer will identify operating problems recorded on the cassette.

Carmakers' Testers

Automotive manufacturers provide electronic testers for use with their various electronic control systems. Chrysler markets a diagnostic readout tester for its engine control system, figure 2-48, to its dealers. Several equipment companies sell equivalent units to independent service technicians.

Testers for Chrysler systems have three general test modes:
- The diagnostic test mode that displays system trouble codes stored in computer memory.
- The circuit actuation test mode (ATM) that operates the ignition coil, fuel injectors, idle

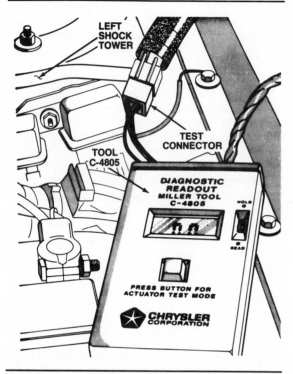

Figure 2-48. The Chrysler special tester attaches to a self-test connector under the hood.

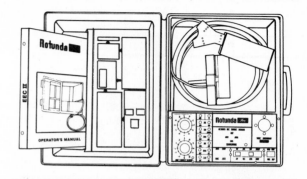

Figure 2-49. A typical Ford EEC tester or breakout box. (Ford)

speed control, and other system actuators.
● The switch test mode that checks the operation of switches and sensors that send information to the computer.

Trouble codes and switch and actuator functions vary, depending on the engine system, year, and model of the vehicle. Test functions for all Chrysler systems, however, follow the same general principles.

Ford offers a variety of EEC testers (often called breakout boxes) for testing its various EEC systems, figure 2-49. These testers plug in-line between the electronic control assembly (ECA) and the vehicle wiring harness, figure 2-50. Used in conjunction with a digital volt-ohmmeter (DVOM), these testers monitor all pertinent EEC signals and are designed to reduce the total number of steps required to locate a faulty component. A diagnostic manual is included with each tester to help maintain and diagnose the particular EEC system for which the tester is designed.

Ford's Self-Test and Automatic Readout (or STAR) tester, figure 2-51 is used with late-model MCU and all EEC-IV systems and shows system trouble codes on its digital display panel. The STAR tester is powered by an internal 9-volt battery and attaches to the vehicle test connector with a special adapter cable.

Ford also offers special testers for particular systems, such as its Electronic Message Center (EMC) tester. Like the breakout boxes described earlier, the EMC tester connects between the EMC control module and the instrument panel harness, and requires the use of a DVOM. The EMC tester monitors sensor signals and provides readout information on the DVOM to indicate if the sensor system is working correctly.

Kent-Moore Tool Group provides a variety of individual component testers for GM vehicles, including an HEI module tester, EGO sensor tester, and Idle Speed Control (ISC) motor tester. When properly connected and used, these testers allow you to monitor component operation or activate a particular device without removing it from the system.

Programmed Engine Analyzers

These large, expensive pieces of shop equipment are preprogrammed for computerized identification of problems affecting all major engine systems. They are offered by equipment manufacturers such as Sun, Allen, and Bear to independent service shops. Ford and General Motors offer the same machines to their dealers under their own brand name.

These so-called analytical analyzers vary considerably in what they will do and how well they do it. While many can handle a high percentage of problems quite well, there are still situations that require interpretation of data by a skilled technician.

In general, all of these analyzers "talk" to the user by asking questions and providing test sequences on a screen. Some even allow the user to "talk back" using a photocell light pen. Once the vehicle identification code has been entered into the analyzer, it compares a car's operational characteristics to diagnostic logic stored in its memory bank, performs the

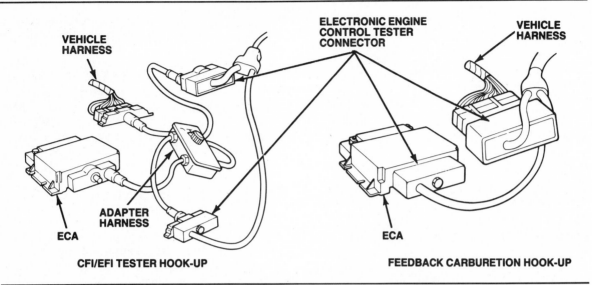

Figure 2-50. EEC tester hookup requires an adapter harness on fuel injection systems. (Ford)

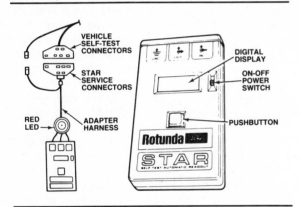

Figure 2-51. The Ford STAR tester appears externally similar to the Chrysler special tester.

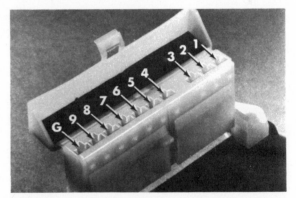

Figure 2-52. The GM diagnostic connector provides voltage signals from: (1) Starter BAT terminal, (2) Ignition switch BAT terminal, (3) Headlamp feed (except Chevette, T1000 and Acadian), (4) Distributor BAT or B+ terminal, (5) Ignition switch IGN 1 terminal, (6) Distributor TACH terminal, (7) not used, (8) Starter solenoid S terminal, (9) Ignition switch START terminal, (G) Ground.

troubleshooting process, and identifies the system or component that is causing the problem.

The analyzers are programmed to recognize out-of-specification conditions, pinpoint the malfunctioning component, and determine the necessary adjustment or repair. In addition, most of them will provide a printout or "hard copy" of the test procedures and results for reference by the serviceman or customer.

This concept has been applied to specific situations, such as the periodic smog test required by California for vehicle registration. In this case, the analyzer's program is designed specifically to test the emission control functions. The user enters the vehicle identification

codes and follows the instructions that appear on the screen. The analyzer monitors the emission systems under predetermined conditions, compares the results to its memory and either passes or fails the vehicle.

VEHICLE TEST AND DIAGNOSTIC CONNECTORS

Most late-model vehicles have test or diagnostic connectors to which you can attach the special testers or several types of standard test equipment.

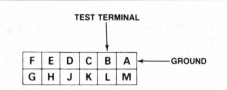

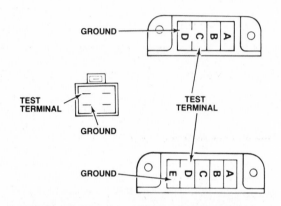

Figure 2-53. GM ALDL or ALCL connector test terminal identification.

GM and Chrysler
Diagnostic Connectors

Diagnostic connectors are provided in the engine compartments of many 1977-1982 GM and 1978-1981 Chrysler vehicles, figure 2-52. These connectors allow you to test several electrical circuits from a single point on the car. Each of the connector terminals is wired in parallel with a voltage test point in the electrical

system. GM vehicles with air conditioning have a second connector to test the air conditioning electrical circuits.

Many equipment companies make special testers or test lead adapters for engine analyzers that plug into the connector. These permit fast hookup and a quick series of prescribed tests. You also can connect a standard voltmeter − lead to the ground terminal and the + lead to any of the other terminals to make several tests from a single point on the car.

Electronic Control System
Test Connectors

All GM cars since 1980 equipped with C-4 or CCC engine control systems have a test connector under the instrument panel. This connector may be called the "Assembly Line Communications Link" (ALCL) or "Assembly Line Diagnostic Link" (ALDL). It has a test terminal that can be connected to a ground terminal to display system trouble codes on the instrument panel's CHECK ENGINE or SERVICE ENGINE SOON lamp. Terminal numbers and locations vary from year to year, figure 2-53.

Most 1984 and later Chrysler front-wheel drive cars have electronic engine control systems with self-diagnostic capability. The self-test connector in the engine compartment lets you attach the special tester required to check the system, figure 2-48.

Ford vehicles equipped with EEC-IV engine control systems and late-model MCU systems have a self-test connector in the engine compartment to which you can connect a standard analog voltmeter or the STAR tester, figure 2-51.

3

Battery Service

A dead battery can cause problems in all areas of a car's electrical system. A quick check of the battery should be your first step before doing any other troubleshooting. If the battery is not in good condition, service or replace it before testing any other circuits. This chapter has information on battery safety, servicing, and replacement.

BATTERY SAFETY

Treat a battery with respect. If spilled, the sulfuric acid in the battery electrolyte can damage the car's paint or corrode metal parts. The acid also can cause severe skin burns and permanent injury to your eyes. Wear safety glasses to protect your eyes when servicing a battery; wear gloves to protect your hands when handling a battery.

If electrolyte contacts your skin or eyes, flush the area with cold water for several minutes, then flood it with a solution of baking soda and water or a neutralizing eyewash. Do not rub the eyes or skin. Call a doctor or ambulance immediately.

When a battery is charging or discharging, it gives off *highly explosive* hydrogen gas. Some hydrogen is present in battery cells at all times. Any spark or flame can cause a battery to explode violently, disintegrating its case and showering bystanders with acid. Follow these important safety precautions to prevent serious personal injury:
● Keep sparks, open flame, and smoking materials far away from batteries at all times.
● Operate charging equipment only in a well-ventilated area.
● Never "short" across battery terminals or cable connectors.
● Never connect or disconnect charger leads at battery terminals while the charger is turned on (which will always cause a spark).
● Remove your wristwatch and any rings before servicing a battery or doing any work near electrical systems. This will help to avoid the possibility of arcing and burns.

Batteries are heavy and awkward to handle. A dropped battery could smash a toe, spill electrolyte, and ruin the battery. Always use a lifting strap or battery carrier, figure 3-1, to make battery handling easier and safer.

Electrolyte in a fully charged battery freezes between −60° and −90°F (−5° and −68°C). In a discharged or partially discharged battery, however, the electrolyte can freeze at 5°F (−15°C) or even warmer. This means that winter temperatures in many areas are cold enough to freeze a weak battery.

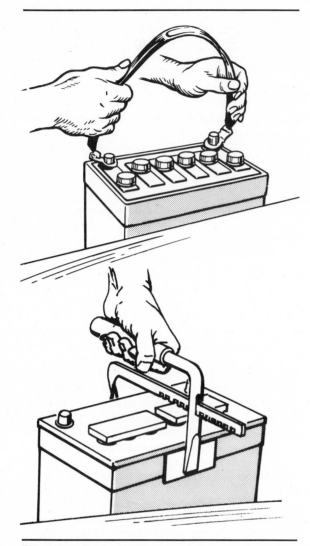

Figure 3-1. Battery carriers are designed to handle a battery without danger to the battery or to the mechanic.

Figure 3-2. These are some of the tools and supplies you will need to service a battery.

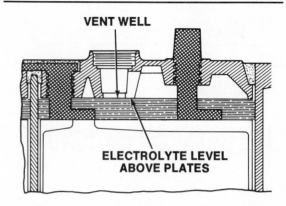

Figure 3-3. Electrolyte should completely cover the battery plates.

Passing current through a frozen battery can cause it to rupture or explode. Before charging or boost-starting a dead battery in winter, always check the electrolyte in all cells for signs of freezing. If ice or slush can be seen, or if the electrolyte level *cannot* be seen, allow the battery to thaw at room temperature before servicing it in any way.

INSPECTION, CLEANING, AND REPLACEMENT

Inspection, cleaning, and replacment are often the only services a battery needs. These simple jobs can be done with the following tools, figure 3-2:
● Baking soda or ammonia solution
● Cleaning brushes
● Connector pliers or wrenches
● Connector puller
● Battery strap or carrier
● Connector and terminal cleaning tool
● Cable clamp spreader
● Anticorrosion coating.

Battery Inspection

Complete battery inspection includes the following points:
1. Check the electrolyte level, figure 3-3. It should be above the tops of the plates or at the indicated level within the cells. If the vent caps are removable, add distilled or mineral-free drinking water to raise the electrolyte level. Do not overfill.
2. Inspect the battery case and cap for dirt or grease that could cause a voltage leak to ground.
3. Inspect for acid corrosion around the battery terminals, figure 3-4, cable connectors, and metal parts of the holddown and battery tray (also called a box).

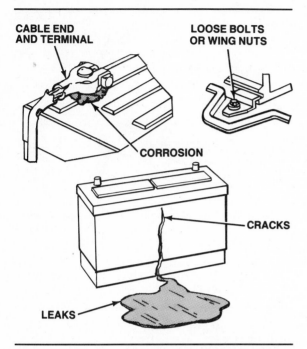

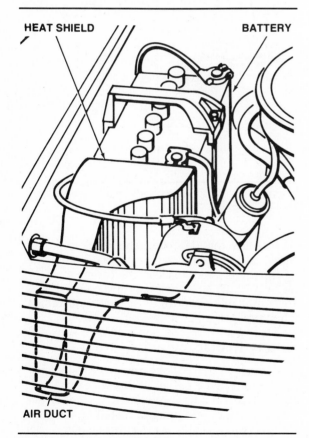

Figure 3-4. Replace an obviously damaged battery.

Figure 3-5. Be sure that battery heat shields are properly installed.

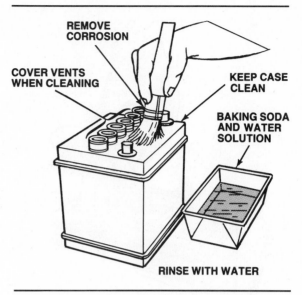

Figure 3-6. A solution of baking soda and water will clean most corrosion off a battery. (Chrysler)

4. Inspect the battery case for cracks, figure 3-4, loose terminal posts, a raised top, and other physical damage. If the battery shows any of this damage, replace it.

5. Check for missing or damaged cell caps. Replace any that are broken or missing.

6. Inspect the cables for broken or corroded wires, worn insulation, and loose or damaged connectors. Replace bad parts.

7. Check all cable connections for looseness and dirt.

8. Inspect the tray and holddown for looseness, damage, and missing parts, figure 3-4.

9. Make sure that heat shields are properly placed on batteries that use them, figure 3-5.

Battery Cleaning

Begin cleaning the battery and cables by neutralizing acid corrosion on terminals, connectors, and other metal parts with baking soda and water or an ammonia solution, figure 3-6. Be careful to keep corrosion off painted surfaces and rubber parts. *Do not let the soda solution enter the battery.*

If corrosion is heavy, it is a good idea to remove the battery from the engine compartment. This will prevent any corrosion from falling into various body and frame crevices where it can react with the metal. Use a stiff-bristled nonmetallic brush, figure 3-7, and remove dirt and grease with a detergent solution or with solvent. Avoid splashing.

After removing corrosion and dirt, rinse the battery and cable connections with fresh water.

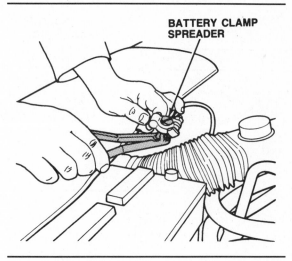

Figure 3-9. A cable clamp spreader tool will open the clamp and ream the inside. (Ford)

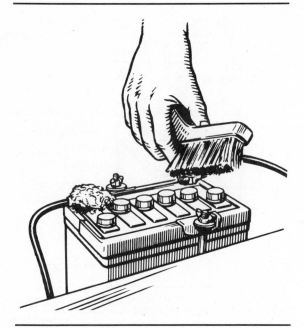

Figure 3-7. A stiff-bristled brush will remove heavy corrosion.

Figure 3-8. A battery connector puller will remove the cable without damaging the battery post.

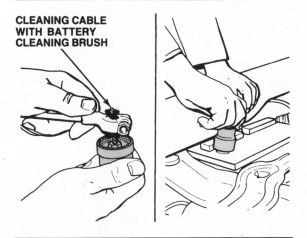

Figure 3-10. This 2-piece brush cleans both battery posts and cable connectors. (Ford)

cable connectors. Use a brush similar to that shown in figure 3-11 to clean side terminals. It works equally well to clean the connectors, figure 3-12. Be sure the posts and connectors are completely clean for good electrical contact when replacing the cables.

Battery Replacement

Before installing a battery, review the safety precautions given earlier in this chapter. To avoid electrical burns, remove rings and wristwatches before removing or installing a battery. Handle batteries only with a lifting strap or battery carrier.

Battery cables are generally color-coded red (positive) and black (negative). Terminal identification is provided by a stamped or raised POS or (+) sign in the battery case be-

Dry with a clean cloth or low-pressure compressed air. If battery terminals and cable connectors are badly corroded, remove the cables from the battery for thorough cleaning. *Remove the ground cable first.* If a cable is stuck on a top terminal battery, use a cable puller, figure 3-8, to remove it. Do not pry it off with a screwdriver or hit it with a hammer.

Use a battery clamp spreader tool to open the cable connector, figure 3-9, and ream the inside. Neutralize corrosion on the cable connectors with a baking soda solution. A combination wire brush with internal and external bristles, figure 3-10, is a handy tool for cleaning top terminal battery posts and the inside of

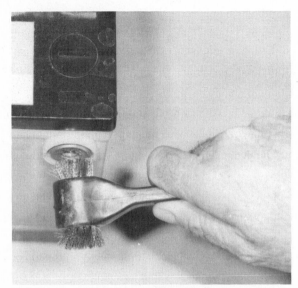

Figure 3-11. This type of brush works well in cleaning side terminals.

Figure 3-12. The same brush can be used to clean the side terminal connectors.

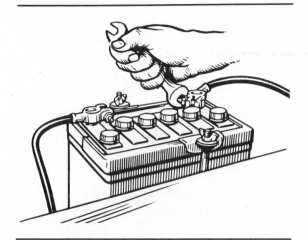

Figure 3-13. Use the proper tool to loosen bolt-type connectors.

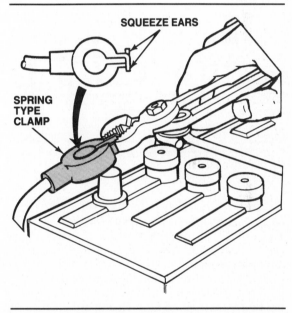

Figure 3-14. A pair of pliers will spread this type of connector. (Chrysler)

side or on top of the positive terminal post, and a NEG or (−) sign beside or on top of the the negative (ground) terminal post. On top-terminal batteries, the positive post is always larger in diameter than the negative post. Many side-terminal batteries also have different size connector threads for the positive and negative terminals. These features help ensure that the correct cable is connected to its corresponding terminal and thus prevent reversed battery polarity from incorrect connections. If there is any question, mark the cable connected to the positive (+) terminal before removing the old battery.

Remove the ground (negative) cable from the battery first; then remove the insulated (positive) cable. Use the correct size wrench for clamp-type connectors, figure 3-13, or pliers for spring-type connectors, figure 3-14. Use a cable puller, figure 3-8, to remove clamp-type connectors that are stuck on battery posts.

Loosen and remove the battery holddown and any heat shields that require removal. Attach a lifting strap or carrier, figure 3-1, and lift the battery from its tray. Inspect and clean the tray, figure 3-15, and both cables, figure 3-10. If new cables are needed, install them at this time.

Attach the strap or carrier to the new battery. Install the battery in the tray and secure the holddown and all heat shield parts. If necessary, spread clamp-type connectors with a spreading tool, figure 3-9, to fit them onto the posts. Never hammer a connector onto a battery post.

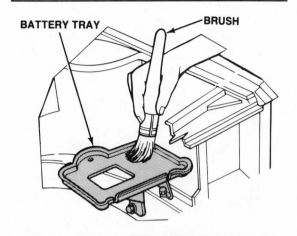

Figure 3-15. Clean all corrosion and dirt from the battery tray (box) before reinstalling the battery. (Chrysler)

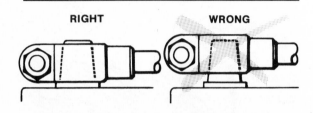

Figure 3-16. The connector must be firmly seated on the battery post.

Connect the insulated (positive) cable to the battery first; then connect the ground (negative) cable. Clamp-type connectors should be flush with or slightly below the tops of the posts, figure 3-16. Do not overtighten the bolts of side terminal clamps or the threads could strip out of the battery. To help prevent corrosion on top terminal batteries, apply a light coat of anticorrosion compound to the terminals and connectors *after* installation.

BATTERY TESTING

The state of charge and the capacity of a battery may be tested by several different methods. The most common are described below.

Specific Gravity Test (Removable Vent-Cap Battery)

A hydrometer is used to measure the specific gravity of the electrolyte in a vent-cap battery. If the battery is a fully closed, maintenance-free design, use the capacity (load) test or the open-circuit voltage test described later in the chapter to determine its state of charge.

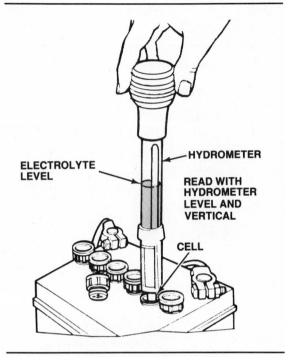

Figure 3-17. Draw enough electrolyte into the hydrometer to float the indicator. (Chrysler)

ELECTROLYTE SPECIFIC GRAVITY	BATTERY STATE OF CHARGE
1.265	100%
1.225	75%
1.190	50%
1.155	25%
1.120	Discharged

Figure 3-18. Electrolyte specific gravity is a direct indicator of battery state of charge.

To perform a specific gravity test, remove the cell caps and check the electrolyte level. If the electrolyte level is too low to take a sample, add water to all cells. Then charge the battery for about 10 minutes at about 5 amperes to mix the water with the electrolyte before testing. Insert the hydrometer into a cell at either end of the battery. Hold the hydrometer vertical and draw enough electrolyte into it to float the indicator, figure 3-17. Gently shake or tap the hydrometer to keep the float from touching the side of the tube. If the hydrometer has a built-in thermometer, draw electrolyte several times to stabilize the temperature reading.

Hold the hydrometer at eye level and read the specific gravity on the indicator. Return the electrolyte to the same cell and measure the other cells. A battery should always be recharged when the specific gravity drops below 1.225. A specific gravity variation of more than 50 points (0.050) between cells indicates a bad

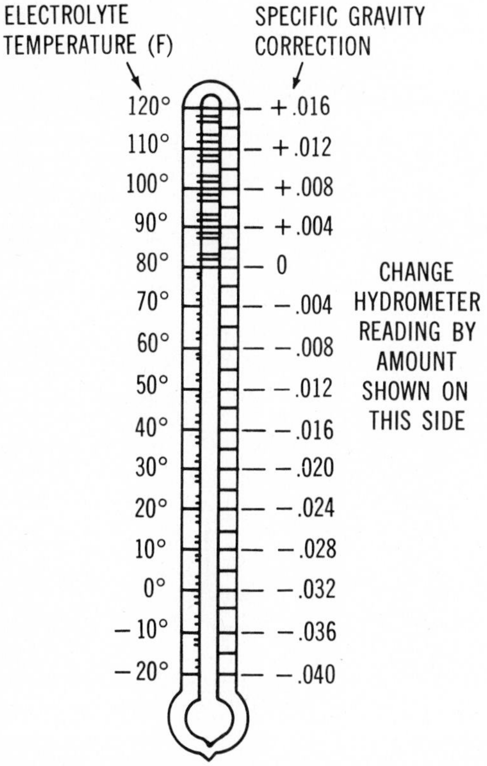

ELECTROLYTE
TEMPERATURE (F)

SPECIFIC GRAVITY
CORRECTION

120° — + .016
110° — + .012
100° — + .008
90° — + .004
80° — 0
70° — − .004
60° — − .008
50° — − .012
40° — − .016
30° — − .020
20° — − .024
10° — − .028
0° — − .032
− 10° — − .036
− 20° — − .040

CHANGE
HYDROMETER
READING BY
AMOUNT
SHOWN ON
THIS SIDE

Figure 3-19. Many hydrometers have a correction table printed on the side.

GREEN DOT — "BLACK" DARK — CLEAR

65% OR ABOVE STATE OF CHARGE — BELOW 65% STATE OF CHARGE — LOW LEVEL ELECTROLYTE

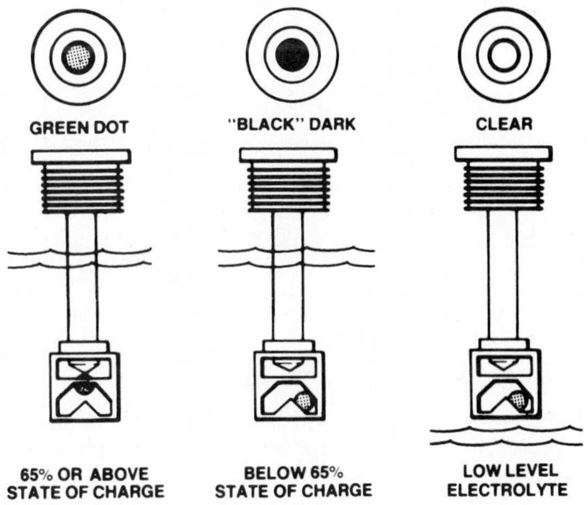

Figure 3-20. Delco "Freedom" batteries have this integral hydrometer built into their tops.

battery that should be replaced. Figure 3-18 shows battery state of charge based on electrolyte specific gravity.

Specific gravity readings are based on an electrolyte temperature of 80°F (27°C). If the temperature is above or below 80°F (27°C), the specific gravity reading must be corrected by adding or subtracting 4 points (0.004) for each 10°F (5.6°C) above or below the standard temperature. For example:

• The indicator reading is 1.230, and the temperature reading is 10°F (− 12.2°C). The specific gravity must be corrected for a variation of 70°F (39.2°C). Since 70 ÷ 10 = 7 (39.2 ÷ 5.6 = 7), that means that 28 points (.004 × 7 = .028) must be subtracted from the indicator reading of 1.230. The true corrected reading is 1.202.

• The indicator reading is 1.235, and the temperature reading is 120°F (49°C). Since the temperature reading is 40°F (22°C) above the standard of 80°F (27°C), 16 points (.004 × 4 = .016) must be added to the indicator reading of 1.235. The true corrected reading is 1.251.

Most hydrometers have a built-in thermometer to determine the electrolyte temperature. Figure 3-19 shows the relationship between that temperature and the correction

necessary for an accurate specific gravity reading.

State-of-charge Indicators

Maintenance-free batteries used on many late-model cars have a visual state-of-charge indicator in the battery top. The indicator shows whether the electrolyte has fallen below a minimum level, and it also functions as a go/no-go hydrometer.

The indicator, figure 3-20, is a plastic rod inserted in the top of the battery and extended into the electrolyte. A colored plastic ball is suspended in a cage from the bottom of the rod. Depending upon the specific gravity of the electrolyte, the ball will float or sink in its cage, changing the appearance of the indicator "eye". Interpret the state of charge indicator as follows:

• Colored dot visible — Any green, red, or blue appearance should be interpreted as a green, red, or blue dot. Some indicators use a red dot inside a larger blue dot. This means that the battery is at or above a 65-percent state of charge and is ready for use or testing. It does *not* automatically mean that the battery is in good condition.

• Dark, colored dot not visible ("black dot") or red dot visible inside larger clear area — Indicates that the battery is below a 65-percent state of charge and must be charged before testing. It does *not* necessarily mean that the battery is bad.

• Clear or light yellow — This means that the electrolyte is below the level of the built-in hydrometer. This may be caused by tipping the

OPEN CIRCUIT VOLTS	STATE OF CHARGE
12.6 or greater	100%
12.4 - 12.6	75 - 100%
12.2 - 12.4	50 - 75%
12.0 - 12.2	25 - 50%
11.7 - 12.0	0 - 25%
11.7 or less	0%

Figure 3-21. Minor changes in the battery open circuit voltage indicate major changes in the state of charge.

battery, a cracked case, or overcharging. This battery should not be recharged. It must be replaced.

Remember, with the exception of a clear or light yellow reading, the state of charge indicator does not tell you whether the battery is good or bad. You must do a capacity test to accurately determine the battery's condition.

Open-Circuit Voltage Test

The open-circuit voltage test can be substituted for the hydrometer specific gravity test with fully sealed, maintenance-free batteries. As a battery is discharged or recharged, the same internal chemical changes that affect the electrolyte specific gravity also result in minor changes in the battery's voltage. Because of this, the battery voltage with no load applied can be used as an indicator of the state of charge.

To do the test, the battery temperature should be 60° to 100°F (16° to 38°C). The voltage also must be allowed to stabilize for at least ten minutes with no load applied. On vehicles with high parasitic drains, it may be necessary to disconnect the battery ground cable. If the battery has just been recharged, apply a load for about 15 seconds to remove the surface charge. Once voltage has stabilized, use a digital voltmeter to measure the battery voltage to the nearest tenth of a volt. Use the chart, figure 3-21, to determine the state of charge.

Just like the specific gravity test performed with a hydrometer, or the state of charge indicator on low-maintenance and maintenance-free batteries, the open-circuit voltage test is only an indicator of the battery's state of charge. It does *not* tell you if the battery has enough current capacity to supply all of a vehicle's needs. If any of these tests indicate less than a 65-percent state of charge, charge the battery and do a capacity test to determine the battery's condition.

Capacity (Load) Test

The capacity, or load, test is the most important and meaningful test used to determine a battery's internal condition. It indicates a battery's

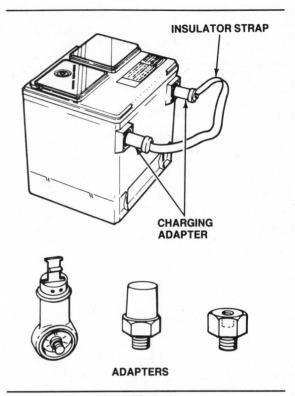

INSULATOR STRAP

CHARGING ADAPTER

ADAPTERS

Figure 3-22. Adapters often are needed when charging side terminal batteries. (Delco)

ability to provide starting current while still maintaining enough voltage to operate the ignition system.

The battery can be tested either in or out of the vehicle, but before beginning the test, it must be at or near a full state of charge. Use the tests already described to determine the battery's state of charge. In addition, the electrolyte temperature should be approximately 80°F (27°C) for best results. A cold battery will show considerably lower capacity.

Perform a capacity test using a volt-amp (battery-starter) tester or a charging-starting-battery (CSB) analyzer. These testers come in a variety of designs, some with variable loads (carbon pile) and some with fixed loads (resistor). Be sure to follow the test equipment manufacturer's instructions for hooking up the tester leads and for conducting the test. General instructions for a capacity test are as follows:

1. With the tester controls off, connect the tester leads to the battery. Observe correct polarity (+) to (+) and (−) to (−) and be sure that the test leads contact the battery posts correctly. Special adapters, figure 3-22, may be required to connect the tester to a side-terminal battery.

BATTERY TEMPERATURE °F (°C)	MINIMUM TEST VOLTAGE
70° (21°) or above	9.6 volts
60° (16°)	9.5 volts
50° (10°)	9.4 volts
40° (4°)	9.3 volts
30° (−1°)	9.1 volts
20° (−7°)	8.9 volts
10° (−12°)	8.7 volts
0° (−18°)	8.5 volts

Figure 3-23. Minimum capacity (load) test voltages vary significantly with battery temperature.

2. If the tester you are using has an adjustment for battery temperature, turn it to the proper setting. Use a thermometer in one of the cells to determine the temperature of a vent-cap battery. On sealed maintenance-free batteries, estimate the temperature as closely as possible, based on outside air temperature.

3. Refer to battery specifications to determine the cranking performance rating of the battery being tested.

4. Turn the load control knob to draw battery current at a rate equal to one-half of the battery's cranking performance rating, as determined in step 3. For example, if the battery is rated 480 cold-cranking amperes, adjust the current draw to 240 amperes.

5. If the cranking performance rating is unknown, estimate the test current as follows:

   a. If the battery is used with a large V-8 engine or any diesel engine — 225 to 300 amperes

   b. If the battery is used with a small V-8 or large 6-cylinder engine — 175 to 225 amperes

   c. If the battery is used with a small 6- or 4-cylinder engine — 170 amperes.

   On a fixed-load tester, set the battery size selector to the appropriate position.

6. Maintain this load for 15 seconds while watching the voltmeter. Turn the control knob off immediately after 15 seconds of current draw.

7. Voltage at the end of the 15 seconds should not fall below 9.6 volts. If voltage is lower, replace the battery.

   If the tester you are using is not temperature-compensating, refer to figure 3-23 for adjusted minimum voltages.

Alternative capacity test

If a suitable tester is not available, the starter motor can be used as a battery loading device for a capacity test. This test is valid only if the battery is at or near a full state of charge, and the starting circuit and starter are known to be in good operating condition.

1. Disable the ignition system so the engine will not start. **CAUTION: Some electronic ignition systems can be damaged during prolonged engine cranking unless properly disabled.** Refer to the vehicle manufacturer's instructions if necessary.

2. Connect a voltmeter to the battery terminals, observing correct polarity (+) to (+) and (−) to (−).

3. Crank the engine continuously for 15 seconds and watch the voltmeter reading at the end of the period.

4. If the voltmeter reading is above the minimum specified in figure 3-23, the battery and cranking circuit are in good condition. If the voltage reading is below this value, the battery may be in poor condition or the starting system may be drawing too much current.

Three-Minute Charge Test

To see if a discharged battery can be recharged or whether it is too badly sulfated to accept a charge, do a 3-minute charge test. This test should *not* be made on maintenance-free batteries, because the test results will not be accurate. A fast battery charger is used to pass a high charging current through the battery for three minutes. If the battery is not badly sulfated, the high current will knock the sulfate deposits off the plates. If the battery is too badly sulfated to accept a fast charge, the sulfate will not be knocked off, and high voltage will be measured across the battery terminals.

   If the battery is to be tested in the car, disconnect both battery cables to avoid damaging the alternator and electrical system. If high voltage is recorded early in the test, *stop the test.* High internal resistance due to sulfation or poor internal connections will develop heat that can boil the electrolyte. Here is how to do the 3-minute charge test:

1. Connect the charger leads to the battery, observing correct polarity (+) to (+) and (−) to (−).

2. Connect a voltmeter across the battery, (+) to (+) and (−) to (−).

3. Turn the charger on and adjust it for the highest charging rate but not exceeding 40 amperes for a 12-volt battery. If the charger has a timer, set it for 3 minutes.

4. After 3 minutes, read the voltmeter. If it is not more than 15.5 volts, the battery can be safely recharged at the maker's suggested charging rate.

5. If the voltage reading is more than 15.5 volts, the battery is bad and should be replaced.

OPEN CIRCUIT VOLTAGE	BATTERY SPECIFIC GRAVITY*	STATE OF CHARGE	CHARGING TIME TO FULL CHARGE AT 80° F**					
			at 60 amps	at 50 amps	at 40 amps	at 30 amps	at 20 amps	at 10 amps
			FULL CHARGE					
12.6	1.265	100%					48 min.	90 min.
12.4	1.225	75%	15 min.	20 min.	27 min.	35 min.	95 min.	180 min.
12.2	1.190	50%	35 min.	45 min.	55 min.	75 min.	145 min.	280 min.
12.0	1.155	25%	50 min.	65 min.	85 min.	115 min.	195 min.	370 min.
11.8	1.120	0%	65 min.	85 min.	110 min.	150 min.		

*Correct for temperature.   **If colder, it'll take longer.

Figure 3-24. Battery charging times vary with state of charge, temperature, and charging rate.

BATTERY CHARGING

Battery charging means applying a charging current rate in amperes for a period of time in hours. For example, a 20-ampere charging rate for three hours would be a 60-ampere-hour charging input to the battery.

Batteries are usually charged at rates from 3 to 50 amperes. Charging rates at the low end of this scale are slow charging; charging rates at the high end of the scale are fast charging. Fast chargers are the most widely used charging equipment in service stations and garages, although most fast chargers can also charge at a slow rate. Many motorists own slow chargers, or trickle chargers, that will charge a battery only at a slow rate.

Generally, any battery can be charged at any current rate if electrolyte gassing and spewing do not occur, and as long as electrolyte temperature stays below 125°F (52°C). When you have the time, however, it is best to charge at a slow rate of 5 to 15 amperes. Figure 3-24 gives typical charging times for various states of charge and charging rates.

Whether charging at a slow or a fast rate, begin by checking the electrolyte level when possible. It should be about ¼-inch (6mm) above the separators in each cell. Charging with the electrolyte level too low may damage the battery plates. Charging with the electrolyte level too high may cause the electrolyte to overflow because of the heat of charging. The proper electrolyte level is especially important for fast charging. Leave the cell caps in place during charging, but *be sure the vent holes are open.* Place a damp cloth over the battery while it is charging to reduce hydrogen escape.

Be sure also that the a.c. power line to which the charger is connected is delivering full power. Do not connect the charger to a heavily loaded circuit. An a.c. voltage drop of 20 percent can reduce the charger's output by 35 to 40 percent. If an extension cord is necessary, use 14-gauge or larger heavy-duty cord not over 25 feet (8 meters) long. The charger power cord and the extension cord should both be the 3-wire type so the charger case can be grounded. Special adapters, figure 3-22, may be required to connect the charger to a side-terminal battery.

Whether fast or slow charging, remember:
- Charge in a well-ventilated area away from sparks and open flame.
- **Be sure the charger is off** before connecting or disconnecting cables at the battery.
- Never try to charge a frozen battery.
- Wear eye protection.

If you are charging the battery while it is in the car:
1. Disconnect both battery cables to avoid damage to the alternator or other electrical parts.
2. Connect the charger cables to the battery, observing correct polarity (+) to (+) and (−) to (−).
3. Turn on the charger and set it for the desired rate.
4. Check the specific gravity and temperature of a vent-cap battery periodically during charging. Estimate the temperature of a maintenance-free battery by touching its case. Stop charging *immediately* if the temperature rises above 125°F (52°C).
5. Check the voltage across the battery terminals with a voltmeter or a battery tester. If voltage rises above 15.5 volts at any time, lower the charging rate until the voltage drops below this maximum value.
6. The battery is fully charged when all cells are gassing freely and specific gravity does not increase for three continuous hours. The fully charged specific gravity should be 1.260 to 1.265, corrected for electrolyte temperature, unless otherwise specified by the battery maker.
7. When charging a closed, maintenance-free battery, follow the maker's specifications for charging rate and time. If the battery has a state-of-charge indicator, charge until the indicator shows a full charge. Repeat the battery load test and continue charging if results are below specifications. In any case, do not exceed the maker's rate or time specifications.

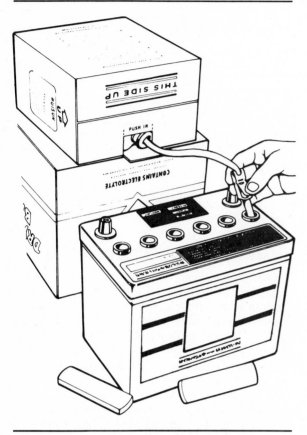

Figure 3-25. Dry-charged batteries must be filled with packaged electrolyte.

8. After charging, wash the battery top with baking soda and water to remove any acid from electrolyte gassing. Rinse with fresh water and dry the battery.

9. On vent-cap batteries, check the electrolyte level and add mineral-free or distilled water as required to bring all cells up to the proper level marks.

Fast-Charging Precautions

Fast charging a battery delivers a higher charging rate for a shorter time. Follow the charger maker's instructions for charging rate and length of time, according to the battery's specific gravity and cranking performance rating.
● Never fast charge a battery that has failed a 3-minute charge test.
● Never fast charge a battery that is sulfated or that has plate or separator damage.
● Watch electrolyte temperature closely and *stop charging* if the temperature rises above 125°F (52°C).

Whenever possible, follow a fast charge with a period of slow charging to fully charge the battery. Most battery chargers have a gradually decreasing charge rate as the battery comes to a full charge. This protects the battery from overcharging.

Maintenance-Free Charging Precautions

Because of their design, maintenance-free batteries require special precautions. As we have already seen, batteries with a state-of-charge indicator should not be recharged if the "eye" is clear or light yellow. This indicates that the electrolyte is below the level of the built-in hydrometer.

A high initial charging current will heat up the electrolyte of a maintenance-free battery and cause it to gas. Since the battery is sealed, venting is minimal with most such designs, and nonexistent with recombinant batteries. Applying a high charging current to a maintenance-free battery can cause internal battery damage and may even result in an explosion and serious injury.

A completely discharged maintenance-free battery may not accept a high charging current. If a load test indicates that the battery is fully discharged, watch the initial charging rate and terminal voltage carefully. If terminal voltage exceeds 15.5 volts with a high charging current, reduce the current and charge the battery for several hours at a setting low enough to keep terminal voltage under 15.5 volts.

ACTIVATING DRY-CHARGED BATTERIES

To ensure the best possible service, activate a dry-charged battery just before you install it in a car. To avoid damage from spilled acid, do not activate the battery after it is in a car.

1. Fill each battery cell to the top of the separators with the packaged electrolyte, figure 3-25. Be sure to read and follow the precautions listed on the electrolyte package, figure 3-26.

2. After filling, charge a 12-volt battery at 30 to 40 amperes until the electrolyte temperature is about 80°F (27°C) and specific gravity is above 1.250.

3. After charging, check the electrolyte level. If it is low, add enough electrolyte to bring the level up to the indicated marks in each cell. After that, service the battery only with mineral-free or distilled water when required to maintain the electrolyte level.

4. When the battery is properly filled and charged, dispose of any excess electrolyte in accordance with local and regional toxic waste

DANGER: POISON
CAUSES SEVERE BURNS
ACID PACKAGE
CONTAINS SULFURIC ACID

AVOID CONTACT WITH THE SKIN OR EYES

ANTIDOTES

EXTERNAL: Flood with water, then cover with moistened sodium bicarbonate. If eyes are involved, wash first with water then with 1 per cent solution of freshly prepared sodium bicarbonate. Call physician immediately.

INTERNAL: Do not use emetics, stomach pump, carbonates or bicarbonates. Give at least 20 to 30 cc (2/3 to 1 ounce) of milk of magnesia or preferably aluminum hydroxide gel diluted with water. If these alkalies are not available, the white of eggs (2 or 3) well beaten may be used. Give large quantities of water. Prevent collapse. Call physician immediately.

FLUSH THE PLASTIC LINER WITH WATER WHEN EMPTY

KEEP OUT OF REACH OF CHILDREN

Figure 3-26. Read and follow the electrolyte package label instructions. (Atlas)

Figure 3-27. Because their battery is located in the trunk, some Ford diesel-powered cars have a remote jump start connector in the engine compartment.

handling procedures. **CAUTION: Do not pour it down a floor drain or utility sink, even if neutralized with baking soda.** This is not only dangerous, but against the law in most areas.

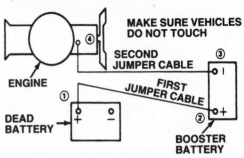

Figure 3-28. Jump-start connection pattern. (Ford)

JUMP STARTING WITH CABLES

It is often necessary to jump start a car with a weak or discharged battery by using a booster battery and jumper cables. There are several good reasons why starting a vehicle by this method is preferable to push-starting it:

● Push-starting most cars with automatic transmissions will not work. Their transmissions have no rear pump to develop hydraulic pressure and turn the engine.

● Push-starting a late-model car with a catalytic converter is likely to draw gasoline through the combustion chambers and deposit it in the converter. This will cause converter overheating and possible damage.

● Push-starting a diesel-powered vehicle is dangerous. The injection system may operate without the necessary lubrication from the fuel, or additional fuel deposited in the cylinders may explode when the engine starts, causing engine damage and possible injury.

Jump-starting a diesel-powered Ford Escort differs slightly from the procedure to be described. This vehicle has its battery located in the trunk and encased in a special protective bag with a vent. To make jump starting easier and safer, a jump terminal connection is provided in the engine compartment near the starter relay, figure 3-27. To use this connection, remove its red neoprene cap and connect the jumper cable here, instead of at the battery positive terminal.

For all other single-battery cars, use the following procedure to avoid damage to the charging and starting systems and to prevent any sparks that might cause a battery explosion. Figure 3-28 shows the proper connections. Always wear safety glasses when making or breaking jumper cable connections.

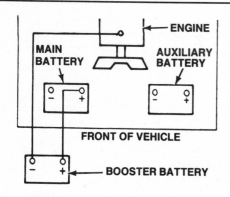

Figure 3-29. Dual-battery jump-start connection pattern. (Ford)

1. Set the parking brake, turn off all accessories and the ignition switch, and place the gearshift lever in Neutral or Park.
2. Connect one end of the first jumper cable to the positive (+) terminal of the discharged battery (point 1, figure 3-28).
3. Connect the other end of the same cable to the positive (+) terminal on the booster battery (point 2, figure 3-28).
4. Connect one end of the other jumper cable to the ground terminal (−) of the booster battery (point 3, figure 3-28). Connect the other end of this cable to a good ground on the *engine block*, of the disabled car, as far from the battery as possible (point 4, figure 3-28). The alternator mounting bracket is usually a convenient place for this.
5. Turn on the ignition and starter of the disabled car. If it doesn't start immediately, and if the booster battery is in another car, start the engine of the other car to avoid excessive drain on the booster battery. Make sure that the cars are not touching each other, because this will create a dangerous electrical connection and possible arcing.
6. After the disabled car is started, remove the jumper cable connection to the engine block *first*. Then remove the other end of that cable from the booster battery.

7. Finally, remove the other cable by disconnecting it first at the booster battery, then at the discharged battery.

Never use more than 16 volts to jump start a car with electronic engine controls or electronic fuel injection. The high voltage can damage the electronic components.

Jump Starting Dual-battery Vehicles

The diesel engines used in many cars and light trucks require a high cranking current (over 900 amperes). This is provided by two 12-volt batteries connected in parallel. You can jump start a diesel engine with two batteries by modifying the previous procedure.

The 12-volt booster battery to be used must have the cranking current capacity required by the diesel engine. A low-capacity battery may not be able to supply enough current to crank the diesel engine, especially in cold weather.

In a dual-battery installation, the positive terminal of the "main" battery is connected to the starter motor solenoid (GM) or starter relay (Ford); the other battery is the "auxiliary" battery. Always connect the booster battery positive cable to the positive terminal of the "main" battery of the diesel engine to minimize starting circuit resistance. Connect the negative jumper cable to a ground point on the engine that is at least 18 inches (45 cm) from both batteries. Figure 3-29 shows the proper connections.

After making the proper jumper cable connections, turn on the ignition switch of the disabled vehicle for about 30 seconds. This will allow the glow plugs to heat the combustion chambers. Start the engine of the booster vehicle and let it run at fast idle while starting the disabled engine. Never use 24-volt booster chargers to jump start a diesel with two batteries. This will cause immediate, severe, and costly damage to diesel engine glow plug systems.

PART TWO

Charging System Service

Chapter

4

A.C. Charging System

ON-CAR INSPECTION AND TESTING

Inspecting and testing the a.c. charging system on the car will help you to pinpoint problems. If the problem is with the alternator or with a solid-state regulator, remove the unit from the car for service or replacement. Off-the-car repairs for alternators are detailed in Chapter 5.

When working with the charging system, remember these safety precautions:
● Keep hands, hair, jewelry, and clothing away from moving parts. Remove any jewelry when servicing the battery.
● Keep the ignition switch off at all times except when specified during actual test procedures.
● Disconnect the battery ground cable before removing any leads from the alternator.
● Remember that the alternator output terminal has voltage present all the time while system connections are still in place.
● Never attempt to polarize an alternator as you would a d.c. generator.
● Make sure to connect the right cable to the right terminal when you install a battery.
● Disconnect the battery ground cable before charging the battery.
● Never operate an alternator without an external load connected to the unit.
● Keep the tester carbon pile off at all times except when specified during procedures.

CHARGING SYSTEM SYMPTOMS AND POSSIBLE CAUSES

Some common warning signs of charging system failures are:
● Ammeter, voltmeter, or warning lamp indications
● Low battery state of charge
● Alternator noise.

These symptoms, their possible causes, and cures are outlined in figure 4-1. The rest of this chapter explains how to test a.c. charging systems with common test equipment and pinpoint the causes of system problems.

CHARGING SYSTEM INSPECTION

1. Check the battery electrolyte level and state of charge as explained in Chapter 3. If the battery is worn out, the charging system may not be at fault.
2. Inspect the alternator drive belt for wear or damage, figure 4-2. If you must adjust the belt, be careful not to pry against the alternator's thin aluminum end-frame housing.

SYMPTOMS	POSSIBLE CAUSE	CURE
• The meter needle flutters • Warning lamp flickers	1. Loose connections in system wiring 2. Loose or worn brushes 3. Oxidized regulator points	1. Repair system wiring 2. Disassemble and test alternator 3. Replace regulator
• Ammeter needle reads discharge • Voltmeter needle shows low system voltage • Warning lamp stays on • Battery is discharged	1. Faulty alternator drive belt 2. Corroded battery cables 3. Loose system wiring 4. Defective field relay 5. Defective battery 6. Wrong battery in car 7. Alternator output low	1. Check and adjust belt 2. Replace battery cables 3. Repair system wiring 4. Replace field relay 5. Replace battery 6. Replace battery 7. Test and repair alternator
• Ammeter needle reads charge • Voltmeter needle shows high system voltage • Battery is overcharged	1. Loose system wiring 2. Poor regulator ground 3. Burned regulator points 4. Incorrect regulator setting 5. Defective regulator	1. Repair system wiring 2. Tighten regulator ground 3. Replace regulator 4. Adjust regulator 5. Replace regulator
• Warning lamp stays on when ignition switch is off	1. Shorted positive diode	1. Disassemble and test alternator
• Alternator makes squealing noise	1. Loose or damaged drive belt 2. Worn or defective rotor shaft bearing 3. Defective stator 4. Loose or misaligned pulley	1. Adjust or replace drive belt 2. Disassemble and inspect alternator 3. Disassemble and test alternator 4. Adjust pulley
• Alternator makes whining noise	1. Shorted diode	1. Disassemble and test alternator

Figure 4-1. Alternator charging system troubleshooting table.

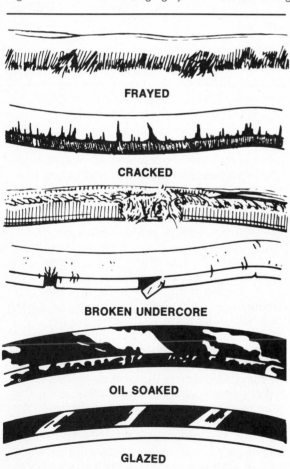

FRAYED

CRACKED

BROKEN UNDERCORE

OIL SOAKED

GLAZED

Figure 4-2. Many kinds of damage can make a drive belt operate inefficiently.

3. Inspect all system wiring and connections. Be sure to inspect fusible links for fusing. Make sure that any multiple plug connectors are latched correctly.

4. Check the alternator and regulator mountings for loose or missing bolts. Replace or tighten as needed.

DRIVE BELTS

The two most important jobs automotive drive belts must perform are to cool the engine by driving the fan and water pump, and to keep the battery charged by driving the alternator. In addition, drive belts also must operate other accessory units, such as the power steering pump, the air conditioning compressor, and the emission control air pump, figure 4-3.

Most automotive accessory drive belts are a simple V-type belt. They may be a smooth or a cogged design, figure 4-4. Since 1979, many vehicles have used a wide belt with multiple V-shaped ribs, figure 4-4. This single belt, called a serpentine belt, is used to drive several or all accessories, figure 4-5. Engines using a serpentine belt have a spring-loaded belt tensioner, which eliminates the need for belt adjustment and simplifies replacement.

Checking Belt Tension

In addition to being in good condition, all drive belts must be in proper adjustment. Correct

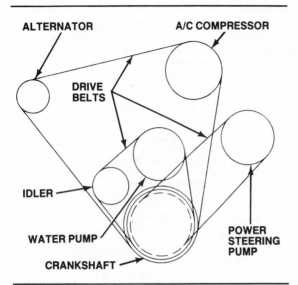

Figure 4-3. Drive belts translate engine power into energy to drive many accessory units.

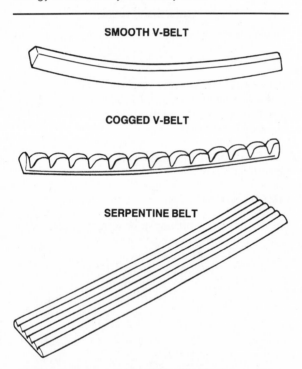

SMOOTH V-BELT

COGGED V-BELT

SERPENTINE BELT

Figure 4-4. These are the three types of drive belts used with automotive systems. (Ford)

belt tension is necessary for satisfactory operation of all belt-driven components. All carmakers specify proper belt tension adjustments for *both new and used* belts.

Specifications for tensioning new and used belts differ. New belt tension specifications apply *only* to replacement belts when first installed. New drive belts will stretch after the

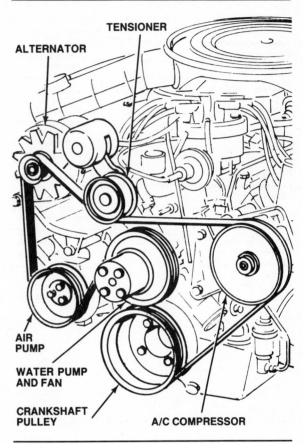

Figure 4-5. The ribbed V-belt, or serpentine belt, drives all accessory units and is tensioned by a tensioner pulley.

first few minutes of operation. Therefore, once a new belt has been tensioned and run, it is considered a used belt and should be adjusted to used belt specifications.

The most widely recommended way to check belt tension is with a strand tension gauge, figure 4-6. There are many commercial tension testers available, but all are used similarly. One common type has a belt hook attached to a spring-loaded plunger and a dial indicator registering in pounds. Press the plunger to engage the hook under the belt, then release the plunger. When using the gauge on a cogged belt, place the hook between two cogs of the belt, figure 4-7. Read the pounds of tension on the dial and compare the reading to the carmaker's specifications. Always take two or more readings, moving the belt each time.

A less accurate, but reasonably reliable, driveway service test is to press the belt with your thumb about midway between the two pulleys. If the belt can be deflected more than ½ inch when applying a pressure of 20 to 22 pounds (about the same force required to re-

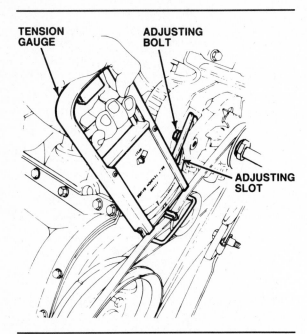

Figure 4-6. The strand tension gauge is the most accurate method of checking drive belt tension.

Figure 4-7. When checking tension of a cogged V-belt, engage the tension gauge hook with a belt notch as shown.

place a crimp-type bottle cap), the belt probably requires retensioning. Placing a straightedge from pulley to pulley, figure 4-8, will help you measure the amount of deflection.

Adjusting Belt Tension

If a check of belt tension indicates a tight or loose belt, the driven accessory must be re-positioned to retension its belt. Belts should be just tight enough to drive the accessory. A properly tensioned belt will run quietly and provide maximum service life. Belts that are too tight, however, put undue stress on the bearings of a component and cause rapid belt wear.

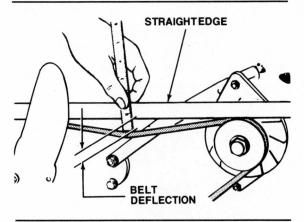

Figure 4-8. If the specification for belt tension is not known, or if a tension gauge is unavailable, press on the belt with a ruler. The belt should not deflect more than ½ inch.

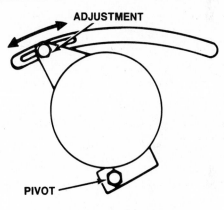

BASIC ALTERNATOR

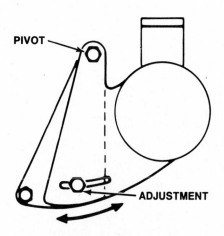

BASIC POWER STEERING PUMP

Figure 4-9. Accessory units generally have a pivot bolt and an adjusting bolt that must be loosened to move the unit.

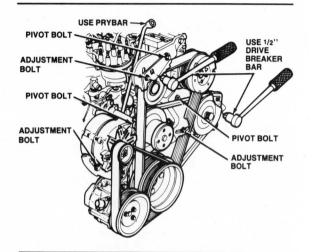

Figure 4-10. To move accessories before adjusting a drive belt, use a breaker bar or ratchet handle at the specified locations.

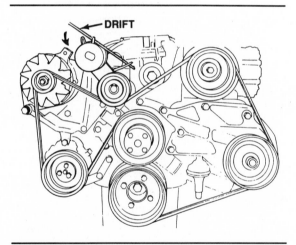

Figure 4-11. Insert a drift in the tensioner slot and press the tensioner to release belt tension replacing a serpentine belt. (Ford)

Belts that are too loose will slip and reduce accessory operating efficiency.

Most accessories are adjusted by loosening one or more retaining bolts and moving the component in an elongated slot in an adjusting bracket, figure 4-9. Tighten the bolts securely after adjustment so that they will not vibrate loose. Some accessories use a slider-type belt adjustment system. To adjust a belt with this system, loosen the nuts on the vertical studs or the alternator locking screw, figure 4-10. A movable bracket attached to the accessory will slide freely on a stationary bracket mounted on the engine. Place a tension gauge on the belt and turn the adjusting nut on the horizontal stud or the adjusting screw until the tension is

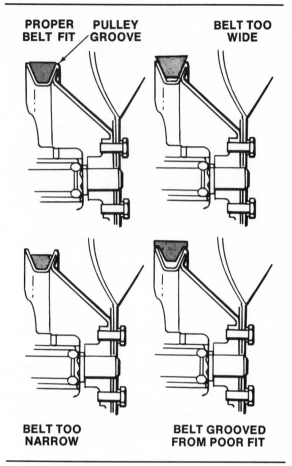

Figure 4-12. The wrong size of drive belt will hamper charging system operation.

correct, then tighten the vertical stud nuts or screws and remove the tension gauge.

Installing Drive Belts

Replace smooth or cogged V-belts by loosening and moving the accessory unit toward the engine to remove the old belt. Then install the new belt. With the new belt in place, move the accessory away from the engine enough to properly tension the belt. Finally, tighten the mounting fasteners to specifications.

Replace a serpentine belt by engaging a slot in the tensioner with a suitable drift, figure 4-11. When you push the drift downward and hold it in that position, it forces the tensioner pulley up. This relieves tension on the belt and allows its removal. To install the new belt, release the tension on the tensioner pulley with the drift. Place the belt under the pulley and route it around the accessories; then remove the drift. This allows the tensioner pulley to apply the correct pressure to the belt.

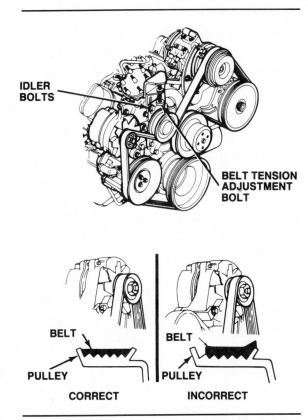

IDLER
BOLTS

BELT TENSION
ADJUSTMENT
BOLT

BELT

PULLEY

CORRECT

BELT

PULLEY

INCORRECT

Figure 4-13. When installing a V-ribbed belt, make sure that all the V-grooves make proper contact. Adjust the idler for the correct tension. (Ford)

When installing a new belt, check the carmaker's specifications for the correct replacement. A correctly installed V-belt should ride on the sides of the pulley, not the bottom, figure 4-12. The top of the belt should be flush with, or not more than $\frac{1}{16}$-inch above, the top of the pulley grooves.

Always replace both belts of a matched pair at the same time. If one belt is bad, you can count on the other being well worn, also. Additionally, you cannot adjust tension equally on mismatched belts. When you install a serpentine belt, be sure that all of its V-grooves contact all the pulleys correctly, figure 4-13.

ALTERNATOR TESTING OVERVIEW

On-car alternator charging system tests are all about the same, regardless of the car being tested. The main differences are the meter test points and the specifications. The next few paragraphs are general descriptions of the most common of these on-car tests.

Then, you will learn the procedures for doing these tests on specific systems. Not all carmakers require all of these tests, and some suggest even more. These will be covered in

detail. If the directions tell you to remove the alternator for more testing, check Chapter 5 for full instructions for removing, disassembling, and testing it.

During the tests, you will have to refer to the manufacturer's specifications for the model you are testing. These specifications are vital to your work. They are the only tool that will tell you where the system is bad.

As you learned in Chapter 1, specifications can be found in the manufacturer's shop manual or in books prepared by independent publishers. Before you begin any test, find the correct specifications. Keep a copy handy while you work, so that you can refer to it quickly.

After completing each alternator test, disconnect all test equipment such as meters, carbon piles, and jumper wires which you might have installed. Be sure to reconnect all wires and connectors which you may have removed during the test.

Circuit Resistance Testing

This is a voltage-drop test of the charging system. The tests are usually done with the engine running at 1,500 to 1,800 rpm and the alternator producing a specific amperage. The insulated circuit test measurement is taken from the battery positive terminal to the battery (output) terminal at the alternator. If the voltage drop exceeds specifications, then test the connections within the circuit to pinpoint the area of resistance.

A voltage-drop test of the ground circuit is made from the alternator frame to the battery ground terminal. A voltage-drop test of the field circuit is made at the regulator. Any loose or corroded connections or damaged wiring must be replaced before the rest of the charging system tests are made, or the test results will not be accurate.

Current Output Testing

Current output tests are made in two stages. Some carmakers suggest doing only one stage or the other. First, a carbon pile is connected across the battery, a voltmeter is connected between the battery positive terminal and ground, and an ammeter is connected between the battery positive terminal and the battery terminal at the alternator. The engine is run at the test speed, and the carbon pile is adjusted either to keep a steady 15-volt level or to get the greatest possible ammeter reading. Compare the ammeter reading to your specifications.

Second, if the ammeter reading does not meet specifications, bypass the voltage

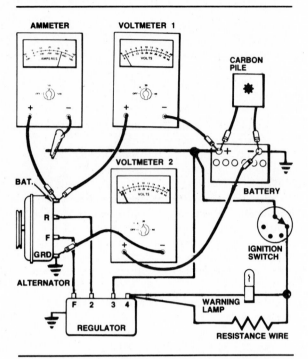

Figure 4-14. Delco-Remy 10-DN circuit resistance test.

regulator. With a remotely mounted regulator, do this with a jumper wire. With an integral regulator, there are several methods to bypass it. With either type, bypassing the regulator connects the field winding to full battery voltage. Run the engine at the test speed and adjust the carbon pile. Compare the ammeter reading to specifications. If it meets specifications, then the voltage regulator may be faulty. If it still does not meet specifications, remove the alternator for further testing.

Voltage Output

The voltage output test is similar to the current output test. It is recommended by some manufacturers to avoid possible damage to an electronic ignition system during a current output test. Run the engine at fast idle, and use either the headlamps or a carbon pile to load the battery. If battery voltage measured at the positive battery terminal is below 13 volts, bypass the regulator and repeat the test. If the battery voltage then increases to about 16 volts, the regulator may be faulty. If the battery voltage remains low, remove the alternator for further testing. Do not allow system voltage to exceed 16 volts during this test.

Field Current Draw

This test is made with the engine off. Often, the carmaker will tell you to bypass the regulator or the warning lamp circuit, or both. Connect an ammeter between either the battery positive terminal and the field, or between the field and ground. When you turn on the ignition switch *without* starting the engine, or bypass the ignition switch and warning lamp with a jumper wire, the ammeter will measure the field current draw. If it is not within specifications, remove the alternator for further testing. If it is within specifications, turn the alternator pulley by hand. If the ammeter reading fluctuates, the brushes and sliprings may need servicing.

Voltage Regulator Test

The regulated voltage can be checked with a voltmeter connected either between the alternator output terminal and ground or between the battery positive terminal and ground. Bring the regulator to operating temperature by running the engine at fast idle with a load on the battery for 10 to 15 minutes. The voltmeter reading at this point is the setting of the normally closed, or series, contacts of an electromechanical regulator.

Then, reduce the load and increase the engine rpm. The voltmeter reading is the setting of the normally open, or grounding, contacts of an electromechanical regulator, or the setting of a solid-state regulator. If the readings do not meet specifications, replace the regulator.

TESTING SPECIFIC ALTERNATORS

Delco-Remy 10-DN Series

Delco recommends that a circuit resistance test, a current output test, a field current draw test, and a voltage regulator test be made on the 10-DN alternator series.

Circuit resistance test
1. Refer to figure 4-14.
2. Disconnect the wire from the battery terminal at the alternator.
3. Connect the ammeter (+) lead to the alternator terminal; connect the ammeter (−) lead to the wire.
4. Connect the carbon pile across the battery terminals.
5. Connect the voltmeter (+) lead to the battery terminal at the alternator; connect the voltmeter (−) lead to the battery (+) terminal.
6. Run the engine at 1,000 rpm.

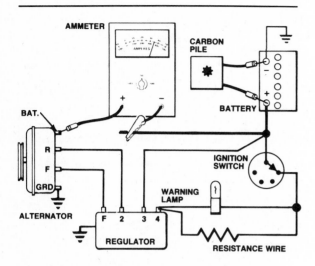

Figure 4-15. Delco-Remy 10-DN current output test with voltage regulator in circuit.

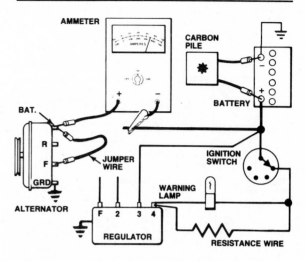

Figure 4-16. Delco-Remy 10-DN current output test with voltage regulator bypassed.

7. Adjust the carbon pile so that the ammeter measures 20 amperes of charging current.

8. Watch the voltmeter reading:

a. If the reading is 0.3 volt or less, the insulated circuit is in good condition; go to step 11.

b. If the reading exceeds 0.3 volt, go to step 9.

9. Touch the voltmeter (+) lead to all of the circuit connections in turn to pinpoint the area of resistance.

10. Repair or replace any loose or corroded connections or damaged wiring before doing the rest of the tests.

11. Connect the voltmeter (+) lead to the battery (−) terminal; connect the voltmeter (−) lead to the ground terminal at the alternator.

12. Observe the voltmeter reading:

a. If the reading is 0.1 volt or less, the circuit's ground connections are good. Stop here, and go on to the next test.

b. If the reading is more than 0.1 volt, go to step 13.

13. Check the circuit's ground connections. Repair or replace any loose or corroded connections or damaged wiring before doing the rest of the tests.

Current output test

1. Refer to figure 4-15.

2. Disconnect the battery ground cable.

3. Disconnect the wire from the battery terminal at the alternator.

4. Connect the ammeter (+) lead to the alternator terminal; connect the ammeter (−) lead to the wire.

5. Reconnect the battery ground cable.

6. Connect the carbon pile across the battery terminals.

7. Run the engine at fast idle.

8. Adjust the carbon pile to get the highest ammeter reading.

9. Compare the ammeter reading to specifications:

a. If the reading is within 10 percent of specifications, both the alternator and the regulator are operating properly. Stop here.

b. If the reading is not within 10 percent of specifications, go to step 10.

10. Turn the ignition switch off. Leave the carbon pile on the battery.

11. Refer to figure 4-16.

12. Unplug the connector from the field terminals at the alternator.

13. Connect a jumper wire from the field F-terminal at the alternator to the battery terminal at the alternator.

14. Run the engine at fast idle and adjust the carbon pile to get the highest ammeter reading.

15. Compare the ammeter reading to specifications:

a. If the reading is within 10 percent of specifications, the alternator is operating properly but the regulator must be tested.

b. If the reading is not within 10 percent of specifications, remove the alternator for further testing.

Field current draw test

1. Refer to figure 4-17.

2. Disconnect the battery ground cable.

3. Disconnect the wire from the battery terminal at the alternator.

4. Connect the ammeter (+) lead to the wire; connect the ammeter (−) lead to the alternator

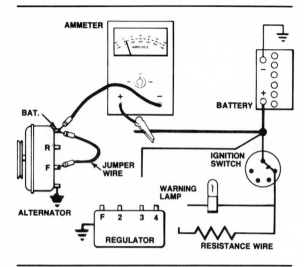

Figure 4-17. Delco-Remy 10-DN field current draw test.

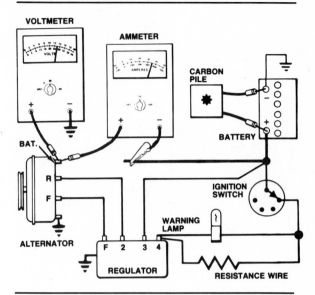

Figure 4-18. Delco-Remy electromechanical voltage regulator test.

terminal. (During this test, field current will flow *from* the battery *to* the alternator.)

5. Unplug the connector from the regulator.
6. Reconnect the battery ground cable.
7. Unplug the connector from the field terminals at the alternator.
8. Connect a jumper wire between the field F-terminal at the alternator and the battery terminal at the alternator.
9. Compare the ammeter reading to specifications:
    a. If the reading matches specifications, the alternator field circuit is in good condition.
    b. If the reading does not match specifications, remove the alternator for further testing.

Electromechanical voltage regulator test

1. Refer to figure 4-18.
2. Disconnect the battery ground cable.
3. Disconnect the wire from the battery terminal at the alternator.
4. Connect the ammeter (+) lead to the alternator terminal; connect the ammeter (−) lead to the wire.
5. Reconnect the battery ground cable.
6. Connect the voltmeter (+) lead to the battery terminal at the alternator; connect the voltmeter (−) lead to ground.
7. Connect the carbon pile across the battery terminals.
8. Bring the regulator to operating temperature by running the engine at 1,500 rpm for 15 minutes with the parking lights on; then turn the lights off.
9. Cycle the regulator by dropping the engine speed to idle, then returning to 1,500 rpm.

10. Adjust the carbon pile to maintain 10 amperes of charging current.
11. Bring the engine speed to 2,000 rpm.
12. The voltmeter reading is the setting of the normally open (shorting) contacts; compare it to the specifications:
    a. If the reading is within specifications and the battery has not been discharging rapidly, go to step 13.
    b. If the reading is not within specifications *or* the battery has been discharging, remove the regulator cover and adjust the upper contact setting.
13. Turn on the parking lights.
14. Decrease the engine speed from 2,000 rpm until the voltmeter reading drops by a few tenths of a volt.
15. The voltmeter reading is the setting of the normally closed (series) contacts; compare it to specifications.
    a. If the reading is within specifications, the voltage regulator is operating properly.
    b. If the reading is not within specifications, remove the regulator cover and adjust the regulator air gap.

Delco-Remy 10-SI, 12-SI, 15-SI and 27-SI Series

Delco recommends that you do a circuit resistance test and a current output test on the SI alternator series. You also can test the solid-state regulator on the vehicle.

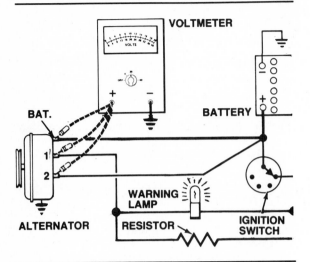

Figure 4-19. Delco-Remy 10-SI circuit resistance test.

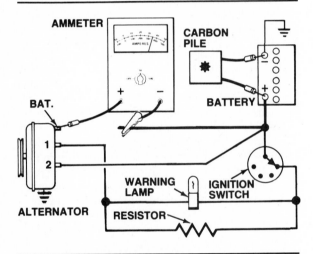

Figure 4-20. Delco-Remy 10-SI current output test with voltage regulator in circuit.

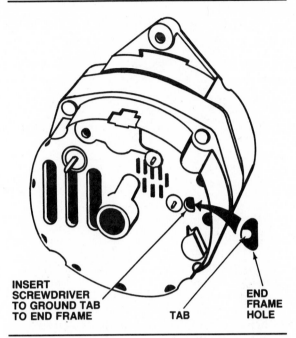

INSERT
SCREWDRIVER
TO GROUND TAB
TO END FRAME   TAB

END
FRAME
HOLE

Figure 4-21. To bypass the 10-SI's voltage regulator, use a screwdriver to ground the tab in the end-frame hole.

Circuit resistance test
1. Refer to figure 4-19.
2. Turn the ignition switch on.
3. Connect the voltmeter (−) lead to ground.
4. Touch the voltmeter (+) lead in turn to:
   a. The battery terminal at the alternator
   b. The number 1 terminal at the alternator
   c. The number 2 terminal at the alternator.
5. A zero voltage reading at any of the test points indicates an open in the circuit between the test point and the battery (+) terminal. Check and repair any opens.
6. If voltage is present at the number 2 terminal and the battery is constantly overcharged, remove the alternator for further testing of the field circuit.

Current output test
1. Refer to Figure 4-20.
2. Disconnect the battery ground cable.
3. Disconnect the wire from the battery terminal at the alternator.
4. Connect the ammeter (+) lead to the alternator terminal; connect the ammeter (−) lead to the wire.
5. Reconnect the battery ground cable.
6. Connect the carbon pile across the battery terminals.
7. Run the engine at moderate speed with all of the accessories operating.
8. Adjust the carbon pile to obtain the maximum possible ammeter reading.
9. Compare the ammeter reading to specifications:
   a. If the reading is within 10 percent of specifications, both the alternator and the regulator are operating properly. Stop here, and go on to the next test.
   b. If the reading is not within 10 percent of specifications, go to step 10.
10. Insert one inch of a screwdriver blade into the test hole on the back of the alternator, figure 4-21. This bypasses the regulator and grounds the alternator field winding.

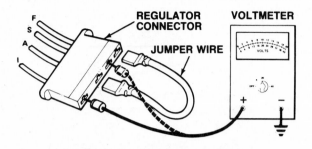

Figure 4-22. Motorcraft regulator circuit test (circuit with warning lamp).

11. Compare the ammeter reading to specifications:
  a. If the reading is within 10 percent of specifications, remove the alternator for further testing of the regulator and field winding.
  b. If the reading is not within 10 percent of specifications, remove the alternator for further testing of the rectifier, the diode trio, and the stator.

Voltage regulator test
The solid-state regulator can be tested on the vehicle.
1. Connect a fast charger and voltmeter to the battery terminals, observing correct polarity (+) to (+) and (−) to (−).
2. Turn the ignition on and *slowly* increase the charge rate.
3. Watch the indicator lamp on the vehicle's instrument panel. When it starts to dim, read the voltmeter.
  a. The lamp should dim between 13.5 and 16 volts.
  b. If the lamp dims at a voltage outside this range, the voltage regulator is defective.

Delco-Remy CS Series

Delco-Remy recommends this general test procedure for CS-series alternators. If the car does not have an indicator lamp, omit steps 3 through 5.
1. Test the battery and charge it if necessary before testing the charging system.
2. Inspect the drive belt and all circuit wiring.
3. Turn on the ignition, but do not start the engine. The indicator lamp should light.
4. If the indicator lamp does not light, disconnect the harness connector from the regulator terminals and ground the L-terminal in the harness.
  a. If the lamp lights, repair the alternator as shown in Chapter 5.
  b. If the lamp does not light, find the open circuit between the grounded L-terminal and the ignition switch.

5. Reconnect the alternator harness connector. Start and run the engine at moderate speed (approximately 2,000 rpm). If the lamp does not turn off, disconnect the alternator harness connector.
  a. If the lamp then turns off, repair the alternator.
  b. If the lamp stays on, check for a grounded L-terminal wire in the harness.
6. If the indicator lamp lights during normal operation, or if the battery is consistently undercharged or overcharged, proceed as follows:
  a. Disconnect the harness from the alternator.
  b. Connect the voltmeter (−) lead to ground.
  c. Connect the voltmeter (+) lead to the L-terminal in the harness connector. Jumper the voltmeter (+) lead to the I-terminal, if one is used.
  d. Turn the ignition on, but do not start the engine. If the meter indicates no voltage, check for an open circuit in the harness.
7. Reconnect the alternator harness and run the engine at moderate speed (approximately 2,000 rpm) with all accessories off.
8. Measure the battery voltage. If it is above 16 volts, replace the regulator.
9. Connect an ammeter in the alternator output circuit (BAT terminal) and use a carbon pile to load the battery for maximum charging current at approximately 13 volts. If charging current is not within 15 amperes of rated output, repair or replace the alternator.

Motorcraft External Voltage Regulator (EVR)

Ford recommends that a regulator circuit test, a voltage output test, a regulator test, and a diode test be made on all of its external regulator alternators.

Regulator circuit test (indicator lamp circuit)
1. Refer to figure 4-22.
2. With the ignition switch off, unplug the connector from the regulator.
3. Connect a jumper wire between the A-terminal and the F-terminal of the connector.
4. Run the engine at idle.
5. Connect the voltmeter (+) lead to the S-terminal of the connector; connect the voltmeter (−) lead to ground.
6. Note the voltmeter reading.
7. Move the voltmeter (+) lead to the I-terminal of the connector.
8. Again note the voltmeter reading.

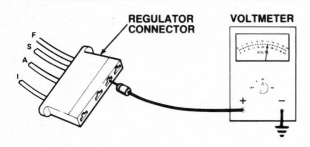

Figure 4-23. Motorcraft regulator circuit test (circuit with ammeter).

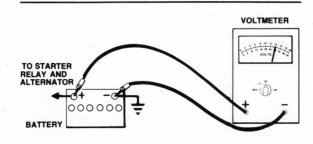

Figure 4-24. Motorcraft voltage output and regulator test with regulator in circuit.

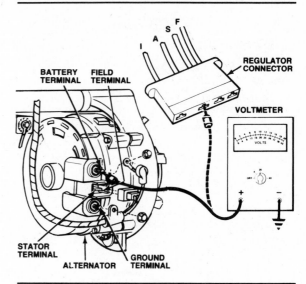

Figure 4-25. Motorcraft voltage test of circuit wiring.

9. Compare the two voltmeter readings taken in steps 6 and 8:
   a. If the S-terminal reading is about 6 volts and the I-terminal reading is about 13 volts, the regulator circuit is all right.
   b. If either reading is zero, repair the wiring to that terminal and repeat the test.
   c. If these readings are within specifications but the voltage output test is not, then replace the regulator and repeat the voltage output test.

Regulator circuit test (ammeter circuit)
1. Refer to figure 4-23.
2. With the ignition switch off, unplug the connector from the regulator.
3. Connect the voltmeter (+) lead to the S-terminal at the connector; connect the voltmeter (−) lead to ground.
4. *Do not start the engine.* Turn the ignition switch on.
5. Watch the voltmeter reading:
   a. If the reading is at or near battery voltage, the regulator circuit is normal.
   b. If the reading is zero, repair the wiring from the ignition switch to the S-terminal at the connector. Test for voltage output.

Voltage output and regulator test
1. Refer to figure 4-24.
2. With the ignition switch off, connect the voltmeter (+) lead to the battery + terminal;

connect the voltmeter (−) lead to the battery (−) terminal.
3. Note the voltmeter reading (battery voltage).
4. Run the engine at 1,500 rpm.
5. Note the voltmeter reading (charging voltage without a load).
6. Run the blower motor at high speed, and turn on the high-beam headlamps.
7. Increase the engine speed to 2,000 rpm.
8. Note the voltmeter reading (charging voltage with a load).
9. Compare the three voltmeter readings:
   a. If the step 5 reading was 1 to 2 volts more than the step 3 reading, and the step 8 reading was 0.5 volt more than the step 5 reading, then the regulator and the alternator are operating properly. Stop here.
   b. If the step 5 reading was more than 2 volts above the step 3 reading, go to step 10.
   c. If the step 8 reading was not 0.5 volt more than the step 5 reading, go to step 13.
10. Check the alternator and the regulator ground connections and repeat the test.
11. If the step 10 retest still shows too much charging voltage without a load:
   a. Turn the ignition switch off.
   b. Unplug the connector from the regulator.
   c. Start the engine and repeat the test.
12. Compare the voltmeter readings to specifications:
   a. If the retest was within specifications, replace the regulator and repeat the test.
   b. If the step 11 retest was not within specifications, check for a short in the wiring between the alternator and the regulator. Repair if necessary.
   c. If a short was found and repaired, replace the regulator and repeat the test.

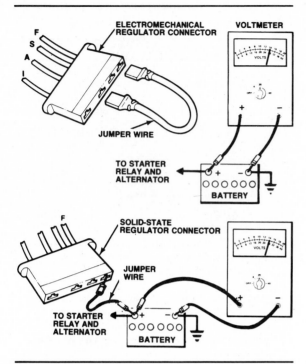

Figure 4-26. Motorcraft output test with regulator bypassed.

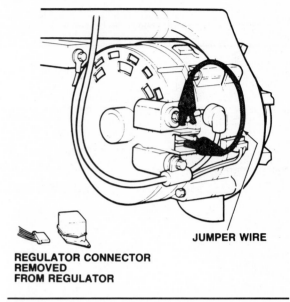

Figure 4-27. Motorcraft voltage output test with field windings connected to full battery voltage.

13. If the charging voltage with a load (step 8) was not 0.5 volt more than the charging voltage without a load (step 5):
    a. Refer to figure 4-25.
    b. Connect the voltmeter (−) lead to ground.
    c. Touch the voltmeter (+) lead to the battery terminal at the alternator and the A-terminal at the regulator connector.
    d. If either reading is zero, repair the wiring between the test point and the battery positive terminal. Then repeat the test.
14. If the test 13 retest still does not meet specifications:
    a. Refer to figure 4-26.
    b. Turn the ignition switch off.
    c. Unplug the connector from the regulator.
    d. With an electromechanical voltage regulator, connect a jumper wire between the A-terminal and the F-terminal at the connector.
    e. With a remotely mounted solid-state voltage regulator, connect a jumper wire between the battery (+) terminal and the F-terminal at the connector.
    f. If the jumper wire sparks and heats, go to step 17.
    g. Repeat the test.

15. If the step 14 readings are still not within specifications:
    a. Refer to figure 4-27.
    b. Remove the jumper wire but leave the connector unplugged.
    c. Connect the jumper wire between the field terminal at the alternator and the battery terminal at the alternator.
    d. Repeat the test.
16. Compare the voltmeter readings to specifications:
    a. If the readings are within specifications, repair the wiring between the alternator and the regulator and repeat the test.
    b. If the readings are still not within specifications, remove the alternator for further testing.
17. If the jumper wire in step 14 sparks and heats:
    a. Refer to figure 4-28.
    b. With the regulator plug disconnected, connect an ohmmeter between the F-terminal at the regulator and the battery (−) terminal. The reading should be between 2.4 and 250 ohms.
    c. Connect the ohmmeter between the I-terminal at the regulator and the F-terminal at the regulator. The reading should be zero ohms.
    d. If either reading does not meet specifications, replace the regulator and repeat the test.

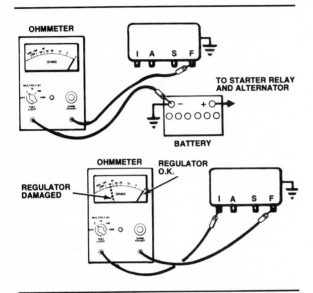

Figure 4-28. Motorcraft regulator test using ohmmeter.

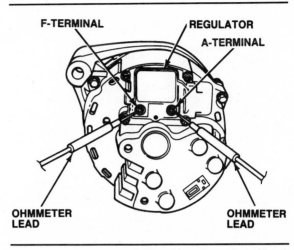

Figure 4-29. Motorcraft IAR under-voltage test. (Ford)

Motorcraft Integral Alternator/Regulator (IAR)

Ford specifies the following circuit test procedure for IAR alternators. Ford also recommends a field circuit drain check to locate the cause of current drain through the alternator field circuit when the ignition is off.

Charging circuit test

1. Connect the voltmeter (+) lead to the battery (+) terminal; connect the voltmeter (−) lead to the battery (−) terminal. Note the voltmeter reading; this is battery voltage.
2. Start the engine and run it at 1,500 rpm with all accessories off. Note the voltmeter reading.
   a. If the reading increases by less than 2 volts over the reading in step 1, continue with step 3.
   b. If the reading does not increase, go to step 5.
   c. If the reading increases by more than 2 volts, go to step 13.
3. Turn all electrical accessories on high and increase engine speed to 2,000 rpm. Note the voltmeter reading.
   a. If the reading increases 0.5 volt or more, continue with step 4.
   b. If the reading does not increase by 0.5 volt, go to step 5.
4. Shut the engine off and connect a 12-volt test lamp in series with the battery (+) cable to check for a battery drain. Locate and correct any current drains.
5. With the ignition switch off, unplug the connector from the regulator at the rear of the alternator.

6. Connect an ohmmeter between the A-terminal and the F-terminal screws on the regulator, figure 4-29.
   a. If the ohmmeter reads 2.4 ohms or less, remove the alternator and replace the regulator, then check the alternator for a shorted rotor or field circuit.
   b. If the ohmmeter reading is more than 2.4 ohms, continue testing.
7. Reconnect the regulator connector at the alternator. Connect the voltmeter (−) lead to the alternator rear housing. Touch the voltmeter (+) lead to the regulator A-terminal screw.
   a. If the voltmeter reads the same as in step 1, continue testing.
   b. If the voltmeter reading is not the same as in step 1, repair the wiring in the A circuit.
8. With the ignition switch off, connect the voltmeter between the regulator F-terminal and ground.
   a. If the voltmeter reads the same as in step 1, continue testing.
   b. If the voltmeter shows no reading, there is probably an open or grounded field circuit in the alternator. Remove the alternator for further testing.
9. With the voltmeter connected as in step 8, turn the ignition switch on. *Do not start the engine.*
   a. If the regulator F-terminal voltage exceeds 1.5 volts, continue testing.
   b. If the F-terminal voltage is 1.5 volts or less, repair the alternator-to-starter relay wiring.
10. With the ignition switch off, unplug the connector from the regulator at the rear of the alternator.
11. Connect a jumper lead between the regulator A-terminal and connector A-lead. Connect

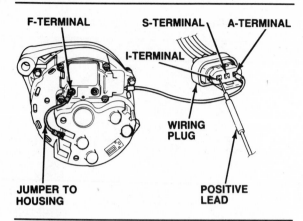

Figure 4-30. Motorcraft IAR regulator S or I circuit test. (Ford)

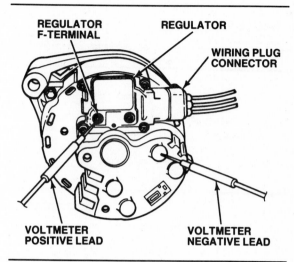

Figure 4-32. Motorcraft IAR field circuit drain check step 1. (Ford)

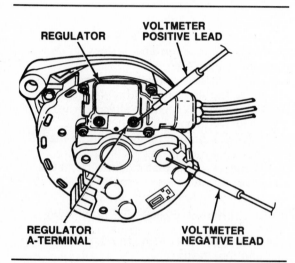

Figure 4-31. Motorcraft IAR over-voltage test. (Ford)

another jumper lead between the regulator F-terminal and the alternator housing, figure 4-30.

12. Start the engine and run it at idle. Connect the voltmeter (−) lead to the battery (−) terminal. Connect the voltmeter (+) lead first to the S-terminal and then to the I-terminal of the connector plug. Note the voltmeter readings.

 a. If the voltage at the S-terminal is approximately one-half that shown at the I-terminal, remove the jumper leads. Shut the engine off, replace the regulator, and reconnect the regulator plug.

 b. If the voltage at the S-terminal is not within specifications, remove the alternator for further testing.

13. Turn the ignition on. *Do not start the engine.* Connect the voltmeter (−) lead to the alternator rear housing. Connect the voltmeter (+) lead first to the output connection at the starter

relay and then to the regulator A-terminal, figure 4-31. Note the voltmeter readings.

 a. If the difference in readings is 0.5 volt or less, continue testing.

 b. If the voltage difference exceeds 0.5 volt, repair the A-circuit wiring.

14. Check for loose regulator ground screws and tighten as required.

Field circuit drain check

1. Connect the voltmeter (−) lead to the alternator rear housing for all steps.

2. With the ignition off, probe the regulator F-terminal with the voltmeter (+) lead, figure 4-32.

 a. If battery voltage is shown, the system is satisfactory. Stop here.

 b. If the reading is less than battery voltage, continue testing.

3. With the ignition switch off, unplug the connector from the regulator.

4. Probe the connector plug I-terminal with the voltmeter (+) lead, figure 4-33. If a voltage reading is obtained, trace the I-circuit lead between the connector plug and the ignition switch to locate and correct the cause of the drain.

5. If no voltage is shown in step 4, move the voltmeter (+) lead to the connector plug S-terminal.

 a. If no voltage is shown, replace the regulator and repeat this step. If the meter still shows no voltage, the alternator rectifier assembly is defective.

 b. If voltage is shown, trace the S-circuit lead to locate and correct the cause of the drain.

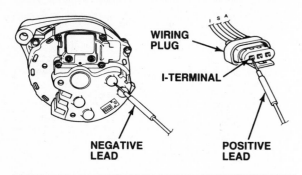

Figure 4-33. Motorcraft IAR field circuit drain check step 2. (Ford)

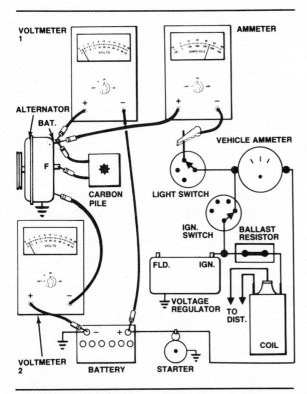

Figure 4-34. Testing circuit resistance of Chrysler with electromechanical regulator.

Chrysler (Electromechanical Regulator)

Early Chrysler alternators with an electro-mechanical voltage regulator should be given a circuit resistance test, a field circuit resistance test, a current output test, a field current draw test, and a voltage regulator test.

Circuit resistance test
1. Refer to figure 4-34.
2. Disconnect the battery ground cable.
3. Disconnect the wire from the battery terminal at the alternator.
4. Connect the ammeter (+) lead to the alter-

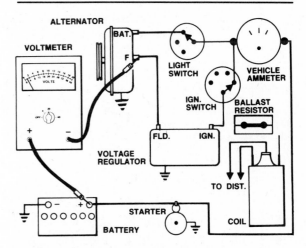

Figure 4-35. Field circuit test of Chrysler with electromechanical regulator.

nator terminal; connect the ammeter (−) lead to the wire.
5. Disconnect the wire from the field terminal at the alternator and insulate the wire.
6. Connect the carbon pile or field rheostat between the field terminal at the alternator and the battery terminal at the alternator.
7. Connect the voltmeter (+) lead to the battery terminal at the alternator; connect the voltmeter (−) lead to the battery (+) terminal.
8. Reconnect the battery ground cable.
9. Turn on the headlamp high beams and run the blower motor at high speed.
10. Start the engine and run it at 1,250 rpm.
11. Adjust the carbon pile or rheostat to maintain 10 amperes of charging current.
12. Compare the voltmeter reading to specifications:
    a. If the reading is 0.3 volt or less, the circuit is in good condition.
    b. If the reading is more than 0.3 volt, check, clean, and tighten the connections within the circuit and repeat the test.
13. Connect the voltmeter (+) lead to the battery (−) terminal; connect the voltmeter (−) lead to the alternator frame.
14. Compare the voltmeter reading to specifications:
    a. If the reading is 0.3 volt or less, the ground circuit is in good condition.
    b. If the reading is more than 0.3 volt, check the ground connections within the charging circuit.

Field circuit resistance test
1. Refer to figure 4-35.
2. With the ignition switch off, disconnect the leads from both ends of the ignition ballast resistor.

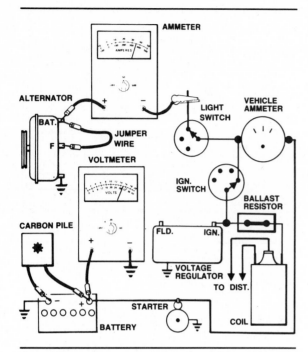

Figure 4-36. Testing current output of Chrysler with electromechanical regulator.

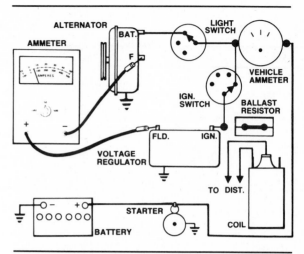

Figure 4-37. Testing field current draw of Chrysler with electromechanical regulator.

3. Connect the voltmeter (+) lead to the battery (+) terminal; connect the voltmeter (−) lead to the field terminal at the regulator.
4. Turn the ignition switch on and observe the voltmeter reading:
   a. If the reading is 0.55 volt or less, the field circuit is in good condition.
   b. If the voltmeter reading is more than 0.55 volt, check, clean, and tighten the connections within the field circuit and repeat the test.

Current output test
1. Refer to figure 4-36.
2. Disconnect the battery ground cable.
3. Disconnect the wire from the battery terminal at the alternator.
4. Connect the ammeter (+) lead to the alternator terminal; connect the ammeter (−) lead to the wire.
5. Disconnect the wire from the field terminal at the alternator and insulate the wire.
6. Connect a jumper wire between the field terminal at the alternator and the battery terminal at the alternator.
7. Connect the voltmeter (+) lead to the battery (+) terminal. Connect the voltmeter (−) lead to ground.
8. Reconnect the battery ground cable.
9. Connect the carbon pile across the battery terminals.

10. Turn on the headlamp high beams and the high-speed blower motor.
11. Start the engine and run it at 1,250 rpm.
12. Adjust the carbon pile so that the voltmeter reads 15 volts.
13. Compare the ammeter reading to specifications:
   a. If the reading is within 5 amperes of specifications, the alternator is operating properly.
   b. If the reading is not within 5 amperes of specifications, remove the alternator for further testing.

Field current draw test
1. Refer to figure 4-37.
2. Disconnect the battery ground cable.
3. Disconnect the leads from both sides of the ignition ballast resistor.
4. Disconnect the wire from the field terminal at the alternator.
5. Connect the ammeter (+) lead to the wire; connect the ammeter (−) lead to the alternator field terminal.
6. Reconnect the battery ground cable.
7. Turn the ignition switch on. *Do not start the engine.*
8. Compare the ammeter reading to specifications:
   a. If the reading is within specifications, the alternator field circuit is in good condition.
   b. If the reading is not within specifications, remove the alternator for further testing.

Electromechanical voltage regulator test
1. Refer to figure 4-38.
2. Disconnect the battery ground cable.
3. Disconnect the wire from the battery terminal at the alternator.

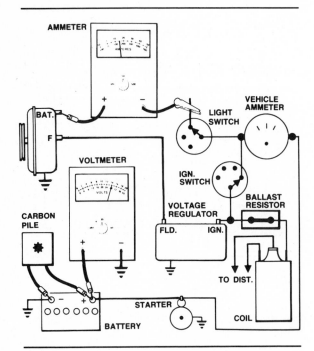

Figure 4-38. Testing Chrysler electromechanical regulator.

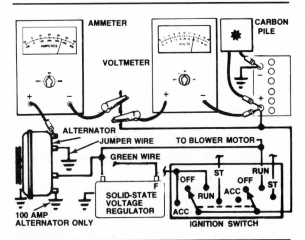

Figure 4-39. Testing circuit resistance of Chrysler with solid-state regulator.

4. Connect the ammeter (+) lead to the alternator terminal; connect the ammeter (−) lead to the wire.

5. Reconnect the battery ground cable.

6. Connect the carbon pile across the battery terminals.

7. Connect the voltmeter (+) lead to the battery (+) terminal; connect the voltmeter (−) lead to ground.

8. Start the engine and run it at 1,250 rpm.

9. Adjust the carbon pile to maintain 15 amperes of charging current.

10. After 15 minutes, cycle the regulator by dropping the engine speed to idle and then returning it to 1,250 rpm.

11. The voltmeter reading is the setting of the normally closed (series) contacts; compare it to specifications:

a. If the reading is within specifications, go to step 12.

b. If the reading is not within specifications, remove the regulator cover and adjust the voltage regulator spring tension.

12. Increase the engine speed to 2,200 rpm.

13. If necessary, adjust the carbon pile to maintain 5 amperes of charging current.

14. Cycle the regulator by dropping the engine speed to idle and then returning to 2,200 rpm.

15. The voltmeter reading is the setting of the normally open (grounding) contacts; compare it to the reading taken in step 11:

a. If the reading increase between step 11 and step 15 is more than 0.2 volt and less than 0.7 volt, the voltage regulator is good.

b. If the reading increase is not within specifications, remove the regulator cover and adjust the normally open contact point gap.

Chrysler Transistorized Regulator

Chrysler alternators with transistorized (solid-state) regulators should be given a circuit resistance test, a current output test, a field current draw test, and a voltage regulator test.

Circuit resistance test

1. Refer to figure 4-39.

2. Disconnect the battery ground cable.

3. Disconnect the wire from the battery terminal at the alternator.

4. Connect the ammeter (+) lead to the alternator terminal; connect the ammeter (−) lead to the wire.

5. Connect the voltmeter (+) lead to the wire from the battery terminal at the alternator; connect the voltmeter (−) lead to the battery (+) terminal.

6. Disconnect the wire from the regulator-to-field terminal at the alternator; insulate the wire.

7. Connect a jumper wire between the regulator-to-field terminal and ground.

8. Connect a carbon pile across the battery terminals.

9. Reconnect the battery ground cable.

10. Run the engine at idle.

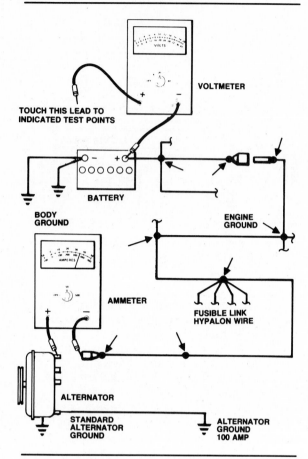

Figure 4-40. Additional test points for circuit resistance test of Chrysler with solid-state regulator.

11. Adjust the carbon pile to maintain 20 amperes of charging current.
12. Watch the voltmeter reading:
    a. If the reading is less than 0.7 volt, the charging circuit wiring is in good condition. Stop here.
    b. If the reading exceeds 0.7 volt, go to step 13.
13. Touch the voltmeter (+) lead to the connectors shown in figure 4-40 to pinpoint the area of resistance.

Current output test
1. Refer to figure 4-41.
2. Disconnect the battery ground cable.
3. Disconnect the wire from the battery terminal at the alternator.
4. Connect the ammeter (+) lead to the alternator terminal; connect the ammeter (−) lead to the wire.
5. Connect the voltmeter (+) lead to the battery terminal at the alternator; connect the voltmeter (−) lead to ground.
6. Disconnect the wire from the field terminal at the alternator and insulate the wire.

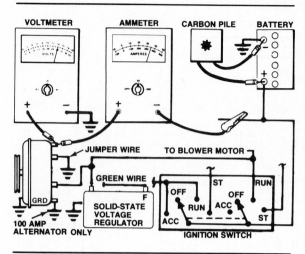

Figure 4-41. Current output test of Chrysler with solid-state regulator.

7. Connect a jumper wire between the field terminal at the alternator and ground.
8. Reconnect the battery ground cable.
9. Connect the carbon pile across the battery.
10. Run the engine at idle.
11. Adjust the carbon pile and engine speed to these levels:
● Standard alternator: 1,250 rpm, 15 volts.
● 100-ampere alternator: 900 rpm, 13 volts.
12. Compare the ammeter reading to specifications:
    a. If the reading is within specifications, the alternator and the regulator are operating properly.
    b. If the reading is not within specifications, remove the alternator for further testing.

Field current draw test
1. Refer to figure 4-42.
2. Disconnect the battery ground cable.
3. Disconnect the wires from both field terminals at the alternator.
4. Connect a jumper wire between one field terminal at the alternator and the battery (+) terminal.
5. Connect the ammeter (+) lead to the second field terminal at the alternator; connect the ammeter (−) lead to the battery (−) terminal.
6. Reconnect the battery ground cable.
7. Slowly rotate the alternator pulley by hand.
8. Compare the ammeter reading to specifications:
    a. If the reading is within specifications, the alternator field circuit is in good condition.
    b. If the reading is not within specifications, remove the alternator for further testing.

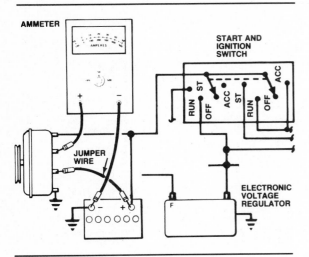

Figure 4-42. Field current draw test of Chrysler solid-state regulator.

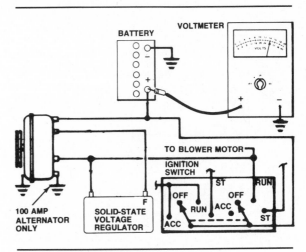

Figure 4-43. Testing Chrysler solid-state regulator.

Voltage regulator test

1. Refer to figure 4-43.
2. Connect the voltmeter (+) lead to the battery (+) terminal; connect the voltmeter (−) lead to ground.
3. Run the engine at 1,250 rpm with all accessories off.
4. Compare the voltmeter reading to specifications:
    a. If the reading is within specifications, the regulator is operating properly. Go to step 6.
    b. If the reading is not within specifications, or if the reading fluctuates, go to step 5.
5. Check the voltage regulator ground and repeat the test.
6. Turn the ignition switch off.
7. Unplug the connector from the regulator and check the connector for bent or distorted terminals. Repair if necessary.
8. Leave the regulator connector unplugged. Turn the ignition switch on. *Do not start the engine.*
9. Touch the voltmeter (+) lead to both of the regulator connector terminals.
    a. If either reading is zero voltage, check the charging circuit wiring and the alternator field circuit for faults. Repair if necessary.
    b. If battery voltage is present at both terminals, replace the regulator and repeat the test.

Chrysler 40/90-Ampere Alternator (Computer Regulator)

Circuit resistance and current output tests for the Chrysler computer-controlled charging system are essentially the same as for systems using external transistorized regulators. You should, however, note the following differences:

● Ground the field circuit at terminal R3 on the dash side of the 8-way black connector, figure 4-44. This corresponds to step 6 of the resistance test for a Chrysler system with a separate transistorized regulator. *Do not ground the blue wire at terminal J2.*

● Maximum allowable voltage drop across the output circuit is 0.05 volt, rather than the 0.7 volt allowed for a circuit with a separate regulator.

Direct testing of the voltage regulating circuitry is generally unnecessary unless the on-board diagnostic capabilities of Chrysler's engine control system detect charging system problems and record fault codes in the system memory. Some of these codes will light the POWER LOSS or POWER LIMITED lamp on the instrument panel; others will not. You can check for charging system fault codes with a special tester (described in Chapter 2) that plugs into the diagnostic connector in the engine compartment. If you do not have the special tester, you can check for fault codes as follows:

1. Test the battery and charge it if necessary before testing the charging system.
2. Turn the ignition switch on-off-on-off-on within 5 seconds to activate the diagnostic system.
3. Observe the POWER LOSS or POWER LIMITED lamp on the instrument panel. It should light steadily for 2 seconds as a bulb and system check.
4. If fault codes have been recorded, the lamp will then indicate the 2-digit code numbers as a series of flashes, with longer pauses between the digits of each code.

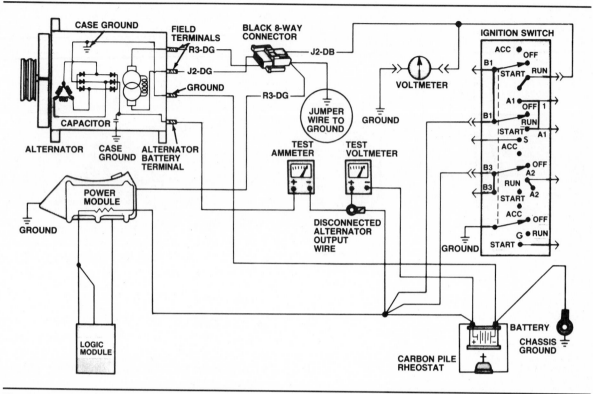

Figure 4-44. Ground terminal R3 at the black 8-way connector when testing Chrysler's computer-controlled charging system.

Charging system fault codes are in the following table. If more than one code is recorded, the lamp will pause 4 seconds between codes. Codes other than those listed in the table involve other portions of the electronic engine control system.

Code	Lamp Lit	Fault
16	Yes	Battery sensing voltage is below 4 or between 7½ and 8½ volts for more than 20 seconds
41	No	Field circuit problem, improper field control
44	No	Battery temperature — sensing signal is below 0.04 volt or above 4.9 volts
46	Yes	Charging voltage is more than 1 volt **above** desired regulating voltage for more than 20 seconds
47	No	Charging voltage is more than 1 volt **below** desired regulating voltage *for more than 20* seconds

Fault codes indicate a problem somewhere within the system. You will have to test individual circuits to pinpoint the cause. Circuit tests and connector terminal numbers vary slightly from one car model to another, depending upon the functions of the engine control system. Consult Chrysler service publications for detailed test instructions.

Chrysler Mitsubishi

As with its domestically produced alternators, Chrysler recommends a circuit resistance test, current output test, and a voltage regulator test for the Mitsubishi alternators used on some of its vehicles.

Circuit resistance test
1. Disconnect the battery ground cable.
2. Disconnect the wire from the battery terminal at the alternator.
3. Connect the ammeter (+) lead to the alternator terminal; connect the ammeter (−) lead to the wire.
4. Connect the voltmeter (+) lead to the wire from the battery terminal at the alternator; connect the voltmeter (−) lead to the battery (+) terminal.
5. Reconnect the battery ground cable.
6. Connect a carbon pile across the battery terminals.

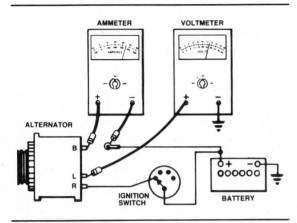

Figure 4-45. Chrysler Mitsubishi voltage regulator test.

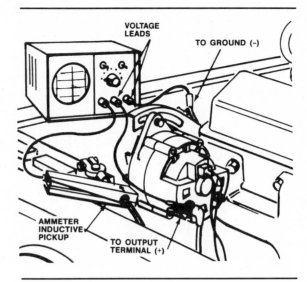

Figure 4-46. Alternator oscilloscope connections.

7. Run the engine at idle.
8. Adjust the carbon pile to maintain 20 amperes of charging current.
9. Watch the voltmeter reading:
   a. If the reading is less than 0.5 volt, the charging circuit wiring is in good condition. Stop here.
   b. If the reading is 0.5 volt or more, go to step 10.
10. Touch the voltmeter (+) lead to all of the circuit connection points between the battery terminal at the alternator and the battery (+) terminal to pinpoint the area of resistance.

Current output test
1. Do steps 1 through 3 of the circuit resistance test just described.
2. Connect the voltmeter (+) lead to the battery terminal of the alternator; connect the voltmeter (−) lead to ground.
3. Reconnect the battery ground cable.
4. Connect a carbon pile across the battery terminals.
5. Run the engine at idle.
6. Adjust the carbon pile and engine speed to 2,000 rpm and 13.5 volts.
7. Compare the ammeter reading to specifications:
   a. If the reading is within specifications, the alternator is operating properly.
   b. If the reading is not within specifications, remove the alternator for further testing.

Voltage regulator test
1. Refer to Figure 4-45.
2. Perform steps 1 through 3 of the circuit resistance test just described.
3. Connect the voltmeter (+) lead to the L-terminal on the alternator; connect the voltmeter (−) lead to ground.

4. Turn the ignition switch on. *Do not start the engine.*
5. Watch the voltmeter reading:
   a. If the reading is above 1 volt, remove the alternator for further testing.
   b. If the reading is 1 volt or less, go to step 6.
6. Short across the ammeter test leads and start the engine.
7. Remove the short from the ammeter test leads and immediately increase the engine speed to 2,000 to 3,000 rpm.
8. Watch the ammeter reading:
   a. If the reading is 10 amps or less, go to step 9.
   b. If the reading is over 10 amps, continue to charge the battery until the reading falls below 10 amps and then go to step 9.
9. Observe the voltmeter reading for the regulated charging voltage:
   a. If the reading is within specifications, the regulator is good.
   b. If the reading is outside specifications, remove the alternator for repairs.

ALTERNATOR SYSTEM TESTING WITH AN OSCILLOSCOPE

Although the oscilloscope is most often used to give the voltage levels of the ignition system, it can also be used to check the alternator voltage output and condition.

Oscilloscope Connections

Many oscilloscopes have an inductive pickup lead that clamps around the alternator output wire or the battery (+) terminal, figure 4-46.

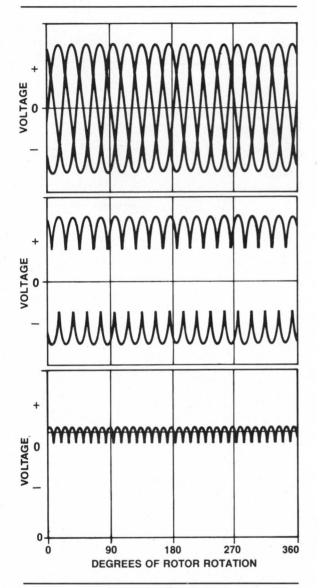

Figure 4-47. The alternator's full-wave rectification causes the rippled oscilloscope trace. (Bosch)

Certain testers may require that the headlamps or some other load be applied.

Voltage Patterns and Diagnosis

The voltage trace shown on the oscilloscope screen is a result of the alternator's rectification process, figure 4-47. A straight, rippled line is normal. If any of the diodes or stator windings are bad, it will affect the trace.

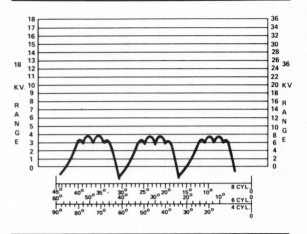

Figure 4-48. An open diode will cause this trace, in which one pulse is missing and the adjacent pulses are compressed. (Allen)

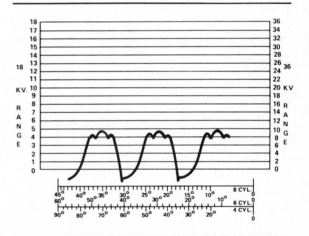

Figure 4-49. If two diodes in the same phase are open, two full pulses will be missing. (Allen)

By studying the trace, you can find what is wrong with the alternator. In general, a shorted diode will have a greater effect on the trace than will an open diode. This is because a shorted diode not only reduces the output of its own phase, but it also affects the output of the following phase. The short allows current to flow back through the stator and oppose the flow of the next phase.

Figures 4-48 through 4-55 show typical faulty alternator traces and explain the causes.

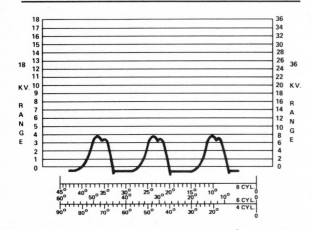

Figure 4-50. When two diodes of the same polarity are open, two output phases will be affected. (Allen)

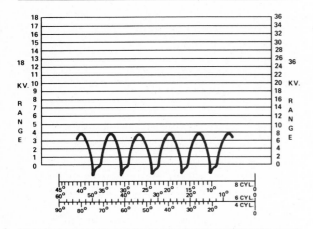

Figure 4-51. This trace is caused by one open positive diode and one open negative diode in different phases.

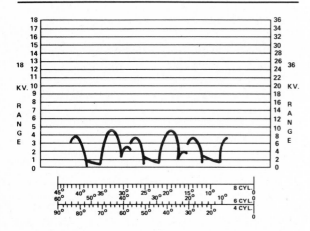

Figure 4-52. One shorted diode will have a great effect upon the trace.

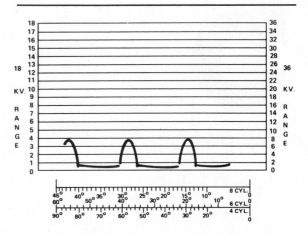

Figure 4-53. When two diodes of the same polarity are shorted, only one phase can produce voltage output.

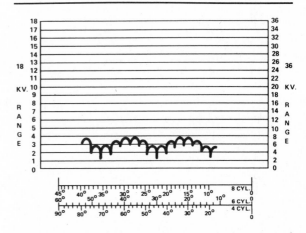

Figure 4-54. This trace shows that none of the diodes has failed, but one diode is offering high resistance to current flow.

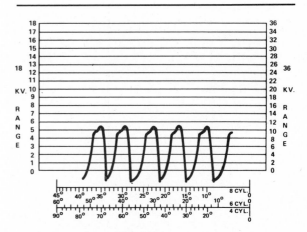

Figure 4-55. The trace caused by shorted stator windings is very similar to that caused by shorted diodes.

5

Alternator Overhaul

This chapter has removal, disassembly, testing, repair, and installation instructions for Delco-Remy, Motorcraft, and Chrysler alternators. Alternator removal, bench testing, and installation procedures are given as general instructions that will help you do these jobs on most domestic cars and light trucks. Overhaul procedures are given as photographic sequences for seven specific alternator models.

ALTERNATOR REMOVAL

You may have to remove, or loosen and relocate, other engine-driven accessory units, such as an air injection pump or air conditioning compressor, to remove the alternator. To remove low-mount alternators, it may be necessary to raise the car with a hoist and work from underneath.

It may help to tag all nuts, bolts, and washers removed from the alternator and other parts. You may also want to tag all drive belts removed from other engine accessory units during alternator service. Observe all electrical safety precautions and shop safety regulations during alternator service. Remove the alternator as follows:

1. Disconnect the battery ground cable.
2. Identify and carefully disconnect all leads from the alternator. Some are held by nuts on terminal studs. Others are plug-in or plug-on connections. Be sure to release any clips or springs holding the plugs in the alternator. You may want to tag the leads for identification at reinstallation.
3. Loosen bolts holding the power steering pump, air pump, or any other unit that interferes with alternator removal.
4. Move other units away from the alternator. You may have to loosen or disconnect some hoses.
5. Remove the air intake duct and protective shield, if the alternator is so equipped.
6. Loosen the adjusting bolt holding the alternator to the alternator support bracket, figure 5-1.
7. Loosen the pivot bolt and push the alternator toward the engine until the drive belts, or belts, can be removed from the alternator pulley.
8. Remove the belt, or belts, from the pulley and let it hang on its engine drive pulley. Make sure all belts are clear of the alternator.
9. Remove the pivot bolt and the adjusting bolt and remove the alternator.

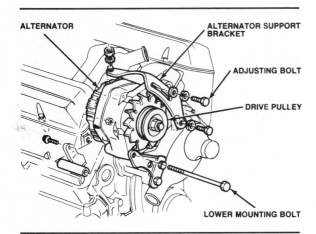

Figure 5-1. Disconnect the ground cable and all leads before removing all bolts securing an alternator to the engine.

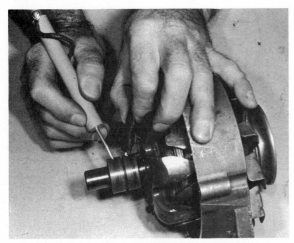

Figure 5-2. Test for rotor continuity by touching one test lamp lead to each slipring.

ALTERNATOR BENCH TEST PROCEDURES

Alternators built by different manufacturers can be tested for rotor continuity, rotor ground, stator continuity, stator ground, capacitor continuity, and rectifier continuity in a similar manner. Remember that alternators with delta stator windings cannot be bench tested for shorts or opens in the stator windings (noticeable discoloration on the assembly generally indicates defective stator windings). Standard procedures also apply to the removal and installation of single diodes that are pressed into heat sinks and end frames.

The following general tests should be made on the alternators covered in the overhaul procedures later in this chapter. These tests can be made at several convenient points during the disassembly and reassembly sequences. Read

Figure 5-3. Test for a grounded rotor winding by touching one test lamp lead to one slipring. Touch the other test lead to the rotor shaft.

these test instructions before overhauling an alternator and refer to them whenever necessary during the overhaul sequence.

Continuity and ground tests can be made with a self-powered test lamp or with an ohmmeter. High resistance or an open circuit is indicated when an ohmmeter gives a very high or an infinite reading or when the test lamp does not light. Continuity is indicated when the test lamp lights or the ohmmeter reads low or zero resistance.

Rotor Continuity

Test the continuity of a rotor winding by touching one test lamp lead to each slipring, figure 5-2. The rotor winding is good if the lamp lights.

Rotor Ground

Test for a grounded rotor winding by touching one test lamp lead to a slipring and the other test lead to the rotor shaft, figure 5-3. If the lamp lights, the rotor winding is grounded.

Stator Continuity

Test stator continuity by touching one test lamp lead to one stator lead or to the neutral junction. Touch the other test lead to each remaining stator lead, in turn, figure 5-4. The stator is open if the lamp does not light at any point.

Stator Ground

Test the stator for grounded windings by touching one test lamp lead to the stator frame. Touch the other test lamp lead to each stator

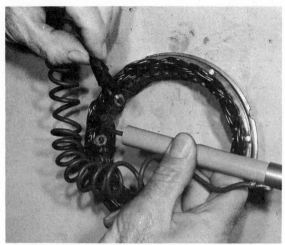

Figure 5-4. Test for stator continuity by touching one test lamp lead to each of the three stator leads.

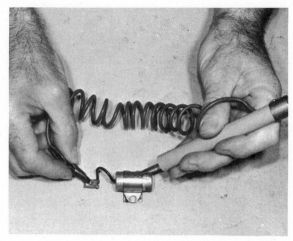

Figure 5-6. Test for a shorted capacitor by touching one test lamp lead to the capacitor case. Touch the other test lead to the capacitor terminal. Reverse the

Figure 5-5. Test for stator ground by touching one test lamp lead to the stator frame. Touch the other test lamp lead to each of the three stator terminals.

Figure 5-7. Test the continuity of individual diodes by touching one test lamp lead to the lead of the diode. Touch the other lead to the heat sink for that diode.

lead, figure 5-5. The stator windings are grounded if the lamp lights at any point.

Shorted Capacitor

Test capacitor continuity by touching one test lamp lead to the capacitor lead and the other test lead to the capacitor case, figure 5-6. The capacitor is shorted if the lamp lights.

If an ohmmeter is used, it should show infinite resistance. A capacitor cannot be tested for an open circuit without the use of a capacitor tester.

Diode and Rectifier Assembly Test and Replacement

Test individual alternator diodes as follows:
1. Touch each test lamp lead to the diode lead

and the other to the diode heat sink, figure 5-7. On some models, the alternator end frame serves as the diode heat sink.
2. Reverse the test leads, figure 5-8. The diode is bad if the lamp lights in both directions or if it does not light at all. The diode is good if the lamp lights in one direction and not in the other.

When an ohmmeter is used, it should show low resistance in one direction and very high or infinite resistance in the other. Special diode testers are also available for these tests. When using a diode tester, follow the manufacturer's directions.

A bad single diode can be replaced by pressing it out of its heat sink with a special tool.

Figure 5-8. Reverse the test lamp leads to check the continuity of an individual diode.

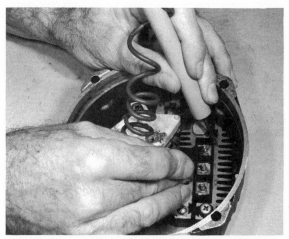

Figure 5-10. Test the rectifier in a Delco-Remy 10-SI alternator by touching one test lamp lead to the base of each diode. Touch the other test lead to the grounded heat sink.

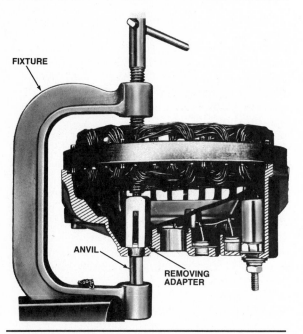

FIXTURE

ANVIL

REMOVING ADAPTER

Figure 5-9. Removing a diode. (Chrysler)

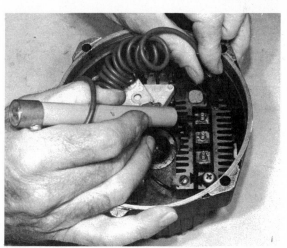

Figure 5-11. Reverse the test leads for each diode in the rectifier.

A diode press is a metal sleeve, or removing adapter, with the same inside diameter as the outside diameter of the diode. The sleeve is placed over the large end of the diode, and the diode is pressed out with a shop press or a special fixture that looks like a C-clamp, figure 5-9.

Test the rectifier of a Delco-Remy SI series alternator as follows:

1. Touch one test lamp lead to the base of a diode terminal. Do not touch the lead to the terminal stud. Touch the other test lead to the outer (grounded) heat sink, figure 5-10.

2. Reverse the test leads for each diode terminal base and the outer (grounded) heat sink, figure 5-11.

3. The lamp should light in one direction but not in the other for each diode. Replace the rectifier with a new one if the lamp lights in both directions, or not at all, for any diode.

4. Repeat steps 1 and 2, using the inner (insulated) heat sink and the base of each diode, figure 5-12. Replace the entire rectifier with a new one if the test lamp lights in both directions or not at all for any diode.

Some SI series alternators have diodes with round, rather than square, bases. Test these rectifiers as we just described, except, touch one test lamp lead to the diode terminal, not to the diode base.

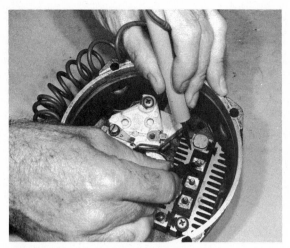

Figure 5-12. Repeat steps 1 and 2 between each diode and the insulated heat sink.

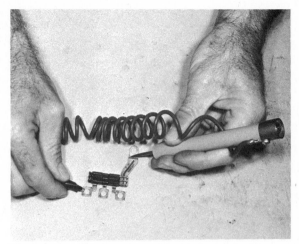

Figure 5-14. Reverse the test leads for each of the three terminals in a diode trio.

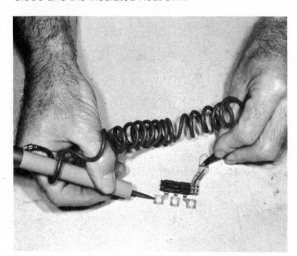

Figure 5-13. Test a field diode, or diode trio, by touching one test lamp lead to the solitary terminal and the other test lead to each of the three diode terminals, in turn.

Test a diode trio, or field diode assembly, as follows:

1. Touch one test lamp lead to the solitary terminal of the diode trio. Touch the other test lead to each of the remaining terminals, in turn, figure 5-13.

2. Reverse the test leads, and repeat step 1 for each terminal, in turn, figure 5-14. If the test lamp lights in both directions, or if it fails to light in one direction for any terminal, the diode trio is defective.

ALTERNATOR OVERHAUL PROCEDURES

The following pages contain photographic procedures for the disassembly, overhaul, and re-

assembly of seven common domestic alternators:

● Delco-Remy Model 10-SI — 1970 and later models with integral solid-state regulator; used by GM

● Delco-Remy Model CS-130 — 1986 and later models with integral multi-function IC regulator; used by GM

● Motorcraft rear-terminal alternator — Used by Ford and AMC with external electromechanical and solid-state regulators

● Motorcraft side-terminal alternator — Used by Ford and AMC with external electromechanical and solid-state regulators

● Motorcraft IAR — 1985 and later models with integral solid-state regulator; used by Ford

● Chrysler late-model standard-duty alternator — 1972 and later models, used with external solid-state regulator

● Chrysler 40/90 amp alternator — 1985 and later models with voltage regulator in the engine electronics (computer controlled)

Chapter 8 of your *Classroom Manual* contains descriptive information and additional drawings of these alternators. You may also find it helpful to refer to the *Classroom Manual* when overhauling an alternator. Before starting any overhaul, be sure you read and understand the test procedures in the preceding section of this chapter, and make the tests at convenient points during the overhaul sequence. Read through the step-by-step procedure for the specific alternator that you will be overhauling before you begin work.

All soldering and unsoldering of electrical parts should be done with a medium-hot soldering iron (approximately 100 watts). Use only rosin-core solder.

DELCO-REMY 10-SI ALTERNATOR OVERHAUL PROCEDURE

1. Draw chalk mark across both end frames and remove four through-bolts that secure frames. Separate end frames.

2. Remove three nuts attaching stator leads to rectifier. Remove stator.

3. Test stator for opens and grounds with self-powered test lamp or ohmmeter.

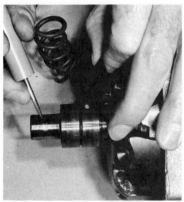

4. This is also convenient time to test rotor for opens and grounds with test lamp or ohmmeter.

5. Remove screw holding diode trio to brush holder. Remove diode trio and test it for opens and shorts.

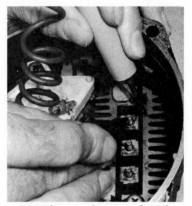

6. Rectifier can be tested with test lamp or ohmmeter while still in end frame.

7. Disconnect capacitor lead from rectifier. Remove screw from capacitor bracket and remove capacitor from end frame.

8. Remove nut, washer, and insulator from BAT terminal on rear of end frame. Then remove BAT terminal. Remove ground screw and rectifier.

9. Remove two screws holding brush holder and regulator. *Be sure* to note position of insulators and insulating sleeves for reassembly.

DELCO-REMY 10-SI ALTERNATOR OVERHAUL PROCEDURE

10. Remove brush holder and regulator. Separate brush holder from regulator and inspect brushes for wear. Replace brushes in matched pairs if necessary.

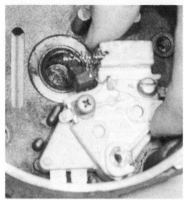

11. Install regulator and brush holder. Replace insulating sleeves and washers if needed. *Be sure* insulating sleeves and washers are reinstalled as removed,

12. Position brushes and springs in brush holder. Insert drill bit or toothpick through rear of end frame to hold brushes above sliprings when rotor is reinstalled.

13. Install rectifier. When rectifier is in place, insert BAT terminal through rectifier and end frame. Install ground screw.

14. Install nut and insulating washer on BAT terminal on rear of end frame.

15. Attach capacitor lead to rectifier and install capacitor mounting screw through bracket.

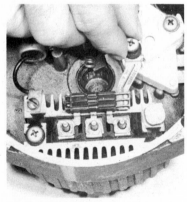

16. Install diode trio. This screw must have insulating sleeve. Other three diode trio leads fit over rectifier terminals.

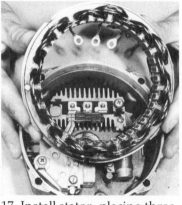

17. Install stator, placing three leads over rectifier terminals. Align notches in stator frame with bolt holes in end frame.

18. To replace parts in drive end frame, *carefully* clamp rotor in vise. Then remove shaft nut, washer, pulley, and fan.

DELCO-REMY 10-SI ALTERNATOR OVERHAUL PROCEDURE

19. Remove collar from shaft behind fan. Then separate rotor and shaft from end frame.

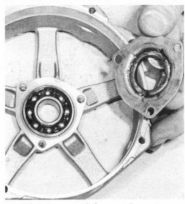

20. If drive end frame bearing is to be replaced, remove three screws holding bearing retainer. Then remove retainer plate.

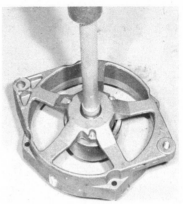

21. Support bearing hub of end frame on suitable fixture and *carefully* drive or press bearing from end frame.

22. To install bearing, tap in carefully with block and hammer or press in with collar over outer race. Old bearing can be relubricated. Do not overfill with grease.

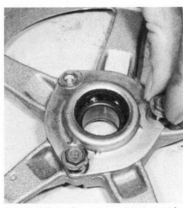

23. Replace bearing retainer if felt seal is hardened or worn. Install three retaining screws.

24. Assemble rotor and shaft into end frame. Install collar on shaft.

25. Attach fan, pulley, washer, and nut. *Carefully* hold rotor in vise; torque shaft nut to 50 ± 10 foot-pounds.

26. Align chalk marks on end frames and assemble end frames.

27. Remove drill bit or toothpick holding brushes away from sliprings. Install and tighten four through-bolts. Overhaul is complete.

DELCO-REMY CS-130 ALTERNATOR OVERHAUL PROCEDURE

1. Remove the through-bolts and carefully separate the drive end frame from the stator end frame.

2. Note the plastic internal fan permanently attached to the rotor shaft; if damaged or overheated, replace the entire rotor assembly as a unit.

3. Remove the pulley retaining nut, spacer, drive pulley, fan and washer from the drive and housing.

4. Separate rotor and end housing; remove spacer (arrow) from rotor shaft. If bearing is worn or damaged, replace end frame and bearing as a unit.

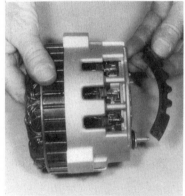

5. This plastic dust cover is installed over the stator lead connections; remove it by carefully prying it off the housing.

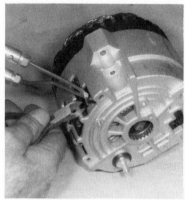

6. Heat one stator lead at a time with a soldering iron, then open the clamp with a pair of diagonal pliers and remove the two wires.

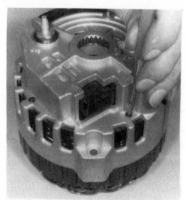

7. Three plastic pins hold the plastic stator cover to the end frame. Use a punch to carefully press the pins from the end frame.

8. Remove the stator (with plastic cover attached) from the end frame. Remove the cover from the stator. If testing is required, refer to Chapter 4.

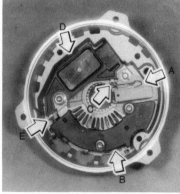

9. The brush holder (A) connects to the rectifier assembly (B) with a slip-on terminal (C). The regulator (D) connects to the rectifier assembly at a soldered terminal (E).

DELCO-REMY CS-130 ALTERNATOR OVERHAUL PROCEDURE

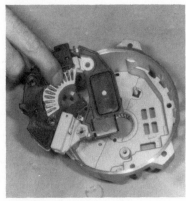

10. Remove the brush holder, rectifier, and regulator as a unit to make it easier to separate the components for testing or replacement.

11. The stator end frame uses no bearing. This rippled aluminum spacer or tolerance ring takes up any play in the machined shaft opening.

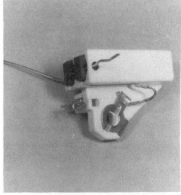

12. The brushes have small holes drilled in them. Insert a bent paper clip as shown to hold them in the brush holder for reinstallation.

13. Once the components are reassembled, be sure to press the stator cover pins completely back into the housing.

14. These stator cover clips must snap into place or you will hear a noise when the rotor is turned.

15. Remove the paper clip to allow the brushes to make contact with the rotor slip-rings.

MOTORCRAFT REAR-TERMINAL ALTERNATOR OVERHAUL PROCEDURE

1. Draw chalk mark across both end frames and remove three through-bolts securing frames.

2. Separate drive end frame and rotor from rear end frame and stator-rectifier assembly. Brushes and springs will pop from brush holder.

3. Remove integral regulator, if present. Remove nuts, washers, and insulators from rear end frame terminals. Tag all fasteners.

4. Separate rear end frame from stator and rectifier assembly.

5. Remove insulators from large BAT terminal (top) and smaller STA terminal (bottom). Remove capacitor. No BAT insulator is used with integral regulator.

6. Unsolder stator leads from printed circuit board terminals. Remove STA terminal from rectifier. Separate stator from rectifier.

7. Remove two screws securing brush holder to rear end frame. Ground brush is attached to one screw. Remove brush holder.

8. Remove brush holder and springs. Note position of insulated brush, insulator, and FLD terminal in end frame. Reinstall the same way.

9. Remove insulated brush, insulator, and FLD terminal. Inspect brushes. Replace both if worn. Replace brush holder if broken.

MOTORCRAFT REAR-TERMINAL ALTERNATOR OVERHAUL PROCEDURE

10. Install brush holder and insulated brush like this. Be sure insulator is in place and that brush lead does not touch end frame.

11. Install ground brush and two screws. Insert drill bit or toothpick through end frame and brush holder to hold brushes.

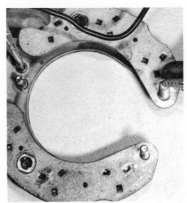

12. Test rectifier by touching one test lamp lead to BAT terminal, other lead to each of three stator winding terminals.

13. Reverse test leads and repeat step 12. Lamp should light at all three positions in one direction, not in the other.

14. Repeat steps 12 and 13 from GRD terminal to all three stator leads. Replace rectifier if it fails any part of tests.

15. Put neutral lead and insulator on STA terminal and install in rectifier. Solder other stator leads to rectifier.

16. Test capacitor and install on BAT and ground terminals. Install insulating washer on BAT terminal.

17. Assemble end frame to stator-rectifier assembly. Be sure all insulators are properly installed. Install nuts, washers, and insulators outside end frame.

18. Test rotor for opens and grounds (as shown here) before reassembling alternator.

MOTORCRAFT REAR-TERMINAL ALTERNATOR OVERHAUL PROCEDURE

19. If drive end frame parts are to be removed, *carefully* hold rotor in vise and remove nut, washer, pulley, fan, and collar.

20. Separate rotor from end frame. Note spacer on shaft. Reinstall in same direction. Leave it on shaft unless replacing it.

21. If front bearing is to be replaced, remove bearing retainer.

22. After old bearing is removed, fit new one into end frame hub.

23. *Carefully* tap bearing into place with wooden block and hammer.

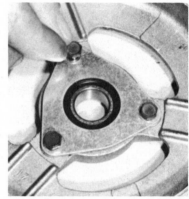

24. Install bearing retainer and tighten three screws carefully.

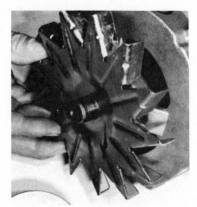

25. Install collar, fan, pulley, and washer. Then carefully hold rotor in vise and tighten nut on rotor shaft.

26. Align chalk marks and assemble drive end frame and rotor with rear end frame and stator-rectifier assembly.

27. Install through-bolts and tighten carefully. Remove drill bit or toothpick holding brushes away from slip rings.

MOTORCRAFT SIDE-TERMINAL ALTERNATOR OVERHAUL PROCEDURE

1. Mark on end frames and remove through-bolts. Separate end frames.

2. Unsolder stator leads from rectifier and remove stator from end frame.

3. Unsolder brush holder lead from rectifier. Remove screws securing brush holder and remove brush holder with brushes.

4. Remove nuts from BAT and GRD terminals outside rear end frame. Remove insulator from BAT terminal.

5. Disconnect capacitor lead from rectifier and remove rectifier. Be sure rectifier insulators in end frame are reinstalled later.

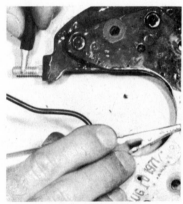

6. Test rectifier by touching one test lamp lead to BAT terminal, other lead to each of three stator winding terminals.

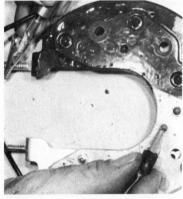

7. Reverse test leads and repeat step 6. Lamp should light at all three positions in one direction, not in the other.

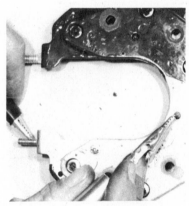

8. Repeat steps 6 and 7 from GRD terminal to all three stator leads. Replace rectifier if it fails any tests.

9. Inspect brushes and replace if worn. Install brush holder with two screws. Insert drill bit or toothpick to hold brushes in place.

MOTORCRAFT SIDE-TERMINAL ALTERNATOR OVERHAUL PROCEDURE

10. Install capacitor. Be sure two insulators are on bosses inside rear end frame.

11. Place rectifier inside end frame with insulating washer on BAT terminal. Secure rectifier to end frame with four screws.

12. Place insulating washer on ouside of BAT terminal. Attach nuts to BAT and GRD terminals.

13. Attach capacitor lead to rectifier with screw. Solder brush holder lead to rectifier.

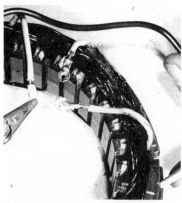

14. Test stator for opens or shorts (shown here) with test lamp or ohmmeter before reassembly. Replace defective stator.

15. Place stator in rear end frame and solder stator leads to three stator terminals on rectifier.

16. Test rotor for grounds and opens (shown here) before reassembling alternator. Drive end frame service is similar to rear-terminal alternators.

17. Align marks on end frames and assemble drive end frame and rotor to rear end frame and stator-rectifier assembly.

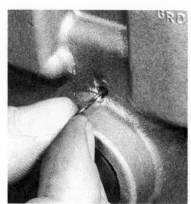

18. Install and tighten four through-bolts. Remove drill bit or toothpick holding brushes away from sliprings.

MOTORCRAFT IAR ALTERNATOR OVERHAUL PROCEDURE

1. Remove the four screws holding the regulator and brush assembly to the rear end frame. Remove the assembly.

2. If replacing the brush, remove the two screws from the regulator. The brushes with leads and screw retaining nuts will come free with the brush holder.

3. The through-bolts have a new style head, but can also be removed with a standard socket.

4. Scribe an alignment mark across the end frames with a grease pencil or chalk, then remove the through-bolts.

5. Carefully separate the end frames. The rotor will remain with the drive end frame; the stator will remain with the rear end frame.

6. To remove the stator from the end frame, you must un-solder the stator leads (arrows) at the rectifier assembly.

7. Heat one stator lead at a time with a soldering iron, then grasp the lead with nee-dlenose pliers and pull it off the rectifier terminal.

8. Once all three leads have been disconnected, you can remove the stator. If it requires testing, refer to Chapter 4.

9. Use a Torx T-20 driver to remove the four rectifier assembly screws. Substitute tools will ruin the Torx screw heads.

MOTORCRAFT IAR ALTERNATOR OVERHAUL PROCEDURE

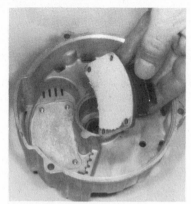

10. Remove the rectifier assembly from the end frame. Note that a silicone grease is used on the base of the assembly.

11. Remove the pulley retaining nut, washer, drive pulley, and fan. Remove the spacer (arrow) from the rotor shaft.

12. Press the rotor from the drive end frame. If it requires testing, refer to Chapter 4.

13. To replace the drive end bearing, remove the three screws and bearing retainer. The bearing is a slip-fit and can be pushed from the frame by hand.

14. When the brush holder is reassembled to the regulator, insert a paper clip as shown to hold the brushes in place for reinstallation to the housing.

15. Install the regulator and brush holder assembly. Tighten the screws, then remove the paper clip to let the brushes engage the sliprings.

CHRYSLER LATE-MODEL STANDARD ALTERNATOR OVERHAUL PROCEDURE

1. Remove two screws, washers, and brush holders from rear end frame.

2. Draw chalk mark across both end frames and remove three through-bolts securing frames. Separate end frames.

3. Remove three nuts securing stator leads to rectifier terminals. Remove stator.

4. Test stator for ground (shown here) and for continuity with test lamp or ohmmeter.

5. To test positive rectifier, touch one test lamp lead to rectifier heat sink. Touch other lead to strap at base of each diode, in turn.

6. Reverse leads. Lamp should light in one direction for each diode, not in other. Replace rectifier if lamp does not light at all or lights in both directions.

7. To test negative rectifier, touch one test lamp lead to rectifier heat sink. Touch other lead to strap at base of each diode, in turn.

8. Reverse leads. Lamp should light in one direction for each diode, not in other. Replace rectifier if lamp does not light or lights in both directions.

9. Remove nut holding capacitor to insulated stud. Remove capacitor. Remove nut from BAT terminal and remove positive rectifier.

CHRYSLER LATE-MODEL STANDARD ALTERNATOR OVERHAUL PROCEDURE

10. Remove four screws securing negative rectifier to end frame. Remove rectifier.

11. If rear bearing is to be replaced, carefully press or drive it from end frame. Install new bearing from outside of end frame.

12. Install mica insulating washer between rectifier and end frame. Install BAT terminal and insulator from outside end frame.

13. Be sure mica insulating washer is on other mounting stud. Then install positive rectifier.

14. Test capacitor for opens and shorts, then install. Secure capacitor and positive rectifier with two nuts to BAT terminal and stud.

15. Install negative rectifier and secure with four screws through top of end frame.

16. Align stator with through-bolt holes. Fit stator dowels into holes in end frame and secure stator leads to rectifier terminals.

17. Test rotor for continuity (shown here) and for ground with test lamp or ohmmeter. Sliprings on Chrysler rotors are at right angles.

18. To disassemble drive end frame, pulley must be removed with *special* puller. *Carefully* clamp end frame in vise and attach puller to pulley hub.

CHRYSLER LATE-MODEL STANDARD ALTERNATOR OVERHAUL PROCEDURE

19. You may need impact wrench to remove pulley with puller. Hold puller with vise grips, *securely*.

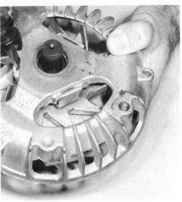

20. Use screwdriver to release three tabs for front bearing grease retainer.

21. If rotor does not separate from front end frame, tap carefully with soft mallet.

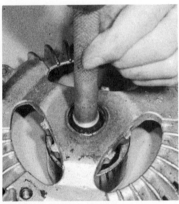

22. To remove bearing, support end frame hub and carefully press or drive bearing from end frame.

23. Carefully drive new bearing into end frame with block of wood and hammer. Assemble rotor with end frame. Then latch grease retainer tabs to end frame.

24. New pulley must be installed on shaft with press. Align dowels on stator with holes in end frame and assemble. Secure with three through-bolts.

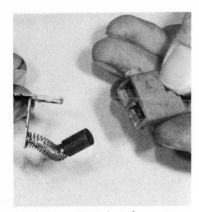

25. Inspect brushes for wear and replace if necessary. Replace as matched pair. Install brushes and springs in brush holders.

26. Install brush holders with brushes on rear end frame. Be sure insulators are between brush holders and screw heads.

27. Be sure BAT terminal and insulator are secure in end frame. Install insulating washer and nut. Overhaul is complete

CHRYSLER 40/90-AMPERE ALTERNATOR OVERHAUL PROCEDURE

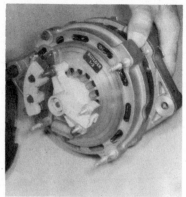

1. Draw a chalk mark across both end frames. Remove dust cover retaining nut from brush holder assembly mounting stud; remove dust cover.

2. Use a deep socket to remove the two brush holder assembly mounting screws. Carefully remove brush holder assembly from rotor shaft.

3. Remove the three screws holding stator leads to the posts on the side of the rectifier assembly. Separate leads from rectifier posts.

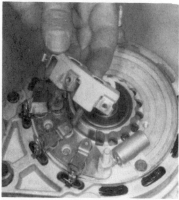

4. Remove the two screws holding the rectifier insulator and assembly to the end shield. Remove the rectifier insulator.

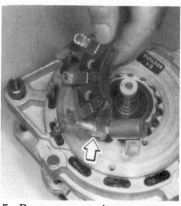

5. Remove capacitor mounting screw from end shield. Remove capacitor and rectifier assembly. They can be separated by removing the large nut (arrow).

6. Remove the four through-bolts (arrows). A deep socket is necessary to remove the two bolts with stud ends.

7. Carefully pry rectifier and drive end shields apart by inserting a screwdriver blade at pry point on each side of end shield and stator.

8. Guide the stator leads through the insulator openings in rectifier end shield as the end shield is separated from the stator assembly.

9. Check the condition of the stator lead insulator assembly. Made of plastic, it can be snapped out of the end shield if replacement is required.

CHRYSLER 40/90-AMPERE ALTERNATOR OVERHAUL PROCEDURE

10. Separate the stator from the drive end shield. If testing is required, refer to Chapter 4.

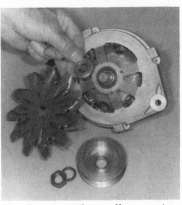

11. Remove the pulley retaining nut, washer, drive pulley, fan, and front bearing spacer. The chamber on the spacer fits against the rotor when reinstalled.

12. Press (do not hammer) the rotor from drive end shield, then remove inner bearing spacer (arrow) from rotor shaft. Refer to Chapter 4 for testing.

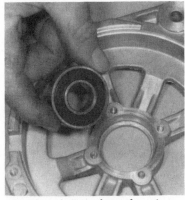

13. If replacing front bearing, remove four bearing retaining capscrews and press bearing from drive end shield. Press new bearing in place and reinstall capscrews.

14. The rotor is more delicate than most. Note ceramic slip-ring end of the shaft (A), which can be easily damaged, and plastic termination plate on rotor (B).

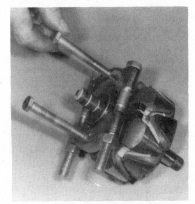

15. Chrysler provides a jig and tool to remove bearings; the universal puller shown will work. Avoid damaging the shaft end and termination plate. Reinstall with the jig.

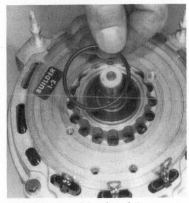

16. Reassemble the drive ends and stator and install the through-bolts, then remove and replace this O-ring from the rectifier end shield.

17. Reinstall rectifier and capacitor assembly. Install rectifier insulator and tighten in place, then install and tighten capacitor screw. Reinstall the three stator to rectifier screws.

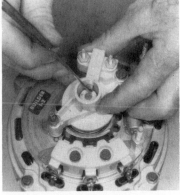

18. Use pointed tool to push brushes back into holder as you slide it over rotor slip-rings. Tighten brush holder screws; reinstall dust cover and retaining nut.

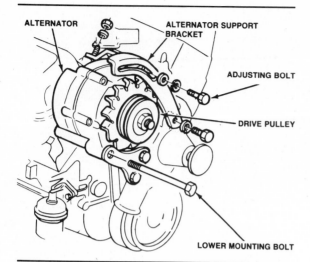

Figure 5-15. Install the alternator on the engine mounting brackets. Loosely secure the alternator with the lower mounting bolt and the adjusting bolt. (Chevrolet)

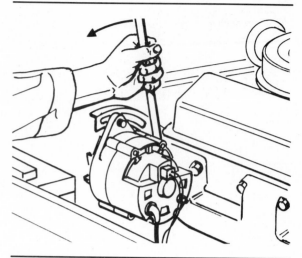

Figure 5-16. Adjust belt tension by carefully prying the alternator away from the engine with a hammer.

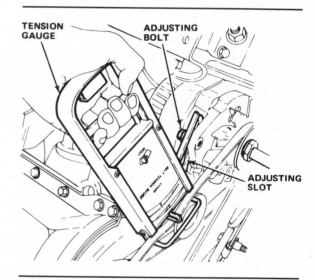

Figure 5-17. Check belt tension with a belt tension gauge. Adjust tension to the manufacturer's specifications. (AMC)

ALTERNATOR INSTALLATION

Spin the shaft of the assembled alternator by hand to be sure the rotor and pulley do not bind. Make sure the brushes contact the sliprings without binding. Be sure the rotor or the fan blades do not snag the stator windings.

Before installing the alternator, inspect the drive belt for wear or damage. Belts that are cracked, broken, glazed, or oil soaked should be replaced as described in Chapter 4. Make sure the pivot bolt is tight before tightening the adjusting bolt for the last time during installation. This prevents binding of the alternator bearings, rotor, shaft, mounting bracket, or adjusting bolt.

Install an alternator as follows:
1. Put the alternator on the engine and the alternator mounting brackets. Loosely secure the alternator with the lower mounting or pivot bolt and the adjusting bolt, figure 5-15.
2. Attach all belts to the alternator pulleys and pull the alternator away from the engine by hand just enough to keep light tension on the belts.
3. Tighten the lower mounting bolt and the adjusting bolt enough to hold the alternator in position under light belt tension.
4. Reposition or reinstall any accessory unit that may have been loosened or removed to aid in removing the alternator.
5. Gently pry the alternator away from the engine with a wooden hammer handle or a pry bar to adjust the final belt tension, figure 5-16. Do not pry against thin-walled sections of the alternator. Tighten the adjusting bolt and the lower mounting bolt.
6. Use a belt tension gauge to check the tension

of all belts on the alternator pulley, figure 5-17. Loosen the mounting and adjusting bolts and readjust, if necessary.
7. Check the belt tension on all other engine accessories that were loosened to install the alternator. Tighten the mounting and adjusting bolts on these accessories. Repeat the belt adjustment and tension checks until all belts are adjusted to specifications.
8. Identify all tagged leads and attach them to their appropriate alternator terminals or plug sockets.
9. Connect the ground cable to the battery.
10. Test the alternator by running the engine. Check for noise or vibration from the alternator.
11. Test the alternator current output and voltage as explained in Chapter 4 of this manual.

PART THREE

Starting System Service

6

Starting System Testing

This chapter has instructions for the on-car testing of starting systems. Figure 6-1 will help you pinpoint the problem in a particular system. Remember, many electrical system problems can be caused by the battery. Test the battery as explained in Chapter 3 before beginning these starting system tests. When these test procedures direct you to remove the starter motor for further testing, refer to Chapter 7 for step-by-step instructions.

SYSTEM INSPECTION

Many problems within the starting system can be found with nothing more than a simple inspection. Inspect the following areas.
1. Battery:
- Loose or corroded terminals
- Loose or corroded cable connections
- Frayed cables
- Damaged insulation.
2. Ignition switch:
- Loose mounting
- Sticking contacts
- Damaged wiring
- Loose connections.
3. Starter motor:
- Loose mounting
- Poor pinion engagement
- Loose wiring and connections
- Damaged wiring and connections.
4. Starting safety switch (if used):
- Poor adjustment
- Loose mounting
- Loose or damaged wiring (electrical switch).
5. Magnetic switches:
- Loose mounting
- Loose connections
- Damaged wiring.

All GM cars have a solenoid mounted on, or enclosed within, the starter motor. All Ford cars have a starter relay mounted on a fender panel, and some older Ford vehicles and diesel models also have a solenoid at the starter. All Chrysler cars have a starter relay mounted on the firewall or a fender panel and a solenoid at the starter. All AMC cars have a starter relay mounted on a fender panel. Most imported cars use a solenoid mounted on the starter.

ON-CAR TESTING

The tests detailed in this chapter can be made using:
- A voltmeter
- An ammeter
- A variable-resistance carbon pile
- Jumper wires
- A remote starter switch.

SYMPTOMS	POSSIBLE CAUSE	CURE
• Nothing happens when ignition switch is turned to Start	1. Battery discharged 2. Open in control circuit 3. Defective starter relay or solenoid 4. Open in motor internal ground connections.	1. Recharge or replace 2. Test control circuit for continuity; repair or replace components as necessary 3. Replace relay or solenoid 4. Replace starter motor
• Solenoid contacts click or chatter but starter does not operate OR movable-pole-shoe starter chatters or disengages before engine has been started	1. Battery discharged 2. Excessive resistance in system 3. Open in solenoid or movable-pole-shoe hold-in winding 4. Defective starter motor	1. Recharge or replace 2. Make voltage drop tests; replace components as necessary 3. Replace solenoid or movable pole shoe starter 4. Replace starter motor
• Starter motor operates but does not turn car engine	1. Defective starter drive 2. Defective engine flywheel ring gear	1. Replace starter drive 2. Replace engine flywheel ring gear
• Starter motor turns engine slowly or unevenly	1. Battery discharged 2. Excessive resistance in system 3. Defective starter 4. Defective engine flywheel ring gear 5. Poor flywheel-starter engagement	1. Recharge or replace 2. Make voltage drop tests; replace components as necessary 3. Replace starter motor 4. Replace engine flywheel ring gear 5. Adjust flywheel-starter engagement
• Engine starts but motor drive does not disengage	1. Defective drive assembly 2. Poor flywheel-starter engagement 3. Shorted solenoid windings 4. Shorted control circuit	1. Replace starter drive 2. Adjust flywheel-starter engagement, if possible, or replace starter motor 3. Replace solenoid 4. Test control circuit; replace components as necessary

Figure 6-1. Starting system troubleshooting guide.

Figure 6-2. A remote starter button is a handy tool when working on the starting system.

All of these units except the remote starter switch and jumper wires may be contained within a single tester. These are often called battery-starter testers.

Pretest Precautions

Almost all starting system tests must be made while the starter motor is cranking the engine. The engine must not start and run during the test, or the readings will be inaccurate.

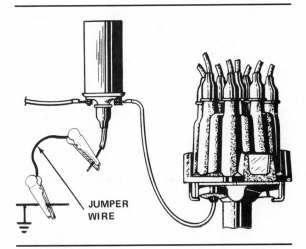

JUMPER WIRE

Figure 6-3. If the ignition system must be disabled, remove the secondary lead from the distributor center tower and ground the lead.

To keep the engine from starting, you can bypass the ignition switch with a remote starter switch, figure 6-2. This is a hand-held, push-button switch with two leads. The leads can be connected so that the button controls current

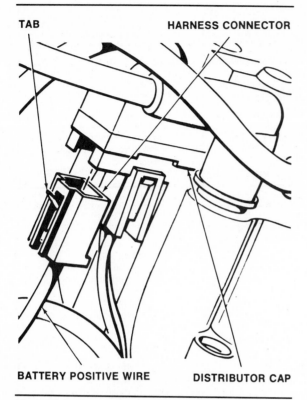

Figure 6-4. To disable the Delco-Remy HEI system, unplug the outermost harness connector from the distributor cap.

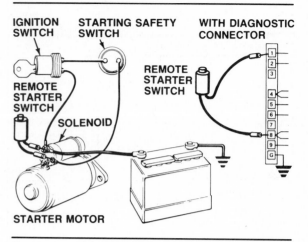

Figure 6-5. Bypassing the ignition system of a GM car.

flow to the starting system but not to the ignition system. On vehicles with the ignition starting bypass in the ignition switch or the starter relay, you must disable the ignition.

On most systems, do this by disconnecting the secondary lead from the center of the distributor cap and grounding the lead, figure 6-3. On electronic ignition or engine control systems, disconnect the wiring harness connector from the distributor. Figure 6-4 shows the removal point on the HEI distributor cap.

Before testing the starting system, be sure the transmission is out of gear (Park or Neutral). A remote starter switch bypasses the starting safety switch. Set the parking brake and block the drive wheels.

Do not crank the starter motor for more than 30 seconds at a time. Allow 2 minutes between tests for the motor to cool. Excessive cranking can overheat the motor and damage it.

If you service the battery, observe the precautions given in Chapter 3.

Disconnect the battery ground cable before making or breaking any connections at the starter motor, solenoid, or relay. Although this is a generally accepted safety procedure, it is often ignored.

Some newer vehicles may have unusual wiring configurations, such as the diesel-powered Escort and Lynx or Tempo and Topaz models. In these vehicles, the starter relay serves only as a junction block. This means that there is power to the starter at all times. If you ground the battery by disconnecting the starter relay wires with the battery connected, nearly 1,000 amperes will flow to ground. This can quickly melt your wrench, damage the engine and electrical system, and cause serious injury.

CRANKING VOLTAGE TEST

The cranking voltage test measures the battery voltage available at the starter during cranking. To obtain accurate results from a cranking voltage test, the battery must be fully charged and in good condition. Use the tests described in Chapter 3 to determine the battery state of charge and capacity, then do the following cranking voltage test.

1. Bypass the ignition switch with a remote starter switch:

    a. On GM and some AMC 4-cylinder cars, figure 6-5, connect the switch between the ignition switch terminal and the starting safety switch terminal on the starter solenoid. If the car has a diagnostic connector, connect the remote starter switch between terminals 1 and 8, figure 6-5.

    b. On Ford, Chrysler, and some AMC cars, figure 6-6, connect the switch leads between the battery terminal at the starter relay and the terminal illustrated.

2. Connect the voltmeter (−) lead to ground;

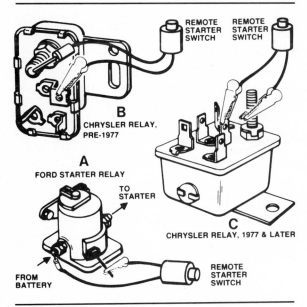

Figure 6-6. Bypassing the ignition system of Ford, AMC, and Chrysler cars.

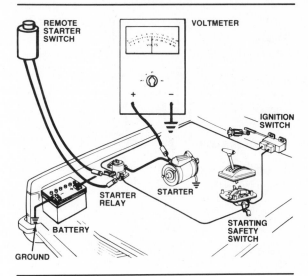

Figure 6-8. Measuring cranking voltage on a Ford or AMC car. (Ford)

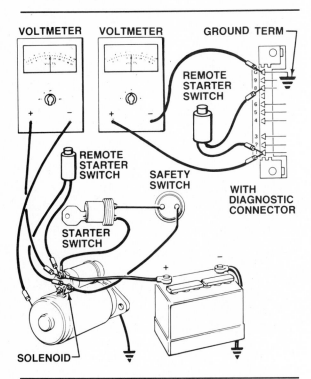

Figure 6-7. Measuring cranking voltage on a GM car.

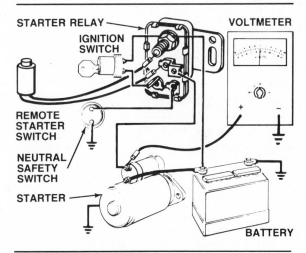

Figure 6-9. Measuring the cranking voltage of a Chrysler car. (Chrysler)

3. Crank the engine and observe the voltmeter reading.

4. Compare the voltmeter reading to the specifications:

  a. If the reading is 9.6 volts or more, but the motor cranks poorly, the problem is in the motor itself and it must be removed for further testing. Refer to Chapter 7.

If the reading is below specifications with a fully charged battery, do a current draw test to determine if the problem is high resistance in the starter circuit, or heavy overloading of the starter by the engine due to seizing, dragging, or preignition.

connect the voltmeter (+) lead to the test point indicated below:

  a. For GM and some 4-cylinder AMC cars, refer to figure 6-7.

  b. For Ford and some AMC cars, refer to figure 6-8.

  c. For Chrysler cars, refer to figure 6-9.

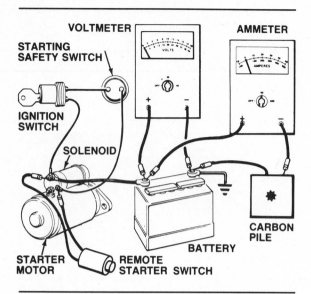

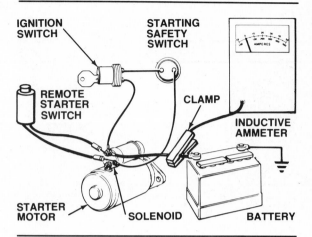

Figure 6-10. The test meter hookup for a starter current draw test.

Figure 6-11. Testing the starter current draw with an inductive ammeter.

CURRENT DRAW TEST

The current draw test measures the amount of current in amperes that the starter circuit requires to crank the engine. This test will help you to isolate the source of a starting problem.

Current Draw Test With A Series Ammeter

1. Bypass the ignition switch with a remote starter switch. Refer to figure 6-5 or 6-6.
2. Refer to figure 6-10 for test connections.
3. Connect the voltmeter (+) lead to the battery (+) terminal; connect the voltmeter (−) lead to the battery (−) terminal.
4. Set the carbon pile to its maximum resistance (open).
5. Connect the ammeter (+) lead to the battery (+) terminal; connect the ammeter (−) lead to one lead of the carbon pile.
6. Connect the other lead of the carbon pile to the battery terminal.
7. Crank the engine and watch the voltmeter reading.
8. With the starter motor *off*, adjust the carbon pile until the voltmeter reading matches the reading taken in step 7.
9. Note the ammeter reading and set the carbon pile back to its open position.
10. Compare the ammeter reading to the manufacturer's specifications. The following table summarizes the most probable cause of too much or too little current draw. If you suspect too much resistance, test the starting system resistance as explained in the circuit resistance tests found later in this chapter. If the problem

is in the starter motor, it will have to be removed for further service. Refer to Chapter 7 for instructions.

PROBLEM	PROBABLE CAUSE
High current draw	Short in starter
	Starter or engine binding
Low current draw	High resistance in starting system
	Battery undercharged or defective

Current Draw Test With An Inductive Ammeter

1. Bypass the ignition switch with a remote starter switch. Refer to figure 6-5 or 6-6.
2. Refer to figure 6-11 for test connections.
3. Connect the ammeter inductive pickup to the battery (+) cable. Be sure the arrow on the inductive pickup is pointing in the right direction as specified on the ammeter.
4. Crank the engine for 15 seconds while watching the ammeter reading.
5. Compare the ammeter reading to the specifications. Use the current draw test explained previously to interpret the readings.

CIRCUIT RESISTANCE TESTS

If the cranking voltage and current tests indicate that the fault lies in one of the electrical circuits of the starting system, use the following tests to pinpoint the problem:
● Insulated circuit test
● Ground circuit test
● Control circuit test.

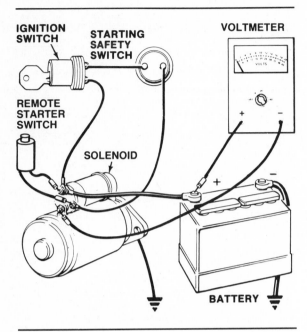

Figure 6-12. Testing the resistance of the starting system insulated circuit.

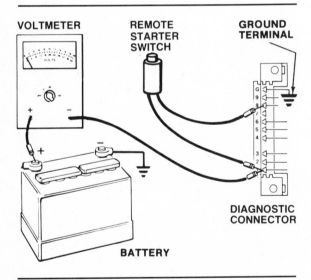

Figure 6-13. Using the GM diagnostic connector to test the resistance of the starting system insulated circuit. (GM)

These tests will locate the point of high resistance in the circuit that is causing too much voltage drop. The resistance usually occurs at one of the connections in the circuits, but internally defective wires and cables will also cause high resistance. A generally accepted standard for voltage drop in starting systems is a maximum of 0.1 volt per connection. Any greater loss will cause starting problems.

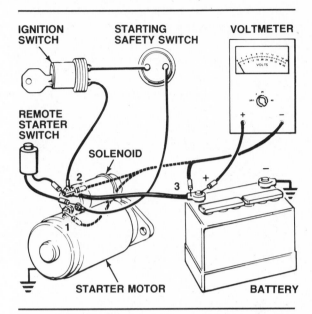

Figure 6-14. Testing the resistance between specific points of the GM starting system insulated circuit.

Insulated Circuit Test

Together, the insulated circuit and ground circuit make up the complete starter motor circuit. The insulated circuit includes all of the high-current cables and connections from the battery to the starter motor. To test this circuit for high resistance:

1. Bypass the ignition switch with a remote starter switch. Refer to figure 6-5 or 6-6.
2. Connect the voltmeter (+) lead to the battery (+) terminal. Connect the meter lead to the post or terminal nut, not to the cable. If you connect to the cable, you will miss a possible area of high resistance in the cable-to-post connection. Then connect the voltmeter (−) lead to the terminal at the starter, figure 6-12. For GM diagnostic connectors, refer to figure 6-13.
3. Crank the engine and watch the voltmeter reading.
4. Compare the voltmeter reading to the specifications:
    a. If the reading is within the specifications, usually 0.2 to 0.6 volt, go to the ground resistance test.
    b. If the reading is above specifications, go to step 5.
5. Move the voltmeter (+) lead to the test points indicated to pinpoint the high resistance. When you past the point of high resistance, the voltage drop will fall to within acceptable limits. Make each test in the order indicated. Take all voltmeter readings while cranking the engine:
    a. For GM and some AMC 4-cylinder cars, refer to figure 6-14.

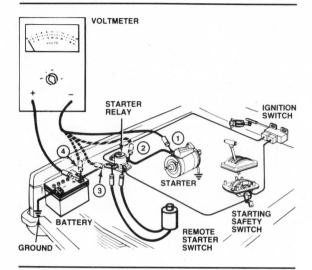

Figure 6-15. Testing the resistance between specific points of the Ford and AMC starting system insulated circuit. (Ford)

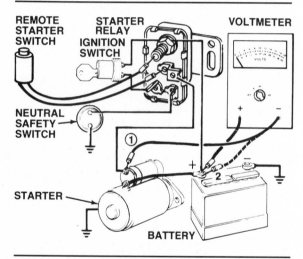

Figure 6-16. Testing the resistance between specific points of the Chrysler starting system insulated circuit. (Chrysler)

b. For Ford and some AMC cars, refer to figure 6-15.

c. For Chrysler cars, refer to figure 6-16.

6. Repair or replace any damaged wiring or faulty connections.

Ground Circuit Test

The ground circuit provides the return path to the battery for the power supplied to the starter through the insulated circuit. It includes the starter-to-engine, engine-to-chassis, and chassis-to-ground terminal connections. To test the ground circuit for high resistance:

1. Bypass the ignition switch with the remote starter switch. Refer to figure 6-5 or 6-6.

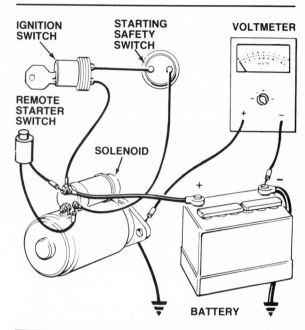

Figure 6-17. Testing the resistance of the ground circuit.

2. Connect the voltmeter (+) lead to the starter housing; connect the voltmeter (−) lead directly to the battery (−) post or terminal nut, figure 6-17. Do not connect the lead to the battery cable, or you will miss any resistance in the cable-to-post connection.

3. Crank the engine and watch the voltmeter reading.

4. Compare the voltmeter reading to the specifications:

    a. If the reading is within the specifications, usually 0.1 to 0.3 volt, go to the control circuit resistance test.

    b. If the reading is above specifications, go to step 5.

5. Tighten the system ground connections, inspect the battery ground cable, and repeat the test. Replace the battery ground cable or engine to chassis ground strap, if necessary.

Control Circuit Test

The control circuit test checks all the wiring and components used to control the magnetic switch. To do the test:

1. Disable the ignition system. Refer to figure 6-3 or 6-4.

2. Connect the voltmeter (+) lead to the battery (+) terminal; connect the voltmeter (−) lead to the switch terminal at the relay or solenoid.

    a. For GM and some 4-cylinder AMC cars, refer to figure 6-18.

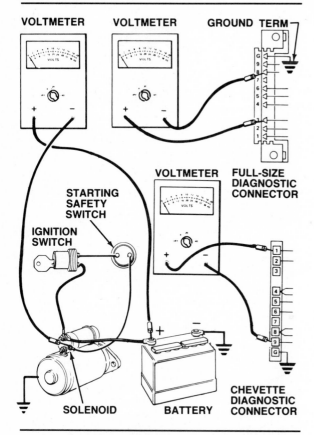

Figure 6-18. Testing the resistance of the GM starting system control circuit.

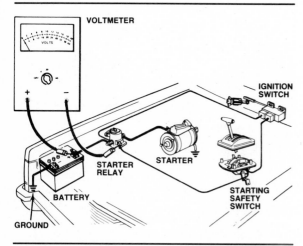

Figure 6-19. Testing the resistance of the Ford or AMC starting system control circuit. (Ford)

b. For Ford and some AMC cars, refer to figure 6-19.

c. For Chrysler cars, refer to figure 6-20.

3. Crank the engine with the ignition switch and watch the voltmeter reading.

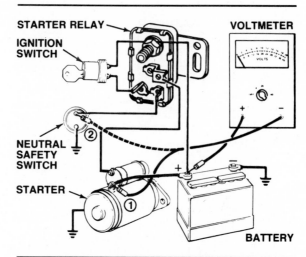

Figure 6-20. Testing the resistance of the Chrysler starting system control circuit. (Chrysler)

4. Compare the voltmeter reading to the specifications:

a. If the reading is within specifications, usually not exceeding 2.5 volts, the control circuit is in good condition.

b. If the reading is above specifications, go to step 5.

5. Touch the voltmeter (+) lead to the test points shown in the drawings to pinpoint the area of high resistance. Take all voltmeter readings while cranking the engine with the ignition switch:

a. For GM and some 4-cylinder AMC cars, refer to figure 6-21.

b. For Ford and some AMC cars, refer to figure 6-22.

c. For Chrysler cars, refer to figure 6-23.

6. Repair or replace any damaged wiring or faulty connections.

STARTING SAFETY SWITCH REPLACEMENT AND ADJUSTMENT

The following paragraphs give general instructions for replacing and adjusting the various types of electrical starting safety switches. When such a switch is used with an automatic transmission or transaxle, it is often called a neutral-start or neutral-safety switch.

Those used with manual transmissions or transaxles are usually clutch interlock switches which require the clutch pedal to be fully depressed to start the engine. A clutch interlock switch is generally connected across the ignition switch and starter motor relay coil to maintain an open circuit when the clutch pedal is released.

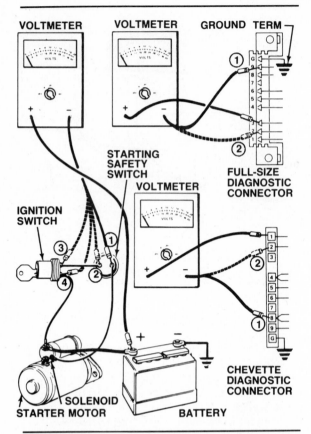

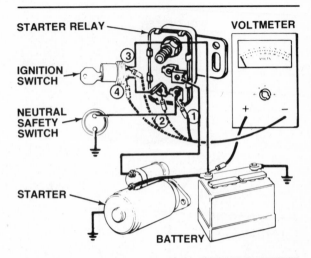

Figure 6-21. Testing the resistance between specific points of the GM starting system control circuit. (GM)

Figure 6-23. Testing the resistance between specific points in the Chrysler starting system control circuit. (Chrysler)

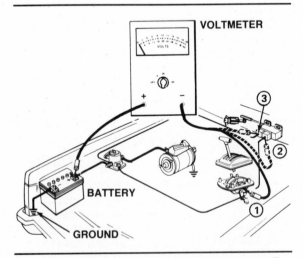

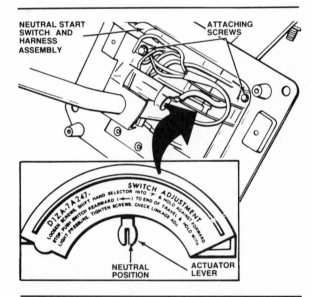

Figure 6-22. Testing the resistance between specific points of a Ford or AMC starting system control circuit. (Ford)

Figure 6-24. Adjusting the Ford floor-mounted starting safety switch. (Ford)

Most neutral-start switches cannot be adjusted. They must be replaced if they do not work properly. The switches used by AMC, Chrysler, and some Ford transmissions (C3,

A4LD, and AOD) are threaded into the transmission housing. If a known-good switch does not operate properly when correctly installed, the transmission internal gear levers must be adjusted.

Other Ford transmissions (C4, C5, and C6) and transaxles (ATX and AXOD) use an adjustable neutral start switch. The switch is generally located on the transmission housing, but some older Ford cars used a floor-mounted switch on the gearshift lever, figure 6-24.

Mechanical blocking devices, as used by GM, should not require service during normal use.

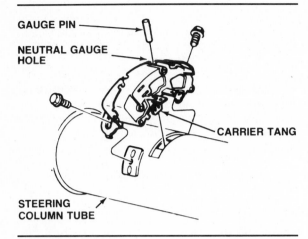

Figure 6-25. Using a gauge pin to adjust a starting safety switch. (Buick)

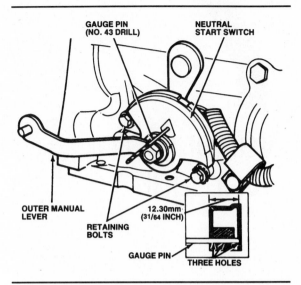

Figure 6-26. The adjustable neutral start switch on some Ford automatic transmissions and transaxles.

Clutch interlock switches cannot be adjusted, but must be replaced.

To adjust the floor-mounted switch on older large Ford models, figure 6-24:
1. Remove the shift lever handle.
2. Remove the dial housing.
3. Remove the pointer backup shield.
4. Loosen the two screws holding the switch to the shift lever housing.
5. Move the shift lever against the forward stop of the Park position and hold it there.
6. Move the switch rearward to the end of its travel.
7. Tighten the two attaching screws.
8. Check that the engine will start only when the shift lever is in Park or Neutral; readjust the switch if necessary.
9. Reinstall the pointer backup shield, the dial housing, and the shift lever handle.

Electrical switches used by Ford and GM have special alignment holes. To adjust these switches:
1. Disconnect the battery ground cable.
2. Loosen the switch attaching screws.
3. Move the switch until the two alignment holes match.
4. Check the hole alignment with a gauge pin of the size specified by the manufacturer, figure 6-25 or 6-26.
5. Tighten the switch attaching screws.
6. Reconnect the battery ground cable.
7. Check that the engine will start only when the shift lever is in Park or Neutral; readjust the switch if necessary.

7

Starter Motor Overhaul

This chapter contains removal, disassembly, testing, repair, and installation instructions for Delco-Remy, Motorcraft, and Chrysler starter motors. Starter motor removal, bench testing, and installation procedures are presented as general instructions to help you do these jobs on most domestic cars and light trucks. Overhaul procedures are presented as photographic sequences for four specific starter motor models.

STARTER MOTOR REMOVAL

You may have to remove, loosen, or relocate heat shields, support brackets, or exhaust pipes to remove the starter motor. It may help to tag nuts, bolts, and washers removed from the starter motor and from other parts. It may also help to tag all wires disconnected from the starter motor. Observe all electrical safety precautions and shop safety regulations during removal of the starter motor. Remove the starter motor as follows:

1. Disconnect the battery ground cable.
2. Raise the car high enough to gain easy access to the starter motor. Support the car on safety stands or a hoist.
3. If necessary, turn the front wheels and disconnect the tie rods for easy access to the starter motor. On some cars, you may have to remove the front wheel nearer the starter motor.
4. Loosen or remove exhaust pipes and other components that interfere with starter motor removal.
5. Remove any plastic protector covering the solenoid or motor terminals. Disconnect all wires from the solenoid or starter motor, figure 7-1. You may want to tag the wires and fasteners removed from the solenoid or motor.
6. Remove bolts securing heat shields and support brackets to the starter motor. Remove the heat shields and brackets.
7. Remove all mounting bolts or nuts securing the starter motor to the engine. Remove the starter motor and any shims that are used. Save the shims for reinstallation.
8. Place the starter motor on a clean workbench or stand where it cannot fall onto the floor. This is especially important with starter motors containing permanent magnets, since the magnets are quite brittle. A sharp blow with a hammer or dropping the motor can destroy the fields.

STARTER MOTOR AND SOLENOID BENCH TEST PROCEDURES

All starter motors listed in this chapter can be given the same standard no-load test, the same

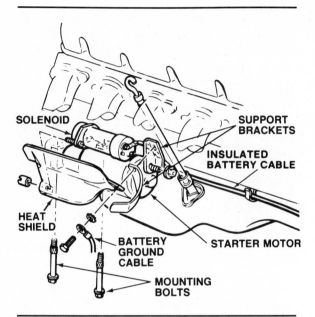

Figure 7-1. Disconnect all wires and remove heat shields and brackets before removing the starter motor from the engine. (Chevrolet)

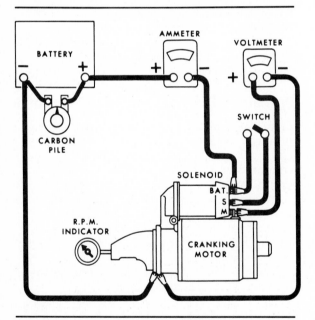

Figure 7-2. No-load test connections for solenoid-actuated starters. (Delco-Remy)

armature growler tests for shorts and opens, and the same tests for grounded or open field circuits.

All solenoids on the motors covered in this chapter can be tested for current draw or continuity.

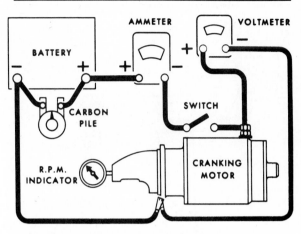

Figure 7-3. No-load test connections for movable-pole-shoe starters. (Delco-Remy)

Starter No-Load Test

The no-load test can be used to locate open or shorted windings, worn bushings, a bent armature shaft, and other problems with the armature and fields. You will need the starter motor maker's specifications for current draw and motor speed for the particular motor you are testing.

The no-load test is made with the starter on the workbench. The starter should be firmly clamped in a vise or similar fixture. Begin the test by connecting a voltmeter, an ammeter, and a switch to a fully charged battery and to the starter. Make connections for solenoid-actuated starters as shown in figure 7-2 and for movable pole shoe starters as shown in figure 7-3. If the solenoid motor terminal is not exposed, connect the voltmeter to the solenoid battery terminal. The carbon pile is optional if you want to regulate battery voltage exactly during the test. Connect an rpm indicator to the pinion shaft to measure motor speed.

Close the switch, note the current draw and motor speed and compare them to the manufacturer's specifications. Interpret test results as explained in the following paragraphs.

A low no-load speed and high current draw can be caused by bearings that are tight, dirty, or worn. A bent armature shaft or loose field pole screws can also cause the armature to drag and result in a low no-load speed and high current draw.

A low no-load speed and low current draw can be caused by an open field winding, high resistance due to poor connections, broken or weak brush springs, worn brushes, high mica on the commutator, a shorted armature, a grounded armature, or a grounded field.

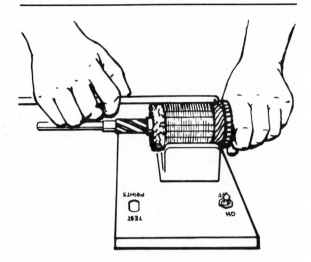

Figure 7-4. Growler test for armature shorts.

Figure 7-5. Armature ground test.

A high no-load speed and high current draw can be caused by shorted fields or by an open shunt field on some starters.

If the starter motor fails to operate with high current draw, the insulated terminal or the fields may be grounded. The shaft bearings may also be frozen.

If the starter motor fails to operate with no current draw, there could be an open field circuit, an open armature coil, broken or weak brush springs, worn brushes, or high mica on the commutator.

Armature Growler Test For Shorts

A growler is an a.c. electromagnet. If the alternating current in a growler is 60-cycle, the current reverses direction 120 times every second. The magnetic field in the electromagnet therefore changes direction 120 times every second. If a starter motor armature is placed in a growler, changing magnetism puts a changing

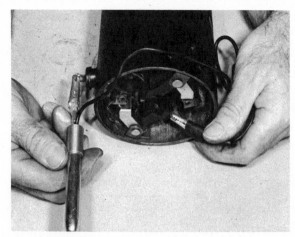

Figure 7-6. Field coil open circuit test.

magnetic force on the armature. This causes a growling noise. Test for shorts as follows:
1. Place the armature on the growler and hold a hacksaw blade flat against the length of the armature core, figure 7-4. Start the growler.
2. Slowly rotate the armature while holding the hacksaw blade against each section of the armature core.
3. If the saw blade jumps or vibrates over any section of the core when the armature is rotated, the armature is shorted.

Armature Test For Grounded Windings

Place one lead of a 110-volt test lamp or a self-powered test lamp, figure 7-5, on the armature core or shaft. Place the other test lead on the commutator. If the lamp lights, the armature is grounded.

You can also test for grounded windings with an ohmmeter. Place one ohmmeter lead on the commutator and the other lead on the shaft. The ohmmeter should show infinite resistance. If the ohmmeter indicates continuity or low resistance, the armature windings are grounded to the shaft.

Field Coil Tests

Test the field coils for open circuits or grounded windings with a 110-volt test lamp or a self-powered test lamp. Most starter motors have two insulated brushes and two ground brushes.

Field coil test for open circuits
Touch one test lamp lead to the insulated brush and the other test lamp lead to the field coil ground lead, figure 7-6. The lamp should light. The coils are open if the lamp does not light. Repeat the test with the other insulated brush, if present.

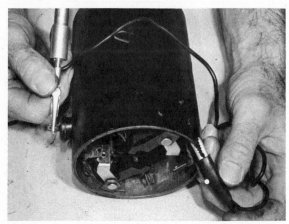

Figure 7-7. Field coil ground test.

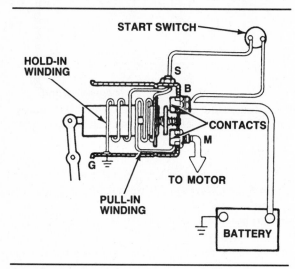

Figure 7-8. Delco-Remy solenoid circuits. (Ford)

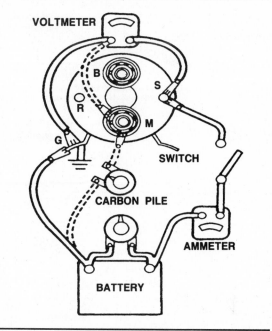

Figure 7-9. Delco-Remy solenoid current draw test. (Ford)

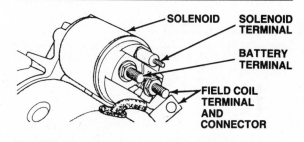

Figure 7-10. Solenoid terminals. (Chrysler)

Field coil test for grounded windings
Disconnect the field ground leads. Touch one test lamp lead to the field insulated lead or solenoid connector and the other test lead to the grounded brush or frame, figure 7-7.

The test lamp should not light. The field coils are grounded if the lamp lights.

Solenoid Tests

The solenoid and its circuit can be tested for current draw and continuity.

Delco-Remy solenoid current draw test
The solenoid electrical circuit is shown in figure 7-8. To check the hold-in winding, disconnect all solenoid leads and connect a voltmeter, an ammeter, a switch, and a carbon pile to the solenoid as shown in figure 7-9. Adjust the carbon pile to reduce battery voltage to 9 volts ±0.1 volt. Compare the ammeter reading to manufacturer's specifications.

To check the pull-in winding, connect a jumper wire between the solenoid switch (S) terminal and the solenoid motor (M) terminal. The current draw will decrease as the temperature of the pull-in winding increases. Maintain battery voltage at 9 volts ±0.1 volt and read the ammeter. To prevent damage to the pull-in winding from overheating, do not keep it energized for more than 15 seconds. Compare the ammeter reading to specifications.

If the ammeter reading is higher than specified on either winding, that winding is shorted or grounded. A lower reading indicates high resistance. If either winding does not meet specifications, replace the solenoid.

Chrysler solenoid current draw test
To check the hold-in winding, disconnect all solenoid leads and the field coil connector from its terminal, figure 7-10. Connect a 6-volt d.c.

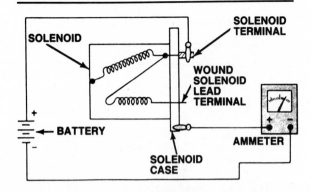

Figure 7-11. Chrysler hold-in coil test. (Chrysler)

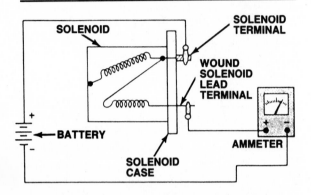

Figure 7-12. Chrysler solenoid pull-in coil test. (Chrysler)

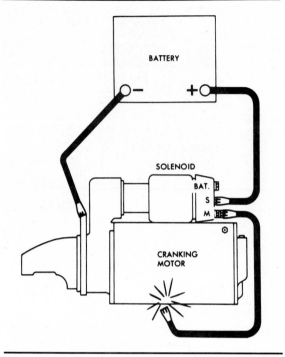

Figure 7-13. Circuit to check pinion clearance. (Chevrolet)

power supply and an ammeter to the solenoid as shown in figure 7-11. Turn the power supply on and watch the ammeter reading. Shut the power supply off and compare the ammeter reading to manufacturer's specifications.

To check the pull-in winding, move the ammeter (−) lead to the wound solenoid lead terminal, figure 7-12. Turn the power supply on a second time and watch the ammeter reading. Shut the power supply off and compare the ammeter reading to manufacturer's specifications.

If either winding does not meet the specifications or the winding appears burnt or otherwise damaged, replace the solenoid.

Solenoid continuity test
To check continuity, disconnect the starter motor-to-solenoid lead at the M terminal, figure 7-8, on Delco-Remy units or the field coil terminal, figure 7-10, on Chrysler units. Connect a 12-volt test lamp between the S and M terminals, figure 7-8, on Delco-Remy units. Connect the test lamp between the solenoid and field coil terminals, figure 7-10, on Chrysler units. The lamp should light, indicating continuity.

Then connect the test lamp between the S terminal (Delco-Remy) or solenoid terminal (Chrysler) and the solenoid case. The lamp should light, indicating continuity. If the lamp does not light in one or both tests, the solenoid has an open circuit and should be replaced.

Delco-Remy Pinion Clearance Test

Test the drive pinion clearance on Delco-Remy starters with the starter motor assembled. Pinion clearance cannot be adjusted on motors with an enclosed shift fork, but it must be correct to avoid a damaged pinion, a stripped flywheel, or a burned-out starter motor.

To test pinion clearance:
1. Disconnect the field coil connector from the solenoid motor terminal. Insulate the connector.
2. Connect a battery from the solenoid switch terminal to the solenoid frame, figure 7-13. Make sure the battery is the same voltage as the solenoid and motor.
3. Momentarily touch a jumper wire from the solenoid motor terminal to the motor frame. The pinion should snap into position and stay there until the battery is disconnected. This test also proves the continuity of the solenoid.
4. Push the pinion back toward the commutator to eliminate slack or end play on the pinion.
5. Measure the distance between the pinion and the pinion stop with a flat feeler gauge,

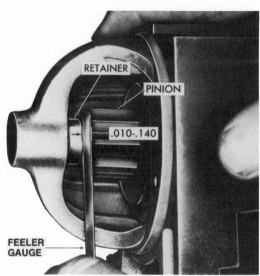

Figure 7-14. Use a feeler gauge to check pinion clearance. (Delco-Remy)

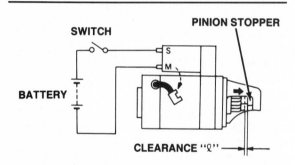

Figure 7-15. Nissan pinion clearance check circuit. (Nissan)

figure 7-14. Clearance should be 0.010" to 0.140" (0.25 mm to 3.55 mm) on standard motors or 0.010" to 0.160" (0.25 mm to 4.05 mm) on permanent-magnet, gear-reduction (PMGR) motors.

6. Disconnect the battery that was connected in step 2.

If the pinion clearance is not within specified limits, check the shift fork, the pivot pin, and the starter drive for improper installation or wear. Replace the shift fork and pin or the drive, if worn.

Nissan Pinion Clearance Test

The drive pinion can be tested and adjusted on some Japanese starters, such as those used by Nissan. Check the manufacturer's specifications to see if pinion clearance is adjustable. The test procedure is the same as that used for Delco-Remy starters but the battery is connected as shown in figure 7-15. Adjustment is made by

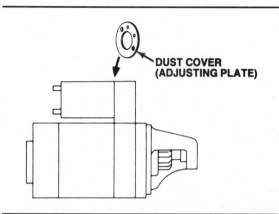

Figure 7-16. If pinion clearance is out of specifications on starters used by Nissan, change the dust cover thickness.

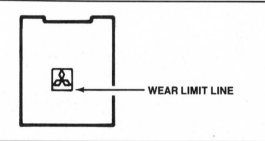

Figure 7-17. Some Japanese starter motors use brushes with a wear limit line to indicate replacement. (Chrysler)

changing the thickness of the dust cover or adjusting plate as shown in figure 7-16.

Brush Service

The brushes are one of the most often replaced items in any electric motor. As a general rule, *all* brushes in a motor should be replaced if *any one* brush has worn to one-half its original length. For a starter motor brush, this is usually ¼ to ⅜ of an inch (6 to 9 mm). The brushes used in some Japanese starter motors have a wear indicator or limit line, figure 7-17. When the brush is worn to this line, it should be replaced.

As a brush wears, spring tension applied to it decreases. This can cause the brush to bounce on the commutator and to arc, which reduces the efficiency of the motor. Brushes should also be replaced if they are oil-soaked, cracked, chipped, or otherwise damaged.

When you install new brushes, match the contour of the brush face with the curve of the commutator, figure 7-18. If the brush angle is reversed, surface contact with the commutator is reduced. This will cause arcing between the commutator segments, premature brush and

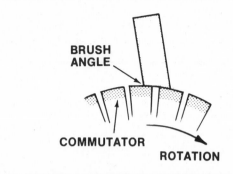

Figure 7-18. The brush angle and contour must match the commutator for proper motor operation.

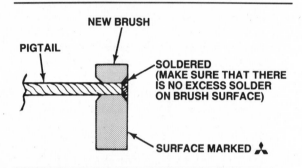

Figure 7-19. After crushing the old brush and cleaning the pigtail, install the new brush and solder it in place. (Chrysler)

commutator wear, and loss of motor efficiency. Always check the brush angle and make sure it is not reversed when reinstalling or replacing brushes.

Brush replacement

Brush replacement requires partial disassembly of a starter motor. Access for checking brush length and condition on older Prestolite and Autolite starters requires only the removal of a metal band around the starter frame. With other units, it is necessary to remove the commutator end plate or cover to gain access for checking brush length and condition. Whenever replacement is required with any unit, the brushes should be removed from their holders. The holder plate can then be removed and the armature taken out of the starter frame to provide access to the insulated brushes.

Permanent-magnet starters differ somewhat. With the Chrysler PMGR starter, the entire brush holder assembly can be removed without removing the armature from the frame. Not so with the Delco-Remy PMGR starter, whose brush holder assembly is secured on the armature shaft by a press-fit commutator end bearing. The entire assembly must be removed from

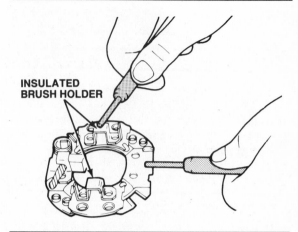

Figure 7-20. Checking the brush plate assembly for grounded brush holders. (Chrysler)

the frame and the bearing pressed off to work on the Delco brush holder assembly.

Ground brushes are generally attached to the starter frame with screws and are easily removed with a screwdriver. With some late-model starters, the ground brushes are an integral part of the brush holder plate and the entire assembly must be replaced to service the brushes.

Insulated brushes are usually found at the end of a field coil lead. To replace this type of brush, it must be cut off as close as possible to the field coil and a new one soldered in place. Replacement brush kits often include small metal clips which are used to attach the new brush to the field coil lead. Rosin-core solder is then applied to the connection with a 100- to 300-watt soldering iron to ensure a permanent joint with good electrical conductivity.

Brush replacement differs with many Japanese starter motors. The old brush is simply crushed with pliers and removed from its pigtail. The end of the pigtail is then cleaned with sandpaper and inserted into a hole in the new brush, figure 7-19. A drop or two of solder is applied in the recessed hole to retain the brush on the pigtail.

Brush holder assembly test

Whenever the brushes are serviced, test the brush holder assembly as well. Use a self-powered test lamp and touch each of the brush holders with one probe while holding the other probe against the holder plate, figure 7-20. The two ground brush holders are grounded 180 degrees apart and should cause the test lamp to light. The insulated brush holders should not cause the test lamp to light. If the lamp lights when checking the insulated brush holders, they are grounded and the entire assembly must be replaced.

When testing the brush holder on the Chrysler PMGR starter, the two ground brushes located side by side are grounded to the brush plate ground. The test lamp should light when connected between a ground brush holder and the plate. The lamp should also light when connected between a field brush holder and the field terminal. If the lamp does not light as specified, replace the brush holder assembly.

STARTER MOTOR OVERHAUL PROCEDURES

The following pages contain photographic procedures for disassembly, overhaul, and reassembly of four common domestic starter motors:

- Delco-Remy solenoid-actuated starter — Used by GM and AMC, it has a solenoid to engage the pinion and close the contact points.
- Motorcraft movable-pole-shoe (positive engagement) starter — Uses a pole shoe in place of a solenoid; used by Ford and AMC.

- Chrysler reduction drive starter — Engaged by a solenoid, it uses a reduction gear along with the starter drive.
- Chrysler permanent-magnet, gear-reduction (PMGR) starter — Engaged by a solenoid, it uses permanent magnets instead of field coils. A planetary gear train transmits power between the motor and the drive pinion. This is a Bosch design used by Chrysler since 1985. Delco-Remy and Bosch PMGR starters are similar.

Chapter 11 of your *Classroom Manual* contains descriptions and more drawings of these starter motors. You may find it helpful to refer to the *Classroom Manual* when overhauling a starter motor. Before starting any overhaul, be sure you read and understand the test procedures in the preceding section of this chapter. Make the tests at convenient points during the overhaul sequence. Read through the step-by-step procedure for the specific starter motor that you will be overhauling before you start work.

All soldering and unsoldering of starter motor components should be done with a medium-to-high-heat soldering iron (approximately 100 to 300 watts) with a fairly large tip. *Use only rosin-core solder.*

DELCO-REMY SOLENOID-ACTUATED STARTER OVERHAUL PROCEDURE

1. Disconnect field coil connector from solenoid motor terminal.

2. Remove two through-bolts and commutator end frame.

3. Remove field frame from drive housing and solenoid. On many motors, you can remove solenoid by removing two screws and turning to unlatch from field frame.

4. Remove two screws and remove solenoid from drive housing. Spring will pop out as solenoid is removed.

5. Solenoid plunger is attached to shift fork. Tilt shift fork and remove armature and drive assembly from drive housing.

6. Remove snapring securing pivot pin in drive housing. Remove pivot pin, then shift fork and plunger.

7. Remove worn commutator end frame bushing with puller. Install new bushing with wooden block and hammer. Replace drive end bushing in same way.

8. Remove thrust collar from end of shaft. Use deep socket and hammer to drive pinion stop collar toward pinion on shaft to expose snapring.

9. Remove snapring from shaft grove. Then slide starter drive and pinion stop collar off shaft.

DELCO-REMY SOLENOID-ACTUATED STARTER OVERHAUL PROCEDURE

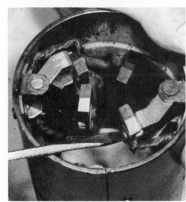

10. Replace brushes if worn to one-half original length. Remove screws holding brushes and leads. Replace leads by disconnecting from ground or field connectors.

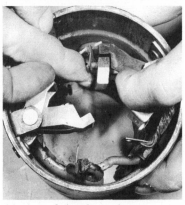

11. Attach leads and new brushes to holders with screws. Broken holders and springs are replaced by pulling pins at base of holders.

12. Apply silicone lubricant to drive end of shaft. Slide starter drive and collar onto shaft with cupped side of collar toward end of shaft.

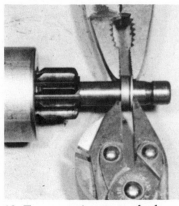

13. Tap snapring onto shaft and slide into groove. Place thrust collar on shaft with flange toward end. Use two pliers to squeeze collars together over snapring.

14. Install shift fork and plunger in drive end housing. Insert pivot pin and secure with snapring, if used. Some pivot pins are tapped in.

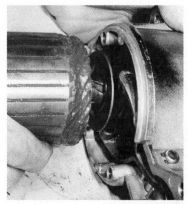

15. Install armature assembly into drive housing. Engage shift fork with collar on drive.

16. Place solenoid spring on plunger and install solenoid on drive housing. Secure with two screws.

17. Install field frame over armature. Hold all four brushes away from commutator. Work slowly; do not force. Do not bend brush holders or nick brushes.

18. Place thrust washer on end of shaft. Install end frame. Secure with through-bolts. Attach motor connector to solenoid motor terminal.

MOTORCRAFT MOVABLE POLE SHOE STARTER OVERHAUL PROCEDURE

1. Ford calls it the "Positive Engagement" starter. Remove brush cover band and pole shoe cover.

2. Hold each brush spring away from brush with hook. Pull each brush from its holder.

3. Remove two through-bolts and commutator end frame. Remove worn end frame bushing with puller. Drive in new bushing.

4. Separate drive end housing from field frame and armature. Plunger return spring will pop out of housing. Don't lose it.

5. Remove pivot pin from field frame and pole shoe plunger. Then remove pole shoe plunger and shift fork assembly.

6. Separate armature from field frame. Test armature and field coils for opens and shorts before reassembly.

7. Remove thrust washer and stopring retainer from end of shaft.

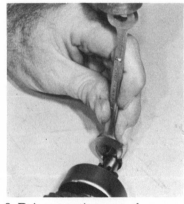

8. Drive stopring out of groove in shaft, as shown. Discard ring; it may break when removed. Then slide starter drive off shaft.

9. Remove ground brush retaining screws. Remove brushes. Replace brushes if worn to one-half original length.

MOTORCRAFT MOVABLE POLE SHOE STARTER OVERHAUL PROCEDURE

10. To remove insulated brushes, unsolder leads from field coils or cut leads as close to field coil connections as possible.

11. Lubricate shaft with Lubriplate and install starter drive on armature. Install new stopring into groove.

12. Install stopring retainer and thrust washer on end of shaft. Install armature and drive assembly into field frame.

13. Install plunger and shift fork on starter frame. Install pivot pin. Be sure shift fork engages starter drive properly.

14. Place plunger return spring on plunger as shown.

15. Fill drive housing bearing ¼ full of grease. Assemble drive housing to field frame. Plunger spring seats in hole at top of drive housing.

16. Place fiber thrust washer on end of shaft, if used. (No washer is used with molded commutator.) Install commutator end frame and two through-bolts.

17. Pull springs away from brush holders and insert brushes in holders. Place springs on brushes. Be sure insulated leads do not touch frame.

18. Install pole shoe cover, gasket, and brush cover band. Secure with screw.

CHRYSLER REDUCTION GEAR STARTER OVERHAUL PROCEDURE

1. Remove two through-bolts and front end frame. Remove armature; note thrust washers on both ends of shaft.

2. Remove worn front end frame bushing with puller. Install new bushing with driver or with wooden block and hammer.

3. Pull field frame far enough from drive end housing to expose field terminal screw. Remove screw and field frame.

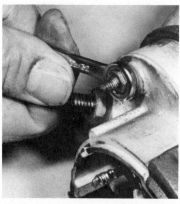

4. Remove nut, washer, and insulating washer from solenoid terminal. Then unsolder solenoid pull-in coil lead from brush terminal.

5. Unwind solenoid pull-in coil lead from brush terminal. Remove brush holder from housing. Some brush holders have more screws to remove.

6. Remove solenoid contact and plunger shaft from solenoid. Tanged washer that fits over shaft hole below solenoid has already been removed.

7. Remove solenoid winding and return spring from drive end housing. Plunger core stays in end housing with shift fork.

8. Remove battery terminal nut from brush holder. Remove brush holder.

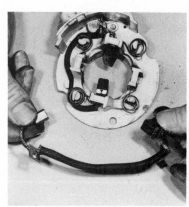

9. Inspect brushes for wear and damaged leads. Replace damaged brushes. Replace all brushes if any are worn to one-half original length.

CHRYSLER REDUCTION GEAR STARTER OVERHAUL PROCEDURE

10. Pry off dust cover. Then use punch or screwdriver to remove snapring holding driven gear to pinion shaft. *Caution*: snapring is under tension and will pop off.

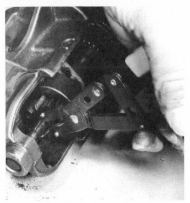

11. Remove C-clip or snapring between pinion and end of drive housing.

12. Tap pinion gear toward driven gear with punch and hammer.

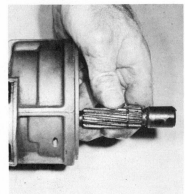

13. Remove shaft from gear end of housing. Remove pinion, clutch, retainer, washers, and two shift fork actuators from other end. Remove gear and friction washer.

14. Pull shift lever toward rear end of housing and remove solenoid plunger core.

15. Remove pivot pin and shift fork. Use pliers or punch and hammer to remove pin.

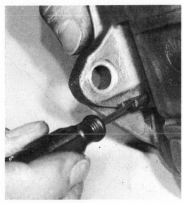

16. Begin reassembly by installing shift fork and pivot pin as removed in step 15. Bend one side of pin after installation.

17. Place driven gear and friction washer in position. Install shaft through front of housing. Install pinion assembly from other end. Engage shift fork with actuators.

18. Friction washer must be on shoulder of shaft splines before driven gear is secured to shaft. Install driven gear snapring.

CHRYSLER REDUCTION GEAR STARTER OVERHAUL PROCEDURE

19. Install pinion shaft C-clip or snapring. Tap pinion shaft into drive end bushing with soft mallet.

20. Install return spring in solenoid plunger core.

21. Assemble battery terminal to brush holder. Install contact plunger in solenoid. Place solenoid on brush holder. Some models are secured with screws.

22. Secure solenoid terminal with insulating washer and nut. Wrap pull-in coil lead around ground brush terminal and solder.

23. Assemble solenoid and brush holder with drive end housing. Some models are attached with screws.

24. Install brushes in slots. Place brush springs away from brushes with screwdriver.

25. Install thrust washer with tangs against brushes. Place springs on brushes. Washer holds brushes from commutator when armature is installed.

26. Test field coils before assembling field frame. Align field frame with end housing and connect field lead to brush terminal with screw.

27. Test armature before assembling. Be sure thrust washers are on both ends of shaft and install armature. Finally, install end frame and two through-bolts.

CHRYSLER PERMANENT-MAGNET, GEAR-REDUCTION (PMGR) STARTER OVERHAUL PROCEDURE

1. Remove the field terminal nut and separate the terminal from the solenoid stud. Remove the field washer.

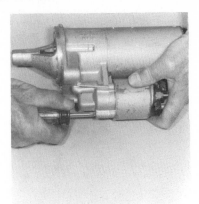

2. Hold the solenoid as shown to counteract the spring pressure, and remove the three mounting screws.

3. Remove the solenoid housing as shown, then work the solenoid off the shift fork and remove it from the starter.

4. Remove the end shield bushing cap, C-washer, and flat washer. Remove bushing seal on the outside of the end shield, if used.

5. Remove the two through bolts and separate the end shield from the starter frame. The arrow shows a bushing seal on the inside of the end shield.

6. Disengage the field terminal insulator from the starter frame and remove the brush plate assembly.

7. Grasp the drive end firmly and carefully separate it from the frame. The permanent magnets will hold the armature in the frame.

8. Each of the six permanent magnets are held in the frame by individual clips. Remove the magnets by sliding them out of the clips.

9. Remove the rubber seal (arrow) from the drive-end housing, then slide the starter drive gear train from the housing.

CHRYSLER PERMANENT-MAGNET, GEAR-REDUCTION (PMGR) STARTER OVERHAUL PROCEDURE

10. Unsnap and remove the metal dust plate from the plastic annulus gear to expose the planetary gears.

11. Use a suitable socket to press the stop collar off the snapring, then remove the snapring and stop collar. Slide the clutch assembly off the output shaft.

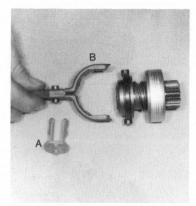

12. The shift lever bushing (A) and shift lever (B) are made of plastic. Separate them from the clutch assembly if replacement is required.

13. To remove the output shaft and planetary gear assembly from the annulus gear, remove the C-clip retainer and washer.

14. To reassemble the drive clutch on the output shaft, use a puller such as the one shown to draw the stop collar up around the snapring.

15. Insert the drive gear train with shift lever and bushing in the drive-end housing, then reinstall the rubber seal.

16. Fit the armature in place, then grasp the frame securely to overcome the magnetic pull and install as shown.

17. Prepare the brush assembly for reinstallation by fitting it over a suitable size socket as shown.

18. Install the brush assembly and remove the socket. Replace the end shield and cap components, then install the solenoid.

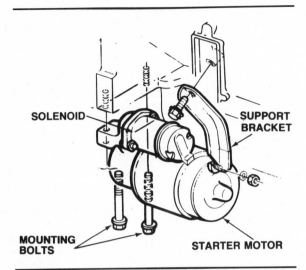

SOLENOID

SUPPORT BRACKET

MOUNTING BOLTS

STARTER MOTOR

Figure 7-21. Install a starter motor by securing the motor and any support brackets to the engine with bolts. Connect all terminal leads to the motor or solenoid. (Chevrolet)

STARTER MOTOR INSTALLATION

To install a starter motor:

1. If they are used, attach the support brackets to the starter motor. Heat shields may be installed before or after the motor, depending upon the motor and engine installation in the car.

2. Install the starter motor and the support brackets with all mounting bolts or nuts, figure 7-21.

3. Check flywheel-to-starter engagement. GM vehicles may use shims to provide correct engagement of the starter pinion gear with the flywheel. These shims are located between the starter drive housing and the engine block. Remove the flywheel cover and check the starter pinion engagement with the flywheel. If the starter motor pinion does not engage the engine flywheel completely, add shims to the upper or outer mounting position. If the starter motor pinion chatters and fails to disengage, add shims to the lower or inner mounting position.

4. Connect all wires to the solenoid or motor terminals. Reinstall plastic protective cover, if used.

5. Connect any parts such as exhaust pipes, tie rods, or wheels that may have been removed to gain access to the starter motor. Lower the car to the ground.

6. Connect the ground cable to the negative battery post.

PART FOUR

Ignition
System and
Electronic
Engine
Control
System
Service

8

Primary Circuit Testing and Service

This chapter provides detailed instructions for on-car testing of the primary circuit of both breaker-point and electronic ignitions. Chapter 9 covers the secondary circuit, and Chapter 10 contains off-car distributor service procedures. Chapter 11 explains testing and adjustment of ignition timing. Chapter 12 provides test and service procedures for the principal electronic engine control systems used by major manufacturers. Figure 8-1 is a troubleshooting table that will help you pinpoint the problem in a particular ignition system.

IGNITION SERVICE SAFETY

To avoid personal injury or damage to the ignition system, always follow these precautions during ignition system tests:

1. Turn the ignition switch off or disconnect the battery ground cable before disconnecting any ignition system wiring, unless the procedure specifically states otherwise. The high-voltage surge that results from making or breaking a connection can damage electronic components.

2. Do not touch any exposed connections while the engine is cranking or running.

3. Do not ground the TACH terminal on Delco-Remy HEI systems. This will destroy the module.

4. Do not short the primary circuit to ground without resistance or the high current will damage wiring and connectors and destroy electronic components.

5. Do not create a secondary voltage arc near the battery or fuel system components. This can cause an explosion.

6. When testing the secondary voltage delivered by the coil, follow the procedure specified by the carmaker. This may be done in one of two ways:

    a. Disconnect a spark plug cable or remove the coil cable at the distributor cap. Hold the disconnected end about ¼ inch (6 mm) from a good engine ground and watch for a spark while cranking the engine, figure 8-2.

    b. Disconnect a spark plug cable and connect it to a spark plug tester (simulator), figure 8-3. Clamp the plug tester to an engine ground and watch for a spark between the shell and the center electrode while cranking the engine.

The procedures given in this chapter are those recommended by the carmakers. Although electronic ignitions require the use of a plug tester to prevent high open-circuit voltage that might damage the coil, this device can be used to check the secondary voltage of any ignition. Plug testers are made by many tool and

CONDITION	CAUSE	CURE
• Engine cranks normally, will not start and run	1. Open primary circuit (breaker-point or solid-state)	1. Check connections, coil, breaker points, pickup coil, module, ignition switch.
	2. Coil grounded	2. Replace coil.
	3. Points not opening	3. Adjust.
	4. Points burned	4. Replace.
	5. Poor timing	5. Adjust timing.
	6. Defective condenser	6. Replace.
	7. Secondary voltage leak	7. Check coil top, distributor cap and rotor, and leads.
	8. Spark plugs fouled	8. Clean and adjust or replace.
	9. Problem in fuel system	
	10. Problem with engine	
• Engine runs, one cylinder misses	1. Defective spark plug	1. Clean and adjust or replace.
	2. Distributor cap or spark plug cable	2. Replace.
	3. Problem with engine	
• Engine runs, different cylinders miss	1. Points dirty, worn, out of adjustment	1. Replace or adjust.
	2. Condenser defective	2. Replace.
	3. Advance units defective	3. Repair or replace.
	4. Defective secondary wiring or insulation	4. Replace as necessary.
	5. Weak coil	5. Replace.
	6. Poor circuit connections	6. Clean and tighten.
	7. Defective spark plugs	7. Clean and adjust or replace.
	8. Problem in fuel system	
	9. Problem with engine	
• Loss of engine power	1. Poor timing	1. Check and adjust.
	2. Defective advance units	2. Repair or replace.
	3. Wrong fuel	3. Use correct fuel.
	4. Wrong engine oil	4. Use correct oil.
• Engine backfires	1. Poor timing	1. Check and adjust.
	2. Ignition crossfire	2. Check secondary insulation and routing of plug wires.
	3. Wrong spark plug heat range	3. Use correct plugs.
	4. Problem with fuel system	
	5. Problem with engine	
• Engine knocks, pings	1. Poor timing	1. Check and adjust.
	2. Defective advance units	2. Repair or replace.
	3. Points out of adjustment	3. Adjust.
	4. Wrong heat range spark plugs	4. Use correct plugs.
	5. Wrong fuel	5. Use correct fuel.
• Contact points burned or oxidized	1. Resistance in condenser circuit	1. Clean and tighten condenser connections; replace if necessary.
	2. High system voltage	2. Check charging system.
	3. Excessive dwell angle	3. Adjust points.
	4. Weak spring tension	4. Adjust or replace.
	5. Oil vapors in distributor from faulty PCV system or overlubricated distributor	5. Check PCV system; remove excess lubricant from distributor.

Figure 8-1. Ignition system troubleshooting chart.

equipment makers, figure 8-4A. You also can make one from an ordinary nonresistor spark plug by cutting off the side electrode and attaching two 10-amp battery clips as shown in figure 8-4B.

PRIMARY CIRCUIT VOLTAGE AND RESISTANCE TESTS

Primary circuit voltage has a direct effect on secondary circuit voltage. A 1-volt loss in the primary circuit can reduce secondary circuit voltage by as much as 10,000 volts (10 kilo-

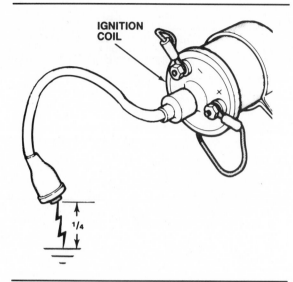

Figure 8-2. To check the secondary spark, hold the coil wire or a spark plug cable about ¼ inch (6 mm) from ground with insulated pliers while cranking the engine.

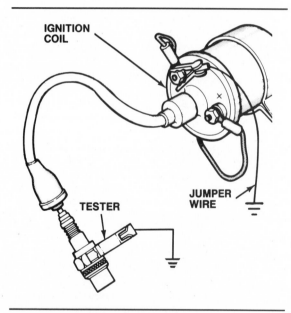

Figure 8-3. Some carmakers recommend the use of a spark plug simulator to check secondary spark.

volts). Voltage losses in the primary circuit can be caused by too much circuit resistance or too little source voltage from the battery or the charging system.

High primary resistance can be caused by:
• Loose, corroded, or damaged wiring connections
• An incorrect or defective ballast resistor
• An incorrect or defective coil, points, or condenser

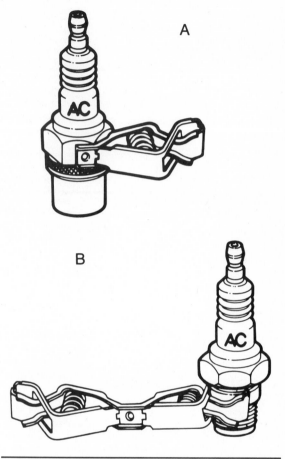

Figure 8-4. Spark plug simulators are manufactured by AC-Delco (A) or can be made by removing the side electrode from a nonresistor plug and attaching two 10-amp battery clips (B).

• A poor ground at the ignition module.
Low source voltage can be caused by:
• Excessive starter motor current draw
• Low charging voltage
• A discharged battery.

Make the following available voltage, voltage-drop, and resistance tests in the order given. Procedures are given for breaker-point ignitions and the most common domestic electronic ignitions. Test principles are similar for all systems, but you should refer to the manufacturer's specific procedures in all cases.

Faults found during these tests could make the vehicle run poorly or fail to start. Make sure that the battery is the correct capacity and that it is fully charged before beginning the tests. Battery testing is explained in Chapter 3 of this *Shop Manual*. Disable the secondary circuit as explained in each test procedure. Make sure the transmission is in neutral or park, the parking brake is set, and the drive wheels are blocked.

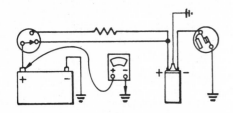

Figure 8-5. Testing battery voltage while cranking.

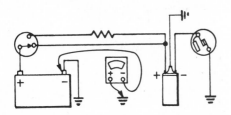

Figure 8-6. Testing voltage drop across the battery ground cable.

Breaker-Point Primary Circuit Voltmeter Tests

Unless otherwise instructed, perform all primary circuit voltmeter tests with the ignition system disabled:
1. Remove the secondary ignition cable from the center tower of the distributor cap.
2. Connect a jumper wire between the cable and a good engine ground.
    To check the battery voltage while cranking:
1. Refer to figure 8-5.
2. Connect the voltmeter (+) lead to the battery (+) terminal, *not* to the cable connector. Connect the voltmeter (−) lead to ground.
3. While cranking the engine, watch the voltmeter reading:
    a. If the reading is 9 volts or more, the battery is in good condition.
    b. If the reading is less than 9 volts, go to step 4.
4. To find the cause of the battery voltage drop:
    a. Check the voltage drop across the battery ground cable as explained in the next chapter.
    b. Test the starter motor for too much current draw as explained in Chapter 6.
    c. Test the charging system for correct charging voltage as explained in Chapter 4.
    To test the voltage drop across the battery ground cable while cranking:
1. Refer to figure 8-6.
2. Connect the voltmeter (+) lead to ground; connect the voltmeter (−) lead to the battery (−) terminal, *not* to the cable connector.

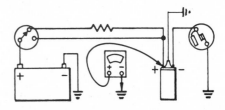

Figure 8-7. Testing available voltage at the coil.

3. While cranking the engine, watch the voltmeter reading:
    a. If the reading is 0.2 volt or less, the battery ground connection and cable are in good condition.
    b. If the reading exceeds 0.2 volt, go to step 4.
4. Clean and tighten the battery ground connection and the battery (−) terminal connection. Repeat the test. Replace the ground cable if necessary.
    To test the available voltage at the coil:
1. Refer to figure 8-7.
2. Connect the voltmeter (+) lead to the coil (+) (battery) terminal; connect the voltmeter (−) lead to ground.
3. Bump the engine with the starter motor until the breaker points are closed.
4. With the ignition switch on, note the voltmeter reading. It should be 5 to 7 volts (one-half battery voltage).
5. Bump the engine with the starter motor until the breaker points are open.
6. With the ignition switch on, note the voltmeter reading. It should be about 12 volts (battery voltage).
7. If either voltmeter reading is not within specifications:
    a. Check the primary ballast resistor circuit connections. Repair or replace any loose or damaged connections.
    b. Test the ballast resistor as explained in this chapter and replace it if necessary.
    c. Test the coil as explained in this chapter and replace it if necessary.
    d. Repeat the test.
    To test the voltage drop across the ignition resistor bypass circuit:
1. Refer to figure 8-8.
2. Connect the voltmeter (+) lead to the battery (+) terminal; connect the voltmeter (−) lead to the coil (+) (battery) terminal.
3. While cranking the engine, watch the voltmeter reading:
    a. If the reading is less than 0.5 volt, the bypass circuit is in good condition.
    b. If the reading is more than 0.5 volt, go to step 4.

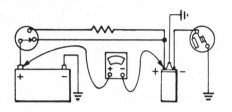

Figure 8-8. Testing voltage drop across the ignition resistor bypass circuit.

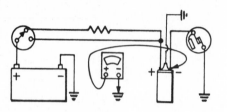

Figure 8-9. Testing voltage drop across the breaker points.

4. To find the area of too much resistance:
a. Check the resistor bypass circuit connections. Repair or replace any loose or damaged connections.
b. Repeat the test.
To measure the voltage drop across the breaker points:
1. Refer to figure 8-9.
2. Connect the voltmeter (+) lead to the coil (−) (distributor) terminal; connect the voltmeter (−) lead to ground.
3. Bump the engine with the starter motor until the breaker points are closed.
4. With the ignition switch on, watch the voltmeter reading:
a. If the reading is less than 0.2 volt, the breaker points are in good condition.
b. If the reading is more than 0.2 volt, go to step 5.
5. Inspect the breaker points for:
a. Loose wiring connections
b. Poor ground connection
c. Poor alignment
d. Burned, pitted, or oxidized contacts
e. Excessive wear.
6. Adjust or replace the breaker points if necessary and repeat the test.
To test the voltage drop across the ballast resistor circuit with the engine running:
1. Refer to figure 8-10.
2. Reconnect the grounded secondary ignition cable to the center tower of the distributor cap.
3. Connect the voltmeter (+) lead to the battery (+) terminal; connect the voltmeter (−) lead to the coil (+) (battery) terminal.

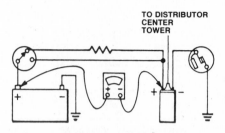

Figure 8-10. Testing voltage drop across the ignition resistor with the engine running.

4. Run the engine at 1,500 rpm and watch the voltmeter reading.
5. Compare the voltmeter reading to the manufacturer's specifications (usually 1.5 to 3.5 volts);
a. If the reading is within specifications, the ballast resistor circuit is in good condition.
b. If the reading is not within specifications, go to step 6.
6. Check the resistor circuit:
a. Repair or replace any loose or damaged connections.
b. Test the ballast resistor as explained in this chapter. Replace it, if necessary.
c. Test the coil as explained in this chapter. Replace it, if necessary.
d. Repeat the test.

Chrysler Original Electronic Ignition Primary Voltage and Resistance Tests

The following procedure can be used to test all Chrysler magnetic pulse electronic ignitions used on all 1972 and later 6- and 8-cylinder engines. If the ignition is incorporated in an electronic lean-burn (ELB) or electronic spark control (ESC) system, refer to the Chrysler test procedures for the particular year and model. The accompanying illustrations show the dual-resistor system. If a single-resistor system is being tested, simply disregard the 5.0-ohm auxiliary resistor circuit.
Chrysler 4-cylinder engines use either a Hall-effect distributor (domestic) or a magnetic pulse distributor (Mitsubishi). Test procedures for both systems are given below.
Before you begin the troubleshooting tests, check the following items:
● Battery cranking voltage (9.5 volts or more)
● Primary wiring and connectors (no damage or loose connections)
● Check for spark at one or more spark plugs with the engine cranking. Use either procedure described earlier.
● Check the air gap between the reluctor and

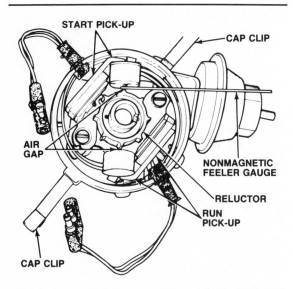

Figure 8-11. Adjusting the reluctor-pickup coil air gap in a Chrysler dual-pickup distributor.

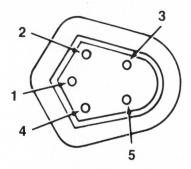

3 NOT USED ON LATER SYSTEMS
WITH SINGLE BALLAST RESISTOR

Figure 8-12. Cavity identification for Chrysler solid-state ignition module connector.

the pickup coil. Adjust the air gap if necessary before testing the primary circuit.

Air gap check and adjustment

The air gap between the reluctor and the pole piece of a Chrysler solid-state distributor is adjustable, but has no effect on the dwell period, which is determined by the control module. The air gap must be set to a specific clearance when a new pickup unit is installed.

During use, the air gap should not change. However, you should check it and adjust it if necessary before making the volt-ohmmeter troubleshooting tests that follow. A nonmetallic or nonmagnetic (brass) feeler gauge must be used, since a steel gauge will be attracted to the permanent magnet, making accurate gap setting impossible.

Chrysler air gap specifications differ according to model and year. Check the specifications. If the distributor uses two pickup coils, check and adjust the air gap for each coil.

1. Bump the engine with the starter motor to align a tooth on the reluctor with the pickup coil.
2. Insert a nonmagnetic feeler gauge of the specified thickness between the pickup coil pole piece and a reluctor tooth, figure 8-11.
3. If the clearance is incorrect, loosen the pickup coil adjustment lockscrew.
4. With the feeler gauge in position, fit a screwdriver blade into the adjustment slot and move the pickup plate until the feeler gauge just contacts the reluctor tooth and pickup coil.
5. Tighten the lockscrew. No force should be required to remove the feeler gauge. The ad-

justment can be checked by using the specified "No-Go" feeler gauge. Do not force the "No-Go" feeler gauge into the air gap.
6. Apply vacuum to the distributor vacuum advance unit and move the pickup plate through its full range of travel. Watch the pickup coil while applying vacuum to make sure it does not hit the reluctor. Recheck the air gap. If the pickup plate is loose, the distributor should be overhauled.

6- and 8-cylinder electronic ignition circuit tests

CAUTION: The ignition switch must be off whenever the connector is removed from, or connected to, the control module.

1. With the ignition switch off, remove the wiring harness connector from the ignition control module.
2. Turn the ignition switch on; connect the voltmeter ($-$) lead to ground.
3. Connect the voltmeter ($+$) lead to the number 1 connector cavity, figure 8-12. With the ignition switch on and all accessories off, the voltmeter reading should be within 1 volt of battery voltage.
   a. If the reading is within specifications, go to step 4.
   b. If the reading is not within specifications, trace and repair the circuit shown in 8-13.
4. Connect the voltmeter ($+$) lead to the number 2 connector cavity, figure 8-12. With the ignition switch on and all accessories off, the voltmeter reading should be within 1 volt of battery voltage.
   a. If the reading is within specifications, go to step 5.
   b. If the reading is not within specifications, trace and repair the circuit shown in figure 8-14.

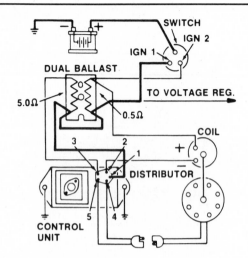

Figure 8-13. Circuit for Chrysler connector cavity number 1.

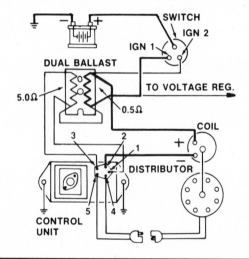

Figure 8-14. Circuit for Chrysler connector cavity number 2.

5. NOTE: Omit this step for systems with 4-pin control modules. Connect the voltmeter (+) lead to the number 3 connector cavity. With the ignition switch on and all accessories off, the voltmeter reading should be within 1 volt of battery voltage.

    a. If the reading is within specifications, go to step 6.

    b. If the reading is not within specifications, trace and repair the circuit shown in figure 8-15.

6. Turn the ignition switch off.

7. Connect the ohmmeter leads to the number 4 and number 5 connector cavities, figure 8-12.

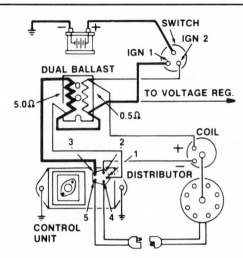

Figure 8-15. Circuit for Chrysler connector cavity number 3.

This measures the pickup coil resistance. Resistance should be 150 to 900 ohms:

    a. If the reading is within specifications, go to step 9.

    b. If the reading is not within specifications, go to step 8.

8. If the pickup coil resistance is out of limits when measured at the connector cavities, disconnect the dual-lead connector at the distributor and check the resistance through the pickup coil leads at the distributor.

    a. If the reading is within specifications, trace and repair the wiring from the control unit to the distributor. Repeat the test at the connector cavities.

    b. If the reading is not within specifications, replace the pickup coil.

9. Connect one ohmmeter lead to ground and touch the other ohmmeter lead alternately to both sides of the pickup coil dual-lead connector at the distributor. The ohmmeter should show infinite resistance at both test points.

    a. If both test points show infinite resistance, go to step 10.

    b. If either test point shows less than infinite resistance, the pickup coil is grounded and must be replaced.

10. Connect one ohmmeter lead to ground; connect the other ohmmeter lead to the control unit connector pin number 5. The ohmmeter should show continuity (zero to 1 ohm) between ground and pin number 5:

    a. If the ohmmeter reading is zero to 1 ohm, go to step 12.

    b. If the ohmmeter reading is more than 1 ohm, go to step 11.

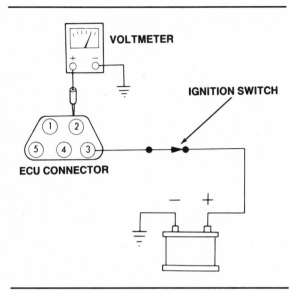

Figure 8-16. Circuit for Chrysler Hall-effect ECU connector cavity number 2.

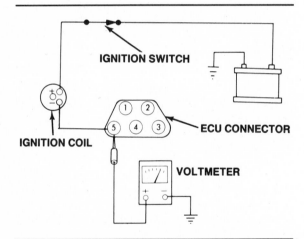

Figure 8-17. Circuit for Chrysler Hall-effect ECU connector cavity number 5.

11. Tighten the control module mounting bolts and repeat step 10:
   a. If the reading is still more than 1 ohm, replace the control module.
   b. If the reading now shows continuity, test the ballast resistor and the coil as described later in this chapter.

4-cylinder Hall-effect electronic ignition circuit tests

CAUTION: The ignition switch must be off whenever the connector is removed from, or connected to, the control module.

1. With the ignition switch off, remove the wiring harness connector from the electronic control unit (ECU).

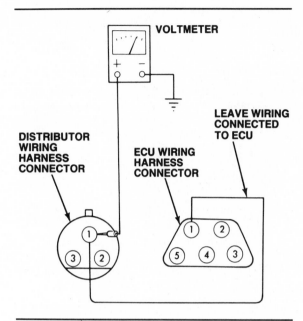

Figure 8-18. Circuit for Chrysler Hall-effect distributor connector cavity number 1.

2. Turn the ignition switch on; connect the voltmeter (−) lead to ground.

3. Connect the voltmeter (+) lead to cavity number 2 of the harness connector, figure 8-16. With the ignition switch on and all accessories off, the voltmeter reading should be within 1 volt of battery voltage.
   a. If the reading is within specifications, go to step 4.
   b. If the reading is not within specifications, trace and repair the circuit shown in figure 8-16.

4. Connect the voltmeter (+) lead to cavity number 5 of the harness connector, figure 8-17. With the ignition switch on and all accessories off, the voltmeter reading should be within 1 volt of battery voltage.
   a. If the reading is within specifications, go to step 5.
   b. If the reading is not within specifications, trace and repair the circuit shown in figure 8-17.

5. Turn the ignition switch off, reconnect the ECU harness connector, and disconnect the distributor connector. Turn the ignition switch on.

6. Connect the voltmeter (+) lead to cavity number 1 of the distributor wiring harness, figure 8-18. With the ignition switch on and all accessories off, the voltmeter reading should be within 1 volt of battery voltage.
   a. If the reading is within specifications, go to step 7.
   b. If the reading is not within specifications, check the wiring harness for continuity be-

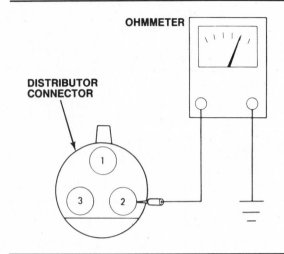

Figure 8-19. Circuit for Chrysler Hall-effect distributor connector cavity number 2.

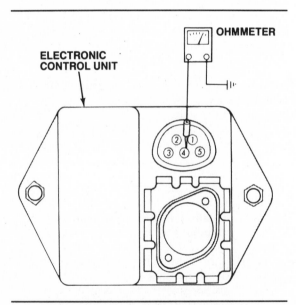

Figure 8-20. Chrysler Hall-effect ECU continuity check.

tween the number 1 cavities of the ECU and the distributor harness connectors. If the wire has continuity, replace the ECU.

7. Turn off the ignition switch. Connect an ohmmeter between cavity number 2 of the distributor harness connector and ground, figure 8-19. There should be continuity.

8. If continuity is not shown in step 7, check for continuity between the ECU number 4 pin and ground with the ohmmeter, figure 8-20.

   a. If there is continuity, check for an open circuit in the wire harness between the ECU number 4 pin and the connector number 2 pin.

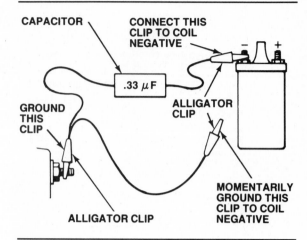

Figure 8-21. Special jumper used to ground the coil negative terminal.

   b. If there is no continuity, remove the ECU and clean its mounting surfaces. Reinstall the ECU and recheck for continuity. If there is still no continuity, replace the ECU.

4-cylinder Mitsubishi electronic ignition circuit tests

1. Remove the coil wire from the distributor cap and hold its end $\frac{3}{16}$ to $\frac{3}{8}$ inch (5 to 10 mm) from a good engine ground.

2. Crank the engine and check for spark.

   a. If spark is constant and strong, go to step 3.

   b. If spark is weak or inconsistent, or there is no spark, go to step 5.

3. Crank the engine and slowly move the coil wire away from ground while watching for arcing at the coil tower.

   a. If arcing occurs, replace the coil.

   b. If there is no arcing, go to step 4.

4. Inspect the secondary spark delivery components to ensure that voltage is reaching the spark plugs.

   a. Repair or replace damaged parts as needed.

   b. If no defects are found, the ignition system is working normally and is not the source of the problem.

5. Turn the ignition switch on and measure the voltage at the coil (−) terminal.

   a. If battery voltage is present, go to step 6.

   b. If there is no voltage, check for an open in the coil or the wiring.

   c. If the voltage is 3 volts less than battery voltage, go to step 8.

6. With the ignition switch on, hold the coil wire $\frac{3}{16}$ to $\frac{3}{8}$ inch (5 to 10 mm) from a good engine ground and use a special jumper wire, figure 8-21, to momentarily ground the coil (−)

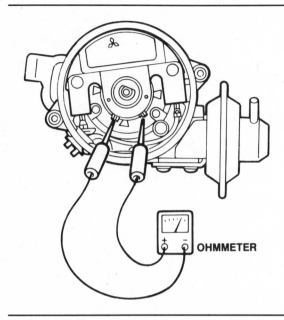

Figure 8-22. Pickup coil resistance check.

terminal. Watch for a spark at the coil wire.
    a. If a spark occurs, go to step 7.
    b. If no spark occurs, go to step 8.
7. Check the voltage at the coil (+) terminal with the ignition switch on.
    a. If battery voltage is present, replace the coil.
    b. If less than battery voltage is indicated, check the wiring and connections for high resistance or opens.
8. Disassemble the distributor as required and use an ohmmeter to check the resistance of the magnetic pickup coil, figure 8-22.
    a. If the resistance is outside of specifications, replace the pickup.
    b. If the resistance is within specifications, replace the ignitor.

Delco-Remy High-Energy Ignition (HEI) Primary Voltage and Resistance Tests

The following tests are for use with basic HEI systems equipped with magnetic pulse generators. Problems in the HEI system can be isolated by performing a coil test, a pickup coil test, and a module test.

Before making any circuit checks, make sure that all primary circuit connectors and secondary cables are securely installed. Be sure that the four distributor cap latches are tight and that the coil and coil cover screws (if they are used) are tight.

To confirm that the problem is in the ignition system, do a spark test:
1. Connect the voltmeter (+) lead to the ignition switch connector on the distributor cap; connect the voltmeter (−) lead to ground.
2. Turn the ignition switch on and watch the voltmeter:
    a. If the reading is approximately battery voltage, go to step 3.
    b. If the reading is zero, trace and repair the circuit between the battery and the distributor, then repeat the test.
3. Disconnect one spark plug cable and connect it to a spark tester, figure 8-3. Attach the tester grounding clip to the engine and crank the engine while watching for a spark between the tester shell and the center electrode:
    a. If sparking occurs, the ignition system is not at fault.
    b. If no sparking occurs, test the ignition coil and the pickup coil as explained in the following procedure.

After performing these preliminary steps, test the HEI system as follows:
1. Connect the voltmeter (+) lead to the BAT terminal on the distributor cap; connect the voltmeter (−) lead to ground.
2. Crank the engine and watch the voltmeter:
    a. If the reading is above 7 volts, go to step 3.
    b. If the reading is zero volts, there is an open in the primary circuit.
    c. If the reading is above zero volts but less than 7 volts, either the battery requires recharging, or there is high resistance in the circuit between the battery and the distributor. Charge the battery as required and retest. If the reading does not change, locate and correct the cause of high resistance in the circuit.
3. Move the voltmeter (+) lead to the TACH terminal on the distributor cap. Turn the ignition switch on (*do not start the engine*) and watch the voltmeter:
    a. If the reading is within 0.5 volt of battery voltage obtained in step 2, go to step 5.
    b. If voltage is 1 volt or less, trace and repair the primary circuit as required, then test the coil.
    c. If voltage is more than 1 volt but less than battery voltage, test the ignition module.
4. If the distributor uses an integral coil, remove the cap and coil by rotating the four cap latches 90 degrees with a suitable tool.
5. To test the resistance of an integral HEI coil:
    a. Make the ohmmeter connections shown in figure 8-23.

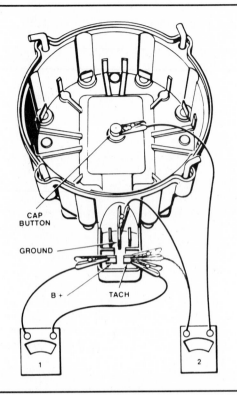

Figure 8-23. HEI integral coil test points.

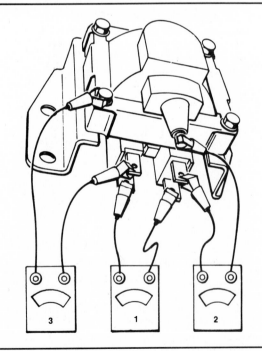

Figure 8-24. HEI remotely mounted coil test points.

b. Test point 1 measures primary resistance. The reading should be zero to 1 ohm (continuity). If not, replace the coil.

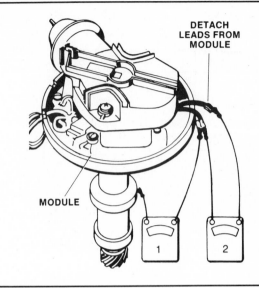

Figure 8-25. HEI pickup coil test points.

c. Test point 2 measures secondary resistance. On coils manufactured before May 1975, measure between the cap button and the TACH terminal. On coils made after May 1975, measure between the cap button and the GROUND terminal. If you are not certain of the manufacture date, measure at both points. Replace the coil only if both readings show infinite resistance or do not match the secondary resistance specification.

6. To test the resistance of a remotely mounted HEI coil:
   a. Make the ohmmeter connections shown in figure 8-24.
   b. Test point 1 measures primary resistance. The reading should be zero to 1 ohm (continuity). If not, replace the coil.
   c. Test point 2 measures secondary resistance. The reading should be within specifications. If not, replace the coil.
   d. Test point 3 should show infinite resistance. If not, replace the coil.

7. To test the HEI pickup coil (pole piece):
   a. Connect a hand-operated vacuum pump to the vacuum advance unit and check the vacuum advance operation. If the vacuum advance unit is faulty, replace it.
   b. Disconnect the two pickup coil leads from the module inside the distributor.
   c. Connect an ohmmeter to test point 1, figure 8-25, and operate the vacuum advance unit through its full range. If resistance between either pickup coil lead and the distributor housing is not infinite, replace the pickup coil.
   d. Connect the ohmmeter to test point 2, figure 8-25, and operate the vacuum advance

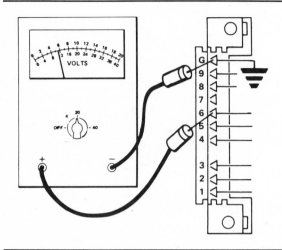

Figure 8-26. GM diagnostic connector test.

unit through its full range. If the pickup coil resistance does not remain within specifications, replace the coil.

8. To test the HEI ignition module, a very accurate, low-scale ammeter is required. An inductive ammeter can only be used if you have a current divider, which allows the meter to accurately measure very small amounts of current. If an inductive ammeter is used, follow the manufacturer's instructions for its use. Proceed as follows:

a. Disconnect the large pink wire (battery positive lead) from the HEI distributor cap.
b. Connect the ammeter (+) lead to the pink wire terminal on the harness side of the connector. Connect the ammeter (−) lead to the distributor terminal. Use jumper wires to make the connections, if necessary.
c. Observe the ammeter under the following conditions. If the meter reading does not meet specifications at any point, replace the module with a known-good module and check the ignition system performance.

Condition	Current Draw
Key on, engine off	0.1 to 0.2 amp
Engine cranking	0.5 to 1.5 amps
Engine at idle	0.5 to 1.5 amps
Engine at 2,000 to 2,500 rpm	1.0 to 2.8 amps

Testing the HEI system at the diagnostic connector

If the engine of a GM car with a diagnostic connector cranks properly but will not start, or if the engine starts but stumbles, a few tests can be made at the connector. These tests will tell you if the HEI system is at fault or if the problem lies elsewhere. If the HEI system is faulty,

or the car does not have a diagnostic connector, use the tests described earlier.

1. Use an oscilloscope to check the available voltage at two separate cylinders, following the manufacturer's recommended procedure:
a. If either is more than 25,000 volts, go to step 2.
b. If both are less than 25,000 volts, go to step 3.
2. Check these items, and repair or replace as required:
a. Defective spark plugs
b. Damaged ignition cables
c. Cracked or dirty distributor cap or rotor.
3. With the engine cranking or idling, connect a voltmeter (+) lead to the diagnostic connector terminal 6; connect the voltmeter (−) lead to terminal G, figure 8-26:
a. If the cranking voltage is more than 7 volts, or the idling voltage is greater than 9.6 volts, the HEI system is faulty.
b. If the cranking voltage is less than 7 volts, or the idling voltage is less than 9.6 volts, proceed with step 4.
4. Move the voltmeter (+) lead to terminal 4:
a. If the cranking voltage is more than 7 volts, or the idling voltage is more than 9.6 volts, go to step 5.
b. If the cranking voltage is less than 7 volts, or the idling voltage is less than 9.6 volts, go to step 6.
5. Inspect the wire between the HEI system and connector terminal 6:
a. If the wire is damaged or grounded, repair it and repeat the test.
b. If the wire is good, the HEI system is at fault.
6. Move the voltmeter (+) lead to terminal 5:
a. If the cranking voltage is more than 7 volts, or the idling voltage is greater than 9.6 volts, go to step 7.
b. If the cranking voltage is less than 7 volts, or the idling voltage is less than 9.6 volts, replace the ignition switch.
7. Check the bulkhead connector for loose or corroded terminals and repair or replace as required.

Ford Solid-State and Dura-Spark Ignition Primary Voltage and Resistance Tests

The following tests are for use with basic Ford solid-state and Dura-Spark systems equipped with magnetic pulse generators. Before testing the primary circuit, make these preliminary checks:
1. Make sure that all connections are clean and

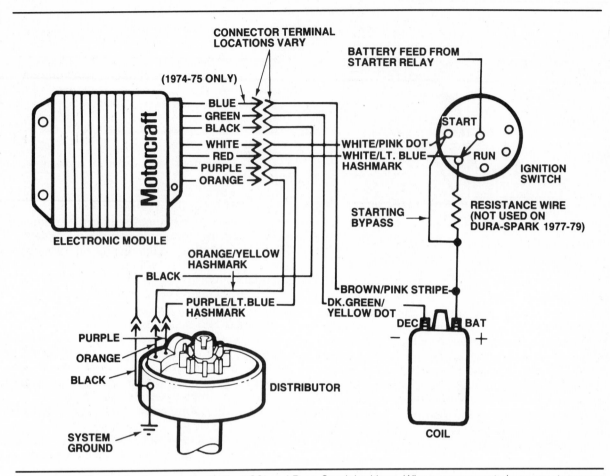

Figure 8-27. The basic circuit used with Ford SSI and Dura-Spark ignitions. Wire arrangements in connectors vary according to model year. (Ford)

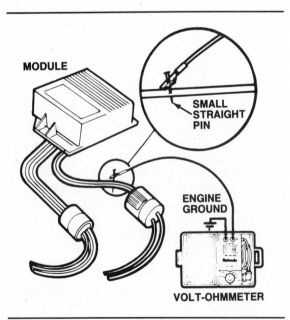

Figure 8-28. A straight pin inserted in the ignition wiring provides a voltmeter connection without damaging the insulation. (Ford)

secure at the coil, control module, and distributor. All connectors in the primary circuit should be lubricated and protected with a conductive lubricant such as Lubriplate D.S. or its equivalent.

2. Be sure that all secondary cables are secure at the coil, the distributor cap, and the spark plugs.

3. Test the coil output by removing the coil secondary cable from the distributor cap, holding it ¼ inch (6 mm) from a good ground with insulated spark plug pliers, and watching for a spark while cranking the engine.

CAUTION: When making the spark intensity test, do not remove the following cables:

- Inline 4-cylinder engines — Nos. 1 and 3
- Inline 6-cylinder engines — Nos. 3 and 5
- V-6 engines — Nos. 1 and 4
- V-8 engines — Nos. 1 and 8.

The magnetic pickup in the distributor is located directly under these plug terminals in the cap. Opening the circuit to these plugs may allow the rotor to crossfire to the pickup coil and damage the assembly.

	Test Voltage Between	Should Be	If Not
Key On	Coil BAT terminal and ground. (Module connected, DEC terminal grounded)	4.9 to 7.9 volts	Low reading - Check primary wiring High reading - Replace resistance wire
	Socket 3 (Red) and ground	Battery voltage ± 0.1 volt	Repair red wire, check connectors
	Socket 5 (Green) and ground	Battery voltage ± 0.1 volt	Check green wire to coil, check coil
Cranking	Socket 1 (White) and ground	8 to 12 volts	Repair white wire, check connectors
	Socket 5 (Green) and ground	8 to 12 volts	Check green wire to coil, check bypass circuit
	Socket 7 (Purple) and Socket 8 (Orange)	0.5 volt ac or any dc voltage	Replace magnetic pickup (stator)
	Test Resistance Between	**Should Be**	**If Not**
Key Off	Socket 7 (Purple) and Socket 8 (Orange)	400 to 800 ohms	Replace magnetic pickup (stator) or repair ground connection
	Socket 6 (Black) and ground	0 ohms	
	Socket 7 and ground	more than 70,000 ohms	
	Socket 8 and ground	more than 70,000 ohms	
	Socket 3 (Red) and coil tower	7,000 to 13,000 ohms	Replace coil
	Socket 5 (Green) and Socket 4 (Blue)	1.0 to 2.0 ohms	
	Socket 5 (Green) and ground	more than 4.0 ohms	Check for short at coil DEC terminal or in wiring to DEC terminal
	Socket 3 (Red) and Socket 4 (Blue)	1.0 to 2.0 ohms	Replace resistance wire

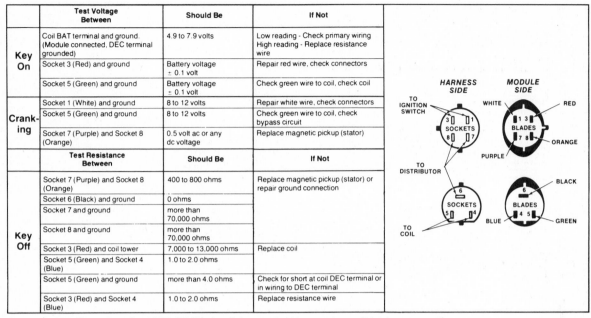

Figure 8-29. Test chart for 1973-74 Ford solid-state ignition systems (black grommet).

5. Inspect the distributor cap, rotor, coil tower, and ignition cables for cracks, moisture, or other damage. Replace as required.

Ford ignition wire color codes
Color coding is the key to tracing the primary circuit. The basic color coding for all Ford systems is:
- White — voltage supply, cranking
- Red — voltage supply, running
- Orange and purple — distributor pickup coil signals
- Green — primary current, coil to module
- Black — ground
- Blue — system protection (1973-75 systems only).

These wires may have different striping or hash marks that vary from year to year, but the main or base color never changes. However, these color codes refer to the wiring on the *vehicle harness side* of the ignition module connectors. In some cases, wire colors change at the module connectors.

Figure 8-27 is a simplified schematic of the 1973 and later Ford SSI and Dura-Spark ignitions. You should only make voltage and resistance tests on the harness side of the connectors, unless the procedure states otherwise. When the Ford test procedure instructs you to make a voltage test with the ignition module connectors connected to the harness, use a small straight pin as shown in figure 8-28 to provide a voltmeter connection. When using this technique, do not allow the pin to ground during testing or a short circuit may damage the electronic components or the wiring.

Ford ignition module connectors and module color codes
To prevent incorrect module use, Ford has switched the position of the pins and sockets in its ignition module connectors, as well as the shape of the connectors, from year to year. The correct connectors and color code of the module grommets are given in the procedure charts discussed below.

Ford primary circuit voltage and resistance tests
If the preliminary checks described earlier did not locate the ignition problem, test the primary circuit as explained in the charts, figures 8-29 through 8-32. All tests at the control module two-, three- and four-wire connectors are made on the *harness side (socket side) of the connectors.* All test at the distributor connector are made on the *distributor side (pin side) of the connector.*

Note that the chart in figure 8-32 applies only to basic Dura-Spark II ignitions with a blue grommet. Systems with limited spark control (those with white and yellow grommets) require a special tester or much more involved test procedures to diagnose. Consult the factory shop manual if you are faced with a no-start problem on one of these systems.

Dura-Spark I stall-shutdown test
Dura-Spark I modules include a special stall-shutdown feature that shuts off the primary current if the engine stalls. A voltmeter can be

	Test Voltage Between	Should Be	If Not
Key On	Coil BAT terminal and ground (Module connected, DEC terminal grounded)	4.9 to 7.9 volts	Low reading - Check primary wiring High reading - Replace resistance wire
	Socket 4 (Red) and ground	Battery voltage ± 0.1 volt	Repair red wire, check connectors
	Socket 1 (Green) and ground	Battery voltage ± 0.1 volt	Check green wire to coil, check coil
Cranking	Socket 5 (White) and ground	8 to 12 volts	Repair white wire, check connectors
	Socket 6 (Blue) and ground (Jumper socket 1 to 8)	more than 6 volts	Check coil connections, check bypass circuit
	Socket 3 (Orange) and Socket 7 (Purple)	0.5 volt ac or any dc voltage	Replace magnetic pickup (stator)
	Test Resistance Between	**Should Be**	**If Not**
Key Off	Socket 3 (Orange) and Socket 7 (Purple)	400 to 800 ohms	Replace magnetic pickup (stator) or repair ground connection
	Socket 8 (Black) and ground	0 ohms	
	Socket 3 and ground	more than 70,000 ohms	
	Socket 7 and ground	more than 70,000 ohms	
	Socket 4 (Red) and coil tower	7,000 to 13,000 ohms	Replace coil
	Socket 1 (Green) and Socket 6 (Blue)	1.0 to 2.0 ohms	
	Socket 1 (Green) and ground	more than 4.0 ohms	Check for short at coil DEC terminal or in wiring to DEC terminal
	Socket 4 (Red) and Socket 6	1.0 to 2.0 ohms	Replace resistance wire

Figure 8-30. Test chart for 1975 Ford solid-state ignition systems (green grommet).

	Test Voltage Between	Should be	If Not
Key On	Socket 4 (Red) and ground	Battery voltage ± 0.1 volt	Repair red wire, check connectors
	Socket 1 (Green) and ground	Battery voltage ± 0.1 volt	Check green wire to coil, check coil
Cranking	Socket 5 (White) and ground	8 to 12 volts	Repair white wire, check connectors
	Coil BAT terminal and ground (Jumper socket 1 to 8)— less than 30 seconds	more than 6 volts	Check coil connections, check bypass circuit
	Socket 3 (Orange) and Socket 7 (Purple)	0.5 volt ac or any dc voltage	Replace magnetic pickup (stator)
	Test Resistance Between	**Should Be**	**If Not**
Key Off	Socket 3 (Orange) and Socket 7 (Purple)	400 to 800 ohms	Replace magnetic pickup (stator) or repair ground connection
	Socket 8 (Black) and ground	0 ohms	
	Socket 3 and ground	more than 70,000 ohms	
	Socket 7 and ground	more than 70,000 ohms	
	Socket 4 (Red) and coil tower	7,350 to 8,250 ohms	Replace coil
	Coil BAT and DEC terminal	.71 to .77 ohms	
	Socket 1 (Green) and ground (2-wire connector connected)	more than 4 ohms	Check for short at coil DEC terminal or in wiring to DEC terminal

Figure 8-31. Test chart for Ford Dura-Spark I ignition systems (red grommet).

used to check the operation of this part of the module circuitry:

1. Make sure that all ignition connectors are properly mated.
2. Connect the voltmeter (+) lead to the coil BAT terminal; connect the voltmeter (−) lead to ground.
3. Turn the ignition switch on.
4. The meter should momentarily deflect and then return to zero if the stall-shutdown feature is operating.
5. If the voltmeter continues to read between 4 and 12 volts, the module may be faulty. Before replacing it, however, perform the troubleshooting tests shown on the Dura-Spark I chart in figure 8-31. Also, repeat the stall-shutdown test with a known-good module to verify the correct circuit operation.

Distributor Hall-Effect Switch Test

A Hall-effect switch, figure 8-33, is used in place of a magnetic pulse generator to provide the primary trigger signals in several late-model distributors used by various carmakers. In some HEI distributors, a Hall-effect switch is used in conjunction with the magnetic pickup coil.

Most Hall-effect switches can be tested by connecting a 12-volt battery across the (+) and (−) source voltage terminals of the switch, and a voltmeter across the (−) and signal voltage

	Test Voltage Between	Should Be	If Not	
Key On	Coil BAT terminal and ground (Module connected DEC terminal grounded)	5 to 8 volts	Low reading - Check primary wiring High reading - Replace resistance wire	
	Socket 4 (Red) and ground	Battery voltage ± 0.1 volt	Repair red wire, check connectors	
	Socket 1 (Green) and ground	Battery voltage ± 0.1 volt	Check green wire to coil, check coil	
Cranking	Socket 5 (White) and ground	8 to 12 volts	Repair white wire, check connectors	
	Socket 3 (Orange) and Socket 7 (Purple)	0.5 volt ac or any dc voltage	Replace magnetic pickup (stator)	
	Test Resistance Between	**Should Be**	**If Not**	
Key Off	Socket 3 (Orange) and Socket 7 (Purple)	<u>1976-80:</u> 400 to 800 ohms <u>1981:</u> 400 to 1000 ohms	Replace magnetic pickup (stator) or repair ground connection	
	Socket 8 (Black) and ground	1 ohm		
	Socket 3 and ground	more than 70,000 ohms		
	Socket 7 and ground	more than 70,000 ohms		
	Socket 4 (Red) and coil tower	7,700 to 9,600 ohms	Replace coil	
	Coil BAT and DEC terminal	1 to 2 ohms		
	Socket 1 (Green) and Socket 4 (Red)	3.0 to 4.0 ohms— 1976 1.7 to 3.7 ohms— 1977-1980	Check for short at coil DEC terminal or in wiring to DEC terminal	
	Socket 4 (Red) and coil BAT terminal	1976: 1-2 ohms 1977-80: 1.05-1.15 ohms 1981: 0.6-1.6 ohms	Replace resistance wire	

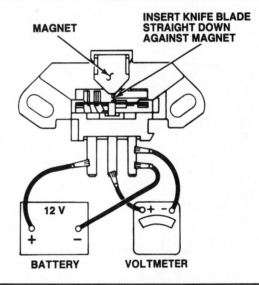

Figure 8-32. Test chart for 1976 Ford solid-state ignition system (blue grommet) and Dura-Spark II systems (blue grommet *only*. Also applies to AMC engines with blue-grommet Dura-Spark II ignitions.

Figure 8-33. A Hall-effect switch used by GM.

terminals, figure 8-34. Insert a steel feeler gauge or knife blade between the Hall-effect switch and magnet. If the switch is good, the volt-meter should read less than 0.5 volt without the feeler gauge or knife blade, and within 0.5 volt of battery voltage with the feeler gauge or knife blade inserted and touching the magnet.

BALLAST RESISTOR TEST AND REPLACEMENT

The ignition ballast resistor can be measured directly with an ohmmeter. The most common problem with the resistor is high, or infinite, resistance caused by an internal open. Whether the resistor is a length of special wire or a ce-

Figure 8-34. To test the output of a Hall-effect switch, apply input voltage and insert a knife or flat feeler gauge against the magnet. (Delco-Remy)

ramic unit, the manufacturer will specify the exact resistance that should be present.

An open circuit will exhibit the following symptoms:
- If the bypass circuit is open, the engine will crank, but will not fire until the key is released and it switches to the run position.
- If the resistor is open, the engine will crank normally, almost start, and then die.

Ballast resistors can be tested with an ohm-meter or by using a voltage-drop test.

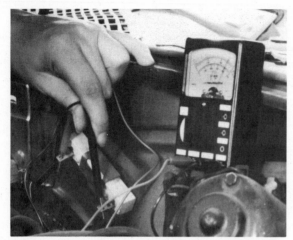

Figure 8-35. Testing the Chrysler unit-type resistor.

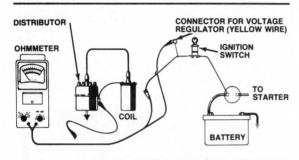

Figure 8-36. Testing a resistance wire with an ohmmeter.

Ballast Resistor Testing

Unit-type resistors

Unit-type resistors (like Chrysler's) contain separate resistors in a ceramic block and can be tested easily with an ohmmeter, figure 8-35. To measure the resistance directly with an ohmmeter:

1. Disconnect the battery ground cable.
2. Disconnect the ignition wiring connectors from the resistor.
3. Connect the ohmmeter leads to the resistor terminals, figure 8-35, and note the meter reading.
4. Compare the reading to the manufacturer's specifications:

   a. If the reading is within specifications, the ballast resistor is good.
   b. If the reading is not within specifications, replace the resistor.

Resistance wires

The ballast resistors used by other carmakers are lengths of resistance wire within the car wiring harness. Use the carmaker's wiring diagrams to help you to locate the ballast resistor.

Resistance wires are often difficult to test with an ohmmeter, especially when one end of

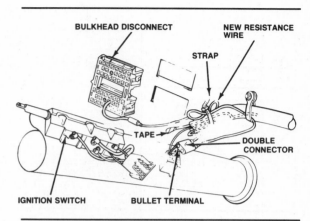

Figure 8-37. Replacing the resistance wire. (Ford)

the wire is attached to the ignition switch in the driver's compartment and the other end of the wire is attached to the ignition coil in the engine compartment. To test this type of ballast resistor, use the voltage-drop method previously described. If both test points are in the engine compartment, you can check the resistance with an ohmmeter as shown in figure 8-36.

Ballast Resistor Replacement

Unit-type resistors are easily replaced. Disconnect the battery ground cable, then disconnect the wires at the resistor and remove the resistor from the firewall. Install the new resistor to the firewall, connect the wires and reconnect the battery ground cable.

To replace a resistance wire, refer to the wiring diagram of the specific model on which you are working. Once you have located the resistance wire, figure 8-37, cut it at both ends and remove it from the harness, then splice in a new length of resistance wire using the procedures given in Chapter 1 of the *Shop Manual*. If the old wire is difficult to remove, you can insulate both cut ends and leave it in the harness.

An alternate method of replacing the original resistance wire is to install a ceramic resistor of the manufacturer's specified value and connect it to bypass the original resistance wire with low-resistance primary wire.

Once you have made the repair, start and run the engine. If the engine will start but not run, check the connections at both ends of the new resistance wire.

COIL TESTS

The resistance, current draw, and polarity of the ignition coil can be tested with an ohmmeter, an ammeter, and a voltmeter. A coil should

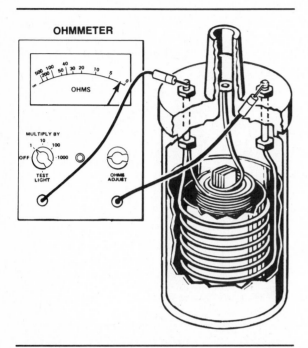

Figure 8-38. Testing the resistance of the coil primary windings.

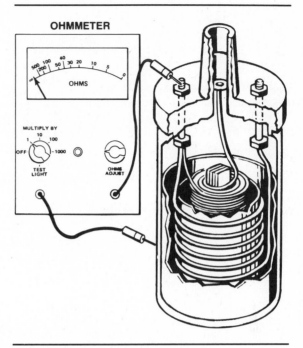

Figure 8-40. Testing the coil for shorted windings.

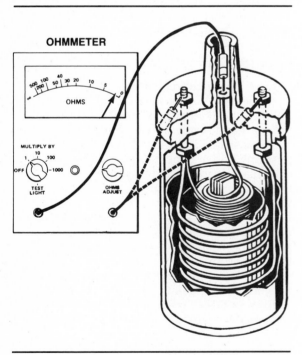

Figure 8-39. Testing the resistance of the coil secondary windings.

be tested at its normal operating temperature because coil resistance changes with temperature. Before testing a coil, make these preliminary checks:

1. Be sure the coil is securely mounted and that all connections are clean and tight.
2. Check for a cracked or burned coil tower.
3. Check for a dented or cracked housing.
4. Check for oil leaks.

Winding Resistance Test

Before you attempt to measure the resistance of the primary and secondary windings, disconnect the battery ground cable or remove the coil from the vehicle. To test the primary winding resistance, connect the ohmmeter across the coil primary terminals, figure 8-38. Set the ohmmeter on its lowest scale and compare the reading to manufacturer's specifications. Replace the coil if the reading is not within specifications.

To test the secondary winding resistance, set the ohmmeter on its highest scale. Connect one ohmmeter test lead to the coil center tower and alternately touch the other test lead to each of the primary terminals, figure 8-39. Compare the lower reading to the manufacturer's specifications; replace the coil if the reading is not within specifications.

To check for shorted windings, set the ohmmeter back on its lowest scale. Connect one test lead to either primary terminal and touch the other test lead to the metal case of the coil, figure 8-40. Any meter reading other than infinite resistance means that the coil windings are shorted to the case and the coil must be replaced.

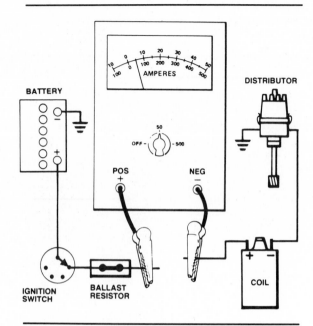

Figure 8-41. Checking the coil current draw.

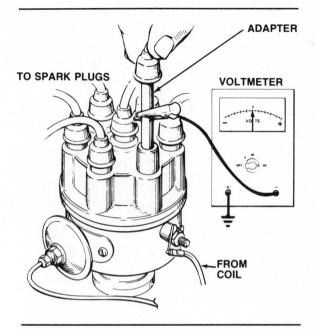

Figure 8-42. Using a positive- and negative-reading voltmeter to check coil polarity.

Current Draw Test

Several manufacturers provide current draw specifications for their ignition coils. These specifications may be given with the engine running, cranking, or with the ignition on and breaker points closed.

To test current draw, disconnect the (+) primary wire from the coil and connect it to an ammeter (+) lead. Connect the ammeter (−) lead to the coil (+) (battery) terminal, figure 8-41. When using an inductive ammeter, fit the inductive pickup over the primary wire to the coil (+) (battery) terminal (leave wire connected). The arrow on the inductive pickup should face in the direction specified by the test equipment manufacturer (generally toward the coil).

Turn the ignition switch on and, depending upon the carmaker's test instructions, either start the engine or close the ignition breaker points. Observe the ammeter reading and compare it to specifications. If there is no reading, the primary circuit is open and the engine will not run.

Higher than specified current draw can be caused by:
• A short circuit in the coil or the ballast resistor
• Use of an incorrect coil or ballast resistor.

Lower than specified current draw results from:
• A discharged battery
• Excessive resistance in the coil primary winding

• Loose or corroded primary connections
• High resistance in the primary wiring or the coil primary winding.

Polarity Test

It doesn't happen frequently, but it is possible to connect the coil backwards, reversing the polarity. If coil polarity is reversed, the engine will start and run, but the required voltage will be increased by 20 to 40 percent. This can cause misfiring under some operating conditions. If coil polarity cannot be determined from the markings at the coil primary terminals, check it with a voltmeter.

The voltmeter used in this test should have a negative as well as a positive scale; that is, the zero voltage position should be in the center of the scale or above the left hand side of the scale. If the voltmeter does not have this feature, it could be damaged during the test.

Later in this chapter, you will learn to test coil polarity with an oscilloscope.

Voltmeter polarity test

To test the coil polarity with a voltmeter:
1. Connect an adapter with an exposed terminal into any spark plug cable, either at the plug or at the distributor cap, figure 8-42.
2. Set the voltmeter on its highest scale and connect the (+) test lead to an engine ground.
3. Start and idle the engine, then momentarily touch the voltmeter (−) lead to the adapter terminal while observing the meter scale.

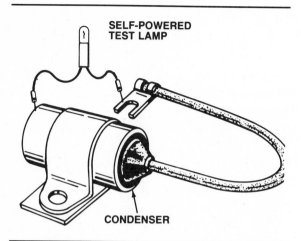

Figure 8-43. Testing the condenser insulation with a self-powered test lamp.

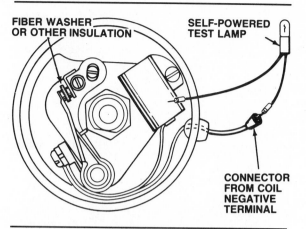

Figure 8-44. If the condenser cannot be removed or disconnected from the distributor, block the points open and use the primary lead from the coil as a test point.

4. If the needle moves toward the positive scale, the coil polarity is correct. If the needle moves toward the negative scale, the coil polarity is reversed.

CONDENSER TESTS

Although many mechanics and technicians routinely replace the condenser in a breaker-point ignition at every tune-up, a condenser can be tested for:
- Series resistance (the condition of the internal connections)
- Capacity
- Insulation condition.

A special condenser tester must be used to test resistance and insulation quality. This device measures actual capacity in microfarads. If such a tester is used, follow the equipment manufacturer's directions.

You can use a self-powered test lamp to make a quick check for an internal short circuit. This checks insulation condition and will tell you if voltage is leaking through the insulation. Connect the self-powered test lamp between the condenser pigtail and the case, figure 8-43. Replace the condenser if the test lamp lights.

If it is not possible to disconnect the condenser lead from the distributor, such as when checking a Uniset point and condenser assembly, then block the breaker points open with a fiber washer, matchbook cover or other insulator, and disconnect the lead from the coil (−) primary terminal to use as a test point, figure 8-44.

This test gives a simple good-or-bad result that may not reveal an intermittent problem. The condenser may have a break in the lead that only fails when it is moist, or the insulation

may leak voltage when it gets hot. Breaker point wear can also be used to determine condenser condition. Points that are badly burned or pitted are an indication that the condenser is shorted or leaking.

BREAKER POINT DWELL TEST AND ADJUSTMENT

Although breaker-point ignitions have not been used in new domestic cars since the mid-1970's, there are still a large number of them in daily service. Measuring and adjusting the dwell angle correctly is an important basic service that affects coil saturation, secondary voltage, and ignition timing.

We will learn how to use an oscilloscope to perform this service later in this chapter, and ignition timing adjustment is covered in Chapter 11. However, breaker point dwell must always be set before adjusting the timing. Dwell angle affects the time at which the points open relative to crankshaft angle. This point opening time is ignition timing.

Installing and Adjusting Breaker Points

Replace breaker points when they become burned or pitted. It is difficult to clean and file used points when they are installed in the distributor, but this can be done in an emergency. Most breaker points have a special hardened contact surface. Once this is filed away, the points will wear out very rapidly. It is usually more practical to simply replace the old point set with a new one.

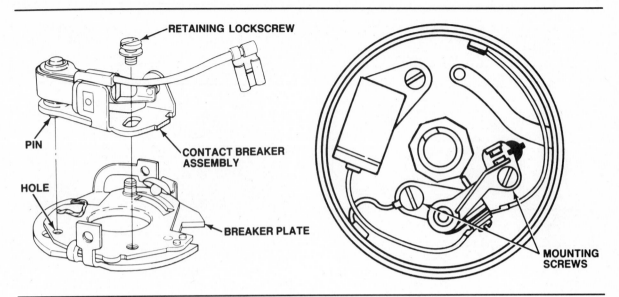

Figure 8-45. Methods of attaching the point assembly to the distributor breaker plate.

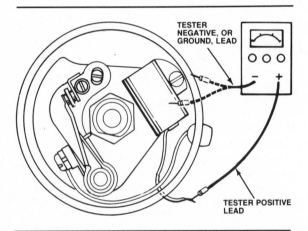

Figure 8-46. Test the spring tension of the breaker point movable arm.

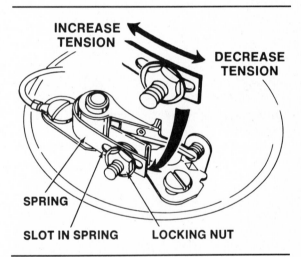

Figure 8-47. Adjusting the movable arm spring tension.

Breaker-point assemblies are usually held to the distributor breaker plate, figure 8-45, by two screws or a single screw and a locating pin. Replacement ignition points for most distributors are preassembled sets. The point alignment and spring tension have been factory-set, but always check them anyway, and align the points if necessary. Dwell adjustment is often the only adjustment required for preassembled points.

Replacement points that come as a 2-piece set need alignment and spring tension adjustment, as well as dwell adjustment. Spring tension can be measured with several types of spring scales made for this purpose, figure 8-46. Check the manufacturer's specification for proper tension. Do not let the scale arm rub against the distributor housing when checking

spring tension or the reading will be inaccurate. Spring tension usually is adjusted by moving a long notch in the end of the spring back and forth on the spring retainer, figure 8-47.

Point alignment can be adjusted with a special tool, figure 8-48. Never bend the movable contact arm. Instead, bend the stationary contact support to correct the alignment.

Do not attempt to set used breaker points with a feeler gauge. The uneven point surface will make the measurement inaccurate, figure 8-49. Used points *must* be set with a tach-dwell meter or an oscilloscope, using the procedure given later in this chapter.

New, properly aligned breaker points can be set with a flat feeler gauge. Check the manu-

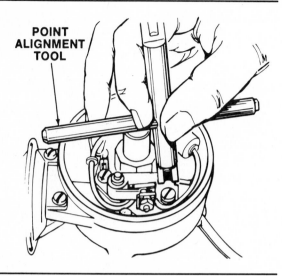

Figure 8-48. Correct point alignment by bending the stationary contact point bracket.

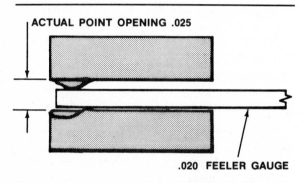

Figure 8-49. Used points should not be set with a feeler gauge. The uneven surface will give an inaccurate reading.

facturer's specification for the correct point gap, then:

1. Remove the distributor cap and rotor.
2. Remove the RFI shield on 1970-73 Delco-Remy V-8 distributors, figure 8-50.
3. Connect a remote starter switch and bump the engine with the starter motor until the breaker point rubbing block is *exactly* on a high point of the cam.
4. Slide the clean, specified feeler gauge between the points, figure 8-51. Adjust the gap by shifting the position of the point assembly. A slight drag should be felt as the gauge is drawn between the points, but the point arm *should not move*.
5. Tighten the holddown screw and recheck the gap. Repeat the adjustment, if necessary.

If an RFI shield is used, make sure there is enough space between the point connector and shield, figure 8-50. If the connector touches

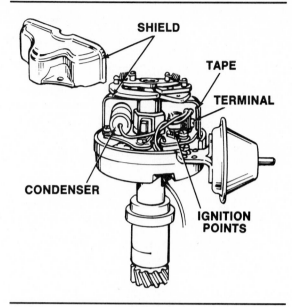

Figure 8-50. Some Delco-Remy distributors have this RFI shield around the points and condenser.

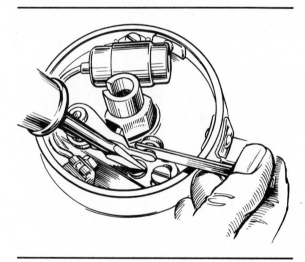

Figure 8-51. Measuring and adjusting the point gap with a flat feeler gauge.

the shield, the primary circuit will be shorted. Be sure the condenser and the primary leads are not caught under the edge of the shield before tightening its two retaining screws. If the Uniset point-condenser assembly is used in place of the separate components, the RFI shield can be discarded.

Checking and Adjusting Dwell

The dwell angle of new points can be checked by measuring the point gap with a feeler gauge, as described earlier. A more accurate way of measuring dwell (especially with used points) is to use an oscilloscope or a tach-dwell tester.

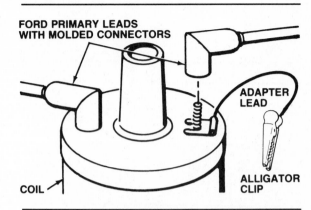

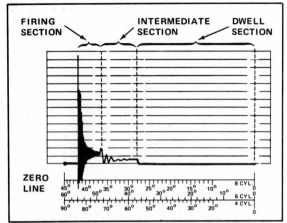

Figure 8-52. This primary superimposed pattern from an 8-cylinder engine shows a dwell angle of 28 degrees.

Figure 8-54. You may need an adapter such as this to hook a tach-dwell meter to a Ford coil on a breaker-point ignition system.

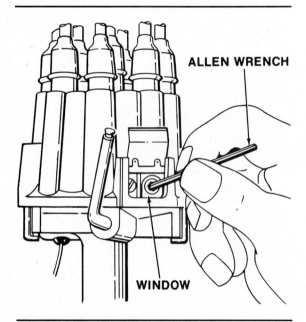

Figure 8-53. This Delco-Remy distributor has points that can be adjusted through a window in the distributor cap while the engine is running.

Oscilloscope test

As we will see in the next section, the dwell portion of an oscilloscope trace can be measured against a degree scale at the bottom of the screen, figure 8-52. On some scopes, the primary superimposed pattern can be seen during cranking, even when the distributor cap and rotor are removed. The point assembly can be shifted until the trace dwell portion matches the manufacturer's specification.

Delco-Remy V-6 and V-8 distributors have a window in the distributor cap, figure 8-53, so that the points can be adjusted while the engine is running. A primary or a secondary trace can be displayed while adjusting the dwell on

these models. If the distributor has an RFI shield, the shield must be removed before servicing and replaced after servicing.

Once dwell is adjusted, the oscilloscope also can be used to check for a dwell variation from cylinder to cylinder, as we will see. The raster pattern is most useful for this test.

Tach-dwell meter test

A tach-dwell meter will measure rpm or dwell angle. The meter usually has only two test leads:
● The positive test lead connects to one of the coil primary terminals (terminal specified by the tester manufacturer). Ford coils will need an adapter, figure 8-54.
● The negative test lead connects to an engine ground. Meters that have other test functions built in may have two additional leads to connect to the battery terminals, or they may operate on a.c.

The tach-dwell meter's electronic circuitry translates the interruptions of primary current flow into rpm or dwell angle measurements. Two different scales are printed on the meter face. The choice of scale is controlled by a knob on the meter. Another knob or switch must be set to the number of cylinders in the engine being tested.

Most tach-dwell meters show a dwell angle reading that is the *average* of all the individual cylinder's dwell angles. This does not alert you to variations in dwell from one cylinder to another, as an oscilloscope can. Only a few console-type dwell meters are able to single out the dwell angle of an individual cylinder. However, no on-car adjustment can correct such variations; the distributor must be removed and overhauled to correct the problem. An average dwell reading is accurate enough for most on-car servicing.

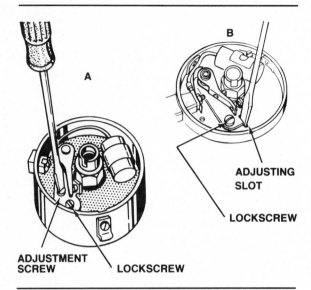

Figure 8-55. The point set in position A is adjusted by turning the eccentric adjustment screw; the point set in position B is adjusted by moving the assembly with a screwdriver set in a slotted hole in the breaker plate.

Dwell Adjustment Procedures

These general procedures can be used with either a scope or a tach-dwell meter. Internal-adjustment (Delco-Remy) distributors require different procedures than external-adjustment distributors.

Internal-adjustment distributors

1. Connect the test leads according to meter instructions.
   a. For an oscilloscope test, select the primary superimposed pattern.
   b. For a tach-dwell meter test, select the dwell position and the correct number of cylinders.
2. Remove the distributor cap and rotor. Remove the RFI shield, if so equipped.
3. Connect a remote starter switch and turn the ignition key on.
4. While observing the scope screen or the meter scale, crank the engine with the remote starter switch.
5. Compare the dwell measurement to the manufacturer's specifications:
   a. If the measurement is within specifications, no adjustment is necessary.
   b. If the measurement is not within specifications, go to step 6.
6. Adjust the point assembly, until the dwell is within specifications:
   a. Some point sets have an adjustment screw, figure 8-55A.
   b. Some point sets have a slotted hole for a screwdriver, figure 8-55B.

7. Tighten the point holddown screw and recheck the dwell measurement. If it does not remain within specifications after the lockscrew is tightened, repeat the adjustment.
8. Disconnect the remote starter switch. Replace the RFI shield (if used), the distributor rotor, and the cap.
9. Start and idle the engine. Compare the dwell measurement to specifications. Repeat the adjustment if necessary.

External-adjustment distributors

1. Connect the test leads according to tester instructions.
   a. For an oscilloscope test, select either the primary or the secondary superimposed pattern.
   b. For a tach-dwell meter test, select the dwell position and the correct number of cylinders.
2. If the distributor has an RFI shield, remove the shield and reassemble the distributor rotor and cap.
3. Start and idle the engine while watching the scope screen or meter scale.
4. Compare the dwell measurement to the manufacturer's specifications:
   a. If the measurement is within specifications, no adjustment is necessary.
   b. If the measurement is not within specifications, go to step 5.
5. While watching the tester, use an Allen wrench to change the point adjustment, figure 8-53:
   a. Turn the screw clockwise to increase the dwell.
   b. Turn the screw counterclockwise to decrease the dwell.
6. When the dwell is within specifications, remove the wrench and close the distributor cap window. The point adjustment is self-locking.
7. Reinstall the RFI shield, if removed in step 2.

Dwell angle variation

Most manufacturers allow a small amount of average dwell variation as engine speed changes. That is, the dwell specification may be 29 degrees to 32 degrees, plus or minus 3 degrees at 2,000 rpm. When you adjust the dwell angle while the engine is cranking, you would set it somewhere between 29 degrees and 32 degrees, say at 30 degrees. Then, use the tachometer setting of the tach-dwell meter to adjust engine speed to 2,000 rpm. Switch to the dwell meter setting and observe the reading. It should be within 3 degrees of your 30 degree dwell setting — from 27 degrees to 33 degrees. If not, the distributor is worn and must be removed for further service.

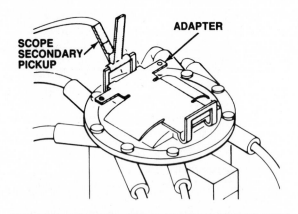

Figure 8-56. Special secondary pickups are required with Delco-Remy HEI coils. (Coats Diagnostic)

Generally, the allowable dwell variation is less for center-pivot breaker plates (Delco-Remy) than it is for side-pivot breaker plates (Chrysler, Motorcraft). In fact, with a side-pivot breaker plate, the dwell will always decrease slightly as the vacuum advance increases. Check the carmaker's specifications for allowable average dwell variation and the engine speed at which it should be tested.

PRIMARY CIRCUIT OSCILLOSCOPE TESTING

We examined the oscilloscope and its basic operation in Chapter 2 of this *Shop Manual*. We know that the ignition system consists of a low-voltage primary circuit and a high-voltage secondary circuit. Voltage varies within these circuits during operation. An oscilloscope displays voltage changes during a period of time, so it is an ideal instrument for testing ignition system operation.

Oscilloscope Connections

All oscilloscope manufacturers provide instructions for the use of their equipment. Although color codes and connector types vary, there are some basic similarities. Most oscilloscopes are installed in multifunction engine analyzer units that also contain voltmeters, ammeters, ohmmeters, tach-dwell meters, vacuum and pressure gauges, timing lights, and exhaust analyzers. The analyzer has various test leads that are connected to different points on the engine, depending upon the test. For comprehensive testing, you may have all leads connected at the same time.

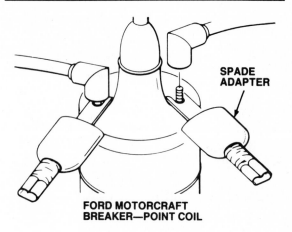

FORD MOTORCRAFT
BREAKER—POINT COIL

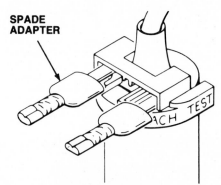

FORD MOTORCRAFT
ELECTRONIC IGNITION COIL

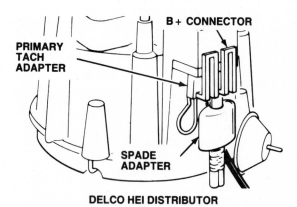

DELCO HEI DISTRIBUTOR

Figure 8-57. Test lead adapters are also required with some primary circuits. (Coats Diagnostic)

Oscilloscopes require that one lead be connected to each of the following:
- Coil (+) or (−) terminal, according to the manufacturer's design
- Ignition cable between the coil and distributor
- Number 1 spark plug cable
- A good engine ground.

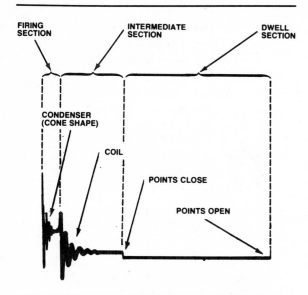

Figure 8-58. The primary superimposed pattern traces all of the cylinders, one upon the other. (Marquette)

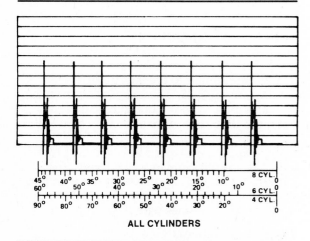

Figure 8-59. The primary parade pattern shows the individual cylinder traces one after the other in firing order. (Marquette)

Late-model scopes all use inductive pickups. Older scopes with series connectors may not be able to test electronic systems. Check the tester manufacturer's recommendations and hookup instructions before beginning any tests.

Adapters are required to make the proper test connections with some ignitions. Delco-Remy HEI systems with the integral cap coil need an inductive adapter for the coil secondary test lead, figure 8-56. Adapters are also required for primary coil connections with Ford and Delco-Remy HEI systems, figure 8-57.

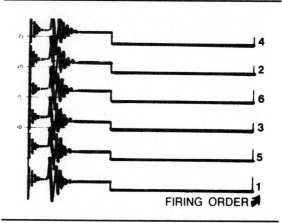

Figure 8-60. The primary raster pattern shows the individual cylinder traces stacked one above the other in firing order. (Marquette)

Oscilloscope Patterns

The voltage traces on the oscilloscope screen are called patterns. Most scopes will display three different patterns for both the primary and the secondary circuits. This makes a total of six patterns available. Each pattern is best used to isolate and identify particular kinds of malfunctions. The three basic patterns are:
1. Superimposed pattern — The voltage traces for all cylinders are superimposed upon each other to form a single pattern, figure 8-58.
2. Parade pattern — The voltage traces for all cylinders are displayed one after the other from left to right in firing order sequence, figure 8-59.
3. Stacked, or raster, pattern — The voltage traces for all cylinders are stacked one above the other in firing order sequence, figure 8-60.

The oscilloscope patterns of electronic ignition systems vary slightly from carmaker to carmaker. Generally, the firing section of the trace can be interpreted in the same way as the firing section from a breaker-point trace, because the same things are happening in both systems. The difference between electronic and breaker-point systems are most noticeable in the intermediate and dwell sections.

Because there is no ignition condenser, there are no condenser oscillations in the intermediate section. The oscillations are all caused by the coil, and can be used to judge coil condition. The beginning of the dwell section in a breaker-point system is the points-close signal. In an electronic system, it is the current-on signal. In both cases, it is a sharp drop to the zero voltage line. The length of the dwell section is not important in most electronic systems, although some systems are designed to lengthen the dwell at higher engine speeds. During the dwell section, some systems have slight voltage

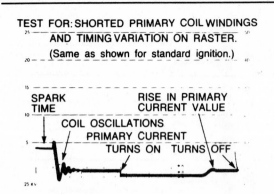

TEST FOR: SHORTED PRIMARY COIL WINDINGS AND TIMING VARIATION ON RASTER.
(Same as shown for standard ignition.)

Figure 8-61. Normal Delco HEI primary superimposed pattern. This also is typical of the AMC-Prestolite and Ford Dura-Spark I/TFI-I systems.

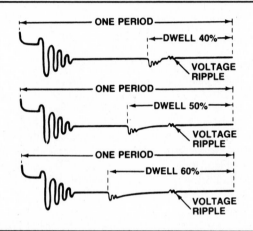

Figure 8-62. The dwell period increases with engine speed in the Delco HEI and Ford Dura-Spark I/TFI-I systems.

ripples or voltage humps. These are normal, as we will see when we look at specific traces. At the end of dwell in a breaker-point system, the beginning of the firing line should be a sharp upward line. In an electronic system, there may be a jagged upward-sloping line leading to the firing spike; again, this is normal in many systems.

Delco-Remy HEI and AMC-Prestolite patterns
Figure 8-61 shows a typical primary super-imposed pattern for the Delco HEI system. Except for the absence of condenser oscillations at the beginning of the trace and the small current hump toward the end of the dwell period, it is quite similar to the pattern for a breaker-point ignition. This pattern is also typical of the AMC-Prestolite ignition and the Ford Dura-Spark I and TFI-I systems.

The primary pattern can be used to check for shorted coil primary windings and, in raster display, for timing variations and distributor wear.

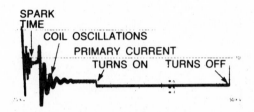

TEST FOR: SHORTED PRIMARY COIL WINDINGS AND TIMING VARIATION ON RASTER.
(Same as shown for standard ignition.)

Figure 8-63. Normal Ford SSI and Dura-Spark II primary superimposed pattern.

The dwell period for the HEI and Dura-Spark I/TFI-I systems changes with engine speed, figure 8-62. At idle and low speed, the dwell period may be only 40 percent of the total pattern. As speed increases, the dwell period will increase to as much as 60 percent of the total pattern.

Motorcraft ignition patterns
The Ford SSI (1973-76) and Dura-Spark II (1977 and later) systems produce a primary pattern that is quite similar to breaker-point ignition patterns, figure 8-63. The coil oscillations may not be as high as with a breaker-point system, but there should be more of them. The dwell period will also be longer.

The Dura-Spark I and TFI-I systems produce a primary pattern similar to the Delco HEI pattern, figure 8-61. A current hump or voltage ripple will appear in the dwell section, and the dwell period increases with engine speed.

Chrysler ignition patterns
A primary superimposed pattern for the basic Chrysler electronic ignition is shown in figure 8-64. Note that there is no intermediate section, as there is in other electronic ignition patterns. The transistor turns on as soon as the spark line stops. There is one set of coil oscillations, caused by the buildup of primary current flow in the coil. The dwell period is a long, straight line with no humps or ripples.

Primary Circuit Abnormalities

Each section of the primary circuit pattern is caused by the operation of a different circuit part. If the part is defective or not properly adjusted, the pattern will be different. You can compare the changed pattern to a normal one and determine why the change occurred. This will tell you which circuit part is defective, and

TEST FOR: TIMING VARIATION ON RASTER
(Same as shown for standard ignition.)

ALL OTHER TESTS: Use secondary patterns

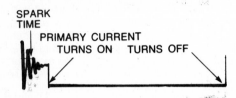

Figure 8-64. Normal Chrysler electronic ignition primary superimposed pattern.

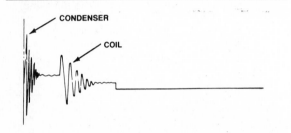

Figure 8-65. In a normal pattern, there should be at least five distinct coil oscillations. (Allen)

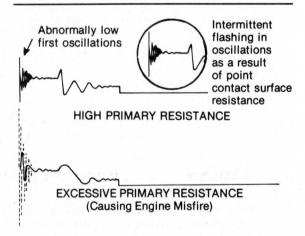

Figure 8-66. Both of these abnormal primary patterns show resistance problems in the primary circuit. (Allen)

how to solve the problem. The following paragraphs describe some common faults that can be pinpointed by examining the primary circuit pattern of breaker point or electronic ignitions.

Firing section

1. The primary superimposed pattern in figure 8-65 shows normal coil and condenser oscillations. The condenser oscillations should start

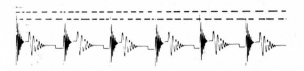

Figure 8-67. When the primary trace is in a parade pattern, the height of the condenser oscillations should not vary greatly from cylinder to cylinder. (Allen)

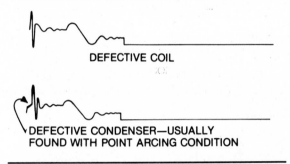

Figure 8-68. A defective coil or a defective condenser can cause a similar pattern. (Allen)

high and taper off as shown. There should be at least 5 distinct coil oscillations, with the first being the largest.

2. In the top pattern of figure 8-66, the condenser oscillations are shortened, or low, and they do not last through the firing section. This can be caused by high condenser resistance or by loose connections in the condenser circuit.

3. In the bottom pattern of figure 8-66, the condenser oscillations (dotted line) are very large. Excessive resistance has made the engine misfire.

4. In figure 8-67, the primary circuit pattern is shown in parade display. The first oscillations in the firing section should all be about the same height:

    a. If the heights all vary at idle to low engine speed, the breaker points may be badly seated, misaligned, or have high resistance.

    b. If the heights all vary at medium to high engine speed, the points may be floating due to low spring tension.

    c. If only one cylinder shows a different height, the distributor cam may be worn or dirty.

Intermediate section

1. There are fewer than 5 distinct coil oscillations in figure 8-68; the coil primary winding may be defective. Figure 8-68 also shows a similar pattern that can be caused by a defective condenser. This is often caused by high resistance in the condenser and is accompanied by point arcing.

HASH SHOWS   POINTS BOUNCE

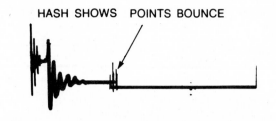

Figure 8-69. The hash marks at the points-close signal indicate bouncing, pitted or misaligned points or a loose breaker plate. (Marquette)

2. In figure 8-69, the points-close signal is not a clean break but has some hash marks above and below the break. This means the points are bouncing, pitted, or misaligned. It can also mean a loose breaker plate.

Dwell section

Figure 8-70 shows the primary circuit in raster display. If the dwell sections of the various cylinders vary by more than 4 to 6 degrees, the distributor is worn. The problem could be a worn cam, worn bushings, or a bent shaft. The dwell period can be measured on the degree scale at the bottom of the scope screen. A similar abnormal pattern can be caused by a loose timing chain.

Primary Circuit Dwell Measurement

Dwell should remain constant on breaker-point and fixed-dwell ignitions. As we saw earlier, however, there is an allowable variation of about 3 degrees with breaker-point systems. This will be shown as a slight offset in the display on a superimposed pattern. If the variation exceeds 3 degrees, switch to a raster pattern and examine individual cylinders for dwell variation at various engine speeds. There should be no more than 3 degrees variation among cylinders at any speed. If there is, check for cam lobe or shaft and bushing wear.

Remember, however, that if the distributor uses a side-pivot breaker plate, dwell will always decrease slightly (3 to 6 degrees) as vacuum advance increases. With center-pivot breaker plates, such variation is probably due to a worn distributor shaft, breaker plate, or vacuum advance unit.

As we have seen, electronic ignition dwell is controlled by the ignition module and cannot be adjusted. However, when a fixed-dwell system shows variations in dwell, it indicates the same kinds of problems described above for breaker-point ignitions.

Variable-dwell electronic ignitions will show an increase in dwell with engine speed, and

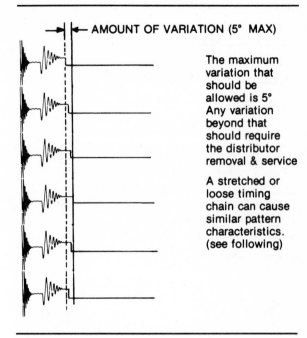

AMOUNT OF VARIATION (5° MAX)

The maximum variation that should be allowed is 5° Any variation beyond that should require the distributor removal & service

A stretched or loose timing chain can cause similar pattern characteristics. (see following)

Figure 8-70. The dwell periods of the individual cylinders should not vary more than 4 to 6 degrees. (Allen)

may even fluctuate somewhat at a uniform speed since dwell is controlled by the module instead of the distributor. If dwell does not increase with increases in engine speed, figure 8-62, the ignition module may be defective.

ELECTRONIC PRIMARY CIRCUIT SERVICE

Electronic primary circuit service is not a periodic requirement, as with breaker-point ignitions. There are three general areas in which problems may occur:
- Primary wiring and connectors — These are the source of high resistance and open or grounded circuits. Problems in this area can be found with simple voltmeter and ohmmeter tests. Many such problems can be solved by cleaning connectors or repairing wiring.
- Distributor signal generator — An open or grounded circuit can be located in the pickup coil or Hall-effect switch by using the procedures described earlier in this chapter. Except for the air gap adjustment on some Chrysler distributors, electronic distributor components are replaced, not adjusted.
- Ignition module — Again, the procedures described earlier will help you determine whether the module is good or defective. Since modules provide the primary circuit ground connection, many problems can be solved by checking and cleaning the ground.

9

Secondary Circuit Testing and Service

SECONDARY CIRCUIT INSPECTION

The secondary circuit of an electronic ignition is essentially the same as that of a breaker-point ignition, but the components don't look alike. Figure 9-1 shows the secondary components:
● The ignition coil secondary windings and coil tower (high-voltage terminal)
● The coil-to-distributor cable and spark plug cables
● The distributor cap and rotor
● The spark plugs.

The secondary circuit has to withstand very high voltage during normal operation. The circuit components must be in good condition, or the system will not work properly. Many secondary circuit problems can be located by a quick visual inspection and a few ohmmeter tests. A more thorough test of the secondary circuit is made during the oscilloscope testing described later in this chapter.

When you are working with the secondary circuit, some precautions are necessary to protect both you and the circuit components:
● Remember that secondary ignition cables carry very high voltage. The voltage can arc across an air gap, so do not bring an exposed cable end near your body while the engine is cranking or running.
● Handle ignition cables carefully. Pulling or kinking cables can cause internal damage that is difficult to detect. The correct way to remove an ignition cable and boot is shown in figure 9-2. Grasp the boot, not the cable. Twist the boot in both directions to relieve any suction seal. Lift the boot straight off the spark plug terminal or distributor cap tower.

Visual Inspection

To inspect the secondary circuit:
1. Check all ignition cables and boots for cracked, burned, or brittle insulation. Make sure all cable connections are secure and well insulated.
2. Inspect the distributor cap for the defects shown in figure 9-3:
    a. A sticking or worn carbon button
    b. Cracks
    c. Carbon tracks from arcing current
    d. Burned or corroded terminals inside the cap
    e. Corrosion inside the cap towers.
3. Inspect the rotor for the defects shown in figure 9-4:
    a. A bent or broken contact strip
    b. A burned or eroded tip
    c. A cracked or broken positioning lug
    d. Carbon tracks or cracks on the body.

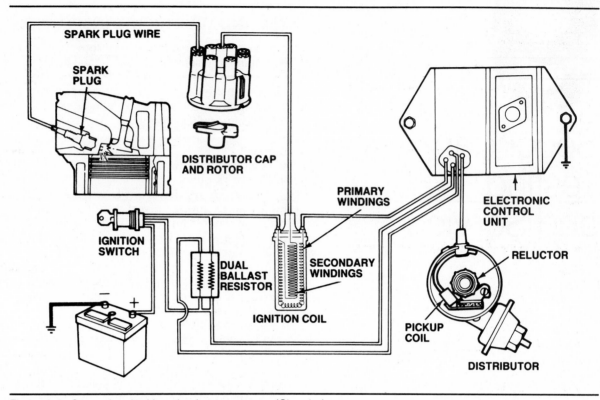

Figure 9-1. Secondary ignition circuit components. (Chrysler)

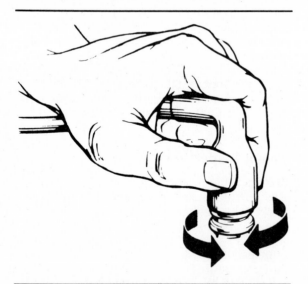

Figure 9-2. Remove ignition cables carefully to avoid damaging the fragile TVRS cable.

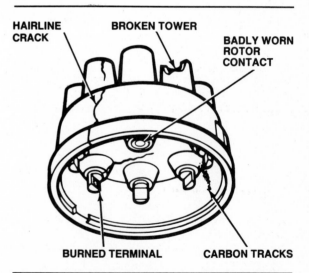

Figure 9-3. Inspect the distributor cap and replace it if you find any of these defects. (Chrysler)

Ohmmeter Tests

In Chapter 8, you learned how to use an ohmmeter to test the resistance of the coil secondary winding. You should also use the ohmmeter to check the ignition cables for resistance. Television-radio suppression (TVRS) cables should measure about 4,000 ohms per foot (30 centimeters). Figure 9-5 is a table that lists ignition cable resistance specifications from several major carmakers. When resistance exceeds specifications, driveability problems can arise from engine misfire, higher burn voltage, and

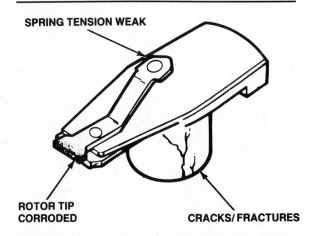

Figure 9-4. Inspect the rotor and replace if any of these defects is found. (Chrysler)

IGNITION COIL RESISTANCE
(OHMS AT 75° F OR 24° C)

	PRIMARY	SECONDARY
AMERICAN MOTORS		
1980-81 4-cylinder	0.4-0.5	8000-9500
1982-83 4-cylinder	0-2.0	6000-30,000
1984 4-cylinder	1.13-1.23	7700-9300
1978-87 6-, 8-cylinder	1.13-1.23	7700-9300
CHEVROLET		
1978-80	0-1.0	6000-30,000
1981-86	0-2.0	6000-30,000
FORD		
1978-79 Dura-Spark I	0.71-0.77	7350-8250
1978-81 Dura-Spark II, III	1.13-1.23	7700-9300
1981 1.6L engine	1.0-2.0	7700-9600
1982-87 TFI ignition	0.3-1.0	8000-11,500
1982-87 Dura-Spark	0.8-1.6	7700-10,500
VOLKSWAGEN∗		
1457cc, 1588cc ex. EI	1.7-2.1	7000-12,000
1978-86 All others	0.52-0.76	2400-3500
∗Ohms at 68° F or 20° C		

Figure 9-5. Ignition coil resistance specifications from several major carmakers.

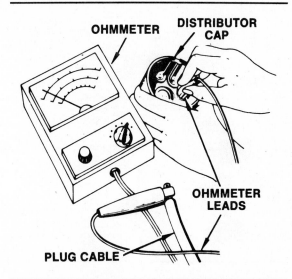

Figure 9-6. Connect one ohmmeter lead to the terminal *inside* the distributor cap when testing the resistance of an ignition cable.

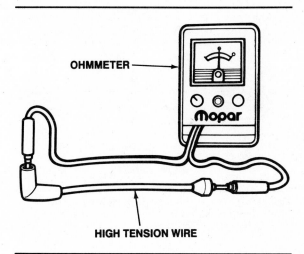

Figure 9-7. With high cable resistance, as measured through the cap, remove and check the cable alone to isolate the problem. (Chrysler)

shorter burn time. Excessive resistance can result from:
• Loose or corroded connections at the distributor cap terminal or spark plug
• Damage to the cable conductor from heat, vibration, or mishandling
• A broken terminal at either end of the cable.
A completely open cable that shows infinite resistance when tested is a serious — and not uncommon — problem. Test cable resistance as follows:
1. Remove the distributor cap from the housing and disconnect the wire to be tested from the spark plug (or coil).
2. Set the ohmmeter on a high scale and connect one lead to the cable at the spark plug terminal. Connect the other ohmmeter lead to the

corresponding terminal *inside* the distributor cap, figure 9-6.
3. Observe the ohmmeter reading:
   a. If the reading is within manufacturer's specifications, the cable is in good condition.
   b. If the reading is not within specifications, check the cable connections and repeat the test. If the reading is still out of specifications, proceed to step 4.
4. Disconnect the cable from the cap and connect the ohmmeter between the cable ends, figure 9-7. Observe the ohmmeter reading:
   a. If the reading is within specifications, replace the distributor cap.

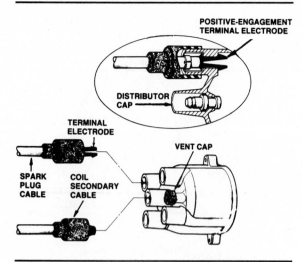

Figure 9-8. Chrysler 4-cylinder distributor use positive-locking spark plug cables which form the distributor cap electrodes. (Chrysler)

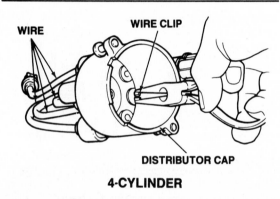

4-CYLINDER

Figure 9-9. To remove a positive locking spark plug cable, remove the cap and compress the terminal ends with pliers. (Chrysler)

IGNITION CABLE, DISTRIBUTOR CAP, AND ROTOR REPLACEMENT

Secondary circuit components can fail because of physical damage or insulation failure. Physical damage can be found by looking for it. Failing insulation can sometimes be seen as carbon tracks, but the most reliable test method is the oscilloscope.

Replacing Ignition Cables

Some Delco-Remy HEI, Ford Dura-Spark, and a few other electronic ignitions use 8-mm ignition cables; all other systems use 7-mm cables. The

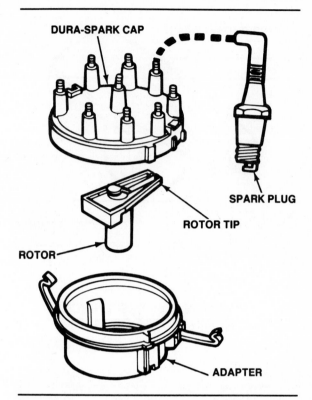

Figure 9-10. Many Ford Dura-Spark distributors use cap adapters, and the ignition cables snap onto the terminals.

8-mm cable insulation gives additional dielectric resistance in a system where secondary voltages can exceed 40 kV. Do not try to install 7-mm cables on a system that uses 8-mm cables; they are not interchangeable.

Ignition cables are manufactured and sold in two ways. You can buy a set of cables made in predetermined lengths with molded terminals and boots at each end. Each set is designed to fit a variety of engines which will be listed on the back of the box. When installing this type of cable, simply remove the old one and install a new cable that is approximately the same length in its place.

You can also buy a set of cables without the preassembled terminals and boots. You should match these cables to the old ones and cut them to length as required. Then slide a boot on each end and install the terminals with a suitable crimping tool.

Ignition cables used with 1980 and later Chrysler 4-cylinder engines have locking terminals, figure 9-8. These cables form the distributor contact terminal within the cap, which has no terminals of its own. To disconnect this type of cable from the cap, you must first remove the cap and then compress the terminal ends with pliers, figure 9-9. Trying to remove a cable

b. If the reading is still out of specifications, replace the cable.

5. Repeat the procedure to check each remaining secondary cable.

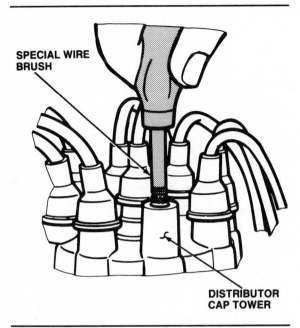

Figure 9-11. Clean light corrosion from cap towers with a wire brush. (Chrysler)

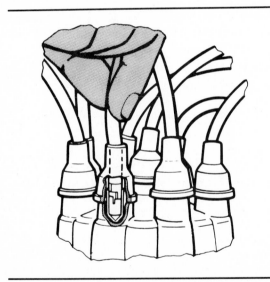

Figure 9-12. Seat the cable terminal firmly into the cap tower, squeezing the boot to release any trapped air. (Chrysler)

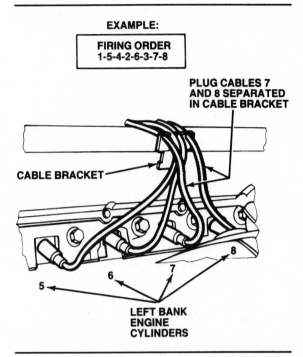

Figure 9-13. Route the spark plug cables correctly to prevent crossfiring. (Chrysler)

of this type in the same way that you would remove a conventional cable can damage the cable, the terminal, and the cap.

Ignition cables used on some 1984 and later Ford engines also have the distributor contact terminal attached, but this is a press-in terminal and can be removed by pulling on the boot, as with a traditional cable.

Some late-model distributor caps use a male ignition cable terminal that looks much like a spark plug, figure 9-10. Ignition cables used

with these caps snap onto the terminal instead of fitting down inside the cap tower.

To install new ignition cables, follow this procedure to avoid confusion and possible incorrect installation:

1. If the distributor cap uses locking terminals, remove the cap. If it is a traditional cap, leave it on the distributor and begin at the front of the engine in cylinder number or in firing order sequence.

2. Disconnect just *one* cable from a spark plug and the distributor cap.

3. Check the cap tower for dirt, corrosion or damage. Clean the tower with a tower cleaning wire brush, figure 9-11, or replace the cap, as neecessary.

4. Fit the new cable to the cap with its terminal seated firmly on or inside the tower, figure 9-12. To make sure the terminal is firmly seated and that the rubber boot seals over the tower, squeeze the boot to remove any trapped air when seating it in place.

5. Connect the other end of the cable to the spark plug. Make sure its terminal and boot fit properly onto the plug terminal.

6. Repeat this procedure for each remaining cable, including the coil cable. Route each cable in the same location as the one removed and fit it into its cable bracket. To prevent the possibility of crossfiring, do not route cables in firing order sequence next to each other, figure 9-13.

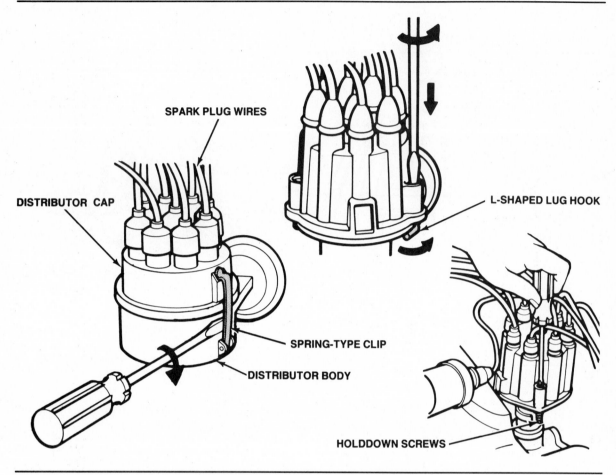

Figure 9-14. Typical distributor cap retainer. (Chrysler)

Make sure that the cables cannot contact the exhaust manifold or interfere with other electrical wiring.

Replacing a Distributor Cap and Rotor

Distributor caps may be held to the housing by spring-type clips, L-shaped lug hooks, or holddown screws, figure 9-14. Caps generally have a locating lug or slot for proper alignment, figure 9-15. Rotors may be retained by holddown screws or may simply slip onto the shaft, figure 9-16. Rotors also use one or more locating lugs, figure 9-17.

The caps used with Ford Dura-Spark and Delco-Remy ignitions are unique. Dura-Spark caps are larger, have male secondary terminals, and may use a cap adapter, figure 9-10. Some Delco-Remy HEI caps have an integral coil, figure 9-18. Such distributors may have wide spacing between the secondary terminals and use special rotors to help prevent crossfiring.

To replace a cap, you either unclip the old one, depress and turn the spring-loaded L-lug hooks with a screwdriver, or loosen the hold-down screws, figure 9-14. On HEI caps with an integral coil, you must disconnect the ignition feed wire and module connector and then remove the coil cover and coil, figure 9-18. Delco HEI caps may use a cable retainer to hold the cables in place. The retainer is removed by depressing the two latches, figure 9-19.

If an adapter is used with a Dura-Spark cap, remove the upper cap portion first, then remove the rotor before removing the adapter, figure 9-10. If this sequence is not followed, the rotor will prevent removal of the cap and adapter as an assembly.

Some V-8 Dura-Spark distributors use a cap and rotor with terminals on two levels. Unlike conventional caps, the terminals are not in firing order sequence. This design is used for two reasons: separating the terminals in this manner allows up to 30 degrees distributor advance, and helps to prevent crossfiring inside the distributor. Such caps have a series of numbers molded into their tops in two rings, figure 9-20. These numbers are *cylinder numbers*, not

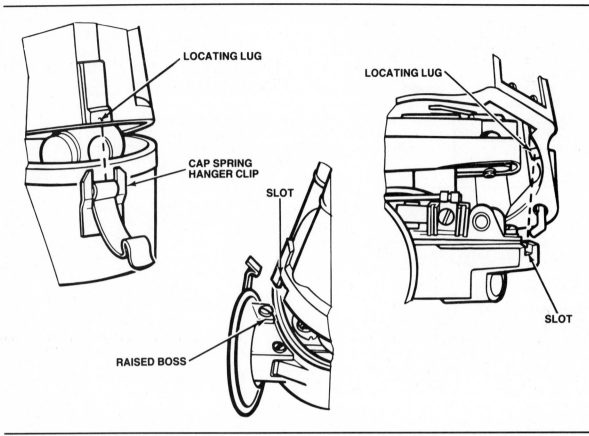

Figure 9-15. Typical distributor cap latches and locking lugs. (Chrysler)

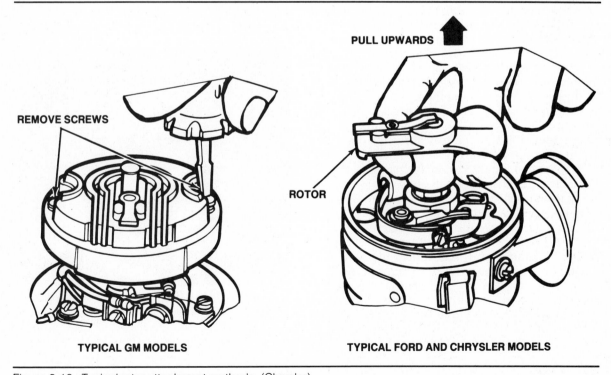

Figure 9-16. Typical rotor attachment methods. (Chrysler)

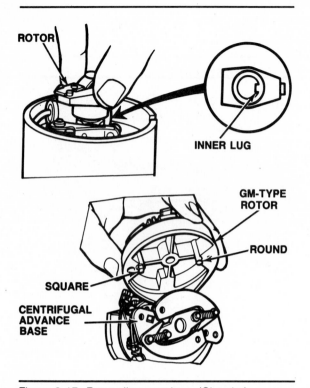

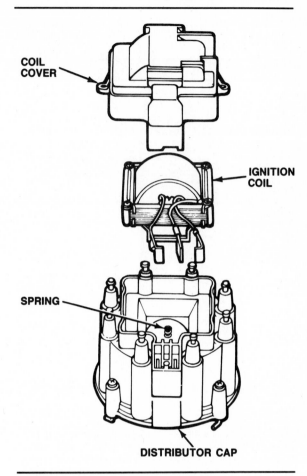

Figure 9-17. Rotor alignment lugs. (Chrysler)

Figure 9-18. The coil is housed under a cover in the distributor cap on many HEI distributors. (Chrysler)

firing order numbers. The inner ring is used with standard 5.0L (302-cid) V-8 engines; the outer ring is used with high-performance 5.0L (302-cid) V8's and 5.8L and 6.6L (351- and 400-cid) V-8's (which have a different firing order). Be very careful when replacing this cap or its cable to avoid making an error.

Press-on rotors usually can be replaced by simply pulling the old one off the distributor shaft, figure 9-16, aligning the lug inside the new rotor with the shaft slot, figure 9-7, and pressing it into place. Make sure the rotor is fully seated. If it is not, it may strike the cap when the engine is started.

This type of rotor occasionally may stick to the distributor shaft. You can often remove a stuck rotor by inserting a screwdriver under both ends and carefully prying it upward. If this does not free the rotor immediately, it is a good idea to crack the rotor with a small chisel and light hammer taps. Attempting to pry the stuck rotor can damage the distributor housing or shaft. If it is necessary to destroy a rotor in this manner to remove it, be sure that all parts and chips are removed from the distributor.

The rotor on Chrysler's 1984 and later optical distributor is both indexed to the shaft and secured by a horizontal capscrew. This location makes it very difficult to remove the rotor with the distributor in the engine.

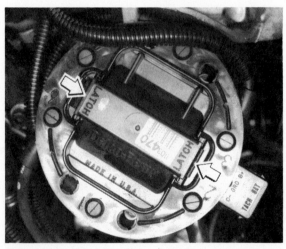

Figure 9-19. The HEI cable retainer is removed by depressing the two latches (arrows).

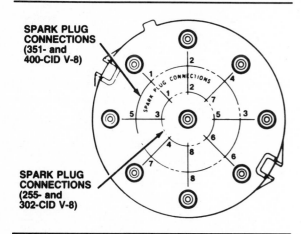

Figure 9-20. Engine cylinder number, *not firing order* numbers, are molded into the top of bilevel Dura-Spark distributor caps. (Ford)

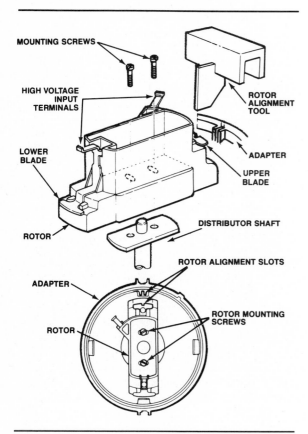

Figure 9-21. Ford EEC-I Dura-Spark rotor alignment. (Ford)

Ford used two different distributors with its early EEC systems. Complete assemblies are interchangeable, but individual components cannot be switched. The rotor in each type distributor requires special replacement and alignment procedures.

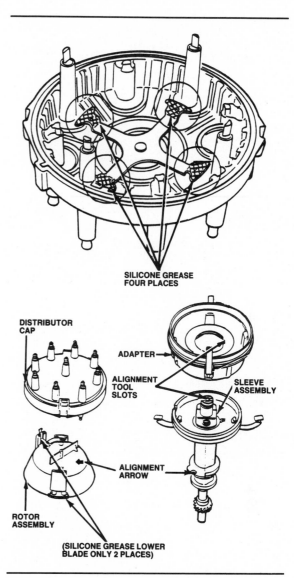

Figure 9-22. Ford EEC-II & III Dura-Spark rotor replacement and sleeve alignment. (Ford)

The early Dura-Spark I rotors attach to the distributor shaft by two screws that fit into slotted holes, figure 9-21. To replace and align the rotor:

1. Remove the distributor cap. Crank the engine until the slot in the rotor upper coil electrode aligns with the cap adapter slot.
2. Remove the screws holding the rotor. Remove the rotor. Be careful not to turn the crankshaft from this point on because it will complicate rotor alignment and retiming.
3. Fit the new rotor in place and install the screws finger tight.
4. Slide the special Ford alignment tool into the distributor adapter and rotor blade slots. This aligns the rotor properly.

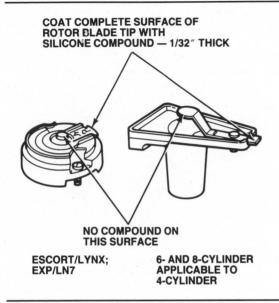

COAT COMPLETE SURFACE OF
ROTOR BLADE TIP WITH
SILICONE COMPOUND — 1/32″ THICK

NO COMPOUND ON
THIS SURFACE

ESCORT/LYNX;   6- AND 8-CYLINDER
EXP/LN7   APPLICABLE TO
                   4-CYLINDER

Figure 9-23. Typical locations for silicone grease on some Ford rotors. (Ford)

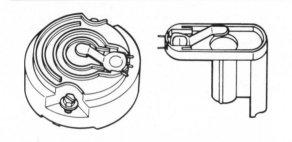

Figure 9-24. Ford's multiple-point or "cat whisker" rotors were designed to suppress RFI without silicone grease. (Ford)

5. Tighten the rotor screws securely and remove the alignment tool.
6. Reinstall the distributor cap.

The second generation Dura-Spark rotors used with EEC-III systems do not generally require alignment, figure 9-22. However, the rotor sleeve on the distributor shaft can be adjusted, if necessary. To replace this type of rotor:

1. Rotate the crankshaft to align the timing marks. Make sure the number 1 piston is on its compression stroke or the rotor will be 180 degrees out of alignment if shaft sleeve adjustment is made.
2. Remove the distributor cap. Grasp the rotor by its lifting tab at the center top and remove it from the shaft.
3. Make sure that the slots on the shaft sleeve align with the slot in the adapter. If they do not, it will be necessary to loosen the two

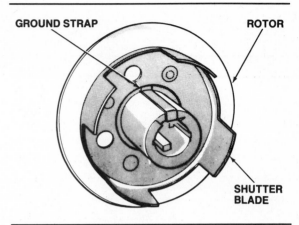

GROUND STRAP   ROTOR

SHUTTER
BLADE

Figure 9-25. Chrysler's Hall-effect rotor contains the shutter blades and must be grounded to the distributor shaft.

sleeve screws, insert the proper alignment tool in the sleeve and adapter slots, and tighten the screws.
4. Align the arrow on the new rotor with the sleeve slot and press the rotor into position.

Some carmakers use a silicone grease on the cap and rotor terminals to suppress radio-frequency interference (RFI). The silicone grease gradually crystalizes and appears similar to corrosion. This is normal and should not be removed. When a new cap or rotor is installed, a thin coat of Dow Corning 111 or G.E. G-627 grease should be applied to the specified areas of the rotor electrode or cap terminals, figure 9-23.

From 1983 to 1985, Ford used a rotor with multiple-point electrodes, figure 9-24, to reduce RFI without the use of silicone grease. They caused other problems, however, and these rotors were discontinued at the end of the 1985 model year. Chrysler Hall-effect distributors use a special rotor with the Hall-effect shutter blade ring attached, figure 9-25. The rotor is grounded through the distributor shaft. If the ground connection has high resistance, it will upset the ignition timing signal and the engine will misfire.

SPARK PLUG SERVICE

Spark plug service is an important part of a complete engine tune-up. Since the spark plugs are the final component in all secondary circuits, if they are not in good condition, the remainder of the circuit cannot perform properly. Vehicle manufacturers' recommendations for plug service intervals vary from 5,000 miles (8,000 kilometers) to as seldom as every 30,000

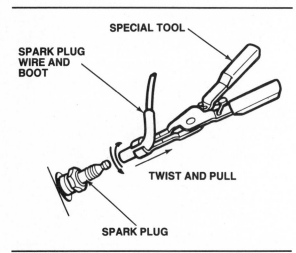

SPECIAL TOOL

SPARK PLUG
WIRE AND
BOOT

TWIST AND PULL

SPARK PLUG

Figure 9-26. Insulated pliers provide extra gripping power and reach while preventing cable damage. (Chrysler)

or even 60,000 miles (48,000 km or even 96,000 km). Spark plug life depends upon:
● Engine design
● Type of driving done
● Kind of fuel used
● Types of emission control devices used.

Generally, the plugs used in late-model engines burning unleaded fuel will last longer than those used in high compression engines that require premium fuel. Follow the car-maker's recommendation for spark plug service intervals.

Spark plug service on many older engines, and on some late-model inline engines with few accessories, is a fairly simple operation. You just remove the plugs with a spark plug socket and a ratchet handle with a convenient extension. Then install the new plugs in the same manner.

Many late-model engines, with a maze of air conditioning and emission control plumbing and several engine-driven accessories, are not such a simple matter when it comes to spark plug service. Some plugs may be hidden behind engine accessories, which must be loosened from their mountings and moved for access to the plugs. Air conditioning compressors, air pumps, and power steering pumps are frequent candidates for relocation during plug service. Whenever you must move one of these accessories, be careful of its plumbing and wiring. Air conditioning lines are particularly bulky and must be handled carefully.

Some spark plugs on some engines are most easily reached from underneath the engine. In these cases, you will have to raise the car on a hoist or with a jack and safety stands and go

beneath the engine to remove and replace the plugs. On a few V-8 engines, it is necessary to loosen the motor mounts and raise the engine to provide access to the rear cylinders for plug removal.

A variety of special wrench extensions and adapters is available to make spark plug service easier. Regardless of the other special tools you may use, you will need a spark plug socket. These come in two sizes:
● A 13/16" socket for 14-mm gasketed and 18-mm tapered-seat plugs
● A 5/8" socket for 14-mm tapered-seat plugs.

Most spark plug sockets have a rubber insert to grip and cushion the plug insulator during service. Spark plug sockets may be either 3/8- or 1/2-inch drive. Many also have an external hex to permit turning with an open-end wrench or a box wrench.

Another item that will make spark plug service easier is a length of rubber or nylon tubing with an inside diameter that fits tightly over the spark plug terminal or insulator. The tubing can be forced over the top of the plug during removal and installation if you cannot reach the plug with your fingers to turn it. The tubing will grip the plug tightly enough to turn it either in or out when the plug is loose.

Removing Spark Plugs

To remove the spark plugs:
1. Disconnect the cables by grasping the plug boot and twisting gently while pulling. Do not pull on the cable itself or you will damage it. Insulated spark plug pliers, figure 9-26, will provide a better grip and are recommended when working near hot manifolds.
2. Loosen each plug one or two turns with a spark plug socket, then blow away dirt from the plugs with compressed air, figure 9-27.
3. Remove the plugs and place each one in a tray or holder in cylinder number order for inspection, figure 9-28.
4. When removing gasketed plugs, be sure the old gasket comes out with the plug. Some older Chrysler engines use gasket-type plugs installed in tubes without gaskets, figure 9-29.

Spark Plug Diagnosis

Examining the firing ends of the spark plugs will tell you a good deal about general engine conditions and plug operating conditions. This is often called "reading" the plugs. Note the amount and kind of deposits and the degree of electrode erosion. The following paragraphs and photographs explain common spark plug conditions.

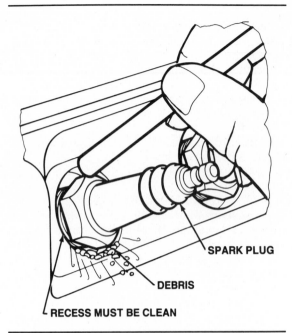

Figure 9-27. Blow all contamination out of the spark plug well before removing the plugs. (Chrysler)

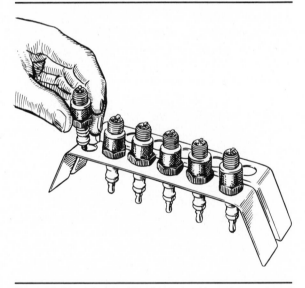

Figure 9-28. A holder like this is handy to keep plugs in order for inspection.

Normal

The visible crusty deposits shown in figure 9-30 are present to some degree on all used plugs. This is normal, however, and does not affect performance. The insulator nose has a light brown-to-grayish color, and there is very little electrode wear. This indicates the correct plug heat range and a healthy engine. If this plug were to be reinstalled, it should be properly cleaned and the electrodes correctly regapped.

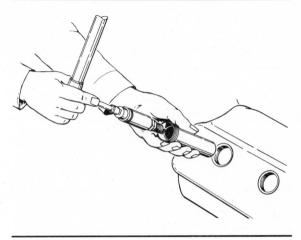

Figure 9-29. Some Chrysler engines have gasket-type spark plugs installed in tubes, using no gaskets.

Figure 9-30. A normal used spark plug. (Champion)

Oil fouled

Excessive oil entering the combustion chamber causes this condition, figure 9-31. In a high-mileage engine, it may be due to piston ring and cylinder wall wear. In a low-mileage or rebuilt engine, normal oil control may not be established. Another cause of oil fouling may be a defective PCV valve. Oil also may seep past worn valve guides, or a ruptured fuel pump diaphragm may allow oil vapor from the crankcase to be drawn to the carburetor. Clean or replace oil-fouled plugs and suggest mechanical repairs to the car owner.

Carbon fouled

Carbon fouling consists of soft, black, sooty deposits, figure 9-32. First, check plug specifications to make sure the correct heat range is being used. A plug that is too cold will easily

Figure 9-31. An oil-fouled spark plug. (Champion)

Figure 9-33. A worn spark plug. (Champion)

Figure 9-32. A carbon-fouled spark plug. (Champion)

Figure 9-34. An ash-fouled spark plug. (Champion)

foul in this way. If the plug is the recommended heat range, check for an overly rich air-fuel mixture caused by a stuck choke or clogged air filter. Other possible causes are weak ignition, inoperative manifold heat control valve or thermostatic air cleaner, retarded timing, low compression, faulty plug wires or distributor cap, or simply, stop-and-go driving.

Worn out
While the color of the insulator nose, figure 9-33, indicates that the heat range is correct and deposits are normal, the rounded and worn electrodes tell you that this plug should be replaced. The voltage required to spark across the gap has doubled and would continue to increase with additional use. Misfiring under load is a clue to worn out plugs. Such plugs also contribute to poor gas mileage, loss of power, and increased emissions.

Ash fouled
Ash deposits, figure 9-34, are light brown to white and are caused by burning certain oil or fuel additives during normal combustion. If they are found on the plug, you can be sure that they cover the entire combustion chamber. Normally, ash deposits are nonconductive, but large amounts may mask the spark and cause misfiring.

Splash fouled
Splash fouling, figure 9-35, is caused by deposits breaking loose from pistons and valves and splashing against hot plug insulators. This often occurs after a tune-up, which restores engine power and higher combustion temperatures. Normally, try cleaning and reinstalling splash-fouled plugs before replacing them.

Figure 9-35. A splash-fouled spark plug. (Champion)

Figure 9-37. A spark plug with the gap bridged. (Champion)

Figure 9-36. A spark plug that has been mechanically damaged. (Champion)

Figure 9-38. A spark plug with a glazed insulator. (Champion)

Mechanical damage
Spark plug damage, figure 9-36, can be caused by a foreign object in the combustion chamber, by a plug of the wrong reach being hit by a piston or valve, or by careless installation. Be careful to prevent dirt from falling into spark plug holes during service and always handle plugs carefully.

Gap bridging
Gap bridging, figure 9-37, is usually due to conditions similar to those described for splash fouling. The difference is one of degree. The deposits form a bridge across the electrodes and cause a short. This condition is common in engines where oil control is poor. Try cleaning and regapping these plugs before replacing them.

Insulator glazing
Shiny, yellow, or tan deposits, figure 9-38, may be insulator glazing. This is usually caused by frequent hard acceleration with a resulting rise in plug temperature. Instead of flaking off, normal plug deposits melt and fuse into a conductive coating that can cause misfiring. Severe glazing cannot easily be removed by normal cleaning, and the plugs may require replacement. Plugs one range colder than recommended may cure a glazing problem.

Detonation
Detonation is a form of spark knock caused by an explosive burning of part of the air-fuel mixture just after ignition occurs. It is caused by the increased heat and pressure in the combustion chamber and exerts extreme pressure on engine parts. In figure 9-39, it has fractured the plug insulator. Contributing factors are over-

Figure 9-39. A spark plug damaged by detonation. (Champion)

Figure 9-41. An overheated spark plug. (Champion)

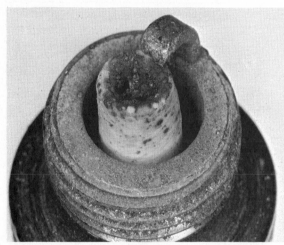

Figure 9-40. A spark plug damaged by preignition. (Champion)

advanced timing, lean carburetion, low gasoline octane, and engine lugging.

Preignition
Ignition of the air-fuel charge before the plug fires can cause this kind of severe damage, figure 9-40. Preignition is usually caused by combustion chamber hot spots or deposits which get hot enough to ignite the air-fuel charge before normal ignition. It can also be caused by crossfiring between plug cables or by a plug heat range much too hot for the engine.

Overheated
An overheated spark plug, figure 9-41, often is indicated by a clean, white insulator tip or excessive electrode wear, or both. The insulator also may be blistered. The plug may be too hot for the engine, but even the correct plug can be overheated by over-advanced timing, a defective cooling system, or lean air-fuel ratios.

Spark Plug Cleaning and Filing

Used plugs that are not excessively worn can be cleaned in a special spark plug cleaner for continued use, but you should be aware that such plugs will require about 40 percent more voltage to fire them. This is one reason why it is more economical to install new spark plugs rather than clean and regap old ones. New plugs also ensure better performance, because there is no way to determine how long cleaned and regapped plugs will perform properly.

Spark plug cleaners are often called "sand-blasters", but the cleaning abrasive used should be an aluminum oxide material similar to that used in the plug insulator. Ordinary blasting sand can adhere to the plug insulator, forming a conductive coating when subjected to combustion temperatures. This will result in a plug misfire.

To properly restore the serviceability of used plugs:
1. Wipe oil and grease from the outside of the plug with a clean cloth. Use a small amount of solvent, if necessary, but do not soak the plugs in solvent or lacquer cleaner. These materials may penetrate the insulator and form conductive deposits that will result in misfiring and short circuits. Dry the plugs with compressed air.
2. Carefully bend back the side (ground) electrode with a special bending tool for better cleaning, figure 9-42.
3. Place the plug in an abrasive-blast machine, figure 9-43, and rotate the plug slowly while applying short bursts of abrasive material.
4. After cleaning, remove all abrasive from the plug with compressed air. Inspect the plug, particularly inside the shell, to make sure all deposits and abrasive have been removed.

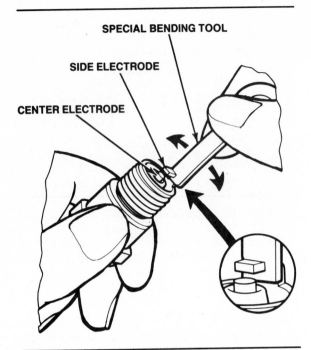

Figure 9-42. Use a special tool to bend the side electrode. (Chrysler)

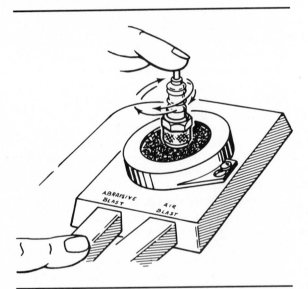

Figure 9-43. Clean the spark plugs in an abrasive blaster.

5. Clean the plug threads with a hand-held wire brush, figure 9-44.
6. File the tip of the center electrode and the inner surface of the side electrode until a shiny surface appears, figure 9-45.

Selecting Replacement Plugs

Do not assume that the last person working on the car installed the correct spark plugs. Spark

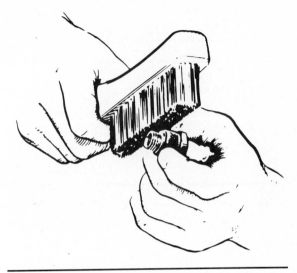

Figure 9-44. Clean the spark plug threads with a wire brush.

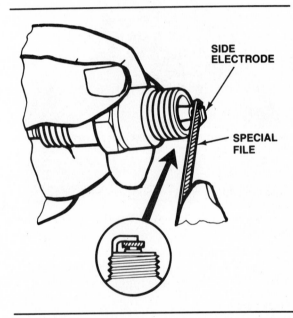

Figure 9-45. File the electrodes lightly before setting the gap on a used plug. (Chrysler)

plug manufacturers and carmakers list the proper spark plugs by part number for use in specific engines. This part number describes the plug features exactly: diameter, reach, heat range, tip design, gap, and resistor or non-resistor type. Always check the vehicle and plug manufacturer specifications before selecting replacement plugs.

In some cases, the basic recommendation may be just a starting point:
● A slightly hotter spark plug may give more satisfactory performance when a vehicle is used

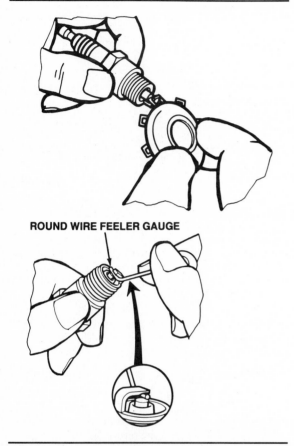

ROUND WIRE FEELER GAUGE

Figure 9-46. Typical spark plug feeler gauges and their use. (Chrysler)

primarily for short trips and stop-and-go driving.
• A slightly colder spark plug may be the best choice for extended highway driving, especially during hot weather.

You should be able to determine the correct heat range from reading the plugs and discussing the use of the vehicle with its driver. Remember, however, that the heat range used should not deviate from the basic recommendation by more than one or two steps.

Copper core spark plugs now being used as original equipment plugs on late-model engines can also be used as service replacement plugs in older engines. Just make sure that the basic features of the copper core plug are the same as the older style plug originally recommended.

Gapping Spark Plugs

Both new and used spark plugs must be correctly gapped to the engine manufacturer's specification:
• Do not assume that new plugs are correctly pregapped

• Do not try to set a wide-gap plug (electronic ignition) to a small-gap specification. This will damage the electrode
• Do not try to set a narrow-gap plug (breaker-point ignition) to a wide-gap specification. This will result in misaligned electrodes
• Do not make "fine" adjustments in gap by tapping the plug's side electrode on a workbench. This can cause internal plug damage.

There are a wide variety of gapping tools available for easy and accurate gap adjustment. The most efficient one, however, is a round wire feeler gauge such as those shown in figure 9-46. The tool should incorporate a bending arm to adjust the ground electrode, figure 9-42. A flat feeler gauge should not be used, as the measurement will be inaccurate. Measure the gap with the round feeler gauge and adjust it by carefully bending the ground electrode.

Installing Spark Plugs

Whether you are installing new or used plugs, it is a good idea to clean the cylinder head plug holes with a thread chaser. This will ensure easy installation, but the tool must be used carefully with aluminum heads to avoid damaging the plug hole threads.

In some cases, the vehicle manufacturer recommends the use of an antiseize compound, especially with aluminum cylinder heads. Be sure to use the specific antiseize compound recommended, because some may not be compatible with aluminum.

To install new or used spark plugs:
1. Carefully wipe any dirt and grease from the engine plug seats with a clean cloth. Do not let this debris fall into the combustion chambers.
2. Be sure the gaskets on gasketed plugs are in good condition and properly installed on the plugs. If possible, install a new gasket on a used plug. Make sure there is only *one* gasket on the plug.
3. If the engine uses gasket-type plugs in metal cylinders, be sure to remove the gaskets before installing the plugs.
4. Install the plugs in the engine by hand. If necessary, use nylon or rubber tubing on the plug terminals or insulators to turn hard-to-reach plugs. If a plug does not turn easily, it may be cross-threaded. Remove the plug and install it a second time.
5. Tighten the plugs with a torque wrench, figure 9-47, to the values listed in figure 9-48.
6. If the gasket plugs have used gaskets or if antiseize compound is used, reduce the torque setting slightly. If thread lubricant is used, re-

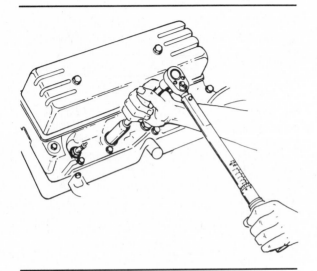

Figure 9-47. Install spark plugs finger-tight, then tighten with a torque wrench to the specified value.

PLUG TYPE	CAST-IRON HEAD		ALUMNINUM HEAD	
	Foot-Pounds	Newton-Meters	Foot-Pounds	Newton-Meters
14-MM GASKETED	25-30	34-40	15-22	20-30
14-MM TAPERED SEAT	7-15	9-20	7-15	9-20
18-MM TAPERED SEAT	15-20	20-27	15-20	20-27

Figure 9-48. Spark plug installation torque values.

duce the torque setting (many spark plug manufacturers do not recommend the use of thread lubricant).

7. If you do not have a torque wrench for plug installation, install the plugs finger-tight. Then tighten 14-mm gasket plugs an additional ¼ turn with a wrench. Tighten 14-mm and 18-mm tapered-seat plugs an additional ¹⁄₁₆ turn *only*. Do not overtighten the spark plugs, particularly in an aluminum cylinder head.

SECONDARY CIRCUIT OSCILLOSCOPE TESTING

We learned to use the oscilloscope in Chapter 8 to test and service the primary circuit. As when checking the primary circuit, you should follow the equipment manufacturer's instructions on connecting the scope leads to the engine. You only need the same minimum connections that are required for the primary circuit:
- Coil (+) or (−) terminal, according to the manufacturer's design
- Ignition cable between the coil and distributor

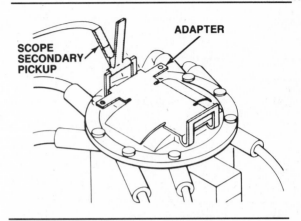

Figure 9-49. Special secondary pickups are required with Delco-Remy HEI coils. (Coats Diagnostic)

- Number 1 spark plug cable
- A good engine ground.

The same adapters, figures 9-49 and 9-50, are required to make the proper test connections. The kilovolt (kV) scales on both sides of the scope screen are used to view the secondary circuit patterns.

Normal Secondary Circuit Patterns

Figure 9-51 is a secondary circuit superimposed pattern. Like the primary circuit pattern, the secondary pattern is also divided into the firing, intermediate, and dwell sections. Secondary circuit voltages, however, are much higher than primary circuit voltages.

The firing section of the secondary superimposed pattern starts with a straight vertical line that indicates the amount of voltage required to create an arc across the spark plug air gap. This is called the firing line or voltage spike. As soon as the arc is established, less voltage is required to maintain it. The horizontal line following the voltage spike represents continued current across the spark plug gap. This is called the spark line and is about one-quarter the height of the voltage spike.

The intermediate section begins when the spark plug arc is extinguished. The remaining voltage is dissipated as oscillations between the coil and condenser in breaker-point systems or within the coil in electronic systems. This series of oscillations starts at the beginning of the intermediate section and gradually diminishes. Because there is no condenser in an electronic ignition, there are no condenser oscillations in the intermediate section. The oscillations are all caused by the coil and can be used to judge coil condition.

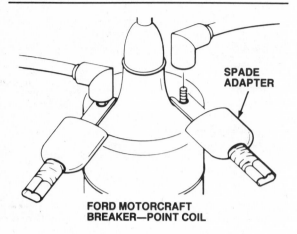

FORD MOTORCRAFT BREAKER—POINT COIL

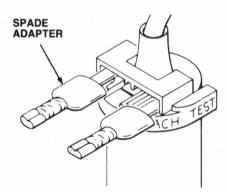

FORD MOTORCRAFT ELECTRONIC IGNITION COIL

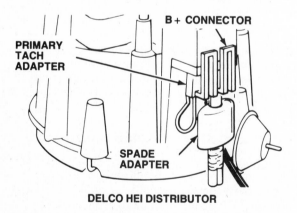

DELCO HEI DISTRIBUTOR

Figure 9-50. Test lead adapters are also required with some primary circuits. (Coats Diagnostic)

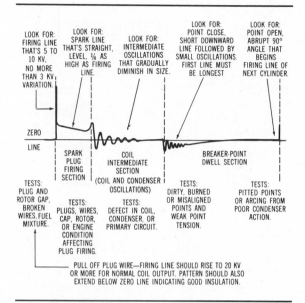

Figure 9-51. This is a normal secondary superimposed pattern, showing the firing, intermediate, and dwell sections. (Sun)

As in the primary pattern, the dwell section of the secondary pattern begins as the points close or the ignition module turns on to close the primary circuit and recharge the coil. The length of the dwell section is not important in most solid-state systems, although some are designed to lengthen the dwell at higher engine speeds. During the dwell section, some systems exhibit slight voltage ripples or humps, which are normal.

There are three basic scope displays for secondary circuit patterns, just as in the primary circuit:

1. Superimposed pattern — The voltage traces for all cylinders are superimposed upon each other to form a single pattern.

2. Parade pattern — The voltage traces for all cylinders are displayed one after the other from left to right in firing order sequence.

3. Stacked, or raster, pattern — The voltage traces for all cylinders are stacked one above the other in firing order sequence.

The secondary pattern can be shifted, expanded, or broken into millisecond increments for diagnostic purposes. The waveform for one cylinder can be separated from a superimposed or parade pattern, a useful feature in analyzing the cables, plugs, and internal condition of an individual cylinder.

Just as the secondary circuits of breaker point and electronic ignitions are essentially similar, so are the secondary scope patterns. Figures 9-52 through 9-54 show typical secondary superimposed patterns for the major domestic electronic ignitions.

Chrysler systems, figure 9-52, have no distinct intermediate section. The coil oscillations begin at the end of the firing section or spark line and gradually turn into a straight line. The lean-burn system, however, does have an intermediate section in the secondary pattern. The

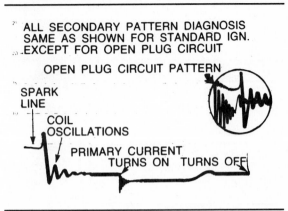

Figure 9-52. Normal Chrysler electronic ignition superimposed pattern. (Marquette)

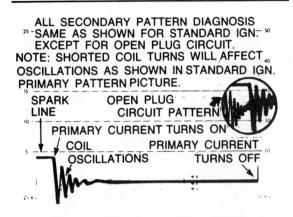

Figure 9-53. Normal Delco HEI secondary superimposed pattern. This is also typical of the AMC-Prestolite and Ford Dura-Spark I systems. (Marquette)

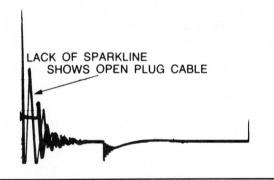

Figure 9-54. Normal Ford SSI, Dura-Spark II and TFI-I secondary superimposed pattern. (Marquette)

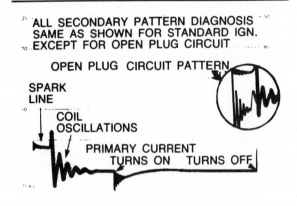

Figure 9-55. These large oscillations with no spark line are caused by an open in one spark plug circuit. (Marquette)

transistor turns on after a short section of coil oscillations. When an early-model lean-burn engine is running on the start pickup instead of the run pickup, its intermediate section is much longer and the dwell period is shorter.

The dwell period for variable-dwell electronic ignitions changes with engine speed. Figure 9-53 shows a typical HEI superimposed pattern. The oscillations that occur at the beginning of the dwell period are coil, not condenser oscillations. Again, the current hump appears in the dwell section of the pattern. This hump or voltage ripple is normal and indicates that the module current-limiting circuits have reduced the primary current. This pattern is also typical of the AMC-Prestolite and Ford Dura-Spark I and TFI-I systems.

The Ford SSI and Dura-Spark II systems produce secondary patterns that are quite similar to breaker-point ignitions. The coil oscillations may not be as high as with a breaker point system, but there should be more of them. The dwell period is longer and has a gentle curve that decreases toward the end of the dwell period.

Secondary Circuit Abnormalities

Variations in the secondary circuit pattern, like those in the primary circuit pattern, can indicate if parts are malfunctioning or incorrectly adjusted. The following paragraphs describe some common secondary circuit problems that can be detected by examining an oscilloscope trace. All traces shown are superimposed, unless the problem can be seen more clearly in a parade, raster or expanded pattern.

Firing section
1. Figure 9-55 shows a large coil oscillation for one cylinder, with little or no spark line. This can be caused by a disconnected or open spark plug cable. Use the secondary raster display to isolate the faulty plug circuit.

Figure 9-56. The open-circuit firing line for cylinder number 6 indicates the coil's maximum available (open-circuit) voltage. (Allen)

Figure 9-57. If this trace appears when a spark plug cable is deliberately disconnected, then the high voltage is leaking away through poor insulation. (Allen)

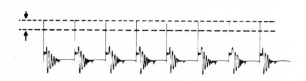

Figure 9-58. The secondary trace firing spikes should not vary greatly from cylinder to cylinder. (Allen)

2. In figure 9-56, the secondary circuit parade pattern shows an open-circuit condition where one spark plug is not firing. This also can be caused by an open or disconnected spark plug cable, or an open between the distributor rotor and the spark plug. This pattern can also be created deliberately to check the coil's maximum voltage output.

3. In figure 9-57, the spark plug cable has been deliberately disconnected, but a parade pattern shows a short spark line still exists. This indicates that the high voltage is causing a current leak to ground somewhere, usually through the ignition cable insulation, the distributor cap, or the rotor. Carbon tracks often will show where this has happened.

4. In figure 9-58, the firing lines (voltage spikes) for all cylinders are compared in a parade pattern. There should not be more than a 20-percent difference between the highest and lowest spikes. If there is, refer to the table in figure 9-59 to diagnose the problem. If you cannot tell whether the problem is fuel related

Cylinders	High	Low	Fluctuating
One/More	Open Plug wire, wide plug gap	Fouled Plug, shorted wire low compression	Fuel Mixture
All Cylinders	Lean fuel mixture car-Carburetor air leak worn plugs.	Rich fuel mixture	Extreme lean mixture, equipped with EGR, sticky valves
All cylinders on same intake runner	Intake manifold leak Unbalanced carburetor		

Figure 9-59. Diagnosis table for firing spike variations. (Allen)

HIGH, SHORT SPARKLINE

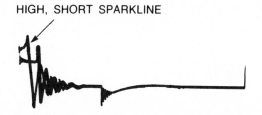

Figure 9-60. A high, short spark line is caused by excessive resistance in one cylinder's circuit. (Marquette)

LONG, LOW SPARKLINE AND SHORT OSCILLATIONS SEPARATED FROM OTHERS SHOW GROUNDED CIRCUIT

Figure 9-61. A long, low spark line is caused by a grounded, or low-resistance, circuit. (Marquette)

or in the electrical system, slowly cover the engine air intake.

   a. If the spikes go down and engine speed decreases, the problem is fuel related.

   b. If the spikes go down and engine speed remains unchanged, the plug gaps may be too great.

   c. If a single spike remains the same height, the cable to that plug may be damaged.

5. In figure 9-60, one spark line is higher and shorter than the rest. This indicates high resistance in the circuit between the distributor cap and the spark plug. A damaged or loose cable or a wide plug gap may be at fault.

6. In figure 9-61, one spark line is lower and longer than the rest. This indicates low resistance in the circuit between the distributor

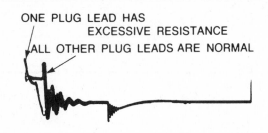

Figure 9-62. A sloping spark line indicates high resistance other than an open circuit in one spark plug circuit. (Marquette)

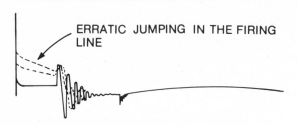

Figure 9-63. An erratic firing line is usually caused by variations in the air-fuel mixture. (Allen)

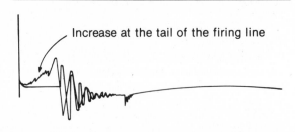

Figure 9-64. A spark line that slopes up toward the end of firing is caused by variations in the air-fuel mixture. (Allen)

Figure 9-65. In this trace, the coil and condenser oscillations are gone, but the dwell buildup is normal. (Allen)

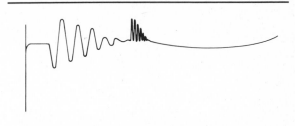

Figure 9-66. This upside-down pattern indicates reversed coil polarity. (Allen)

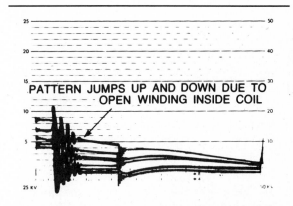

Figure 9-67. A jumping, erratic pattern is caused by an intermittent open in the coil secondary winding. (Marquette)

cap and the spark plug. Carbon tracks in the distributor, poor cable insulation, or a fouled spark plug may be to blame.

7. In figure 9-62, the spark line for one cylinder starts higher than the others and angles downward more sharply. This indicates high resistance other than an open circuit. Look for corrosion on the cable terminals and in the distributor cap.

8. In figure 9-63, the spark line of one cylinder jumps erratically. If the fuel mixture in this cylinder is erratic because of a sticking or worn valve, the mixture will offer varying amounts of resistance to the spark. This will change the spark line from one firing to the next. This trace could also be caused by air leaks or fuel induction problems.

9. In figure 9-64, the spark line of one cylinder slopes up rather than down. If this occurs at high engine speed, a valve may be sticking open. This would cause a leaner mixture at the end of combustion and greater resistance to the spark. This trace also could be caused by air leaks or fuel induction problems.

Intermediate section

1. In figure 9-65, the coil and condenser oscillations are not present but the dwell section is normal. This indicates a faulty condenser or condenser circuit.

2. In figure 9-66, the secondary circuit pattern is displayed upside-down. This indicates that coil polarity is reversed, usually because of reversed primary connections at the coil.

3. In figure 9-67, the entire pattern is jumping on the screen. This can be caused by an intermittent open in the coil secondary winding.

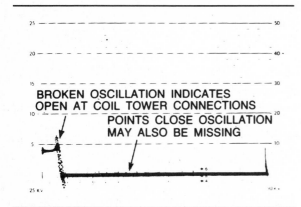

Figure 9-68. This trace shows a reduced coil oscillation and no points-close oscillations. (Marquette)

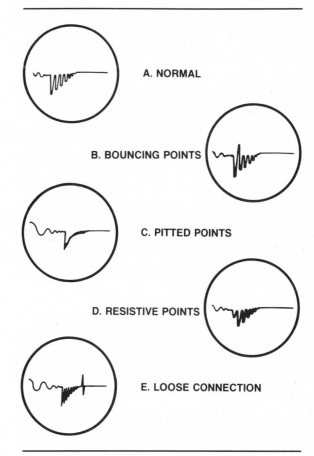

Figure 9-69. Points-close signal comparison. (Allen)

4. In figure 9-68, the coil oscillations are reduced and the points-close or module-on signal is missing. This can be caused by a problem between the coil and the distributor cap.

Dwell section
1. A secondary raster display can be used to check the dwell variation between cylinders with a breaker-point system. If the dwell varies by more than 4 to 6 degrees, it indicates mechanical wear in the distributor. If the periods do not vary, check the dwell against the manufacturer's specifications. Use the degree scale at the bottom of the screen to measure dwell.
2. A close examination of the points-close signal in a breaker-point secondary superimposed pattern can reveal other ignition system problems. When the points close, a buildup of primary coil current causes a slight voltage in the secondary circuit. At the points-close signal, there should be at least three downward oscillations, all below the dwell line, and the first should be the longest. Figure 9-69 shows a normal points-close signal, some abnormal patterns and their causes.

Special Secondary Tests

Secondary scope patterns can be used for special tests of the ignition and engine operation.

Coil output and secondary leakage tests
Test the maximum available voltage (coil output) of a breaker-point system by disconnecting one cable from a spark plug while the engine is idling and noting the open-circuit voltage on a secondary parade pattern.

To do the same test on an electronic ignition, use the spark tester or spark plug simulator described in Chapter 8. However, don't connect it to the same plug cable to which the scope lead is connected. Use the secondary parade pattern on the high-kV scale. Figure 9-56 shows this pattern with open-circuit voltage displayed on the number 6 cylinder. The minimum coil output voltage should be 20 to 25 kV for most ignitions; a few electronic systems will deliver slightly more. If the voltage is lower, look for:
- A defective coil
- A leaking condenser
- A bad ballast resistor
- Insufficient dwell
- Other high primary resistance
- Secondary circuit leakage.

Compare the maximum available voltage to the firing voltage of the other cylinders. Remember, maximum coil output is available voltage while firing voltage is required voltage. The difference between these two figure is the reserve voltage. Whenever available voltage drops below required voltage, the engine will misfire. A properly tuned ignition system on an engine in good operating condition should have a 60 percent voltage reserve.

You can also check available voltage while cranking, by observing the highest voltage

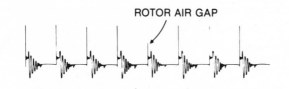

Figure 9-70. The voltage required to jump the rotor air gap can be measured by deliberately grounding a spark plug cable. (Allen)

Figure 9-71. Checking the required voltage during sudden acceleration. (Allen)

peak while the engine is being cranked. The available voltage should be about the same during cranking as with the engine running. If it is not, look for one of the problems mentioned above, a bad battery, or high resistance in the starting bypass circuit.

Rotor air gap test
Resistance is created by the gap between the rotor tip and the distributor cap plug terminals. Some resistance is designed into the system, but when resistance exceeds the design factor, it can raise the required voltage (and therefore reduce the voltage reserve).

Air gap resistance cannot be measured directly, but the voltage required to bridge the gap can be measured. Ground one end of a heavy jumper wire and inset the other end into a spark plug tower at the distributor. With the secondary parade pattern set on the low-kV scale, note the voltage spike at the grounded cylinder, figure 9-70. This is the voltage required to jump the rotor air gap. It may be as low as 3 kV for breaker-point ignitions and as high as 6 to 8 kV for electronic ignitions. If it is excessively high compared to the plug-firing voltages, replace the cap and rotor.

Rotor air gap measurements also can be used for other distributor tests. Connect a hand-operated vacuum pump to the vacuum advance diaphragm. Operate the advance mechanism through its full range while watching the air gap voltage on the scope. It should be no

greater at full advance than twice what it was with no advance. If it is, check the rotor and cap, look for a bent or worn breaker plate or distributor shaft, or incorrect dwell on a breaker-point system.

To check for worn distributor bushings or a worn or bent shaft, check the air gap for two cylinders 180 degrees apart in the distributor cap. The difference in air gap voltages should not be greater than 1 to 2 kV if the distributor is good.

Snap acceleration test
A parade pattern can be used to locate worn spark plugs with this test. Note the plug firing voltage at 1,000 rpm, then quickly open and close the throttle to place a momentary load on the engine. The firing lines should jump abruptly at the moment the throttle is opened and then return to their previous level at idle, figure 9-71. if one or more firing lines exceeds the others, look for:
- Worn spark plugs or excessive plug gaps
- High-resistance or broken plug cables
- A worn distributor cap
- A loose distributor shaft
- A lean air-fuel ratio.

If one or more firing lines are lower than the others, look for:
- Fouled spark plugs or narrow plug gaps
- A secondary leakage to ground
- A rich air-fuel ratio.

10

Distributor Service

This chapter contains procedures to remove, disassemble, test, repair, and install the major domestic breaker-point and electronic distributors. These are general instructions that will help you do these jobs on most cars and light trucks. Overhaul procedures are presented as photographic sequences for two breaker-point and six electronic distributor models.

BREAKER-POINT SERVICE IN THE VEHICLE

In Chapter 8, you learned the basic steps involved in installing and adjusting breaker points. Since most breaker points are replaced with the distributor in the engine, we will open this chapter with a photo sequence showing in-car breaker-point service and adjustment before moving on to distributor service out of the car.

A Bosch 4-cylinder distributor installed in a VW Rabbit is featured in this sequence. It is a typical example of the basic breaker-point distributors used in import cars even after domestic manufacturers had switched to solid-state distributors. The principles shown in this sequence can be applied to almost all breaker-point systems.

BOSCH BREAKER-POINT SERVICE—DISTRIBUTOR IN ENGINE

1. Unsnap the clip on each side of the distributor cap with a screwdriver as shown, then remove the cap with cables attached.

2. Check the cap for carbon tracks, corrosion, cracks or other damage, then wipe it with a clean, dry shop cloth. Do not moisten cloth with solvent.

3. Pull the rotor straight up and off the distributor shaft and check for the same defects as the cap. Replace rotor and cap if either is defective.

4. Remove the dust cap or RFI shield, if the distributor has one. Clean cap with shop cloth and place to one side.

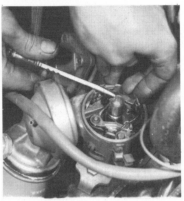

5. The primary lead can be pried out of the terminal on this distributor. Other distributors may use a connector screw that must be loosened to remove the lead.

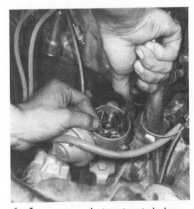

6. Loosen point set retaining screw. Remove screw and old point set. Because of limited access, you cannot replace the external condenser without removing this distributor.

7. Proper cam lubrication is important. You can lubricate the cam surface or the rubbing block on the new point set.

8. Install the new point set with its locating pin engaging the hole in the breaker plate.

9. Replace, but do not tighten, attaching screw. Rotate crankshaft to place rubbing block on high point of cam lobe.

BOSCH BREAKER-POINT SERVICE—DISTRIBUTOR IN ENGINE

10. Set the point gap to specifications and check with a flat feeler gauge. When gap is correct, tighten point set retaining screw.

11. Reconnect the point set primary lead to the primary terminal.

12. Use a screwdriver blade to place 1 or 2 drops of engine oil on the felt pad inside the distributor shaft.

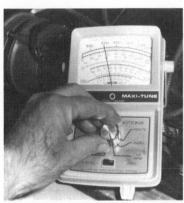

13. Reinstall dust plate, rotor, and cap. Connect a dwellmeter and check the dwell adjustment while cranking the engine.

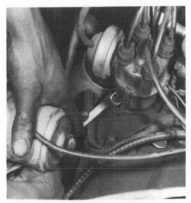

14. Loosen the distributor holddown capscrew just enough to allow the distributor to be rotated in the engine.

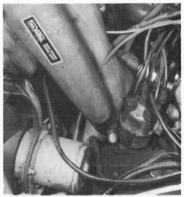

15. Connect a timing light, start the engine and adjust the initial timing. When correct, shut off the engine and tighten the holddown capscrew.

Figure 10-1. On an HEI distributor, unlatch and set aside the spark plug retainer.

Figure 10-2. Disconnect the ignition and pickup coil connectors on the HEI distributor.

DISTRIBUTOR REMOVAL

The principles of distributor removal are the same for all systems, although the exact details will vary somewhat according to manufacturer and engine. Just as with spark plug or charging system service, you may have to remove, loosen or relocate other engine accessories. On many engines, it is necessary to remove the air cleaner or air intake ducts. It may be helpful to tag all electrical leads and vacuum lines that are disconnected during distributor removal. Be sure to observe all electrical safety precautions and shop safety regulations during distributor removal.

Before removing the distributor, unclip or release the distributor cap and set it to one side with the spark plug cables attached. When removing a Delco-Remy HEI distributor with an

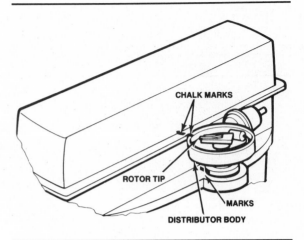

Figure 10-3. Make the alignment marks shown here before distributor removal. (Chrysler)

integral-coil cap, it is often easier to unlatch the spark plug cable retainer from the distributor cap, figure 10-1, and set the retainer and cables to one side, removing the cap with the distributor. Regardless of which you choose to do, remember to disconnect the ignition feed and pickup coil connectors from the terminal on the side of the HEI cap, figure 10-2.

Once the distributor cap is safely out of the way, you should establish a reference point for correct distributor reinstallation. Do this by making a chalk or pencil mark or a light scribe mark on the rim of the distributor housing in line with the rotor tip, figure 10-3. (Most Bosch distributors have a notch in the rim of the distributor housing indicating the number one spark plug terminal location.) Make another pair of marks in line with each other on the base of the housing and the engine block. If you cannot reach the base of the housing, simply note the position of the vacuum advance unit relative to the engine.

Many mechanics make a habit of always cranking the engine so that the rotor points in the same direction on any engine they are servicing: for example, parallel with the engine centerline and pointing forward. Another way to establish a reference position for reinstalling the distributor is to crank the engine until the timing marks are aligned at the initial timing setting for the number 1 cylinder. Then mark the rotor position on the rim of the distributor housing. This takes a bit more time, but it aids static timing when you reinstall the distributor.

Most distributors are driven by a helical gear, or bevel gear, that engages a spiral gear on the camshaft or auxiliary shaft in the engine, figure 10-4. When the distributor is removed, the

Figure 10-4. Most distributors use a drive gear that engages with a corresponding gear on the engine camshaft or auxiliary shaft.

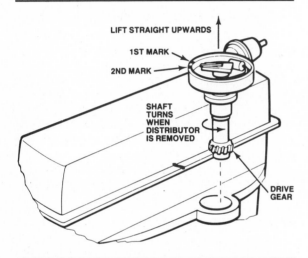

Figure 10-5. Mark the position of the rotor on the rim of the distributor housing as it moves when the distributor is removed. (Chrysler)

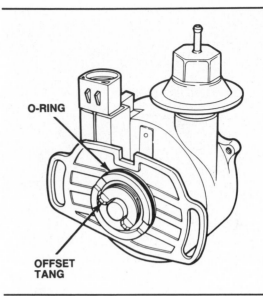

Figure 10-6. Some 4-cylinder distributors couple directly to the rear of the camshaft with an offset tang. (Ford)

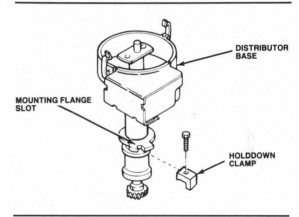

Figure 10-7. A typical distributor holddown and capscrew. (Ford)

shaft will rotate as the gear slides out of engagement with the camshaft or auxiliary shaft gear. This causes the rotor tip to move about ¼ inch (6 mm) in the direction opposite to its normal rotation, as measured relative to the distributor rim.

When removing such a distributor, stop when the gear is free of its mating gear in the engine and make a second mark on the distributor rim in line with the rotor tip, figure 10-5. This second mark will be used to align the rotor when reinstalling the distributor. As the distributor seats in the engine, the rotor tip should move and align with the first mark made. These little extra steps can save you considerable time and avoid problems when the distributor is reinstalled.

Horizontally mounted distributors used on some late-model 4-cylinder engines couple directly with the end of the camshaft by an off-

set tang on the distributor shaft, figure 10-6. Since the distributor drive connects directly to the rear of the camshaft, it is not necessary to make alignment marks. Cylinder positioning has no effect on distributor removal or installation. If the engine is turned over while the distributor is removed, it can be reinstalled without any problem. Just make sure the distributor drive tang engages the camshaft slot.

Horizontally mounted distributors usually have a pair of slotted ears that fit over two studs and are retained by nuts. Remove the distributor from the engine simply by removing the two nuts. Other distributors are generally held in the engine with a holddown clamp and capscrew. The clamp rides over a mounting flange on the distributor base, figure 10-7. After

Figure 10-8. Disconnect the primary lead from the distributor side of the coil.

the capscrew and clamp have been removed, the distributor should come free easily. On some GM 4-cylinder engines, however, the fuel pump must be removed to provide clearance for distributor removal.

Distributors that are not removed periodically tend to stick in the engine due to heat, dirt, and varnish deposits. If the distributor does not move easily, you must loosen it before you can remove it from the engine. There are several ways to do this, but *never* yank it from the engine. If you encounter this situation, try to loosen the distributor housing from the engine by holding it and gently twisting it with a rocking motion. If that does not work, squirt penetrating oil on the housing where it meets the engine and gently rock the distributor again. On some distributors, you also can attach an oil filter wrench to the housing, and *carefully* twist the housing to loosen it. As a last resort, *gently* tap the distributor housing with a soft-faced hammer.

A metal sealing ring or a neoprene O-ring may be installed between the bottom of the distributor housing and the engine, figure 10-6. Do not lose a metal sealing ring, because it must be used again. Inspect neoprene O-rings and replace them if damaged, or an oil leak may develop at the distributor base.

Some engines use an intermediate shaft between the oil pump and the distributor. The shaft should remain in the engine when the distributor is removed. However, if the inside of the engine has a lot of sludge buildup, the shaft may stick in the distributor drive gear and pull out of the oil pump as the distributor is removed. If the shaft comes all the way out with the distributor, there is no problem because it can be easily reinstalled. But if it comes part way out and then drops off the distributor into the engine, you have a serious problem. The shaft will generally fall into the front of the

oil pan or timing cover, which must be removed to retrieve it.

To avoid such problems on a small-block Ford V-8 or other engine that uses an intermediate shaft, carefully lift the distributor slowly and just enough to reach under the housing to the bottom of the drive gear. If the intermediate shaft is stuck in the distributor, grasp it and lift it out with the distributor. Since it has already pulled free of the oil pump, do not attempt to push it back in place.

To reinstall an intermediate shaft, hold the top end firmly with a gripping tool and lower the shaft into the engine. Engage the bottom of the shaft with the oil pump and release the gripping tool. Make sure the shaft is completely seated before reinstalling the distributor. If there is any question in your mind about the drive gear arrangement used on a particular engine, refer to the manufacturer's shop manual for exact information.

Use the following procedure to remove any distributor:

1. Release the distributor cap clips or holddown latches or screws. Remove the cap with wires attached and set it to one side. On HEI distributors with an integral coil:

   a. You may want to remove the cable retainers from the cap as described earlier.

   b. Unlatch the ignition feed wire (large pink wire) connector and any other wires connected to the distributor cap with a small screwdriver; then remove the connectors from the cap.

2. Align the distributor rotor as described earlier and make the necessary alignment marks.

3. Make sure the ignition switch is off. To prevent the engine from being cranked with the distributor out, it is a good idea to disconnect the battery ground cable at this time.

4. On breaker-point ignitions, disconnect the primary lead from the distributor side of the coil, figure 10-8.

5. On solid-state distributors, disconnect the pickup coil connector at the distributor. Some electronic distributors have two connectors to disconnect.

6. Disconnect any vacuum lines attached to the distributor.

7. Loosen the distributor holddown capscrew with a suitable tool. On some distributors, you can do this with a socket, extension, and ratchet. In crowded engine compartments, you may need an offset distributor wrench, figure 10-9.

8. Remove the holddown clamp and capscrew, figure 10-10.

9. Carefully loosen and remove the distributor

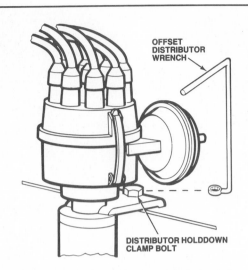

Figure 10-9. An offset distributor wrench may be needed to loosen the holddown capscrew. (Chrysler)

Figure 10-11. Remove the distributor carefully and slowly.

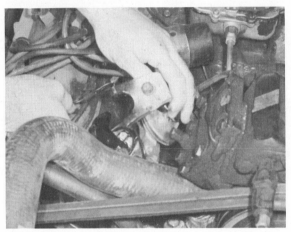

Figure 10-10. Remove the holddown clamp and capscrew.

from the engine, figure 10-11. It may be necessary to rock the distributor gently to loosen it from the engine.

10. Clean all oil, grease, dirt, and rust from the distributor shaft and housing with solvent and a brush. Keep solvent away from vacuum advance units, bushings, and electronic components.

11. If the distributor is to be serviced, install it in a bench vise with protective (soft) jaws. If protective jaws are not available, wrap the distributor housing with shop cloths.

12. If the distributor is to be tested and adjusted, install it in a distributor tester.

BREAKER-POINT DISTRIBUTOR OVERHAUL PROCEDURES

The following pages contain photographic pro-

cedures to disassemble, overhaul, and reassemble two common domestic breaker-point distributors:

● Delco-Remy 8-cylinder model — Used by GM and AMC until 1975; features external point adjustment.

● Motorcraft 8-cylinder model — Used by Ford until 1975; features internal point adjustment. Six-cylinder models are similar.

Chapter 13 of your *Classroom Manual* has information and more drawings of these distributors. You may also find it helpful to refer to the *Classroom Manual* when overhauling a distributor.

The section of this chapter following the illustrated overhaul procedures contains test procedures using a distributor tester. The distributor tester (also called a synchrograph or synchroscope) is the most useful piece of test equipment for complete distributor service. Many of the distributor test procedures should be done before the distributor is disassembled, to find out how much overhaul is needed. Other service procedures using the tester (such as point adjustment) are done after the distributor is reassembled. Many distributors can be overhauled while mounted in the tester.

Before overhauling a distributor, read and understand the test and adjustment procedures in the following section. The sequence of steps that you use for distributor test, overhaul, and adjustment should be organized for the best use of your shop time and facilities. If you don't have a distributor tester, you can mount the distributor in a vise for overhaul. Use soft jaw covers on the vise or wrap the distributor housing in clean shop cloths to prevent damage. Read the step-by-step procedure for the distributor that you will be overhauling before you begin work.

DELCO-REMY 8-CYLINDER DISTRIBUTOR OVERHAUL PROCEDURE

1. Mount distributor in vise or tester and remove cap by turning two latch screws with screwdriver. Remove two screws from rotor. Remove rotor.

2. Unhook advance springs from pins on shaft and cam base. Mark springs and pins so that springs are reinstalled in original positions.

3. Remove advance weights. Mark weights so that they are reinstalled in their original positions.

4. Some distributors have 2-piece RFI shields that must be removed for access to breaker plate. Remove primary lead and condenser lead from breaker-point terminal.

5. Loosen or remove two screws and slide point assembly off breaker plate. In Uniset assembly, condenser is attached to points.

6. Remove screw securing condenser to breaker plate. Remove condenser.

7. Remove screw securing vacuum advance unit inside distributor. Then remove screw securing vacuum unit to rim of housing.

8. Disengage vacuum advance link from breaker plate. Then use screwdriver to release grommet on primary lead from housing. Remove primary lead.

9. To begin reassembly, press grommet of new primary lead into housing from inside. Engage vacuum advance link with breaker plate.

DELCO-REMY 8-CYLINDER DISTRIBUTOR OVERHAUL PROCEDURE

10. Place locator dimple on advance unit in hole in housing.

11. Hold primary lead aside and install screw securing vacuum unit inside distributor.

12. Attach breaker plate ground lead to screw and install screw to secure vacuum unit to rim of distributor.

13. Attach condenser to breaker plate with screw. Engage breaker point assembly with two screws on breaker plate. Tighten screws.

14. Slip primary lead and condenser lead into spring-loaded terminal on breaker points.

15. Apply *one drop* of lubricant to spring pins on distributor shaft and cam base.

16. Assemble weights on cam base and shaft. Be sure they are returned to their original positions.

17. Install springs on pins in their original positions. Align square and round locators on rotor with holes in cam base. Install rotor with two screws.

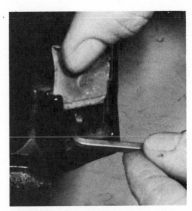

18. With distributor in engine, dwell is adjusted through window in cap. Adjust dwell by turning adjustment screw with allen wrench. Install RFI shield after adjustment.

MOTORCRAFT 8-CYLINDER DISTRIBUTOR OVERHAUL PROCEDURE

1. Remove spring clip securing vacuum advance link. Remove two screws securing vacuum advance. Remove vacuum advance.

2. Disconnect primary lead and condenser lead from terminal.

3. Remove points and condenser from breaker plate. Disconnect one end of ground wire. Remove primary lead from housing.

4. Remove two screws securing breaker plate and ground wire. Remove breaker plate and ground wire.

5. Clean breaker plate and inspect for wear. Lubricate pivot points *sparingly*.

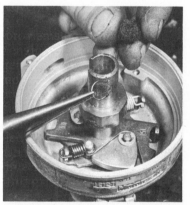

6. Remove lubricating wick and cam retainer from center of cam.

7. Mark one advance weight, its spring, its spring bracket, and its pivot pin. Remove both weight springs.

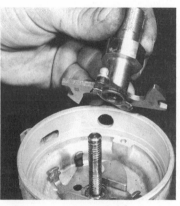

8. Remove cam and thrust washer from shaft.

9. Remove drive gear, if worn, by driving out roll pin securing gear to shaft. To remove shaft, drive out pin securing collar to shaft.

MOTORCRAFT 8-CYLINDER DISTRIBUTOR OVERHAUL PROCEDURE

10. Replace O-ring on housing, if worn. Press worn bushing out of housing. Press in new one.

11. Reassemble shaft and housing. Install drive gear and collar with roll pins. Lubricate shaft. Install thrust washer and cam on shaft.

12. Lubricate weight pivot pins and spring pins *sparingly*. Reinstall springs in their original positions, as marked at disassembly.

13. Apply small amount of distributor cam lubricant to cam. Install cam retainer and lubricating wick. Apply one or two drops of oil to wick.

14. Install breaker plate assembly. Secure plate to distributor with two screws. One end of ground wire goes under screw by primary lead hole.

15. Inspect primary lead for wear. Replace worn lead.

16. Engage vacuum advance link with pin on breaker plate; secure with spring clip. Attach vacuum unit to housing with two screws.

17. Install points and condenser. Secure ground wire to one breaker-point screw. Attach primary and condenser leads to terminal.

18. Place rubbing block on high point of cam. Adjust point gap to specifications with feeler gauge and screwdriver. Install rotor.

Figure 10-12. A distributor tester is a valuable piece of equipment for complete distributor service. (Sun)

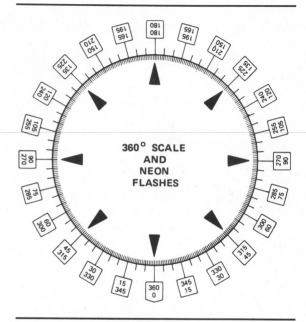

Figure 10-13. The synchronizing scale on the distributor tester is a movable ring, graduated in 1-degree increments. The arrow-shaped flashing lights indicate the distributor firing for each engine cylinder.

BREAKER-POINT DISTRIBUTOR TEST AND ADJUSTMENT

The distributor tester, or synchrograph, figure 10-12, is an electronic test machine in which you can mount a distributor for testing and service when it is removed from an engine. Many of the overhaul steps listed in the preceding section of this chapter can be done with the distributor mounted in a tester. Before overhauling any distributor, you should test it for cam, shaft, and bushing wear and for centrifugal and vacuum advance operation to find out how much overhaul is required.

The distributor tester has a fixture for mounting the distributor and a motor to drive it for testing. The motor or drive mechanism is reversible so that the distributor can be rotated clockwise (right-hand drive) or counterclockwise (left-hand drive), as needed. The drive speed also is variable so that the distributor can be rotated at different speeds. Rotation speed is shown on the tester's tachometer.

Electrical test leads from the tester are connected to the breaker-point primary lead and to ground on the distributor housing. These leads provide primary current through the points for testing. This primary connection through the breaker points operates the tachometer and the dwellmeter that are built into the tester. The circuit also operates the stroboscopic synchronizing scale that surrounds the distributor drive fixture on the tester.

The synchronizing scale is a 360-degree ring, with each degree marked. Each time the breaker points open, the tester circuitry triggers an arrow-shaped neon light. There will be as many light flashes per revolution as there are lobes on the distributor cam, figure 10-13. For most distributors, there are as many cam lobes as there are engine cylinders. Therefore, each flash represents the firing of each cylinder in firing order sequence. Because of the stroboscopic effect of the flashing lights, the arrows appear to stand still as they flash. At medium and high distributor speeds, the arrows for all cylinders appear to be always lit.

The scale ring on the tester can be moved so that you can align it at the starting points for the number of cylinders in the engine. For an 8-cylinder engine (8-lobe distributor cam), the flashes appear 45 degrees apart. For an even-firing 6-cylinder engine, the flashes are 60 degrees apart, and 90 degrees apart for a 4-cylinder engine. Remember that the degrees and speed of distributor rotation are one-half the degrees and speed of engine rotation.

Because the flashing lights on the synchronizing scale show the distributor firing for each cylinder, variations in dwell and timing can be seen among the cylinders. When the distributor centrifugal and vacuum advance mechanisms are operated, the flashing lights will move around the scale. This enables you to test the exact amount of spark advance at any distributor speed and with any amount of vacuum.

Figure 10-14. Installing a distributor in the tester.

Figure 10-15. Tighten the drive chuck on the distributor drive gear or shaft. Do not allow the distributor to bottom in the chuck.

Many testers have a built-in vacuum pump to operate the vacuum advance unit. Others may have a condenser tester and an ohmmeter.

The following paragraphs explain the operation of the distributor tester and its use for specific tests and adjustment.

Pretest Inspection

Before testing any distributor, check it for obvious problems:
1. Look for binding or excessive end play and side play in the shaft and worn or chipped drive gear teeth.
2. Check the cam lobes for wear.
3. Check for a loose breaker plate and worn breaker plate bearings.
4. Look for signs of inadequate lubrication.
5. Check the condition of electrical leads and connections.
6. Inspect the condition of the breaker-point surfaces.

Distributor Installation in the Tester

Before mounting the distributor in the tester, clean off any dirt, oil, or grease. Dirt and grime can damage the tester and make distributor service more difficult. Mount the distributor in the tester as follows:
1. Raise the clamp arms so that the distributor will clear the chuck.
2. Place the distributor in the clamp arms so they will grip the largest machined surface on

the distributor body, figure 10-14. Use a sleeve adapter to protect any O-rings on the distributor. Some tester manufacturers will specify that the vacuum unit should be pointing in a certain direction.
3. Tighten the clamp arms *lightly*.
4. If necessary, slip rubber tubing over the distributor drive gear to protect it from the chuck.
5. Lower the distributor until the gear or shaft is in the tester chuck. Do not allow the shaft to bottom in the chuck. Use a drive adapter, if necessary.
6. Tighten the chuck, figure 10-15, and the clamp arms.
7. Remove the distributor rotor. Turn the distributor shaft by hand to be sure it rotates freely.
8. If required, calibrate the tester dwellmeter as follows:
    a. Connect the two tester leads together.
    b. Turn the dwellmeter switch to the "Calibrate" position.
    c. Turn the motor switch to the proper direction of rotation.
    d. Turn the dwellmeter calibration knob until the meter reads on the "Set" line.
    e. Before testing, turn the dwellmeter switch to the correct position for the number of engine cylinders.
9. Connect the tester's insulated lead (usually red) to the distributor primary lead. Connect the tester's ground lead (usually black) to a grounding stud on the tester or to the distributor housing, figure 10-16.

Figure 10-16. Connect the tester leads to the distributor as shown here.

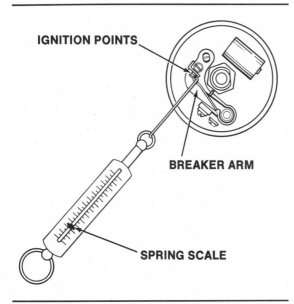

Figure 10-17. Measuring breaker-point spring tension.

Point Spring Tension Test

If the old points are going to remain in the distributor, their spring tension should be checked. Tension also should be checked (and adjusted, if necessary) after installing new points. Spring tension usually is specified in the 15- to 25-ounce (425- to 710-gram) range, but check the manufacturer's specifications for the exact setting. You can check spring tension quickly and easily with a distributor tester and a spring tension scale:

1. Rotate the distributor shaft to close the points.
2. Set the tester "motor" switch to the correct rotation direction.

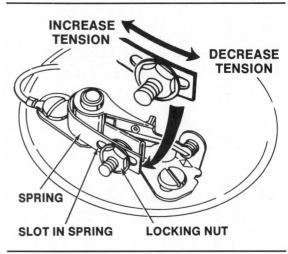

Figure 10-18. Breaker-point spring tension adjustment.

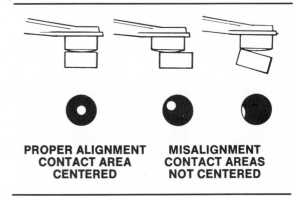

Figure 10-19. Breaker-point alignment and misalignment.

3. Hook the tension scale over the movable point arm and slowly pull at a right angle to the point arm, figure 10-17. Do not drag the scale on the distributor housing.
4. Note the scale reading when the tester arrow flashes or the dwellmeter starts to drop to zero.
5. If tension is out of specifications, adjust it by moving the slotted hole in the spring, figure 10-18. If tension cannot be adjusted within limits, replace the point set.
6. Check for binding at the pivot point by slowly closing the points and noting the spring tension scale reading when the dwellmeter starts to rise from zero.
7. If the spring tension is the same when the points open as when they close, there is no pivot point binding. If the tension varies, there is binding. Binding often can be corrected by lubricating the pivot point with *one drop* of penetrating oil. If this does not cure the problem, replace the point set.

Figure 10-20. Turn the speed control knob to control distributor rotation speed.

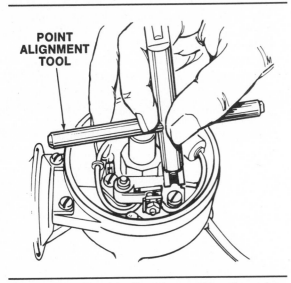

POINT ALIGNMENT TOOL

Figure 10-21. Bend the fixed (ground) breaker point to adjust point alignment. Do not bend the movable point arm.

Breaker-Point Alignment

The breaker-point surfaces should be aligned so that the centers of their surfaces contact squarely, figure 10-19. Misalignment will shorten breaker-point life and can cause erratic ignition operation. Align the breaker points as follows:

1. Operate the distributor at about 1,000 rpm in the distributor tester, figure 10-20.
2. View the points from above and from one side. You should see a small spark near the centers of the contact surfaces.
3. If the spark is near the centers of the sur-

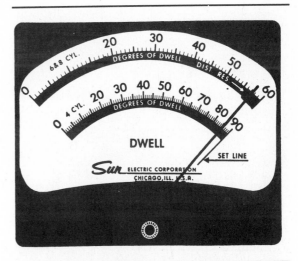

Figure 10-22. The dwell meter should read within the "Points Resistance" area if the distributor resistance is within limits. (Sun)

faces, the points are correctly aligned.
4. If the spark if off-center, bend the ground (fixed) breaker point with a bending tool, figure 10-21, to correct the alignment. Do not bend the movable point arm.

Rubbing Block Alignment

The point set rubbing block must contact the cam squarely to ensure long point life and to prevent dwell change. To check rubbing block alignment, operate the distributor at about 1,000 rpm in the tester and look at the rubbing block and cam contact surfaces. They should meet squarely. If not, replace the point set. Also check the breaker plate for looseness or misalignment.

Breaker Point and Distributor Resistance Test

Test the resistance of the point contact surfaces and of the primary connections within the distributor. High resistance will harm the overall ignition performance. Make these tests after the distributor has been run in the tester for a few minutes to burn any oxidation off the contact surfaces of the points.

1. Stop the distributor with the breaker points closed.
2. Turn the dwellmeter switch to the "Calibrate" position.
3. The dwellmeter should read within the "Distributor Resistance" area at the end of the scale, figure 10-22. Normal resistance is the same as the 0.2-volt drop that you can measure with a voltmeter when testing the distributor in the car.

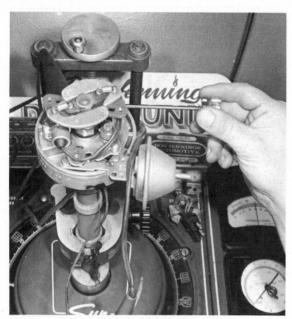

Figure 10-23. Adjusting the dwell on a Delco-Remy external adjustment distributor.

4. If the dwellmeter does not read within the correct area, take the following steps to locate and correct the high resistance:
   a. Repeat the test with the red tester lead connected directly to the movable breaker point.
   b. If the results are within limits, replace the distributor primary wire. Be sure the connection to the points is clean and tight.
   c. If the results in step 4a are out of limits, clean the points by drawing a smooth, clean piece of heavy paper between the closed contact surfaces. Do not try to file the points or clean them with emery cloth.
   d. If the results are still out of limits, repeat the test with the red test lead connected to the grounded breaker point. If the results remain out of limits, check for a loose or dirty attachment of the breaker plate to the distributor housing.
   e. If the distributor resistance is still out of limits after these tests, replace the breaker points and repeat the sequence.

Dwell Adjustment

Dwell adjustment with the distributor mounted in the tester is the fastest and most precise way to set dwell. If you plan to leave the old breaker points in the distributor, make all of the preceding tests and adjustments described in this section *before* making the final dwell adjustment. If you have installed new breaker points, you will find it easier to make an initial dwell adjustment before checking spring tension,

alignment, and the other points we already described. You should also recheck the dwell setting as the final step before removing the distributor from the tester.

Do not lubricate the cam and breaker point rubbing block before making the final dwell adjustment. Allowing the distributor to operate for a few minutes without lubricant between the cam and rubbing block will burnish the rubbing block surface and reduce its initial wear when the distributor is put back into service. This means that the dwell adjustment will not change as quickly or as much between distributor service intervals. Lubricate the cam and rubbing block after dwell adjustment.

You will need the carmaker's specifications for the dwell angle of the particular distributor being serviced. These are listed in various specification manuals, such as Chek-Chart's **Car Care Guide**, by distributor part number or by car make, model, engine, and year. The dwell angle will be listed as a range (28 degrees to 32 degrees, for example) or as a nominal setting with a tolerance (30 degrees ±2 degrees). In both cases, adjust the dwell toward the lower end of the specification. In the example above, set the dwell at 28 degrees, 29 degrees, or 30 degrees. This will allow for rubbing block wear and the gradual increase in dwell angle during distributor use.

Adjust the dwell angle in a single-point distributor as follows:
1. Set the dwellmeter switch for the correct number of engine cylinders or distributor cam lobes.
2. Make sure the tester leads are correctly connected and that the tester is set for the correct direction of rotation.
3. Operate the tester to rotate the distributor at about 300 rpm.
4. Watch the dwellmeter and adjust the dwell angle to specifications as follows:
   a. Delco-Remy external adjustment distributor — Fit an Allen wrench into the point adjusting screw, figure 10-23. Turn the screw clockwise to increase dwell angle or counterclockwise to decrease dwell angle.
   b. Internal adjustment distributor — Loosen the point mounting screw, if required. Turn the point adjusting screw, figure 10-24A, or move the point base by inserting a screwdriver in the slotted hole, figure 10-24B. Tighten the mounting screw after adjustment.

Dwell Angle Variation Test

Manufacturers allow for a small change in the dwell angle as engine speed increases. This is

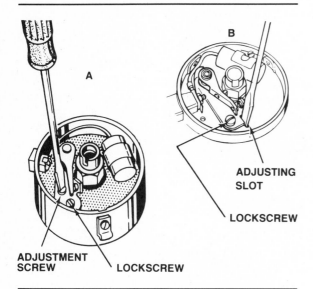

Figure 10-24. Dwell adjustment points for an internal adjustment distributor.

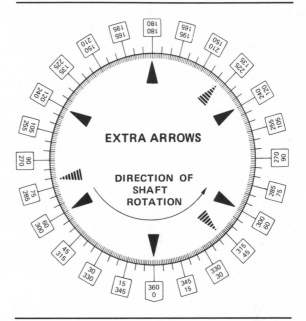

Figure 10-25. Extra arrows, or ghost flashes, on the synchronizing scale indicate point bounce.

called dwell variation. The amount of allowable dwell variation differs for various distributors. Once again, you must know the specifications. Generally, the amount of dwell variation is greater for distributors with side-pivot breaker plates than for those with center-pivot breaker plates. Too much dwell variation is usually caused by a worn or loose breaker plate, worn bushings, or a bent distributor shaft.

Test for dwell variation as follows:
1. Operate the distributor at 300 rpm or the speed at which you adjusted the dwell angle.
2. Watch the dwell meter while slowly increasing distributor speed to 2,500 rpm.
3. If the dwell changes more than the allowable variation, look for a worn shaft, bushing, or breaker plate.
4. Reduce the distributor speed to 200 rpm.
5. Connect the tester vacuum line to the distributor vacuum advance unit.
6. Watch the dwellmeter while applying 15 to 20 inch (380 to 510 mm) Hg of vacuum.
7. If dwell changes more than the allowable variation, look for a loose breaker plate or worn breaker plate bearings.

Point Float Test

This is similar to the dwell variation test and determines whether the points are closing at the proper time. If they remain open longer than they should, the dwell angle will be reduced.
1. Operate the distributor at 300 rpm or the speed at which you adjusted the dwell angle.
2. Watch the dwellmeter while slowly increasing distributor speed to 2,500 rpm.

3. Watch for a sudden decrease in the dwell angle.
4. If the dwell angle drops sharply, the points have floated, or remained open, for part of the dwell period. This is usually caused by weak spring tension or binding at the breaker point pivot.

Point Bounce Test

Use this test to determine whether the points close, bounce open, and then reclose at the start of the dwell period.
1. Operate the distributor from 300 rpm to 2,500 rpm.
2. Watch the flashing arrows; look for double flashes or ghost arrows, figure 10-25.
3. There should be as many sharp flashing arrows as there are lobes on the distributor cam. Any extra arrows or double (uneven) flashes at any point indicate that the points are bouncing. This is usually caused by incorrect spring tension, misaligned points, or binding at the breaker-point pivot.

Cam Lobe, Bushing, and Shaft Wear Test

This test will determine whether all of the cam lobes are an equal distance from each other, or whether any of them are worn. It will also show wear in the distributor bushings or shaft.
1. Operate the distributor at 1,000 rpm.
2. Rotate the degree ring on the synchronizing

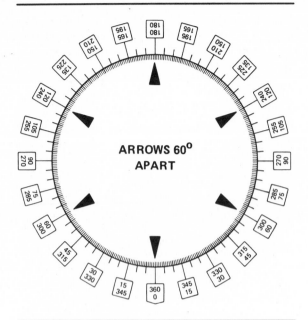

Figure 10-26. The flashing arrows should be evenly spaced around the degree ring. This pattern is for a 6-lobe distributor cam.

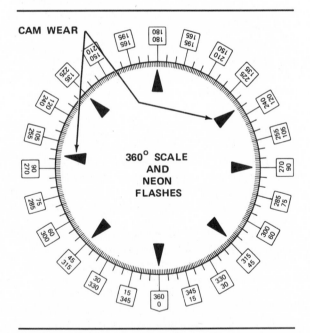

Figure 10-27. Cam wear is indicated if some arrows flash late, while others flash at the correct position.

scale until the zero point aligns with any one of the flashing arrows, figure 10-26.
3. Watch the position on the degree ring of each of the other flashing arrows. They should be evenly spaced, ±1 degree, as follows:
● 4-lobe cam — every 90 degrees
● 6-lobe cam — every 60 degrees (even firing)
● 8-lobe cam — every 45 degrees.

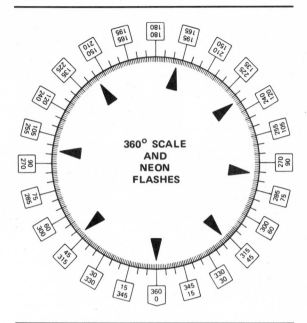

Figure 10-28. Shaft or bushing wear is indicated if the entire pattern is shifted like this.

4. If the flashing arrows are evenly spaced and within 1 degree of their correct positions, figure 10-26, the distributor cam, shaft, and bushings are not worn.
5. If the flashing arrows are not in their correct positions, look for these two general conditions:
   a. If any one arrow, or several arrows at random locations, are out of position, it means a worn cam lobe, figure 10-27. These arrows will flash later than they should on the degree ring.
   b. If the entire pattern of flashing arrows gradually shifts out of position from the zero point on the degree ring, figure 10-28, and the arrow at the 180-degree point is the farthest out of position, look for a bent shaft or worn bushings.

Distributor Spark Advance Tests

The distributor centrifugal and vacuum advance mechanisms can both be tested and adjusted in the distributor tester. Distributor advance specifications are called advance curves and are essential for precise testing. Curves are listed for each distributor by the manufacturer's part number. You must know its part number before you can test a distributor. You will find the part number on the side of the distributor housing.

Distributor advance specifications may be given in engine speed and degrees, or in distributor speed and degrees. To use a distributor tester, you need specifications in distributor

DISTRIBUTOR PART NO.	CENTRIFUGAL ADVANCE IN DISTRIBUTOR DEGREES AT DISTRIBUTOR RPM						VACUUM ADVANCE— (MAX. DIST. DEG AT IN. Hg)
	START	INTERMEDIATE	INTERMEDIATE	INTERMEDIATE	INTERMEDIATE	MAXIMUM	
1112062 (Delco)	0–2.4 @ 625	7.5–10 @ 950	8–10 @ 960	—	—	13–15 @ 2200	10° @ 13–14.75″
1111956 (Delco)	0–3.5 @ 550	1.3–4.8 @ 583	9.5–11.5 @ 1000	—	—	15–17 @ 2200	13° @ 16–17.5″
721F-AHA (Ford)	0–1 @ 500	1–3 @ 750	5–7 @ 1000	6–8 @ 1250	7–9 @ 1500	9.5–11.5 @ 2000	4.2°–7.2° @ 10″
D30F-BA (Ford)	0–1.5 @ 500	4–6 @ 750	4.5–6.5 @ 1000	5.2–7.4 @ 1250	6–8.2 @ 1500	7.2–10 @ 2000	6.5°–9.2° @ 10″
3656780 (Chrysler)	1–3.5 @ 500	10–12.5 @ 800	—	11.2–13.2 @ 1250	—	13–15 @ 1750	9.5°–12.5° @ 15″
3755365 (Chrysler)	1–4 @ 650	8–10 @ 800	8.7–10.7 @ 1000	7.5–11.5 @ 1250	—	12–14 @ 2000	9.5°–12.5° @ 15″

Figure 10-29. Typical manufacturer's distributor advance specifications.

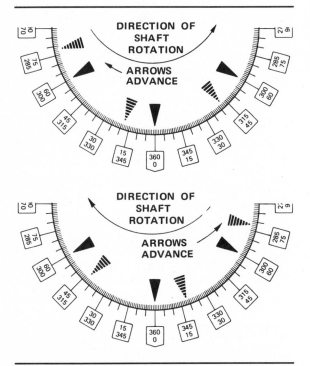

Figure 10-30. The arrows will advance in the direction opposite to shaft rotation. (Sun)

speed and degrees. If the specifications are given in engine speed and degrees, simply divide them both by two.

Centrifugal advance curves begin with a starting point that lists zero degrees of advance (sometimes 0 to 1 degree) at a given speed. This means that there should be no advance below this speed and that the advance should start at this speed. One or more intermediate points are then tested, giving the number of degrees of advance at higher speeds. Finally, the full centrifugal advance is listed at a specific speed. There should be no more advance above this speed.

Vacuum advance curves are listed as the number of degrees of advance with a certain amount of vacuum applied to the diaphragm, such as: 8 degrees at 16 inch (405 mm) Hg

vacuum. Vacuum advance is tested with the distributor operating below the starting speed for the centrifugal advance. This prevents any centrifugal advance from being added to the vacuum advance and giving false test results. Figure 10-29 shows typical centrifugal and vacuum advance specifications for several distributors.

Centrifugal advance test and adjustment

1. Operate the distributor at about 200 rpm.
2. Rotate the degree ring so that the zero point is aligned with any of the flashing arrows.
3. Increase the distributor speed to the specified starting point of the advance curve.
4. Record the position of the arrow on the degree ring. It should remain at zero or show only about 1 degree of advance.
5. Increase the distributor speed to the next specified point and record the position of the arrow on the degree ring. It should indicate the specified amount of spark advance. If the distributor rotates clockwise, the flashing arrows will advance counterclockwise around the degree ring, figure 10-30. If it rotates counterclockwise, the arrows will advance clockwise.
6. Repeat step 6 for the remaining intermediate points in the advance specifications.
7. Increase the distributor speed to the speed listed for full centrifugal advance and record the position of the arrow on the degree ring.
8. Increase the distributor speed 200 to 400 rpm above the full centrifugal advance speed. There should be no more spark advance.
9. Reduce the distributor speed to each point listed in the specifications, recording the position of the arrow on the degree ring as the speed is decreased. The arrows should move backward smoothly, showing the same amount of advance at each point of decreasing speed that they showed with increasing speed. If the arrows move unevenly or if they do not show the same amount of advance at each point with decreasing speed, the advance weights are sticking or the springs may be weak or broken.

Figure 10-31. Adjusting the centrifugal advance on an internal adjustment distributor.

If the amount of centrifugal advance is out of limits at any point in the specifications, the advance mechanism must be cleaned and lubricated or adjusted, or the springs and weights must be replaced. If the advance is bad at low speeds, but good at high speeds, look for wear, binding, or dirt. If the advance is bad at all speeds, look for broken or binding springs or weights.

You can adjust the advance on many internal adjustment distributors by reaching through a slot in the breaker plate with a screwdriver and bending the spring anchors, figure 10-31. Bend the anchors outward to increase spring tension and slow down the advance. Bend the anchors inward to decrease spring tension and speed up or increase the advance. Adjust both the primary and the secondary advance weights. Repeat the tests after adjusting or replacing any parts.

If the advance is out of limits on a Delco-Remy external adjustment distributor, you may be able to correct it by stretching or shortening the ends of the springs. However, this is not a very precise way to adjust the centrifugal advance. It is better to replace the springs with new ones of the correct part number. You also may need to replace the weights to correct the centrifugal advance.

Vacuum advance test and adjustment
1. Operate the distributor at about 200 rpm. Keep distributor speed constant during this test.
2. Rotate the degree ring until the zero point is aligned with any one of the flashing arrows.
3. Connect the tester vacuum line to the dis-

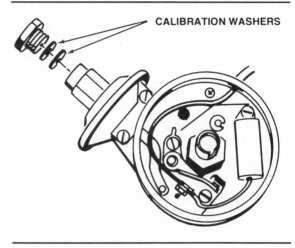

Figure 10-32. Vacuum advance adjustment with calibration washers.

tributor vacuum advance diaphragm and adjust the tester vacuum pump for zero inch Hg or mm Hg of vacuum.
4. Slowly increase the vacuum, noting the amount of vacuum when the arrow first moves off the zero point.
5. Increase vacuum to the first test point in the specifications and record the position of the arrow on the degree ring.
6. Repeat step 5 for each remaining intermediate point in the vacuum advance specifications.
7. Increase the vacuum to the full amount specified and record the position of the arrow on the degree ring.
8. Reduce the vacuum to zero. The arrow should return to the zero position of the degree ring.
9. Stop the distributor rotation.

If the amount of vacuum advance is out of limits at any point in the specifications, the vacuum unit must be adjusted or replaced. Delco-Remy vacuum advance units must be replaced if out of limits; most Ford vacuum advance units can be adjusted by one of two methods, depending upon design.

Autolite and Holley distributors used before 1972 are adjusted by changing calibration washers inside the vacuum advance unit. This type of unit has a removable hex-head plug in the end of the housing, figure 10-32. Some Chrysler and Prestolite distributors also can be adjusted in this way. To adjust this type of unit, remove the plug from the end of the housing. Add washers to decrease advance; remove washers to increase advance. Often, removing one washer and replacing it with another of a slightly different thickness will provide a fine degree of adjustment.

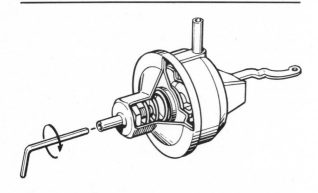

Figure 10-33. Vacuum advance adjustment with an internal screw.

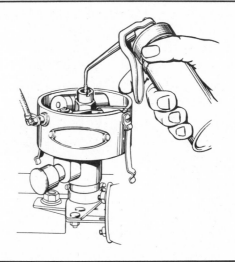

Figure 10-35. If the distributor has a felt wick in the top of the shaft, apply two or three drops of light engine oil.

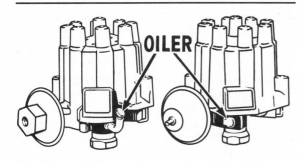

Figure 10-34. If a distributor has an oil or grease cup, apply the recommended lubricant during service.

Autolite and Motorcraft distributors used from 1972 until the late 1970's are adjusted by inserting an Allen wrench through the vacuum hose nipple in the end of the housing and turning an internal nut, figure 10-33. Turn the wrench clockwise to increase advance or counterclockwise to decrease it. Make adjustments in small increments and check advance after each change.

After advance is adjusted at one vacuum setting, check the advance points at other specified vacuum settings. Do not change the distributor speed from the original rpm setting while checking the vacuum advance points. If the other vacuum advance points are not within limits, there is leakage in the vacuum unit or line, or a defective spring. Replace a bad vacuum unit.

On dual-diaphragm distributors, which provide both vacuum advance and retard, test the retard diaphragm before adjusting the advance diaphragm. If the retard diaphragm is not working correctly, the advance diaphragm cannot be adjusted accurately. Retard diaphragms are not adjustable, and the entire vacuum unit must be replaced if it is bad.

Distributor Cleaning and Lubrication

Rust, dirt, grease, and varnish tend to collect inside a distributor while it is operating. Accumulated dirt and grime will affect centrifugal advance operation and can cause crossfiring and short circuits in the electrical connections. Always clean a distributor thoroughly when servicing it.

Distributor lubrication is equally important. Proper lubrication is essential for correct operation. Too much lubrication is as bad as not enough lubrication. The centrifugal force of distributor rotation will spray excess lubricant around the inside of the distributor, creating more dirt and causing burned points and short circuits.

The moving parts of a distributor should be cleaned and lubricated (with one exception) *before* the dwell and advance mechanisms are adjusted. The exception is point rubbing block and cam: lubricate these *after* dwell adjustment.

Clean the inside of the distributor with solvent and a small brush. Wipe dirt off with a clean, lint-free cloth. Remove the vacuum advance unit before cleaning or be careful not to get solvent on the diaphragm. Make sure that all dirt and solvent residue is removed from all electrical connections. Dry the inside of the distributor with low-pressure compressed air.

When servicing an older distributor with an oil cup or a grease cup for bushing lubrication, figure 10-34, use the oil or grease specified by the carmaker. Distributors may have a felt wick in the top of the shaft, figure 10-35. Apply two or three drops of light motor oil to the wick.

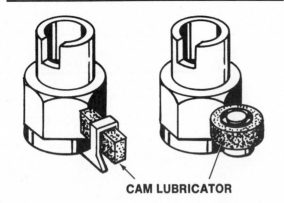

CAM LUBRICATOR

Figure 10-36. These felt lubricators for the cam should be replaced during service.

Other distributors have a felt lubrication wick that rubs against the cam during operation, figure 10-36. Replace these lubricators during service; do not try to oil them.

Lubricate the contact and pivot points of the centrifugal advance weights and springs with a light coat of distributor cam lubricant or one or two small drops of penetrating oil. Lubricate the breaker point pivot with *one drop* of penetrating oil, or a light film of distributor cam lubricant when the points are replaced.

If the distributor has no grease or oil cup, apply a few drops of motor oil to the shaft through the drive end of the housing and rotate the shaft manually to ensure adequate lubrication before reinstalling the distributor. After the final dwell adjustment is made, apply a light film of special distributor cam lubricant to the cam lobes and rubbing block. Remember to be very careful in keeping all lubricants off the points, cap, rotor, and all electrical connections.

Before reinstalling the distributor in the engine, install the RFI shield, if used, and the rotor.

SOLID-STATE ELECTRONIC DISTRIBUTOR OVERHAUL PROCEDURES

The following pages contain photographic procedures to disassemble, overhaul, and reassemble six common domestic solid-state distributors:
- Delco-Remy 8-cylinder HEI model — Used by GM since 1974.
- Delco-Remy 4-cylinder HEI-EST model — Contains both a magnetic pulse signal generator and a Hall-effect switch.
- Motorcraft Dura-Spark model — Used by Ford since 1977. This distributor also is typical of the earlier solid-state ignition (SSI) distributor used by Ford since 1974 and AMC since 1978.
- Motorcraft Universal TFI-I model — Introduced on 1982 4-cylinder Escort engines. This distributor contains a magnetic pulse signal generator; TFI-IV models are similar but have a Hall-effect switch.
- Chrysler 8-cylinder electronic ignition model — Used by Chrysler since 1972. This distributor is also typical of Chrysler lean-burn distributors.
- Chrysler 4-cylinder Hall-effect model — Variations of this distributor have been used since 1978. The one shown in the sequence is a 1986 version used on the 2.5-liter engine.

Chapter 13 of your *Classroom Manual* has information and more drawings of these distributors. You may also find it helpful to refer to the *Classroom Manual* when overhauling a distributor.

The section of this chapter following the illustrated overhaul procedures contains test procedures using a distributor tester. The distributor tester was described fully earlier in this chapter. Many of the test procedures should be done before the distributor is disassembled, in order to find out how much overhaul is needed. Other service procedures using the tester are done after the distributor is reassembled. Many distributors can be overhauled while mounted in the tester.

Before overhauling a distributor, read and understand the test and adjustment procedures in the following section. The sequence of steps that you use for distributor test, overhaul, and adjustment should be organized for the best use of your shop time and facilities. If you don't have a distributor tester, you can mount the distributor in a vise for overhaul. Use soft jaw covers on the vise or wrap the distributor housing in clean shop cloths to prevent damage. Read the step-by-step procedure for the distributor that you will be overhauling before you begin work.

DELCO-REMY 8-CYLINDER HEI DISTRIBUTOR OVERHAUL PROCEDURE

1. Carefully pry module connector from cap terminal with screwdriver. Release four latches. Remove cap and coil from distributor. Inspect cap for signs of crossfiring.

2. Remove three screws trom coil cover. Remove four coil mounting screws. Coil is grounded with lead to one screw and at other screw near screwdriver. Remove coil.

3. Remove rubber seal, carbon button, and spring. Replace seal if brittle. Button and spring are secondary coil lead. Replace if worn or spring is broken.

4. Remove rotor from weight base. Unplug pickup coil leads from module. Test pickup coil resistance with ohmmeter across these leads. If not within limits, replace coil.

5. Unplug connector from B+ and C terminals on module. Remove primary lead grommet from distributor housing.

6. Remove two screws securing module. Remove module. Note silicone grease on module and mounting base. Grease must be applied when module is installed.

7. Remove screw securing RFI capacitor. Lift capacitor and primary lead harness from distributor.

8. Unplug capacitor from primary lead. Inspect and test capacitor and primary lead for wear, continuity, and short circuits. Replace worn or damaged parts.

9. Remove two springs and weight retainer. Remove weights. Mark springs, pins, and weights so that they are reinstalled in their original positions.

DELCO-REMY 8-CYLINDER HEI DISTRIBUTOR OVERHAUL PROCEDURE

10. Shaft must be removed to remove pickup coil and pole piece. Support gear as shown. Drive roll pin from gear and shaft.

11. Remove gear, shim, and tanged washer. Note positions for reassembly. Dimple toward bottom of gear must align with rotor tip when reassembled.

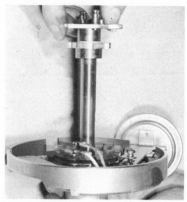

12. Remove shaft, trigger wheel, and weight base from distributor. Do not bump or nick bushings when removing shaft. Trigger wheel can be separated from shaft.

13. Remove three screws securing pole piece to pickup coil. Remove pole piece. Remove rubber gasket beneath pole piece.

14. Remove pickup coil from retainer. During operation, retainer is rotated by vacuum advance mechanism.

15. Carefully pry this small wave-washer from its slot. It holds pickup coil retainer to bushing at top of housing.

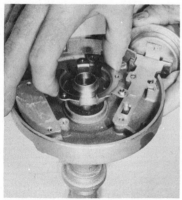

16. Remove pickup coil retainer from vacuum advance link. Remove two screws securing vacuum unit. Remove vacuum unit.

17. Lubricate or replace felt washer beneath pickup coil retainer. Apply silicone grease to module mounting base.

18. Install vacuum advance unit. Install pickup coil retainer and its retaining ring. Install pickup coil and gasket.

DELCO-REMY 8-CYLINDER HEI DISTRIBUTOR OVERHAUL PROCEDURE

19. Assemble trigger wheel and weight base to distributor shaft.

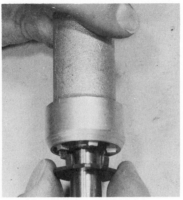

20. Insert shaft into housing. Be careful not to hit bushings. Assemble tanged washer, shim, and gear on shaft.

21. To be sure gear is correctly installed, place rotor on top of weight base. Be sure dimple on gear aligns with rotor tip. Drive roll pin through gear and shaft.

22. Install weights in their original positions on weight base. Place retainer over pins and shaft. Install springs in their original positions.

23. Plug capacitor into primary lead harness. Attach capacitor to distributor with screw. Insert harness grommet into slot in housing.

24. Place module on mounting base and secure with two screws. Attach primary connector to one end, pickup coil leads to other end.

25. Thoroughly inspect rotor for signs of carbon tracking and crossfiring. Check the underside for signs of burn-through. Replace rotor if it has any of these signs.

26. Be sure carbon button, spring, and rubber seal are in good condition and correctly installed. Install coil in cap.

27. Install four coil mounting screws. Install coil cover. Install cap on distributor and secure four holddown latches.

DELCO-REMY 4-CYLINDER HEI-EST DISTRIBUTOR OVERHAUL PROCEDURE

1. Pull the rotor straight off the shaft. Unclip and disconnect the leads on both sides of the HEI-EST module (A), then remove the module screws (B).

2. Remove the HEI-EST module from the distributor base. Clean the base of any silicone lubricant left by the module.

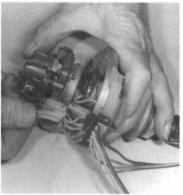

3. Carefully unclip the electrical connector from the Hall-effect switch. This switch is used to provide the EST signal.

4. Remove the two screws holding the Hall-effect switch to the pick-up coil assembly. Remove the Hall-effect switch from the distributor.

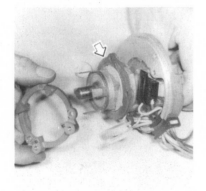

5. Remove the three screws holding the pole piece and magnet. Remove the pole piece first, then remove the magnet (arrow).

6. Loosen the screw holding the wiring harness to the distributor housing. Remove the wiring harness from the housing.

7. Remove the drive gear roll pin (arrow) with a suitable punch. Remove the drive gear, small washer, spring assembly, and large washer.

8. Deburr the distributor shaft with crocus cloth to prevent damage to the housing bushings when the shaft is removed.

9. Carefully withdraw the shaft with the attached Hall-effect shutter and trigger wheel from the distributor housing.

DELCO-REMY 4-CYLINDER HEI-EST DISTRIBUTOR OVERHAUL PROCEDURE

10. Remove the magnetic pulse pick-up coil from the cup on the distributor base.

11. Use a small screwdriver as shown to remove the O-ring on the housing base. Install a new O-ring.

12. Apply a new coat of silicone lubricant to the module base; reinstall it to the distributor base.

MOTORCRAFT DURA-SPARK DISTRIBUTOR OVERHAUL PROCEDURE

1. Beneath cap, adapter ring, and rotor, Dura-Spark distributor is typical of earlier Motorcraft solid-state units. Remove cap.

2. Remove rotor before removing adapter ring. Early Dura-Spark adapter rings are secured by second pair of clips.

3. Remove two screws and remove adapter ring from housing. This is late-model 6-cylinder unit.

4. Using two screwdrivers, carefully pry trigger wheel (armature) from sleeve.

5. When removing armature, note small roll pin that secures armature to sleeve. Do not lose it.

6. Remove two screws securing pickup coil (stator) and pickup plate to housing. Stator and plate are serviced as assembly.

7. Disengage stator pin from vacuum link. Test stator resistance with ohmmeter. It should be 400 to 800 ohms. Also check for ground to plate. Replace if defective.

8. Remove two screws securing vacuum advance unit. Remove vacuum unit from distributor.

9. Mark advance weights, springs, and pins for correct reassembly. Unhook springs from anchor tabs and pins.

MOTORCRAFT DURA-SPARK DISTRIBUTOR OVERHAUL PROCEDURE

10. Remove felt wick and retaining clip from sleeve. Lift sleeve off shaft and weight base.

11. Tanged washer may stay on weight base or come off with sleeve. Be sure it is installed before reassembly. Lubricate shaft and weight pivot pins sparingly.

12. Install sleeve on shaft. Rubber stop (near screwdriver) must be in place and in good condition or centrifugal advance will be excessive.

13. Reinstall retaining clip and wick in sleeve. Lubricate wick with 2 or 3 drops of lightweight oil.

14. Lubricate spring ends and pins *sparingly* with penetrating oil. Reinstall springs in their original positions marked at disassembly.

15. Install plate and stator assembly on housing. Engage stator pin with vacuum link. Press stator lead grommet into cutout in housing. Tab on grommet is system ground.

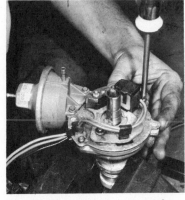

16. Attach vacuum unit with two hex-head screws. Secure stator base plate to housing with two screws.

17. Align roll pin slot in armature with slot in sleeve and press armature down onto sleeve.

18. Insert pin into place in armature and sleeve. Tap in with small punch and hammer. Reinstall rotor, adapter, and cap.

MOTORCRAFT UNIVERSAL TFI-I DISTRIBUTOR OVERHAUL PROCEDURE

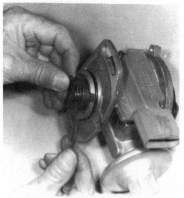

1. Use the point of an awl or a small screwdriver to lift up one end of the retaining spring, then carefully remove spring without stretching it.

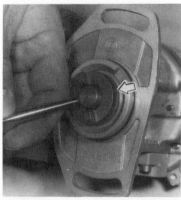

2. Make a small punch mark on the edge of the distributor shaft bottom to align with the metal drive coupling pin (arrow).

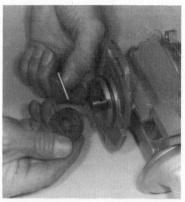

3. Remove the drive coupling pin with a suitable punch and hammer. Remove the coupling from the shaft.

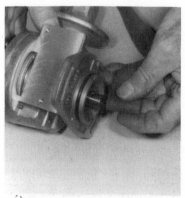

4. Deburr the end of the distributor shaft with crocus cloth to prevent damage to the housing seal and bushing when the shaft is removed.

5. Carefully remove the distributor shaft with its advance mechanism from the distributor housing.

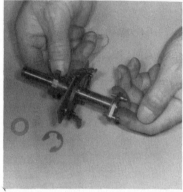

6. Unclip the advance weight springs, then remove the circlip and washer holding the shaft assembly to the armature assembly.

7. Check the shaft and armature assemblies for wear at all pivot points (arrows). The centrifugal advance weights are mounted on plastic bushings.

8. An Allen wrench is required to remove the two screws holding the TFI module to the distributor housing.

9. Apply a straight downward motion to disengage the module pins from the stator assembly. Do not rock the module or the pins may be damaged.

MOTORCRAFT UNIVERSAL TFI-I DISTRIBUTOR OVERHAUL PROCEDURE

10. Remove vacuum advance screw (A); disengage advance arm from stator assembly (B) by pressing the arm with a small screwdriver blade.

11. Remove the advance unit from the distributor housing. Check the O-ring (arrow) for damage or deterioration; replace if required.

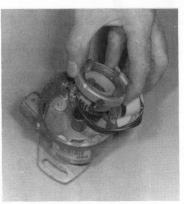

12. Remove the screws holding the stator assembly. Carefully lift the assembly up and out of the distributor housing.

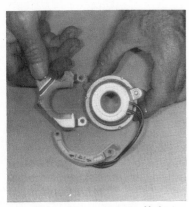

13. Slide the retainer off the bottom of the stator assembly. Check the plastic pad on the retainer for wear or damage; replace if needed.

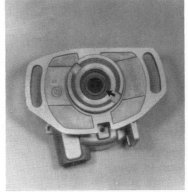

14. Check the shaft seal and bushing (arrow). They are not serviceable and the distributor housing must be replaced if either is worn or damaged.

15. Coat the module base and the distributor housing with silicone grease before reinstalling the module.

CHRYSLER 8-CYLINDER ELECTRONIC DISTRIBUTOR OVERHAUL PROCEDURE

1. Remove cap and rotor. Lean-Burn distributor is similar to this Chrysler conventional electronic distributor, except Lean-Burn has no advance mechanisms.

2. Using two screwdrivers, carefully pry reluctor (trigger wheel) and keeper pin off sleeve.

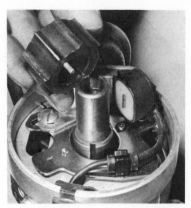

3. Note two slots inside reluctor and one slot at base of sleeve. Pin must be in reluctor slot by arrow that corresponds to direction of rotation.

4. Pull pickup coil lead grommet from slot in distributor housing. Remove screw securing pickup coil to pickup plate. Remove pickup coil.

5. Remove two screws securing vacuum advance unit to distributor. Disengage vacuum link from pickup plate. Remove vacuum unit.

6. Remove two screws securing pickup plate assembly. Remove plate assembly and inspect pivot point for looseness and wear.

7. Remove felt wick and sleeve retainer from center of sleeve. Early Lean-Burn distributors have advance weights; later ones do not.

8. Remove sleeve from distributor shaft. Inspect for wear or damage.

9. Disengage springs from anchor pins. Remove weights and springs from pivot pins. Mark springs, pins, and weights for reinstallation in original positions.

CHRYSLER 8-CYLINDER ELECTRONIC DISTRIBUTOR OVERHAUL PROCEDURE

10. Clean and reinstall weights and springs. Lubricate pins lightly with distributor lubricant. Remove nylon bushing from shaft. Inspect for wear; replace if worn.

11. Lightly lubricate shaft. Then install sleeve on shaft. Install sleeve retainer and felt wick. Apply 2 or 3 drops of lightweight oil to wick.

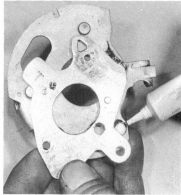

12. Replace pickup plate if pivot is worn. Loose pivot may cause pickup coil to hit reluctor. Lubricate pivot before installing plate.

13. Slide plate assembly into distributor and secure with two screws.

14. Engage vacuum link with movable plate. Secure vacuum unit to distributor with two screws.

15. Test pickup coil resistance with ohmmeter. It should be from 150 to 900 ohms. Install pickup coil and screw. Press lead grommet into slot.

16. On V-8 distributors, place pin in reluctor slot at arrow that matches rotation. If reluctor is installed wrong, timing will be off.

17. Align pin with slot in sleeve and press reluctor carefully into place.

18. Align reluctor tooth with pickup coil. Adjust air gap with nonmagnetic feeler gauge. Loosen screw and move pickup coil with screwdriver in slot. Tighten screw.

CHRYSLER ELECTRONIC SPARK ADVANCE (ESA) DISTRIBUTOR (HALL-EFFECT) OVERHAUL PROCEDURE

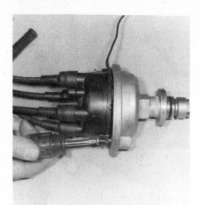

1. Loosen the two screws holding the distributor cap to the base. Lift the cap straight off to prevent rotor damage.

2. Pull the rotor straight off the distributor shaft. It has an internal tang that indexes with a slot in the shaft.

3. Remove the Hall-effect pickup assembly. This unit is held in place by the distributor cap screws and will be loose when the cap is removed.

4. Punch a small mark (arrow) on the base of the shaft to align with the drive tang roll pin.

5. A fixture such as this is useful to remove and install the drive tang roll pin without damage.

6. Remove the drive tang from the shaft, then deburr the end of the shaft with crocus cloth before removing it from the housing.

7. The shutter blade is retained in place on the distributor shaft by a small roll pin (arrow).

8. When reisntalling the Hall-effect pickup, be sure to align the raised tang with the countersunk hole in the housing.

9. Note the cap slot which must align with the tang on the Hall-effect pickup assembly when the cap is reinstalled.

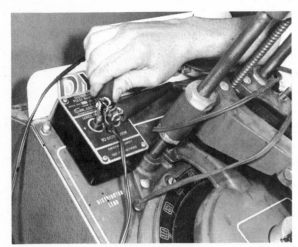

Figure 10-37. Connect distributor tester leads to the amplifier module according to the equipment maker's instructions.

SOLID-STATE DISTRIBUTOR TEST AND ADJUSTMENT

The distributor tester described earlier can be used to test the centrifugal and vacuum advance mechanisms of a solid-state distributor (if used), as well as to check for shaft and bushing wear. Since solid-state distributors have no breaker points, there are no breaker-point tests and adjustments.

Install a solid-state distributor in the tester in the same way that would a breaker-point distributor. The electrical connections differ, however. The pickup coil produces a small trigger voltage, which is not strong enough to drive the circuitry of many testers. An additional electronic amplifier module is required for solid-state distributor testing. Many late-model testers have this additional capability built in. An accessory amplifier can be attached to older testers to adapt them for solid-state testing.

Follow the test equipment manufacturer's instructions for circuit connections. Figure 10-37 shows the tester leads connected to an accessory amplifier. The amplifier leads are then connected to the distributor pickup coil leads, figure 10-38. Many late-model testers also have the capability to check out the ignition system control module.

A distributor tester is an ideal way to check for intermittent opens or short circuits caused by vibration at high speed or movement of the vacuum advance unit. Such conditions cannot easily be tested with the distributor in the vehicle, but they can be located with a distributor tester using the ohmmeter to check pickup

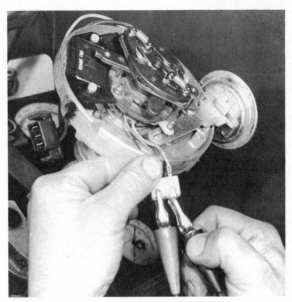

Figure 10-38. Connect amplifier module leads to distributor pickup coil leads.

coil resistance. Wiggle the pickup connector leads while testing coil resistance and checking for short circuits.

The distributors used with electronic timing systems have no advance mechanisms, and may not even have a signal generator. They simply distribute the secondary voltage to the spark plugs. Distributors with a signal generator can be checked for shaft and bushing wear, but the other tests described below are not applicable.

Inspect the distributor as described earlier in the chapter before testing it.

Bushing and Shaft Wear Tests

Test a solid-state distributor for bushing and shaft wear and alignment as described earlier for breaker-point distributors.

Centrifugal and Vacuum Advance Test and Adjustment

Except for those used with electronic timing control systems, solid-state distributors have the same kinds of spark advance mechanisms that breaker-point distributors have. They are tested and adjusted in the same way.

You will need the manufacturer's specifications, or advance curve, for the distributor to be tested. Specifications are listed by distributor part number, located on the side of the distributor housing.

In a Delco-Remy HEI distributor, the vacuum advance rotates the pickup coil retainer. In

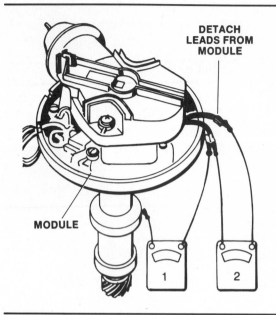

Figure 10-39. Pickup coil test points for the HEI distributor.

Figure 10-40. Coat the top, bottom, and sides of a Dura-Spark rotor with a silicone lubricant.

other solid-state distributors, the vacuum advance unit rotates the pickup coil or sensor baseplate. Connect the tester vacuum line to the vacuum unit and test the vacuum advance just as you would for a breaker-point distributor.

Centrifugal advance mechanisms on solid-state distributors can be adjusted in the same way as breaker-point distributors, except on some Chrysler models in which the eccentric pins that anchor the springs must be turned with a special tool.

Pickup Coil Tests

Many distributor testers have an ohmmeter for testing the pickup coil resistance. Test the resistance by touching the ohmmeter leads to the pickup coil leads, figure 10-39. Resistance must be within the manufacturer's specifications. If it is not, replace the pickup coil.

Test for a grounded pickup coil by touching one ohmmeter lead to the distributor housing and the other alternately to each pickup coil lead, figure 10-39. The ohmmeter must show infinite resistance. If any continuity is shown, the pickup coil is grounded and must be replaced.

Solid-State Distributor Cleaning and Lubrication

Solid-state distributors should be cleaned and lubricated in the same way as breaker point

distributors. Follow the instructions provided earlier. Since there are no breaker points, no cam or rubbing block lubrication is required. Solid-state distributors do not have provisions to lubricate the shaft and bushings.

Solid-state distributors must be thoroughly cleaned, and *all* solvent residue completely removed. Be extremely careful not to over-lubricate any of the locations within a solid-state distributor. Any dirt, solvent residue or lubricant that gets on a low-voltage connection can disrupt ignition operation.

Many solid-state distributors require that a silicone lubricant be applied to specific locations within the distributor. Ford, AMC, and other manufacturers specify the use of silicone lubricant at the ignition module primary connectors and at the distributor connectors to prevent corrosion and moisture that might interfere with voltage signals. The Delco-Remy HEI and Motorcraft TFI distributors require a silicone lubricant between the module and its mounting base. The grease also helps to dissipate heat.

Many Ford Dura-Spark distributors also require a silicone lubricant on the rotor tip (except multipoint, or "cat-whisker", rotors) and cap electrodes, figure 10-40, for RFI suppression. Follow the carmaker's specific direction for special solid-state distributor lubrication.

DISTRIBUTOR INSTALLATION

After the distributor has been serviced, follow these general directions to install the distributor:

1. Make sure the ignition switch is off. You may have disconnected the battery ground cable when you removed the distributor.
2. Rotate the distributor shaft until the rotor is aligned with the mark that you made on the housing when you removed it.
3. Align the distributor housing with your reference point on the engine.
4. Make sure the sealing ring or Neoprene O-ring is in position on the distributor, if one is used. Insert the distributor into the engine.
5. When installing a horizontal distributor that couples directly to the end of the camshaft, align the tangs on the distributor shaft with the slots in the end of the camshaft and simply seat the distributor against the cylinder head. Proceed to step 8.
6. Engage the distributor drive with the camshaft or auxiliary shaft and oil pump drive. If the distributor uses a helical drive gear, the rotor may rotate out of position when the distributor is inserted in the engine. If this happens, note the amount that the rotor moves. Then raise the distributor up and move the rotor backwards the same amount (usually 15 to 20 degrees) and lower the distributor back into place.
7. Make sure the distributor is fully seated in the engine and engaged with the camshaft and oil pump drive. You may have to wiggle the shaft slightly to engage the oil pump or bump the engine with the starter to turn the distributor slightly for shaft engagement.
8. Install the distributor clamp and holddown bolt. On horizontal distributors, install the attaching nuts.
9. Connect the distributor primary lead to the coil or the pickup coil lead connector to the module harness. On solid-state distributors, connect any other wires that were disconnected during removal.
10. Connect the vacuum lines to the vacuum advance unit, if so equipped.
11. Install the cap with attached spark plug wires on the distributor and secure it with the clips, latches, or holddown screws.
12. Reconnect the battery ground cable, if it was disconnected.

STATIC TIMING

If the engine was not cranked while the distributor was out, it should start and run if the distributor was reinstalled correctly. Then check and adjust initial timing with a timing light. If the engine was cranked while the distributor was out, you have to reestablish the basic timing position (except on horizontal distributors that couple directly to the rear of the camshaft). This is called static timing. Proceed as follows:

1. Bring the number 1 piston to top dead center on the compression stroke. If the engine is timed on any cylinder other than number 1, use that cylinder for static timing.
2. Align the timing marks at the specified initial timing position.
3. Install the distributor so that the rotor points at the number 1 spark plug terminal in the cap. Make a reference line on the distributor housing to align the rotor with the cap off.
4. Loosen the distributor holddown clamp and bolt.
5. For a breaker-point distributor, turn the ignition on with the points closed. Slowly turn the distributor opposite from rotor rotation until an arc jumps across the point contact surfaces.

For a solid-state distributor, rotate the distributor body so that the pickup coil piece is exactly aligned with one trigger wheel tooth.
6. Tighten the holddown clamp and bolt.

The distributor should now be timed closely enough for the engine to start and run. You will learn about complete adjustment and testing of ignition timing in Chapter 11.

11

Ignition Timing — Test and Adjustment

We have discussed how to test and service the primary (Chapter 8) and secondary (Chapter 9) circuits, and how to service the distributor (Chapter 10). This chapter covers the final steps of ignition service — testing and adjusting ignition timing.

Timing adjustment generally is the final step in servicing the ignition. However, it also may be necessary to check timing and spark advance at other times, such as during routine service of a vehicle, to isolate the cause of a problem.

IGNITION TIMING TESTS AND ADJUSTMENTS

Ignition timing can be adjusted statically (engine off) or dynamically (engine running). Static timing is usually set only when a distributor is being reinstalled in an engine. Final adjustment of the timing usually is made with a stroboscopic timing light while the engine is running. Some carmakers, however, provide only static timing specifications for older models and for late-model vehicles with certain electronic engine control systems. Static timing procedures are explained in Chapter 10. Timing generally is set in relation to the number 1 cylinder. International Harvester V-8 engines are one notable exception: they are timed from the number 8 cylinder.

Using a Timing Light

Dynamic timing is done with a stroboscopic timing light triggered by voltage from the number 1 spark plug cable. The light can be attached to an oscilloscope console, or it can be a separate piece of equipment. It can draw current from the car battery, or it can run on alternating current.

Simple timing lights do nothing more than flash every time number 1 spark plug fires. They can be used to check and adjust initial timing and to make simple tests of the advance mechanisms. However, to make precise tests of the advance mechanisms and of timing control systems, you will need an adjustable timing light.

An adjustable timing light contains additional solid-state circuitry which allows you to set the light to flash at a time *after* the number 1 spark plug fires. For example, you may have the light hooked up to an engine that has an initial timing of top dead center. The adjustable timing light is set to flash when the number 1 spark plug fires. When it flashes, the timing marks are aligned at top dead center. Now set the adjustable timing light for 5° on the light's

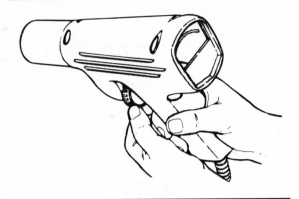

Figure 11-1. This adjustable timing light can be set so that it will flash at some time *after* the firing of the number 1 spark plug. The amount of delay in engine crankshaft degrees is shown on the meter. (Chrysler)

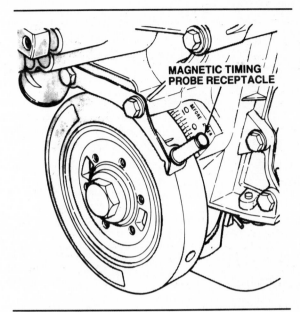

Figure 11-3. A typical magnetic timing probe receptacle. (Chrysler)

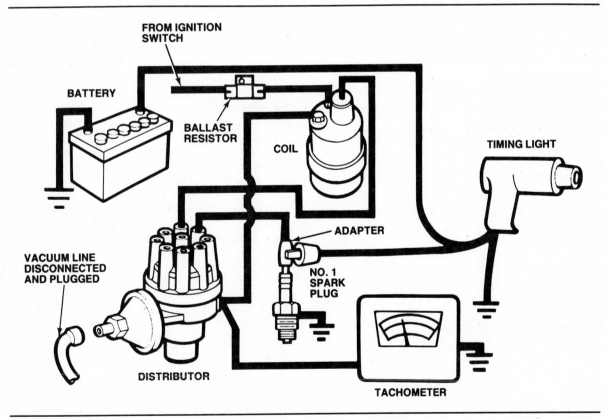

Figure 11-2. The timing light is connected to the battery and the number 1 cylinder spark plug cable. Some lights work on alternating current instead of the car's battery. (Chrysler)

meter, figure 11-1. The light will flash five engine rotation degrees later, and the timing marks will be aligned at 5° atdc. The actual timing of the engine has not changed; the time at which the light flashes has changed. The adjustable timing light can be used to test advance mechanisms and timing control systems, as we will see.

DISTRIBUTOR PART NO.	CENTRIFUGAL ADVANCE IN DISTRIBUTOR DEGREES AT DISTRIBUTOR RPM						VACUUM ADVANCE (MAX. DIST. DEG AT IN. Hg)
	START	INTERMEDIATE (1)	INTERMEDIATE (2)	INTERMEDIATE (3)	INTERMEDIATE (4)	MAXIMUM	
1112164 (Delco)	0–2.5 @ 600	7.0–10 @ 900	8–10 @ 1000	—	—	14–18 @ 2200	10° @ 13–15"
1111958 (Delco)	0–3.0 @ 650	1.5–7.0 @ 600	9–13 @ 1000	—	—	15–19 @ 2300	13° @ 16–18"
D50F-BA (Ford)	0–1.5 @ 500	4–5 @ 750	5–7 @ 1000	6–8 @ 1250	6–10 @ 1500	10–12 @ 2000	6°–8° @ 10"
D60F-AH (Ford)	0–1 @ 500	1–4 @ 750	4–6 @ 1000	5–7 @ 1250	8–9 @ 1500	10–13 @ 2000	8°–9° @ 10"
3666782 (Chrys)	1–3 @ 500	10–12 @ 800	—	11–13 @ 1250	—	14–16 @ 1800	9°–12° @ 15"
3755470 (Chrys)	1–4 @ 650	8–11 @ 800	8–12 @ 1000	12–14 @ 1250	—	14–18 @ 2000	9°–12° @ 15"

Figure 11-4. Typical centrifugal and vacuum advance specifications in distributor degrees and distributor rpm.

DISTRIBUTOR PART NO.	CENTRIFUGAL ADVANCE IN CRANKSHAFT DEGREES AT ENGINE RPM					
	START	INTERMEDIATE (1)	INTERMEDIATE (2)	INTERMEDIATE (3)	INTERMEDIATE (4)	MAXIMUM
1112164 (Delco)	0–5 @ 1200	12–20 @ 1800	16–21 @ 2000	—	—	28–36 @ 4400
1111958 (Delco)	0–6 @ 1300	3–10 @ 1200	18–24 @ 2000	—	—	30–38 @ 4600
D50F-BA (Ford)	0–3 @ 1000	8–10 @ 1500	10–14 @ 2000	12–17 @ 2500	18–21 @ 3000	20–24 @ 4000
D60F-AH (Ford)	0–2 @ 1000	2–7 @ 1500	8–12 @ 2000	10–14 @ 2500	16–18 @ 3000	20–26 @ 4000
3666782 (Chrys)	2–6 @ 1000	20–24 @ 1600	—	22–26 @ 2500	—	28–32 @ 3600
3755470 (Chrys)	1–8 @ 1300	16–20 @ 1600	16–22 @ 2000	24–28 @ 2500	—	28–32 @ 4000

Figure 11-5. Typical centrifugal and vacuum advance specifications in crankshaft (engine) degrees and engine rpm.

ENGINE	TRANS	YEAR	DISTRIBUTOR PART NO.	ADVANCE DEGREES @ 2500 RPM	
				TOTAL	CENTRIFUGAL
200-cid	AT	1980–81	D9BE-DA	24.8–33.5	4.8–11.0

Figure 11-6. To use these typical spark advance specifications in engine speed and degrees, add the basic timing.

To connect both kinds of timing lights, attach the timing light lead to the number 1 spark plug cable, either at the plug or at the distributor cap. If you have an older model timing light without an inductive pickup that clamps around the plug cable, you should use an adapter between the cable and plug or distributor cap, figure 11-2. *Never puncture a spark plug cable or boot with a sharp probe to connect a timing light.* Now connect the timing light to its power source — the car battery or an a.c.-powered console.

Using a Magnetic Timing Meter

Most late-model engines have a magnetic timing probe receptacle, figure 11-3. The magnetic timing probe is a pickup coil that is inserted into the receptacle. A notch, tab, or magnetic particle in the crankshaft, flywheel, or vibration damper generates a pulse signal every time it passes the end of the probe. On many engines, the notch, tab, or particle that creates the signal is offset from the actual number 1 cylinder tdc position by a specified number of degrees. Most magnetic timing meters require you to set the offset specifications on the meter before checking the timing. These specifications may be found in the meter instructions or in carmakers' service manuals.

Checking timing in this way is much faster and more accurate than using a stroboscopic timing light. You simply connect the meter to the engine and insert the probe in the receptacle according to the equipment instructions. If the instructions tell you to adjust the crankshaft offset on the meter, do so. Then start and run the engine just as you would to check timing with a light and read the meter. Since you don't have to hold a timing light with one hand, you can use both hands to adjust the distributor.

Spark Advance Specifications

In order to correctly set or check timing, you must have the manufacturer's specifications. These are provided in several different ways:
- Centrifugal advance in distributor degrees at distributor rpm, figure 11-4. These are to be used with a distributor tester and must be doubled if the distributor is checked while still in an engine.
- Centrifugal advance in crankshaft degrees at crankshaft rpm, figure 11-5. These are to be used with the distributor in the engine and must be divided by two when the distributor is checked in a distributor tester.
- Vacuum advance in distributor or crankshaft degrees at specified vacuum levels (in. Hg or mm).
- Total advance and centrifugal advance at a specified engine speed, such as 2,500 rpm, figure 11-6. These let you check overall advance

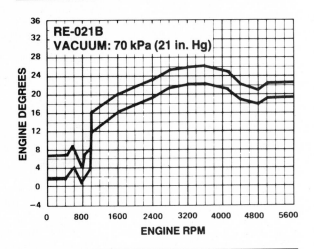

Figure 11-7. A vacuum advance curve for one distributor. (AMC-Renault)

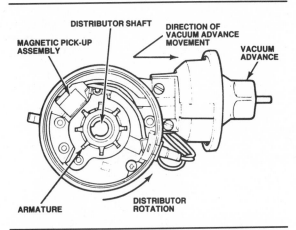

Figure 11-8. The rotor always rotates opposite to the direction of the vacuum advance linkage movement. (Chrysler)

operation quickly, but cannot be used to check advance at different speeds with differing loads. Vacuum advance is determined by subtracting centrifugal advance from the total amount of advance.

Specifications generally are given in table form, although they may also be plotted as a curve on a graph, figure 11-7.

Because carmakers may use a variety of distributors with different centrifugal and vacuum advance curves in a particular engine during a single model year, advance specifications are provided by distributor part number. This number is stamped on the distributor body or on a metal tag fastened to the distributor.

When checking spark advance with the distributor in the engine, you add or subtract the initial or basic advance from the distributor specifications. For example, if the distributor centrifugal advance is 22 *crankshaft* degrees btdc at 2,500 engine rpm, and initial timing is 6 degrees btdc, add the two numbers to determine spark advance:

22 degrees distributor advance + 6 degrees btdc initial timing = 28 degrees engine spark advance @ 2,500 rpm.

Suppose that the same distributor is installed in an engine with an initial timing of 2 degrees atdc (retarded). To determine the engine spark advance, you subtract the initial timing from the distributor advance specification:

22 degrees distributor advance − 2 degrees atdc initial timing = 20 degrees engine spark advance @ 2,500 rpm.

Initial Timing Test and Adjustment

Before you test and adjust initial timing, you should service the primary circuit. If working

with a breaker-point ignition, make sure that dwell is correctly set. The engine must be idling at its correct speed and at normal operating temperature.

Although all timing adjustments involve the same principles, you should have the carmaker's specifications before setting initial timing on a particular vehicle. If the information you need is not provided on the engine decal (or if the decal is missing or unreadable), refer to the carmaker's shop manual or a manual such as the **Car Care Guide**.

To determine the direction of distributor rotation on a unit with a vacuum advance mechanism, note the location of the advance unit. The distributor rotation is always in the opposite direction of vacuum advance linkage movement, figure 11-8. If the advance unit is on the right side of the distributor, the direction of distributor rotation is counterclockwise. If it is on the left side of the distributor, the direction of rotation is clockwise.

To determine the direction of rotation on a distributor with a centrifugal advance mechanism, grasp the rotor and try turning it. The advance weights will prevent you from turning it backward, so the direction in which the rotor will move a few degrees is the direction of rotation. Rotational direction also can be determined by cranking the engine with the distributor removed and noting the direction in which the rotor moves.

Timing generally is set at a normal slow idle, sometimes called "curb" idle, but some carmakers, such as Oldsmobile for a number of models, specify that timing be set at higher speeds (above 1,000 rpm).

Timing is set on most engines with the distributor vacuum lines disconnected and

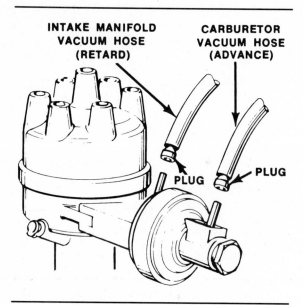

INTAKE MANIFOLD
VACUUM HOSE
(RETARD)

CARBURETOR
VACUUM HOSE
(ADVANCE)

PLUG

PLUG

Figure 11-9. Most cars are timed with the distributor vacuum lines disconnected and plugged.

plugged, figure 11-9. However, some car-makers specify that the vacuum advance lines remain connected. On dual-diaphragm distributors, the manifold vacuum line that provides spark retard usually must be disconnected and plugged. Note the position of vacuum lines before disconnecting them so you can reinstall them correctly.

If you remove the air cleaner to get to the distributor, plug any vacuum lines that you disconnect.

When timing distributors that have advance or retard solenoids, follow the manufacturer's directions about whether to disconnect or energize the solenoid.

Find the timing marks on the engine and crankshaft pulley or balancer. The timing marks on many late-model engines are difficult to find or see, often hidden behind a maze of belts and engine accessories. If you cannot reach the timing marks to clean them by hand, spray them with carburetor or choke cleaner to make them easier to see. If you have access to them, wipe the marks clean and mark them with chalk or paint. Timing marks on some engines, particularly in vans, must be viewed from the bottom of the engine.

On engines with electronic timing control, you may have to disconnect a specified connector at the distributor or ignition module to check basic timing. This puts the module into a bypass or "default" timing mode in which it does not control timing. On some engines with electronic timing control, it is not possible to check or set basic timing. When a distributor is

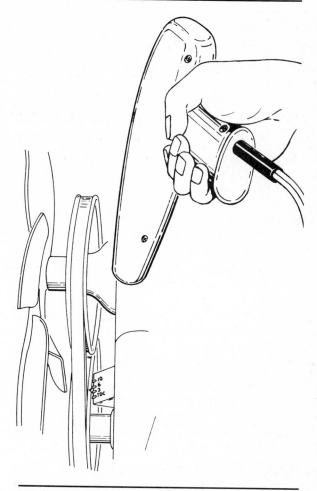

Figure 11-10. Aim the timing light at the timing marks and observe their position as the light flashes.

removed from such an engine, it is static-timed upon installation and the electronics take over from there. This will be covered later in the chapter.

Check the tune-up specifications for the exact timing setting and engine speed for the particular vehicle model. On late-model engines, the timing setting is given on a Vehicle Emission Control Information (VECI) label or decal located in the engine compartment. This is generally the specification that should be followed, even if it differs from printed specifications in a manual.

To adjust the initial timing:
1. Connect a tachometer and a timing light.
2. Start the engine and run it *at the specified speed.* Many late-model engines may be timed at speeds above or below the normal slow-idle speed.
3. Aim the flashing timing light at the timing marks and observe their position, figure 11-10.

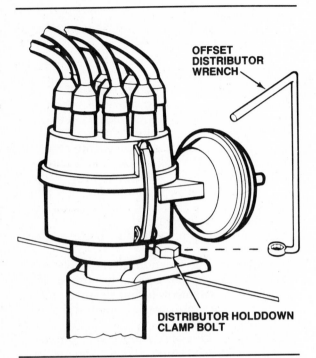

Figure 11-11. An offset distributor wrench is often required to loosen the distributor holddown capscrew. (Chrysler)

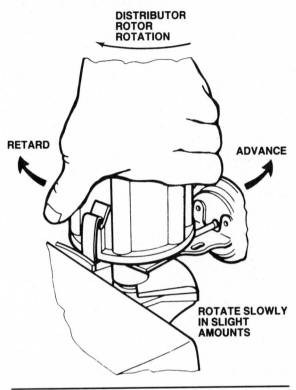

Figure 11-12. Rotate the distributor body slowly. As little as ¼ inch (13 mm) makes a big change in timing. (Chrysler)

If adjustment is necessary:
   a. Loosen the distributor holddown bolt with a distributor wrench, figure 11-11, or with a ratchet, extension, and U-joint socket.
   b. To advance the timing, manually turn the distributor *against* rotor rotation, figure 11-12.
   c. To retard the timing, turn the distributor *with* rotor rotation, figure 11-12.
   d. Tighten the holddown bolt and recheck the timing.
4. After adjusting timing, reconnect all vacuum lines and readjust the idle speed if necessary. If idle speed is readjusted, recheck the timing afterward.

Centrifugal and Vacuum Advance Mechanism Tests

Dwell, initial timing, and idle speed must be adjusted before spark advance is tested. If the engine has a timing control system that affects vacuum advance for emission control, this should be checked after the centrifugal and vacuum systems have been tested.

Timing advance tests with an adjustable timing light

1. Connect a tachometer and an adjustable timing light to the engine.
2. Start and idle the engine; verify the initial timing setting.

3. Increase engine speed to the rpm specified for checking total advance.
4. Watch the timing marks and adjust the timing light advance meter until the timing marks are aligned at the step 2 initial timing setting.
5. Read the degrees of total advance recorded on the timing light meter and compare to specifications:
   a. If the reading is within specifications, you may want to test the individual advance devices anyway.
   b. If the reading is not within specifications, you must test the individual advance devices to determine which is at fault.
   To test the individual advance mechanisms:
1. With the engine at idle, disconnect and plug the distributor vacuum lines.
2. Increase engine rpm to the specified test speed.
3. Note the timing mark alignment and adjust the advance meter control to align the marks at the initial timing setting.
4. Read the degrees of advance recorded on the timing light meter. This is the *centrifugal advance only*; compare it to specifications:
   a. If the reading is within specifications, go to step 5.

b. If the reading is not within specifications, the centrifugal advance mechanism must be adjusted or replaced.

5. While still at the specified test speed, unplug and reconnect the vacuum advance line to the distributor vacuum unit.

NOTE: This step cannot be done if the car has a speed- or transmission-controlled spark system that denies vacuum advance. In this case, you must test the vacuum advance mechanism with a hand-operated vacuum pump (as explained in following paragraphs), or by connecting a manifold vacuum line to the distributor advance diaphragm.

6. Again note the timing marks and adjust the advance meter until the marks are aligned at the initial timing setting.

7. Subtract the centrifugal advance reading in step 4 from the new reading. The result is the amount of vacuum advance; compare it to specifications:

a. If the reading is within specifications, the vacuum advance unit is working correctly.

b. If the reading is not within specifications, the vacuum advance unit must be adjusted or replaced.

Some 1970 and later cars with spark timing control emission systems do not provide vacuum advance with the vehicle stationary and the transmission in Neutral. To test such a car, raise the vehicle on a hoist and operate it in gear at specified speeds, or bypass the vacuum control devices. Vacuum switches and valves often can be bypassed by connecting a hose directly from the carburetor spark port or from a manifold vacuum port to the distributor vacuum unit. Vacuum advance units can also be checked with a hand vacuum pump, as we will soon see.

Distributor advance specifications may be given at several different test speeds. If so, perform the tests at all given speeds to ensure precise control of ignition timing.

If the distributor being tested has a dual-diaphragm vacuum advance unit, check the vacuum retard as follows:

1. Disconnect and plug both vacuum hoses at the distributor, figure 11-9.

2. Run the engine at idle. Watch the timing marks with an adjustable timing light and connect the manifold vacuum hose to the inner (distributor side) vacuum chamber.

3. Timing should immediately retard from the initial setting. Check the amount of retard with the timing light advance meter; compare it to specifications.

a. If the reading is within specifications, the vacuum retard is working properly.

b. If the reading is not within specifications, replace the vacuum unit.

Timing advance tests
without an adjustable timing light

If an adjustable timing light is not available, a nonadjustable timing light can be used to check the general operation of the centrifugal advance, vacuum advance, and vacuum retard mechanisms. Exact degrees, however, cannot be measured.

1. Connect a tachometer and timing light to the engine.

2. Start and idle the engine.

3. Disconnect and plug the distributor vacuum lines.

4. Increase engine speed to 2,000 or 2,500 rpm while watching the timing marks. The marks should advance smoothly and steadily, indicating that the centrifugal advance mechanism is working.

5. Hold the engine speed above idle. Unplug and connect the vacuum advance line to the distributor.

6. The timing marks should advance an additional amount and engine speed should increase, indicating that the vacuum advance is working.

7. To check the vacuum retard on dual-diaphragm units, return the engine speed to idle.

8. Unplug and connect the manifold vacuum line to the retard vacuum chamber. Timing should retard about 6 to 12 degrees (or as specified by the carmaker) and engine speed should decrease.

Vacuum advance test with
a hand vacuum pump

A hand-operated vacuum pump can be used to test the precise vacuum advance curve of a distributor.

1. Disconnect and plug the vacuum line from the vacuum advance unit. Connect the tester hose to the advance unit, figure 11-13, using an adapter if required.

2. Close the pump release valve and operate the pump to apply 15 to 20 in. (380 to 510 mm) Hg vacuum.

3. Watch the gauge for at least 10 seconds. If the reading drops, the diaphragm is leaking and the advance unit must be replaced.

4. Using an adjustable timing light, check the centrifugal spark advance at the specified test rpm points. Leave the vacuum line to the advance diaphragm disconnected and plugged.

5. Record the centrifugal advance setting at 1,000 rpm or other engine speed specified for testing the vacuum advance unit.

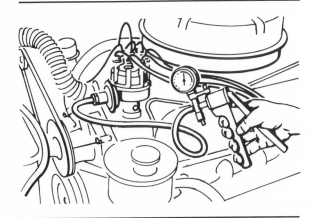

Figure 11-13. Use a hand vacuum pump to check the condition of the vacuum advance unit.

6. With the engine at the test speed, apply vacuum to the advance diaphragm with the hand pump. Apply the amount of vacuum specified for that test speed.

7. Record the total advance at each test point. Subtract the reading from the centrifugal advance recorded in step 5. The difference is the amount of vacuum advance. If the reading does not meet the specifications at all test points, the vacuum unit must be adjusted or replaced.

Spark Timing Emission Control System Tests

The centrifugal and vacuum advance tests described earlier check the advance mechanism in the distributor. They do not test the additional spark timing control systems used as part of many emission control systems. Test the various switches, solenoids, and valves in these systems with the following methods. Because many of the systems exist in different configurations from one car model to another, you must know the exact system configuration and specifications for the car you are testing. You will find this information in carmakers' shop manuals or independent service guides.

You can make a quick overall test of system operation by driving or operating the car and checking for vacuum advance cutoff at low speed or in the low gears and then for vacuum advance at higher speeds or in high gear. Most spark timing control systems include one or more of the following parts:

- Transmission- or speed-controlled switch
- Vacuum solenoid
- Thermostatic vacuum switch
- Delaying or reversing relay
- Spark delay valve.

Systems with spark delay valves usually do not have a transmission or speed switch, or a vacuum solenoid. Other systems may have additional valves and switches. Regardless of how the system is wired and plumbed together, you can test its overall operation by checking for vacuum at the distributor at certain times, and for absence of vacuum at other times.

Transmission- or Speed-controlled vacuum advance system test

You will need a timing light or a vacuum gauge, or both, for this test. Check the system as follows:

1. Connect the timing light to the ignition if the car is being tested in the shop.

2. If you are going to drive the car to test it, connect a vacuum gauge to the vacuum solenoid with a long hose and route the gauge into the driver's compartment. Be careful not to pinch the hose.

3. Operate the car as follows:

　a. For transmission-controlled systems with manual transmissions, start the engine and shift the transmission through all the gear ranges.

　b. For speed-controlled systems and for transmission-controlled systems with automatic transmissions, raise the car on a hoist and run it through the required speed or gear ranges.

　c. For all front-wheel-drive (FWD) cars, drive the car on the road through the required speed or gear ranges.F

NOTE: Operating the car on a hoist, on a dynamometer, or on the road is necessary for most systems with automatic transmissions because the transmission switch is actuated by high-gear hydraulic pressure, which is not available until the transmission actually upshifts into high gear. Some systems with automatic transmissions also provide vacuum advance in reverse. You can test for this by placing the transmission in reverse while stationary on the shop floor. Do not test *front-wheel-drive cars in operation on a hoist* because of the danger in working around the engine compartment while the wheels are turning.

4. With the spark timing control system in operation, check the vacuum solenoid with one of the following methods. You may need the help of an assistant:

　a. Watch the engine timing marks with the timing light. Advance should increase when vacuum is applied (high gear or cruising speed) and decrease when it is cut off (low gears or lower speeds).

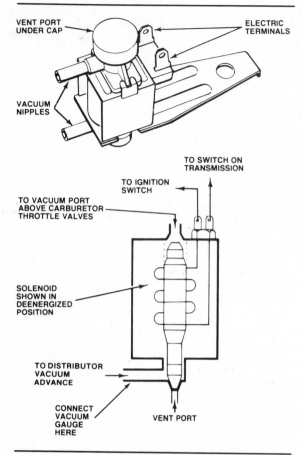

Figure 11-14. A vacuum solenoid test diagram (bottom) and a typical solenoid (top).

b. Watch the vacuum gauge connected to the distributor port of the solenoid, figure 11-14. The gauge should show no vacuum in low gears or at low speed, and it should show a reading in high gear or at cruising speed.

If these tests show that the solenoid is applying vacuum to the distributor at the correct speed or gear ranges, the system is working properly. If the vacuum is not applied properly, and you have tested the vacuum advance unit, do the following tests.

Vacuum solenoid test
Test a vacuum solenoid for proper air-vacuum flow and for internal leaks around the plunger. Replace a solenoid if it does not pass this test sequence:
1. Disconnect the hoses and electrical connectors from the solenoid.
2. Connect a hose to the distributor vacuum port on the solenoid, figure 11-14, and blow air through it. Air should come out of the:
   a. Carburetor vacuum port, if the solenoid must be energized to deny vacuum.

b. Vent port, if the solenoid must be de-energized to deny vacuum.
3. Connect a jumper wire from one solenoid electrical terminal to ground.
4. Connect a second jumper wire from the other solenoid terminal to the battery positive terminal.
5. Again blow air through the hose. Air should now come out of the:
   a. Vent port, if the solenoid must be energized to deny vacuum.
   b. Carburetor vacuum port, if the solenoid must be deenergized to deny vacuum.
6. Blocking the airflow through the appropriate port while still blowing into the hose should block all airflow. If not, the solenoid has internal leakage.

To test a vacuum solenoid for correct plunger operation:
1. Disconnect the 2-wire connector from the vacuum solenoid.
2. Connect a jumper wire from one solenoid terminal to ground.
3. Connect a second jumper wire to the other solenoid terminal. Momentarily touch this lead to the battery positive terminal.
4. Listen for a click every time the circuit opens and closes. Repeat several times. The plunger should operate promptly each time. If it does not, replace the solenoid.

Transmission switch tests
The TCS systems of AMC, GM and some 1972 Chrysler models, and the Ford TRS systems use transmission-operated switches to actuate a solenoid that controls vacuum spark advance. Most transmission switches are *normally closed* in low and intermediate gears to *energize* the solenoid and *deny* vacuum advance. The switches on some systems (mostly Chevrolet), however, are *normally open* in low and intermediate gears to leave the solenoid *deenergized* yet still *deny* vacuum advance. To further complicate the picture, some systems use a *normally closed* switch to activate a *reversing relay* that *deenergizes* the solenoid to *deny* vacuum advance in low gear.

To test the operation of a transmission control switch:
1. Connect a voltmeter or test lamp in series with the switch feed wire, figure 11-15. The test lamp should use an 1893 bulb or equivalent which draws only 0.8 ampere. If the bulb draws more current than this, the transmission control switch contacts could be damaged.
2. With the ignition switch on, operate the transmission through all gear ranges.

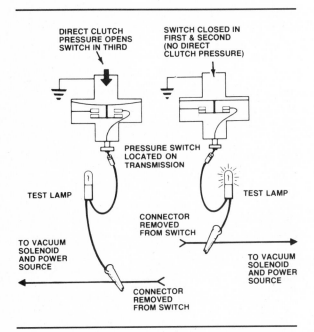

Figure 11-15. Testing a normally closed TCS switch.

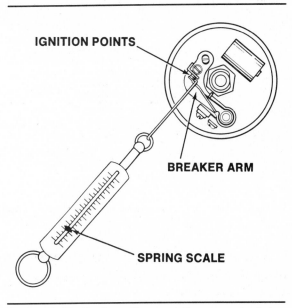

Figure 11-16. Testing a thermostatic vacuum switch.

3. The lamp will go on and off, or the voltmeter will show a reading, as the switch closes and opens.

4. Some automatic transmission systems in which the switch is operated by high clutch pressure may not operate unless the car is lifted on a hoist and driven through the gear ranges.

5. Some switches can be adjusted; most must be replaced if they do not operate properly.

Thermostatic vacuum switch test

Thermostatic vacuum switches come in many shapes, sizes, and names. TVS devices are also called PVS, CTO, TIC, and TVV units. Thermostatic switches are activated by engine coolant or by air temperature. The vacuum switch may be opened or closed by high or low temperatures, depending upon its use and the system design. Therefore, the manufacturer's specifications and test procedures must be followed to correctly interpret the results.

Coolant-controlled switches should be tested with the engine cold, at normal operating temperature, and in some cases, at high temperature. When the test procedure requires you to test at high temperatures, do not allow the engine to overheat. This is most important on cars with catalytic converters.

Apply vacuum to the specified switch port, figure 11-16. Note the gauge reading when the switch is both energized and deenergized. Compare these readings to the manufacturer's specifications to determine if the switch is operating correctly.

Relay tests

Relays do various jobs in spark timing control systems. Delaying relays have special circuitry that keeps the contact points from closing for a specific length of time (usually about 20 seconds). Delaying relays are used when the ignition switch is first turned on, to allow vacuum advance for a short time when the car is first started. The vacuum solenoid is not energized to deny vacuum advance until the delaying relay's points have closed.

Reversing relays are used in a few systems where the operation of the speed or transmission control switch does not match the operation of the vacuum solenoid. That is, the transmission control switch is opened when the vacuum solenoid must be energized. A reversing relay, with normally closed points that *open* when current flows through the relay coil, can be used in this type of system, figure 11-17.

To test a delay relay, turn the ignition switch on without starting the engine. Count the number of seconds before the vacuum solenoid clicks. If necessary, the relay can be tested with a 12-volt test lamp:

1. Connect a test lamp between the relay armature and ground, figure 11-18.

2. Turn the ignition switch on without starting the engine.

3. Count the number of seconds before the lamp lights and compare to manufacturer's specifications. If it does not match the specifications, replace the relay.

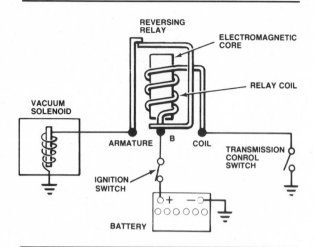

Figure 11-17. When current flows through the coil circuit of this reversing relay, the armature opens and no current flows to the vacuum solenoid.

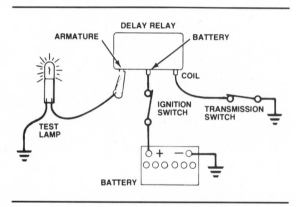

Figure 11-18. Testing a delay relay.

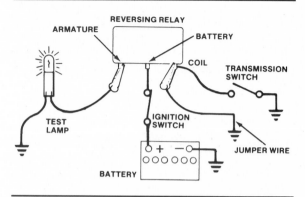

Figure 11-19. Testing a reversing relay.

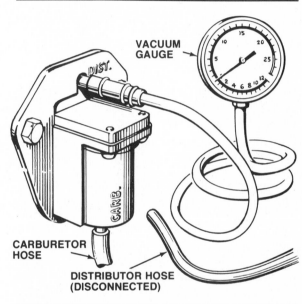

Figure 11-20. Testing an OSAC valve.

A reversing relay can also be tested with a 12-volt lamp:
1. Connect a test lamp between the relay armature and ground, figure 11-19.
2. With the transmission in neutral, turn the ignition switch on. The test lamp should light.
3. Connect a jumper wire between the relay coil terminal and ground. The test lamp should go off.
4. Replace the relay if it does not work as described.

Spark delay valve tests
Chrysler OSAC valves and the spark delay valves used by various other carmakers delay vacuum advance with restriction in the vacuum line. Test them by attaching a vacuum gauge to the distributor side of the valve and applying vacuum to the valve inlet, or carburetor side. The length of time required for the vacuum gauge to rise to a steady reading is noted and compared to the carmaker's specifications.

To test an OSAC valve on the car:
1. Connect a vacuum gauge to the distributor port of the valve, figure 11-20.
2. Run the engine at 2,200 rpm and note the time required for the vacuum gauge to rise to a steady reading. Several different OSAC valves are used, providing different delay times for different engines.
3. If the OSAC valve has a temperature override feature, it should permit immediate vacuum advance below 16° C (60° F). Heat and cool the temperature sensing portion of the valve to check its operation above and below 16° C (60° F).

To test the spark delay valve used by other manufacturers:
1. Connect a hand vacuum pump to the black side of the valve or the side marked CARB.

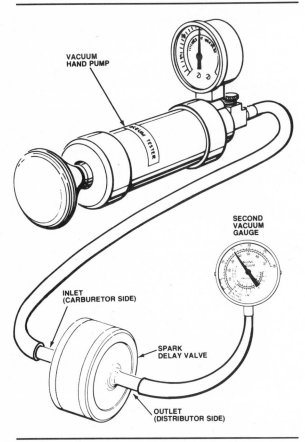

VACUUM
HAND PUMP

SECOND
VACUUM
GAUGE

INLET
(CARBURETOR SIDE)

SPARK
DELAY VALVE

OUTLET
(DISTRIBUTOR SIDE)

Figure 11-21. The vacuum gauge should show a slow buildup of vacuum.

Connect a vacuum gauge to the other side of the valve, figure 11-21.

2. Apply 10 to 15 in. (255 to 380 mm) Hg vacuum with the hand pump. The gauge reading should rise slowly to a steady reading. Ford provides specifications for the number of seconds required for various valves to rise to 6 inches (150 mm) of vacuum at the gauge when 10 inches (255 mm) is applied on the carburetor side.

3. To check the valve's release operation, reverse the pump and gauge connections at the valve. When vacuum is applied, the gauge reading should rise immediately.

4. Some GM vacuum delay valves have a cold temperature override feature similar to that of an OSAC valve. When the valve is cooled to below 10° C (50° F), there should be no delay in the application of vacuum to the distributor side.

5. For some cars, the manufacturers recommend that spark delay valves be replaced at regular intervals. The valves are usually color coded to indicate different delay valve times. Always make sure that the correct delay valve is installed and that it is installed in the right

direction. Since spark delay valves have been used for jobs other than simple vacuum advance delay, all valves are not installed in the same way. Doublecheck the installation instructions given by the manufacturer.

TIMING AND TEST ADJUSTMENT WITH ELECTRONIC ENGINE CONTROLS

Ignition timing has been integrated into the electronic engine control system as a computer function on most late-model engines. In many systems, the distributor contains no advance mechanisms: spark advance is a computer function. Basic timing specifications are still provided, although timing may or may not be adjustable, depending upon the system. If basic timing is out of specifications, you may need to replace the distributor, ignition module, or system computer to correct the problem.

The first step in checking ignition timing of an engine with electronic timing control is the same as it is with any ignition: obtain the correct specifications. These will be found on VECI labels, in factory shop manuals, or in independent publications such as the **Car Care Guide**. In the remainder of this chapter, we will discuss the principles of checking electronic timing control to help you make better use of the manufacturer's specific procedures.

General Motors Electronic Timing

Several procedures are provided by GM to test the timing on its electronically controlled engine systems. If an HEI distributor used on a carbureted engine has a 4-wire terminal connector, figure 11-22, the connector must be disconnected to put the system into the bypass timing mode and isolate the ignition module from the computer. Since this returns control to the ignition module, you can check timing at the specified rpm.

Disconnecting the 4-wire connector on fuel-injected engines will not work, because the engine will not run. The computer requires a signal from the distributor to time the injectors. Use one of these three methods to check timing on fuel-injected GM engines:

1. Connect a jumper wire across two terminals of the diagnostic connector.

2. Open a special connector in the distributor wiring harness.

3. Ground a test connector in the engine compartment.

The procedures to be used vary considerably on GM engines built after 1982. Knowing the specific procedure to be used is extremely im-

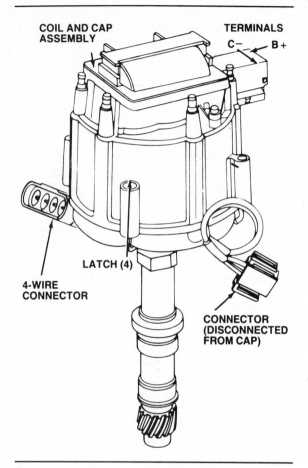

Figure 11-22. Disconnect the 4-terminal connector on HEI distributors to set timing on carbureted engines.

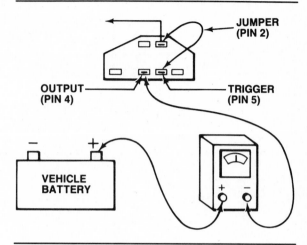

Figure 11-23. Jumper wire and voltmeter connections on Ford's EEC-IV system. (Ford)

portant on these engines, since using the wrong method can put the system into a fixed timing mode that is *not* basic timing. In other cases, the timing check method is rather obscure unless you know the carmaker's specific procedure. For example, some Cadillacs let you check timing by programming test codes into the automatic climate control system. The computer then flashes the timing as a digital display on the dashboard panel.

Ford Electronic Timing

Various procedures are used with the Ford systems. Engine timing is adjustable on some systems but not on others. A special tester is needed to check the timing completely on Ford's electronic engine control (EEC) I and II systems. However, it is possible to check basic timing by removing the calibration assembly from the computer and using a timing light to check timing mark alignment.

Check basic timing on EEC III in the same manner — by removing the calibration assem-

bly. By applying vacuum to the manifold absolute pressure (MAP) sensor with a hand-operated vacuum pump, you can make the system go into a self-test mode and check its advance at approximately 2,000 rpm without a load. The timing light can be used to check advance while the system is self-testing.

A diagnostic connector is provided in the engine compartment of Ford vehicles with EEC-IV. To check spark advance, connect the + lead of an analog voltmeter to the battery (+) terminal. Depending upon the particular car involved, use one or the other of the following methods:

    a. Connect a jumper wire between pin 2 and pin 5 of the diagnostic connector and connect the voltmeter (−) lead to pin 4, figure 11-23.

    b. Insert one end of a jumper wire into pin 4 of the diagnostic connector and clamp the voltmeter (−) lead to the other end, then connect a second jumper wire between pin 2 of the diagnostic connector and the self-test input connector, figure 11-24.

The system will then go into self-test mode, if the engine is at normal operating temperature and is running at idle. When engine speed increases to 2,000 rpm, use the timing light to read the spark advance according to the timing mark alignment and compare to specifications.

You can check basic timing on EEC-IV systems by disconnecting an inline base timing connector, figure 11-25. This interrupts the ECA's timing advance-and-retard signal and locks the ignition into its basic timing with no electronic control. Use a timing light to check timing mark alignment at the specified engine speed.

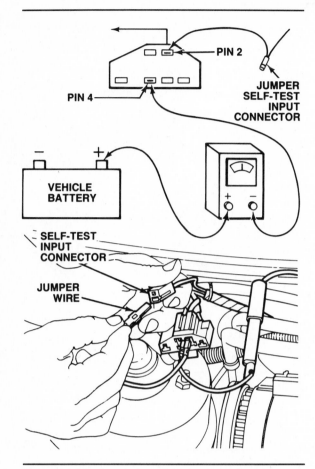

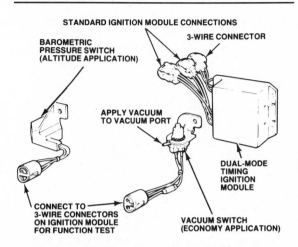

Figure 11-26. The vacuum switch or barometric pressure switch must be disconnected on Ford dual-mode ignitions. (Ford)

Figure 11-24. A variation of the jumper wire and voltmeter connections on Ford's EEC-IV system. (Ford)

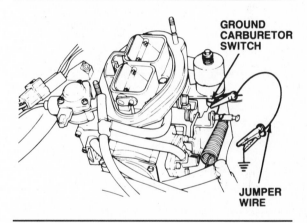

Figure 11-27. Ground the carburetor switch for basic timing check. (Chrysler)

On Ford ignition systems with dual-mode modules, the module must be disconnected from the vacuum switch or barometric pressure switch, figure 11-26. On some systems, a jumper wire must be installed across the black and yellow terminals; on others, no jumper wire is necessary. Once the connector is un-plugged, you can check timing with the timing light, but Ford's procedures must be followed exactly or you may damage the system or set timing incorrectly.

Chrysler Electronic Timing

The principal requirement to test timing of all Chrysler computer-controlled ignitions is to ground the carburetor idle-stop switch, figure 11-27. With the switch grounded and the en-gine at normal operating temperature and run-ning at idle, the timing should be within ±2

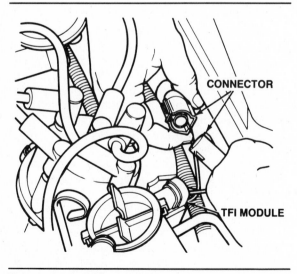

Figure 11-25. EEC-IV inline base timing connector location. (Ford)

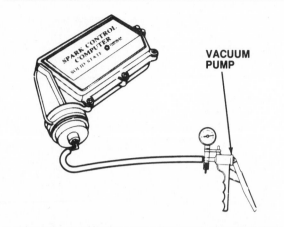

Figure 11-28. Chrysler V-6 and V-8 vacuum transducer connection. (Chrysler)

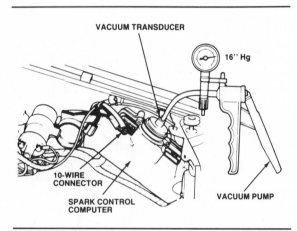

Figure 11-29. Chrysler 4-cylinder vacuum transducer connection. (Chrysler)

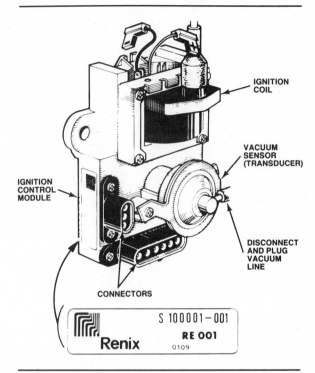

Figure 11-30. To check AMC-Renault 4-cylinder timing, disconnect the vacuum line from the transducer. (AMC-Renault)

degrees of the specified setting. If not, loosen the distributor holddown capscrew and adjust the timing just as you would for a system without electronic control.

To check spark advance, remove the jumper wire from the carburetor switch and place a matchbook cover between the switch and the idle screw. Disconnect and plug the vacuum line at the vacuum transducer, then connect a hand vacuum pump to the vacuum transducer and apply 16 in. (405 mm) Hg vacuum. Figure 11-28 shows the V-6 and V-8 connection; figure 11-29 shows the 4-cylinder connection.

Increase engine speed to 2,000 rpm and check timing with the timing light. Subtract the specified basic timing from what the timing light shows and you have the amount of advance. If this figure does not agree with the specifications, replace the computer.

Remove the hand vacuum pump and matchbook cover from the system; it should return to

basic timing. If it does not, look for oxidation on the carburetor switch contact, preventing it from grounding when the throttle is closed. If the switch contact is not oxidized, the switch may be defective.

While this method is the most common one used on Chrysler systems, there are variations specified for particular models. For example, some 4-cylinder engines require that you disconnect and reconnect the engine coolant temperature sensor. When the timing check is completed, you must do the same to the computer power supply connector located near the battery. This example points out why it is important to locate and use the *exact* procedure specified by the manufacturer.

American Motors Electronic Timing

AMC engines with the Ford SSI or Delco HEI systems can be checked with the same procedures used for Ford or GM vehicles.

Although timing is not adjustable on AMC-Renault 4-cylinder vehicles, you can check basic timing on these engines. To do so, disconnect the vacuum line from the ignition control module transducer, figure 11-30, and check timing at slow (curb) idle. If it is not within specifications, follow the carmaker's procedure to locate the defective part.

12

Electronic Engine Control System Testing and Service

In Chapter 11, you learned that the manufacturer's test and adjustment procedures are required to service an electronic ignition. This is also true when dealing with electronic engine control systems. In addition, you must understand the system components, know how they interact, and know how the system as a whole functions. Although this chapter cannot possibly contain *all* of the procedures required to service *all* of the various engine control systems, it will acquaint you with them and assist you in using the manufacturer's information and procedures more efficiently.

TROUBLESHOOTING PRINCIPLES

Before you can service an electronic engine control system, you must know what it does — the systems it monitors and the functions it controls. The job of any engine control system is to efficiently manage the functions it controls. Early engine control systems managed one or two functions, such as ignition timing or fuel metering. The most recent systems are multi-function and fully integrated. They monitor and manage a variety of interrelated engine operating conditions, including ignition, fuel metering, EGR, air injection, and fuel-vapor canister purge. Some even manage torque converter lockup, automatic transmission or transaxle shifting, and cruise control. The operation and service principles of all engine control systems are basically the same, no matter how many vehicle systems they manage. Chapter 17 of the *Classroom Manual* should be used in conjunction with this chapter to help you recognize the functions of any system.

When dealing with an engine control system, don't overlook the basic checkout procedure that should be followed *whenever* you are troubleshooting an automotive problem. Adding electronic controls to an engine does *not* change the basic structure or operation of the engine. To determine the cause of a problem, always make a general visual check of all components, wiring and connectors, and engine fluid levels before checking the control system. There is no sense in checking the control system for a problem if the problem is outside the system.

Area Tests and Pinpoint Tests

You learned to test from the general to the specific in Chapter 1. This principle is indispensable in checking the operation of an engine control system, if you expect to locate the cause of a problem and correct it efficiently.

We start by checking general system operation. These are called area tests. Area testing leads us to check a particular subsystem, circuit, or component. These are called pinpoint tests. Since all manufacturers have organized their system troubleshooting procedures in this manner, it is possible to break down the testing of any engine control system into three overall steps:

1. Perform an overall system, or area, diagnostic test based on the driver's complaint.
2. Use the results of the area test to do one or more specific subsystem, or pinpoint, tests as required.
3. Make the necessary adjustments or repairs based on the pinpoint testing and then do a system operational check to verify that the system is again working properly.

As a result of your pinpoint tests, it may be necessary to perform service procedures you have already learned for engines without a control system, such as idle adjustment or basic ignition timing. However, each procedure will relate to the control system and its proper operation.

ELECTRONIC SYSTEM SERVICE PROCEDURES

In addition to the general shop and vehicle system safety precautions you learned in Chapter 1, servicing an electronic control system requires that you follow the precautions listed below. This will prevent possible expensive damage to the vehicle systems or any test equipment being used, as well as making your job easier.

● Electrical connections:
1. Check for and retrieve any stored trouble codes from the computer before disconnecting the battery, since that will erase the stored codes from the computer memory. All programmed electronic devices such as radios, clocks, and air conditioning controls will have to be reset once the battery is reconnected.
2. Make sure the ignition switch is *off* before disconnecting the battery. If the switch is on, the resulting high-voltage surge may damage electronic components. For the same reason, you should not disconnect or reconnect any electrical connectors with the ignition on *unless* the manufacturer's procedure tells you specifically to do so.
3. Make sure all connectors are clean and properly connected. If they are not, high resistance can affect the operation of electronic systems which function with low voltage and very low current levels. Many problems can be solved by paying attention to connectors and wiring.

● EGO sensors:
1. Do not short across the terminals of a 2-wire exhaust gas oxygen (EGO) sensor or connect any test equipment to any EGO sensor unless the equipment is approved for this use. A high-impedance digital volt-ohmmeter (DVOM) with an input impedance of at least 10 megohms per volt can be used with most EGO sensors. The current draw of low-impedance test equipment may burn the sensor out.
2. Avoid using any rubber lubricants, belt dressings, or other sprays containing silicone near an EGO sensor. The silicone compounds tend to collect on the ambient air side of the sensor. This causes an incorrect voltage signal which the computer generally interprets as a lean-mixture signal. As a result, the computer will over-enrich the mixture.
3. Leaded gasoline used in a vehicle with an EGO sensor has the opposite effect of a silicone spray. The lead collects on the exhaust side of the sensor, causing an incorrect voltage signal which the computer will interpret as a rich-mixture signal. As a result, the computer leans out the mixture excessively.

● Exhaust system:
1. Do not modify the exhaust system of any vehicle with electronic engine controls. Removing the muffler or the catalytic converter or installing headers changes the exhaust backpressure. This may affect the operation of the exhaust gas recirculation (EGR) system, which is designed to function with a specific amount of backpressure.
2. Remember that you are dealing with a catalytic converter. This emission control device operates at a very high temperature and remains hot for a long time after the engine is shut off. Working on a vehicle with a converter requires special precautions:
   a. Avoid contact with the converter to avoid serious personal injury.
   b. Correct any misfiring condition at once.
   c. Do not crank the engine for more than 15 seconds without starting it, because this will allow fuel to enter the converter.
   d. After performing a power balance test, run the engine for at least 20 seconds at fast idle to clear the converter.

● Cooling system:
1. Proper engine temperature is imperative to engine control system operation. Since many engine control sensors are activated by coolant temperature, do not remove the thermostat or install one that does not meet the manufacturer's temperature specifications. If the engine does not warm up enough for the sensors to signal the computer, the vehicle will never

switch out of open loop, and in some cases, the system may record trouble codes.

SELF-DIAGNOSTIC SYSTEMS

The computers used in late-model engine control systems are programmed to check their own operation, as well as the operation of each sensor or actuator circuit. The extent to which a system can do this depends upon the system design. Generally, the computer does one or more of the following:

- Recognizes that a particular signal, such as engine speed, is not being furnished.
- Recognizes that a signal is improbable, such as input from a barometric pressure sensor that indicates the vehicle is being driven at an altitude of 25,000 feet.
- Recognizes that a signal is out of limits for too long, such as a too-rich or too-lean EGO sensor signal.
- Tests sensor or actuator circuit continuity by sending a test voltage signal or monitoring a return voltage signal.

Some test procedures may have you deliberately create an improbable or conflicting signal to trigger the selftest mode. Whenever the computer recognizes a signal that is outside its limits, it records a trouble or fault code in its memory. In addition, some systems turn on a warning or CHECK ENGINE or SERVICE ENGINE SOON lamp on the instrument panel to alert the driver to the need for service. Troubleshooting an engine control system starts with retrieving and reading these trouble codes. When you are dealing with a self-diagnostic control system, trouble code retrieval is your *area test*.

Almost all carmakers have equipped their engine control systems with self-diagnostic capabilities. The extent of this capability differs with the control system and the carmaker. We will use GM, Ford, and Chrysler systems as examples throughout this chapter. Once you understand the basic principles involved, you should be able to transfer this knowledge to the systems used by other carmakers.

Trouble Code Precautions

When properly used, trouble codes will help you to organize your thinking and approach to the problem efficiently. In this respect, they are valuable diagnostic aids, but a trouble code cannot think and test for you. It is simply a key to where the problem lies and indicates that a particular circuit or component should be checked. This means that it is only a general indicator that narrows down the possibilities; it does not

point directly to the exact or precise cause of a problem. The following examples should clarify what a trouble code actually does, and *does not*, do.

Rich or lean exhaust indication

Most engine control systems use one or two codes to indicate when oxygen in the exhaust varies from a 14.7:1 ratio during closed-loop operation. The code tells you that something is wrong with engine operation, but only points you in a general direction.

For example, if a "rich exhaust" trouble code is retrieved from the computer, it means one or more of the following problems exist:

- The EGO sensor, wiring, or connector is defective
- The air filter is dirty
- The choke is stuck closed, or not opening fully
- An excessive amount of fuel vapor is being purged from the vapor-storage canister
- The PCV system is overloaded or an excessively worn engine is allowing too much blowby
- The carburetor or injection system metering device is defective
- The system computer is defective.

On the other hand, a "lean exhaust" trouble code means one or more of the following problems exist:

- The EGO sensor, wiring, or connector is defective
- There is a vacuum leak in the intake system
- The engine is misfiring
- The EGR system is malfunctioning
- The carburetor or injection system metering device is defective
- The system computer is defective.

Once you have retrieved the trouble code and determined what it means, you must then perform one or more pinpoint tests to locate the exact cause of the problem. As you can see, a trouble code eliminates some possible causes while indicating *several other* probable causes. For this reason, manufacturers organize their test procedures to begin with the most probable cause.

High or low coolant temperature indication

A self-diagnostic system generally has one or more trouble codes to tell you that there is a problem with either the coolant temperature sensor or the temperature-sensing circuit. System designs vary. Some may only tell you that there is a malfunction, while others will indicate that the problem is one of high or low temperature. To interpret the information, however, you must know the kind of sensor used in

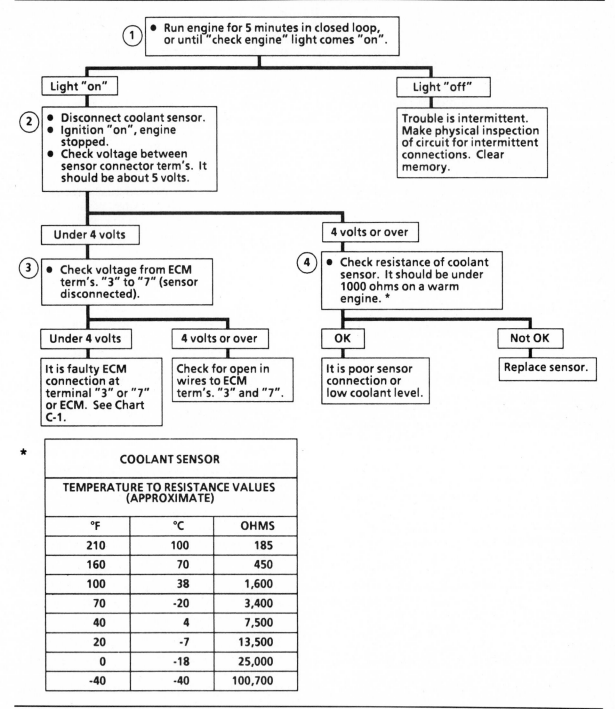

Figure 12-1. Typical GM troubleshooting chart for CCC system trouble code 15, an open coolant sensor circuit. (Chevrolet)

the system and how it operates. This information is available in the manufacturer's specifications and procedures.

As an example of what the trouble code is telling you, high-temperature malfunctions can result from:
• Engine overheating caused by a thermostat

that is stuck closed or opening at high temperature, a low coolant level, blocked radiator airflow, clogged hoses, or restrictions in the water jackets or passages.
• A defective coolant temperature sensor, its wiring, or its connector.
• A defective system computer.

TEST STEP	RESULT ▶	ACTION TO TAKE
DA1 SERVICE CODE 24: CHECK AMBIENT TEMPERATURE		
• Ambient temperature must be greater than 50°F for this test.	Yes ▶ No ▶	GO to DA2. RERUN Quick Test.
DA2 CHECK FOR V REF AT THROTTLE POSITION SENSOR		
• Refer to illustration Q. • Key Off, wait 10 seconds. • DVOM on 20V scale. • Disconnect TP sensor. • Key On, Engine Off. • Measure voltage at the TP harness connector between VREF and signal return.	Less than 4.0V or greater than 6.0V ▶ 4.0V to 6.0V ▶	GO to Pinpoint Test Step C1. RECONNECT TP sensor, GO to DA3.

Figure 12-2. The first two steps in Ford's pinpoint test for an EEC-IV air-charge (intake air) temperature sensor fault. (Ford)

Low-temperature malfunctions can result from:
• A thermostat that has been removed, or one that opens at low temperature.
• A defective ambient air temperature sensor.
• A defective coolant temperature sensor, its wiring, or its connector.
• A defective system computer.

The logic of a troubleshooting chart provided by the manufacturer is shown in figures 12-1 and 12-2. While some test procedures may seem complicated or even duplicate each other, they will help you solve the problem in the most efficient way — if you follow them exactly, without skipping or mixing steps along the route.

Open-loop and closed-loop faults

Many conditions indicated by a trouble code are the kind that will prevent the engine control system from switching into closed-loop operation. Other problems may exist in the closed-loop mode, but they will not show up as a trouble code until the problem which keeps the system in open-loop operation is corrected. When you understand this, you can see why it is vital that you check system performance after correcting a problem. If you do not check system performance, it is possible that the car will leave your shop with only one of several problems solved. This usually results in a comeback and a dissatisfied customer.

Kinds of Trouble Codes

Trouble codes can be categorized in several ways. You should be aware of the difference between a hard failure, which prevents the engine from running, and a soft failure, which allows the engine to run, but poorly.
• Hard failure — If the computer loses the signal that tells if the engine is cranking or running, and thus has no way to determine how to control ignition timing, the engine will not start and run.
• Soft failure — If the computer receives a too-low signal from the coolant temperature sensor, it will switch to open loop, or not switch out of open loop. The engine will run, but performance and fuel economy will suffer.

Some soft failures are more easily noticed than others, since they may reduce power or gas mileage. Others may not be noticed at all if the system contains built-in bypass circuitry. In this case, the warning or CHECK ENGINE light comes on to alert the driver of the need for service, but the vehicle continues to run satisfactorily because the computer is accepting a substitute input signal. Either a hard or a soft failure will set a trouble code in systems with self-diagnostic capabilities.

Hard and soft failures will produce either a continuous or an intermittent code. The *continuous* code indicates that the malfunction was and is present. This type of code generally results from total failure of a component or subsystem. An *intermittent* code indicates that the

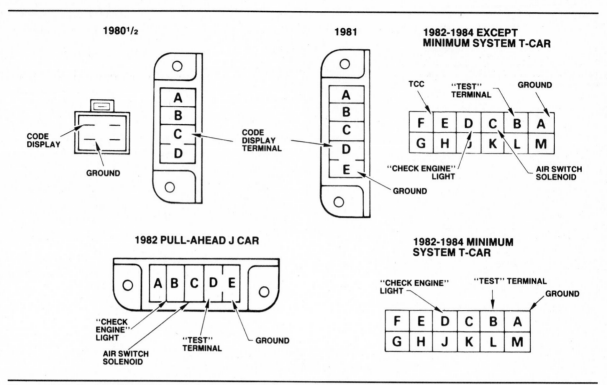

Figure 12-3. Typical GM CCC diagnostic connector terminal locations. (GM)

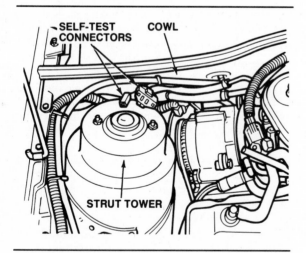

Figure 12-4. Typical Ford EEC-IV self-test connector location. (Ford)

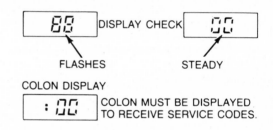

Figure 12-5. Ford's STAR tester readout display. (Ford)

malfunction took place and disappeared. This type of code usually means that a component or subsystem is functioning erratically. Intermittent malfunctions that occur when the engine is in closed-loop operation will not produce a trouble code if the engine returns to the open-loop mode.

In order for the system to record an intermittent trouble code, the computer must have long-term memory, or memory that is not lost when the ignition is turned off. Long-term

memory will store an intermittent code for 50 to 60 engine-start cycles (key off, on, and off) after it has been set. Early control systems did not have long-term memory; late-model systems do. On some C-4 systems without long-term memory, such as the 1980 GM X-cars, a jumper wire can be connected to the computer memory to maintain applied voltage with the ignition off, thus activating long-term memory. All GM CCC systems (except the "minimum function" Chevette and T1000 systems) have long-term memory and can store intermittent codes.

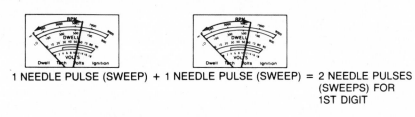

1 NEEDLE PULSE (SWEEP) + 1 NEEDLE PULSE (SWEEP) = 2 NEEDLE PULSES (SWEEPS) FOR 1ST DIGIT

2-SECOND PAUSE BETWEEN DIGITS

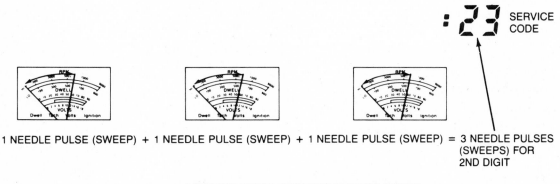

SERVICE CODE

1 NEEDLE PULSE (SWEEP) + 1 NEEDLE PULSE (SWEEP) + 1 NEEDLE PULSE (SWEEP) = 3 NEEDLE PULSES (SWEEPS) FOR 2ND DIGIT

4-SECOND PAUSE BETWEEN SERVICE CODES, WHEN MORE THAN ONE CODE IS GENERATED

Figure 12-6. An analog voltmeter can be used to signal numerical trouble codes by its pulsating needle. (Ford)

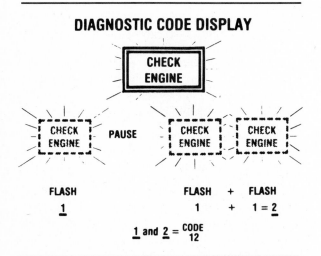

Figure 12-7. GM uses a CHECK ENGINE light to flash trouble codes. (GM)

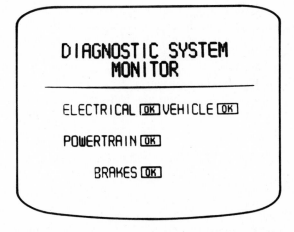

Figure 12-8. Touching one of the systems on the diagnostic page of Buick's graphic control center display will bring up trouble codes, if any are stored. (GM)

Manufacturers use various terms to describe their trouble codes, which can be confusing. For example, Ford refers to continuous codes (as we described them above) as "on-demand codes", and intermittent codes (as described above) as "continuous codes". Other manufacturers may use the term "stored codes" to describe intermittent codes (as described above).

Reading Trouble Codes

Each manufacturer publishes a list of trouble codes used with each system and has devised special procedures for retrieving and reading the codes. Most vehicles have a diagnostic test connector of some kind which is used to connect test equipment into the system. On GM

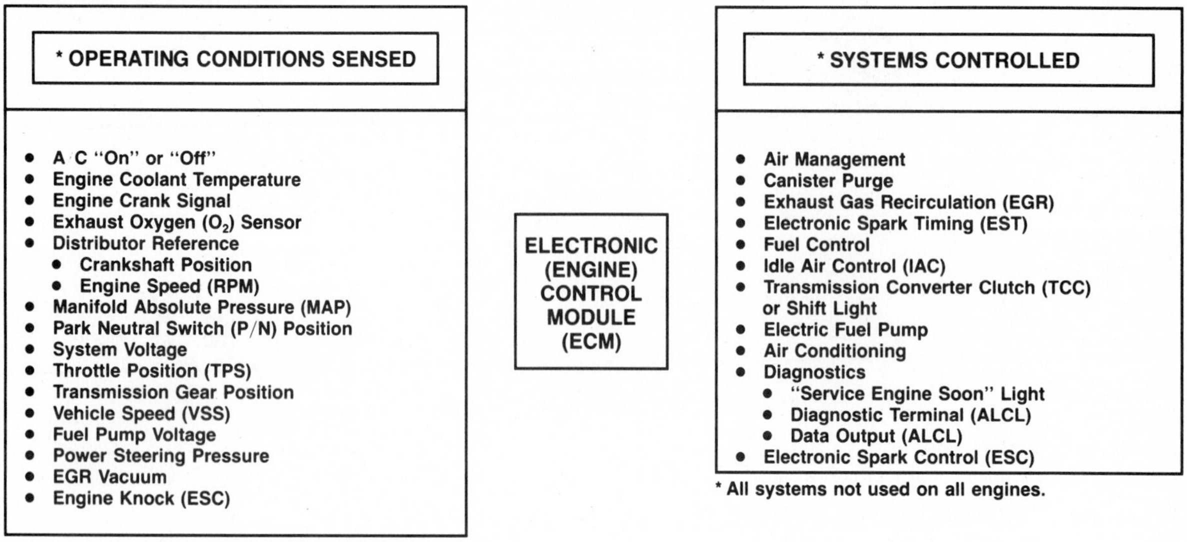

```
┌─────────────────────────────────┐        ┌─────────────────────────────────┐
│ ┌─────────────────────────────┐ │        │ ┌─────────────────────────────┐ │
│ │ * OPERATING CONDITIONS SENSED│ │        │ │   * SYSTEMS CONTROLLED      │ │
│ └─────────────────────────────┘ │        │ └─────────────────────────────┘ │
│                                 │        │                                 │
│ ● A·C "On" or "Off"             │        │ ● Air Management                │
│ ● Engine Coolant Temperature    │        │ ● Canister Purge                │
│ ● Engine Crank Signal           │        │ ● Exhaust Gas Recirculation (EGR)│
│ ● Exhaust Oxygen (O₂) Sensor    │        │ ● Electronic Spark Timing (EST) │
│ ● Distributor Reference         │        │ ● Fuel Control                  │
│     ● Crankshaft Position       │        │ ● Idle Air Control (IAC)        │
│     ● Engine Speed (RPM)        │        │ ● Transmission Converter Clutch (TCC)│
│ ● Manifold Absolute Pressure (MAP)│      │     or Shift Light              │
│ ● Park Neutral Switch (P/N) Position│    │ ● Electric Fuel Pump            │
│ ● System Voltage                │        │ ● Air Conditioning              │
│ ● Throttle Position (TPS)       │        │ ● Diagnostics                   │
│ ● Transmission Gear Position    │        │     ● "Service Engine Soon" Light│
│ ● Vehicle Speed (VSS)           │        │     ● Diagnostic Terminal (ALCL)│
│ ● Fuel Pump Voltage             │        │     ● Data Output (ALCL)        │
│ ● Power Steering Pressure       │        │ ● Electronic Spark Control (ESC)│
│ ● EGR Vacuum                    │        │                                 │
│ ● Engine Knock (ESC)            │        │ * All systems not used on all engines.│
└─────────────────────────────────┘        └─────────────────────────────────┘
```

ELECTRONIC
(ENGINE)
CONTROL
MODULE
(ECM)

Figure 12-9. Operating conditions sensed and systems controlled by the CCC ECM. (Chevrolet)

vehicles, a diagnostic code display terminal is found in a 4-, 5-, or 12-terminal connector installed under the instrument panel, figure 12-3. Ford generally has the connector in the engine compartment, figure 12-4. Carmakers and a variety of test equipment manufacturers offer special testers that plug into the test connector to retrieve the codes. While these testers are more efficient, you often can use an analog voltmeter or other general-purpose test equipment for the same purpose.

A trouble code generally is displayed in one of four basic ways. It may be seen as a:
1. Numerical display on a special tester, figure 12-5
2. Pulsating voltmeter needle, figure 12-6
3. Pulsating instrument panel CHECK ENGINE light, figure 12-7
4. Digital display on an instrument panel, figure 12-8.

TESTING THE GENERAL MOTORS CCC AND C-4 SYSTEMS

Recent GM CCC systems monitor up to 15 engine functions and vehicle conditions, controlling as many as 11 output functions, figure 12-9. This is called a "full-function" system. The "minimum-function" CCC system used on 1982 and later Chevettes and T1000 cars and the early C-4 systems do not monitor or control all functions.

Reading GM Trouble Codes — Diagnostic (Area) Tests

A CHECK ENGINE lamp is provided on the instrument panel of all GM vehicles with C-4 and CCC systems. This lamp alerts the driver of a malfunction, but it also can be used to retrieve and read trouble codes by grounding a test terminal under the instrument panel, figure 12-3. This is known as an assembly line communications link (ALCL) or assembly line diagnostic link (ALDL) connector. Early C-4 systems used a single-wire connector near the computer or control module.

Note that the ground terminal is located right next to the test terminal on all ALCL and ALDL connectors. When a jumper wire is inserted in the test and ground terminals, the CHECK ENGINE light flashes to display the trouble codes. Full-function CCC systems display both continuous and intermittent codes; C-4 and minimum-function systems display only codes for malfunctions that exist during testing.

To check the diagnostic circuit operation and read the trouble codes:
1. Turn the ignition key on but *do not start the engine.* The CHECK ENGINE lamp should come on, along with the other warning lamps. This bulb check tells you the lamp is working. *Turn the ignition key off.*
2. Insert a jumper wire between the test and ground terminals in the connector, figure 12-3.
3. Turn the ignition key on again without starting the engine and watch the CHECK ENGINE lamp. It should flash one short flash, followed

---

TROUBLE CODE IDENTIFICATION

The "CHECK ENGINE" light will only be "ON" if the malfunction exists under the conditions listed below. It takes up to five seconds for the light to come on when a problem occurs. If the malfunction clears, the light will go out and a trouble code will be set in the ECM. Code 12 does not store in memory. If the light comes "ON" intermittently, but no code is stored, go to the "Driver Comments" section. Any codes stored will be erased if no problem reoccurs within 50 engine starts.

The trouble codes indicate problems as follows:

TROUBLE CODE 12 No distributor reference pulses to the ECM. This code is not stored in memory and will only flash while the fault is present.

TROUBLE CODE 13 Oxygen sensor circuit — The engine must run up to five minutes at part throttle, under road load, before this code will set.

TROUBLE CODE 14 Shorted coolant sensor circuit — The engine must run up to five minutes before this code will set.

TROUBLE CODE 15 Open coolant sensor circuit — The engine must run up to five minutes before this code will set.

TROUBLE CODE 21 Throttle position sensor circuit — The engine must run up to 25 seconds, at specified curb idle speed, before this code will set.

TROUBLE CODE 23 Open or grounded M/C solenoid circuit.

TROUBLE CODE 24 Vehicle speed sensor (VSS) circuit — The car must operate up to five minutes at road speed before this code will set.

TROUBLE CODE 32 Barometric pressure sensor (BARO) circuit low, or altitude compensator low on J-Car.

TROUBLE CODE 34 Manifold absolute pressure (MAP) or vacuum sensor circuit — The engine must run up to five minutes, at specified curb idle speed, before this code will set.

TROUBLE CODE 35 Idle speed control (ISC) switch circuit shorted. (Over 50% throttle for over 2 sec.)

TROUBLE CODE 41 No distributor reference pulses to the ECM at specified engine vacuum. This code will store in memory.

TROUBLE CODE 42 Electronic spark timing (EST) bypass circuit or EST circuit grounded or open.

TROUBLE CODE 43 ESC retard signal for too long; causes a retard in EST signal.

TROUBLE CODE 44 Lean exhaust indication — The engine must run up to five minutes, in closed loop, at part throttle and road load before this code will set.

TROUBLE CODE 44 & 55 (At same time) — Faulty oxygen sensor circuit.

TROUBLE CODE 45 Rich exhaust indication — The engine must run up to five minutes, in closed loop, at part throttle and road load before this code will set.

TROUBLE CODE 51 Faulty calibration unit (PROM) or installation. It takes up to 30 seconds before this code will set.

TROUBLE CODE 54 Shorted M/C solenoid circuit and/or faulty ECM.

TROUBLE CODE 55 Grounded V ref (terminal "21"), faulty oxygen sensor, or ECM.

Figure 12-10. The basic trouble codes of a full-function CCC system. (GM)

by a pause and then two short, rapid flashes, figure 12-7. This is code 12, a system self-check which tells you that the diagnostic function is operating as designed. It indicates no distributor pulses, or tach signal, to the computer (since the engine is not running, there should be no tach signal to the computer during this procedure).

4. Let code 12 flash three times. If there are other trouble codes stored in the memory, the lamp will pause and then flash the remaining codes three times each. When all trouble codes have been displayed, the lamp will pause and

flash code 12 four more times. If the lamp flashes code 12 four times initially, pauses and then flashes code 12 four more times, there are no trouble codes stored in the memory.

Figures 12-10 and 12-11 are typical trouble codes for full-function and minimum-function CCC systems. Figure 12-12 gives the trouble codes for most C-4 systems. Note that all systems use code 12 as a self-test and that many codes indicate the same problems in all systems.

Except for the 50-series codes, all codes are flashed in numerical sequence in GM systems.

TROUBLE CODE IDENTIFICATION

The "CHECK ENGINE" light will only be "ON" if the malfunction exists under the conditions listed below. It takes up to five seconds for the light to come on when a problem occurs. If the malfunction clears, the light will go out and a trouble code will be set in the ECM. Code 12 does not store in memory. If the light comes "ON" intermittently, but no code is stored, go to the "DRIVER COMMENT" section. Any codes stored will be erased when the ignition is turned "OFF".

The trouble codes indicate problems as follows:

TROUBLE CODE 12 No distributor reference pulses to the ECM. This code is not stored in memory and will only flash while the fault is present.

TROUBLE CODE 15 Open coolant switch circuit — The engine must run for five minutes before this code will set.

TROUBLE CODE 21 Throttle position sensor circuit at WOT — The engine must run for 10 seconds, below 1000 RPM, before this code will set.

TROUBLE CODE 23 M/C solenoid circuit. (Must be in closed loop mode to set code.)

TROUBLE CODE 44 Lean exhaust indication — The engine must run up to one minute, in closed loop, at part throttle above 2000 RPM before this code will set.

TROUBLE CODE 45 Rich exhaust indication — The engine must run up to one minute, in closed loop, at part throttle above 2000 RPM before this code will set.

TROUBLE CODE 51 Faulty calibration unit (PROM) or installation. Turns ECM off.

Figure 12-11. The basic trouble codes of a minimum-function CCC system. (GM)

GM C-4 SYSTEM TROUBLE CODES

TROUBLE CODE	PROBLEM — SEE SPECIFIC DIAGNOSTIC CHART
12	No tachometer signal to ECM.
13	Oxygen sensor circuit. The engine must run for about 5 minutes at part throttle for this code to show.
14	Shorted coolant sensor circuit. The engine must run for about 2 minutes for this code to show.
15	Open coolant sensor circuit. The engine must run for about 5 minutes at part throttle for this code to show.
21	Throttle position sensor circuit (V-6).
22	Grounded closed-throttle or wide-open-throttle switch circuit (4-cylinder).
21 & 22 (same time)	Grounded wide-open-throttle switch circuit (4-cylinder).
23	Carburetor solenoid circuit.
44	Lean oxygen sensor signal.
45	Rich oxygen sensor signal.
51	On service-replacement ECM, check calibration unit. On original-equipment ECM, replace ECM.
54	Faulty carburetor solenoid or ECM.
52, 53	Replace ECM.
55	Faulty throttle position sensor (V-6) or ECM.

Figure 12-12. The basic trouble codes of the GM X-car C-4 system. (GM)

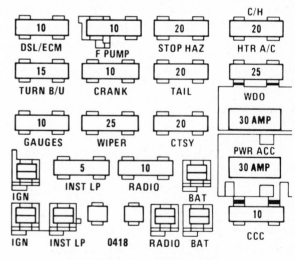

FRONT VIEW OF FUSE BLOCK

Figure 12-13. The computer memory can be cleared on some cars by removing a specific fuse. (Chevrolet)

A 50-series code will flash immediately after code 12 because it indicates a problem in the electronic control module (ECM), or computer, that must be corrected before proceeding to any other code.

You should write the codes down as they flash for two reasons: to remember them and

1983 DIAGNOSTIC CODES

CODE	CIRCUIT AFFECTED
■■ 12	NO DISTRIBUTOR (TACH) SIGNAL
☐ 13	O_2 SENSOR NOT READY
☐ 14	SHORTED COOLANT SENSOR CIRCUIT
☐ 15	OPEN COOLANT SENSOR CIRCUIT
■■ 16	GENERATOR VOLTAGE OUT OF RANGE
☐ 18	OPEN CRANK SIGNAL CIRCUIT
☐ 19	SHORTED FUEL PUMP CIRCUIT
■■ 20	OPEN FUEL PUMP CIRCUIT
☐ 21	SHORTED THROTTLE POSITION SENSOR CIRCUIT
☐ 22	OPEN THROTTLE POSITION SENSOR CIRCUIT
☐ 23	EST/BYPASS CIRCUIT PROBLEM
☐ 24	SPEED SENSOR CIRCUIT PROBLEM
☐ 26	SHORTED THROTTLE SWITCH CIRCUIT
☐ 27	OPEN THROTTLE SWITCH CIRCUIT
☐ 28	OPEN FOURTH GEAR CIRCUIT
☐ 29	SHORTED FOURTH GEAR CIRCUIT
☐ 30	ISC CIRCUIT PROBLEM
■■ 31	SHORTED MAP SENSOR CIRCUIT
■■ 32	OPEN MAP SENSOR CIRCUIT
■■ 33	MAP/BARO SENSOR CORRELATION
■■ 34	MAP SIGNAL TOO HIGH
☐ 35	SHORTED BARO SENSOR CIRCUIT
☐ 36	OPEN BARO SENSOR CIRCUIT
☐ 37	SHORTED MAT SENSOR CIRCUIT
☐ 38	OPEN MAT SENSOR CIRCUIT
☐ 39	TCC ENGAGEMENT PROBLEM
■■ 44	LEAN EXHAUST SIGNAL
■■ 45	RICH EXHAUST SIGNAL
■■ 51	PROM ERROR INDICATOR
▼ 52	ECM MEMORY RESET INDICATOR
▼ 53	DISTRIBUTOR SIGNAL INTERRUPT
▼ 60	TRANSMISSION NOT IN DRIVE
▼ 63	CAR AND SET SPEED TOLERANCE EXCEEDED
▼ 64	CAR ACCELERATION EXCEEDS MAX. LIMIT
▼ 65	COOLANT TEMPERATURE EXCEEDS MAX. LIMIT
▼ 66	ENGINE RPM EXCEEDS MAXIMUM LIMIT
▼ 67	SHORTED SET OR RESUME CIRCUIT
.7.0	SYSTEM READY FOR FURTHER TESTS
.7.1	CRUISE CONTROL BRAKE CIRCUIT TEST
.7.2	THROTTLE SWITCH CIRCUIT TEST
.7.3	DRIVE (ADL) CIRCUIT TEST
.7.4	REVERSE CIRCUIT TEST
.7.5	CRUISE ON/OFF CIRCUIT TEST
.7.6	"SET/COAST" CIRCUIT TEST
.7.7	"RESUME/ACCELERATION" CIRCUIT TEST
.7.8	"INSTANT/AVERAGE" CIRCUIT TEST
.7.9	"RESET" CIRCUIT TEST
.8.0	A/C CLUTCH CIRCUIT TEST
-1.8.8	DISPLAY CHECK
.9.0	SYSTEM READY TO DISPLAY ENGINE DATA
.9.5	SYSTEM READY FOR OUTPUT CYCLING OR IN FIXED SPARK MODE
.9.6	OUTPUT CYCLING
.0.0	ALL DIANOSTICS COMPLETE

■■	TURNS ON "SERVICE NOW" LIGHT
∷	TURNS ON "SERVICE SOON" LIGHT
▼	DOES NOT TURN ON ANY TELLTALE LIGHT

NOTE: CRUISE IS DISENGAGED WITH ANY "SERVICE NOW" LIGHT OR WITH CODES 60-67.

Figure 12-14. The CCC system used by Cadillac contains air conditioning and cruise control trouble codes, as well as engine codes. (Cadillac)

because the computer memory will have to be cleared in order to determine whether the code is continuous or intermittent. To continue with the general diagnostic test:

1. Once you have written down the trouble codes, if any, and watched code 12 signal the end of code display, shut off the ignition and disconnect the jumper from the test connector.
2. With the ignition off, the computer memory can be cleared in one of four ways, depending upon the vehicle being tested:
   a. Remove a specific fuse from the fuse block, figure 12-13.
   b. Disconnect a specific connector at the ECM.
   c. Disconnect a memory connector located near the battery positive terminal.
   d. Disconnect the battery ground cable. (This will also erase the memory of other electronic devices in the vehicle.)
3. Reinstall the fuse or reconnect the connector or battery cable and start the engine. Watch the CHECK ENGINE lamp. If it lights, the fault is continuous; that is, it is still present. If it does not light, previously displayed codes indicated intermittent faults that are not present at the time of testing.

Suppose, however, that the CHECK ENGINE lamp does not behave as we have described it. This is entirely possible; here are some of the variations that may occur:

● The lamp does not light during the bulb check (key on, engine off). If this happens, a special diagnostic chart is provided to troubleshoot the lamp before moving on to other tests.

● The lamp glows dimly without displaying any codes. There is either a bad ground at the computer or the voltage supplied to the computer is less than 9 volts. Check the ground and charge the battery.

● The lamp flashes erratically, displaying unlisted trouble codes. There is probably a voltage interference. It is most likely coming from the ignition system, a CB radio, an open diode in the A/C compressor clutch circuit, or a misrouted CCC wire harness that is too close to other engine wiring.

● The lamp does not light but the owner has a driveability complaint. In this case, a special "driver comment" diagnostic chart is provided to troubleshoot the most likely causes of specific symptoms.

Cadillac diagnostic displays

Cadillac has devised an easier-to-read display system for trouble codes on its late-model vehicles with CCC systems and digital fuel injection (DFI). While you need to have the Cadillac test

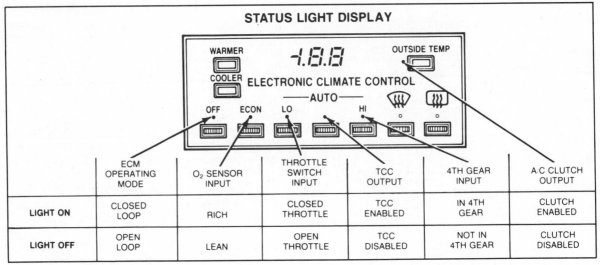

Figure 12-15. The Cadillac air conditioning control panel is used to display digital trouble codes. (Cadillac)

	ECM OPERATING MODE	O₂ SENSOR INPUT	THROTTLE SWITCH INPUT	TCC OUTPUT	4TH GEAR INPUT	A·C CLUTCH OUTPUT
LIGHT ON	CLOSED LOOP	RICH	CLOSED THROTTLE	TCC ENABLED	IN 4TH GEAR	CLUTCH ENABLED
LIGHT OFF	OPEN LOOP	LEAN	OPEN THROTTLE	TCC DISABLED	NOT IN 4TH GEAR	CLUTCH DISABLED

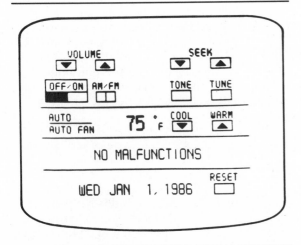

Figure 12-16. The summary page of Buick's graphic control center is displayed after a self-test initiated by touching the vehicle's door handle. (GM)

procedures to work with the extensive trouble codes provided by the system, figure 12-14, its operation is quite simple. With the ignition on, you press the OFF and WARMER buttons on the A/C electric climate control (ECC) panel. The digital display then shows the CCC trouble codes, figure 12-15, instead of time and temperature data.

The Cadillac system has other features. It can be used while the car is being driven. It also checks transmission switch and cruise control operation. To differentiate between hard and soft failures, Cadillac uses a SERVICE NOW (hard) lamp and a SERVICE SOON (soft) lamp instead of the single CHECK ENGINE lamp found on other GM systems.

Advanced versions of this system called the "Driver Information Center" are used on 1985 and later Cadillacs and Oldsmobile Toronados.

CRT diagnostic displays

The 1986 Buick Riviera uses a graphic control center containing a cathode ray tube, or CRT, display screen. A mylar panel over the display screen contains ultra-thin wires which are row- and column-encoded to provide six different "pages" or displays on the screen, depending upon the voltage signal sent to the control circuitry. Touching the door handle activates power to the displays, which are brought up on the screen as soon as the driver's door is closed. The electronic instrument cluster goes into a silent self-test while the screen displays the Riviera logo. If the driver does not ask for a specific display within 30 seconds, the system switches to the first, or summary, "page", figure 12-16. By touching any of the switch functions labeled on the edge of the screen, the driver can call up:

● Climate control
● Trip monitor
● Diagnostics
● Radio
● Gauges.

When the diagnostic page is called up, a menu appears containing four main and one optional categories, figure 12-8. The driver can check the monitored system within any of these areas by touching the desired one. Each category displays a box that shows "OK" if the system is working properly, or flashes if there is a problem. When the electrical category is displayed, status boxes indicate the operating condition of the CCC system and subsystems. If a box flashes, a problem exists in that area. The

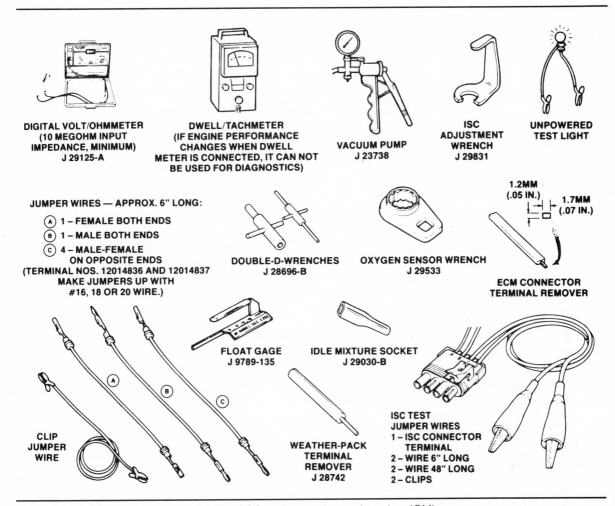

DIGITAL VOLT/OHMMETER
(10 MEGOHM INPUT
IMPEDANCE, MINIMUM)
J 29125-A

DWELL/TACHMETER
(IF ENGINE PERFORMANCE
CHANGES WHEN DWELL
METER IS CONNECTED, IT CAN NOT
BE USED FOR DIAGNOSTICS)

VACUUM PUMP
J 23738

ISC ADJUSTMENT WRENCH
J 29831

UNPOWERED TEST LIGHT

JUMPER WIRES — APPROX. 6" LONG:
(A) 1 – FEMALE BOTH ENDS
(B) 1 – MALE BOTH ENDS
(C) 4 – MALE-FEMALE ON OPPOSITE ENDS
(TERMINAL NOS. 12014836 AND 12014837 MAKE JUMPERS UP WITH #16, 18 OR 20 WIRE.)

DOUBLE-D-WRENCHES
J 28696-B

OXYGEN SENSOR WRENCH
J 29533

1.2MM (.05 IN.) 1.7MM (.07 IN.)

ECM CONNECTOR TERMINAL REMOVER

CLIP JUMPER WIRE

FLOAT GAGE
J 9789-135

IDLE MIXTURE SOCKET
J 29030-B

WEATHER-PACK TERMINAL REMOVER
J 28742

ISC TEST JUMPER WIRES
1 – ISC CONNECTOR TERMINAL
2 – WIRE 6" LONG
2 – WIRE 48" LONG
2 – CLIPS

Figure 12-17. These tools are required for CCC system testing and service. (GM)

touch-sensitive screen of the CRT allows you to press the flashing box to display trouble codes and other diagnostic information. If problems exist, additional display screens lead you through the troubleshooting routines.

GM CCC System Pinpoint Tests

Once you have recorded the trouble codes and determined whether they are continuous or intermittent, you can proceed with the diagnostic chart provided for each code. Some circuits may use two codes for differing problems, figure 12-10 and 12-14. Each code has its own separate chart to help you locate the problem. If there is no code for a particular circuit or subsystem, refer to the "driver comment" chart which will direct you to the appropriate chart or charts to be used.

CCC system problems can be solved without the use of special test equipment for troubleshooting. Figure 12-17 shows the basic equipment required to service a CCC system. While the GM special tool numbers are shown for many items, you can make several yourself, (such as jumper wires), and equivalent test equipment is available from various manufacturers. The dwellmeter is used to test the carburetor mixture control solenoid, as we will see later in the chapter.

Before referring to a diagnostic chart, you should make sure all vacuum lines are in good condition and are properly routed, with no leaking connections. You should also make sure that all electrical connectors are free from low or high resistance and are connected securely.

A diagnostic chart is useless if the fault does not exist at the time of testing. Intermittent faults that were recorded earlier, but are not present during testing, cannot be solved with the charts. Some codes require specific engine operating conditions for a given length of time before they are recorded in memory, figure 12-10. An intermittent code may be recorded in memory, but it must occur during testing if you are to find the cause.

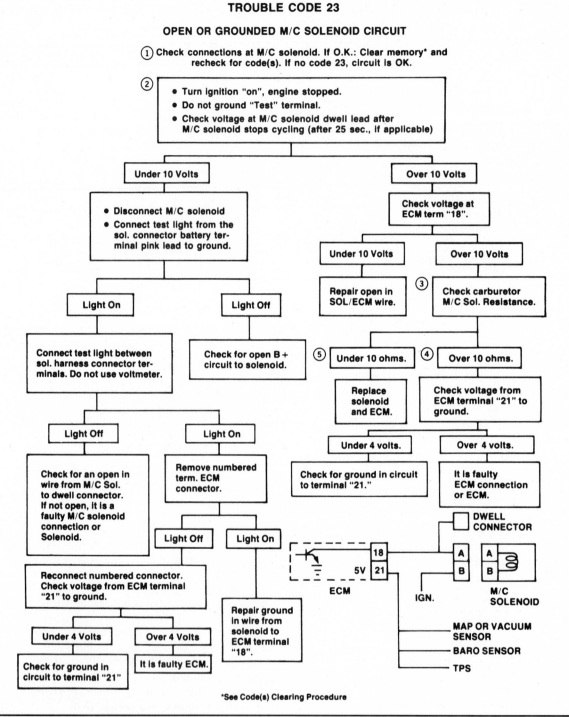

Figure 12-18. Typical GM troubleshooting chart for CCC system trouble code 23, an open or grounded mixture control solenoid circuit. (GM)

We'll use code 23 to show you how to use a diagnostic chart. Code 23 deals with an open or shorted mixture control solenoid circuit used with a CCC feedback carburetor, figure 12-18.

Here is how you proceed:
1. Check for broken wiring and loose or corroded connections at the mixture control solenoid. Repair or replace as required.

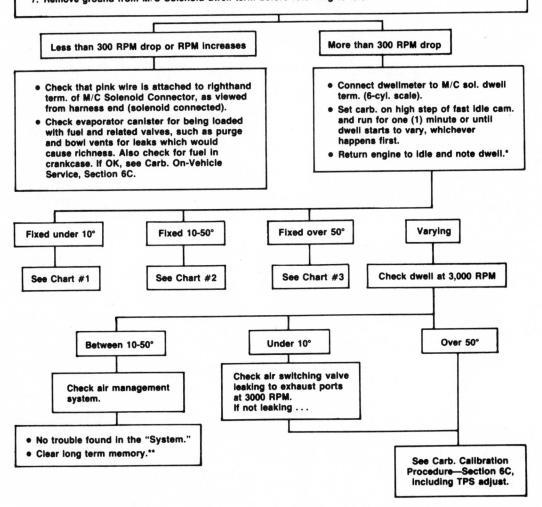

SYSTEM PERFORMANCE CHECK
(EXCEPT CKG TRUCK)

1. Start engine.
2. Ground "test" term. (Must not be grounded before engine is started.)
3. Disconnect purge hose from canister and plug it. On E2SE carburetors, disconnect bowl vent at carburetor.
4. Connect tachometer.
5. Disconnect Mixture Control (M/C) Solenoid and ground M/C Solenoid dwell term.
6. Run engine at 3,000 RPM and, while keeping throttle constant, reconnect M/C Solenoid and note RPM. If car is equipped with an electric cooling fan, it may lower RPM when it engages.
7. Remove ground from M/C Solenoid dwell term before returning to idle.

Less than 300 RPM drop or RPM increases

- Check that pink wire is attached to righthand term. of M/C Solenoid Connector, as viewed from harness end (solenoid connected).
- Check evaporator canister for being loaded with fuel and related valves, such as purge and bowl vents for leaks which would cause richness. Also check for fuel in crankcase. If OK, see Carb. On-Vehicle Service, Section 6C.

More than 300 RPM drop

- Connect dwellmeter to M/C sol. dwell term. (6-cyl. scale).
- Set carb. on high step of fast idle cam. and run for one (1) minute or until dwell starts to vary, whichever happens first.
- Return engine to idle and note dwell.*

Fixed under 10° → **See Chart #1**

Fixed 10-50° → **See Chart #2**

Fixed over 50° → **See Chart #3**

Varying → **Check dwell at 3,000 RPM**

Between 10-50°
- Check air management system.
  - No trouble found in the "System."
  - Clear long term memory.**

Under 10°
- Check air switching valve leaking to exhaust ports at 3000 RPM. If not leaking . . .

Over 50°
- See Carb. Calibration Procedure—Section 6C, including TPS adjust.

*Oxygen sensors may cool off at idle and the dwell change from varying to fixed. If this happens, running the engine at fast idle will warm it up again.

**See Code(s) Clearing Procedure.

Figure 12-19. The CCC system performance chart. (GM)

2. Turn the ignition key on, but do not start the engine.

3. Connect your voltmeter to the green single-wire terminal open connector at the rear of the engine compartment. This is the mixture control solenoid dwell test connector and is used to measure solenoid dwell, or duty cycle, during a system performance test.

4. Note the voltmeter reading:
   a. If the reading exceeds 10 volts, check the voltage at the ECM terminal 18.
   b. If the reading is less than 10 volts, locate

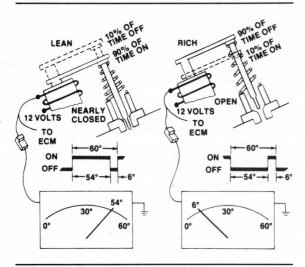

Figure 12-20. Mixture control solenoid duty cycle is indicated by a dwell measurement. (GM)

and repair an open circuit between the mixture control solenoid and the ECM.

5. If the voltage at ECM terminal 18 exceeds 10 volts, test the mixture control solenoid resistance with an ohmmeter.

　a. If the resistance is under 10 ohms, replace both the mixture control solenoid and the ECM.

　b. If the resistance exceeds 10 ohms, measure the voltage between ECM terminal 21 and ground with the voltmeter.

6. If the voltage between terminal 21 and ground is under 4 volts, look for a ground in the circuit leading to terminal 21. If voltage exceeds 4 volts, either repair the ECM connection (if required) or replace the ECM.

GM CCC System Performance Test

Use the system performance test to check system operation under four basic conditions:

1. When the owner has a driveability complaint but no trouble code is found.

2. After completing each pinpoint test and making the necessary repairs.

3. As a method of verifying system operation after all service has been completed.

4. As preventive maintenance (a routine performance check).

　The CCC system performance test is shown in figure 12-19 and contains three basic sections:

1. A carburetor lean-drop test at 3,000 rpm (part throttle)

2. A mixture control solenoid dwell test at idle

3. A mixture control solenoid dwell test at 3,000 rpm (part throttle).

Follow the 7 steps at the top of the chart to complete section 1 of the test. When the mixture control solenoid is disconnected, the carburetor goes to a full rich condition. Reconnecting the solenoid with the dwell test lead grounded drives the carburetor to a full lean position, with a corresponding drop in engine rpm. The rpm drop should be more than 300 rpm if the lean mixture control is satisfactory at part throttle. If the drop is less than 300 rpm, there is a problem in the carburetor or the solenoid circuit that is preventing proper lean mixture control.

Section 2 of the test leads you to another series of mixture control solenoid dwell tests at idle. The solenoid dwell should vary between 10 degrees and 50 degrees at idle. If the dwell reading does not vary, the test refers you to another diagnostic chart to determine whether the problem is with the solenoid, canister purging, or the PCV system.

Section 3 of the test has you check mixture control solenoid dwell at 3,000 rpm. Again, it should vary between 10 degrees and 50 degrees if the carburetor is properly controlling the fuel metering. If the solenoid dwell is fixed, you are directed to another diagnostic chart to determine the reason.

Testing a Mixture Control Solenoid with a Dwellmeter

A dwellmeter is used to test the operation of a mixture control solenoid (and any other solenoid that operates with a varying duty cycle). To use the dwellmeter properly, you must understand the relationship of the "dwell" readings to the operation of the solenoid.

　As we learned in Chapter 4 of the *Classroom Manual*, solenoid operation is precisely controlled through a procedure called pulse width modulation (PWM). This means that the solenoid is continuously cycled on and off a fixed number of times per second. That percentage of the total cycle time during which a solenoid is energized is called its duty cycle. A dwellmeter can be used to measure the duty cycle.

　While a mixture control solenoid operates at a fixed rate of 10 cycles per second, the duty cycle varies, as shown in figure 12-20. The dwell reading on the meter represents the duty cycle, or the time when the energized solenoid moves the carburetor metering rods to the lean mixture position.

　To check a mixture control solenoid with a dwellmeter:

1. Connect your dwellmeter to the mixture control solenoid dwell test connector. This is a

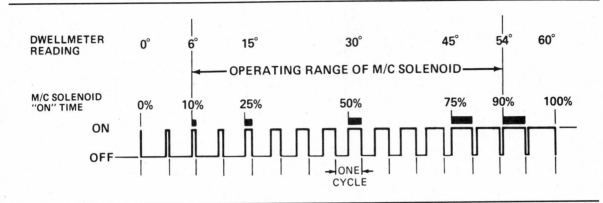

Figure 12-21. The mixture control solenoid dwell readings indicate the duty cycle percentage. (GM)

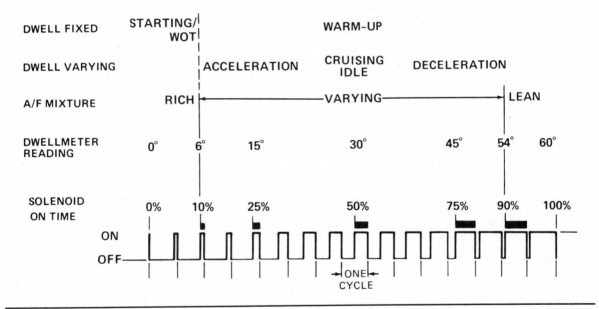

Figure 12-22. Dwellmeter readings and solenoid duty cycles change according to open- and closed-loop operating conditions. (GM)

green single-wire terminal open connector at the rear of the engine compartment and it connects the dwellmeter to the solenoid supply voltage.

2. Set the meter on the 6-cylinder scale to provide a dwell range of 0 degrees to 60 degrees. Remember that while you are reading dwell in terms of degrees, what you are really seeing is the percentage of on-time, or the duty cycle. The degree readings must be converted to percentages as follows:

0 degrees	=	0 percent
6 degrees	=	10 percent
15 degrees	=	25 percent
30 degrees	=	50 percent
45 degrees	=	75 percent
54 degrees	=	90 percent
60 degrees	=	100 percent

This relationship is demonstrated in figure 12-21; each 1-degree change in dwell equal to a 1.67-percent change in duty cycle. Or, in other words, every 3-degree change in dwell equals 5-percent change in duty cycle.

Since the mixture control solenoid operates at a fixed rate of 10 cycles per second, it moves the carburetor metering rods up (rich position) and down (lean position) 10 times per second. The ECM varies the duty cycle according to input from the EGO sensor when in closed loop, or other engine sensors when in open loop.

Figure 12-22 shows the relationship of solenoid operation to different open-loop (fixed dwell) and closed-loop (varying dwell) conditions, as well as the relationships of solenoid on-time to dwell readings. The mixture control solenoid used with CCC systems should vary in dwell between 5 or 6 degrees (full rich) and

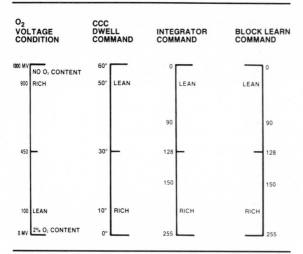

Figure 12-23. The relationship between EGO sensor voltage, dwell, and the ECM integrator and block learn function of fuel-injected CCC systems. (GM)

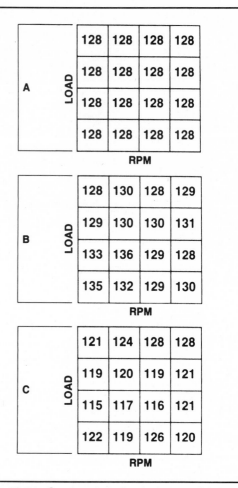

Figure 12-24. Correct air-fuel ratio, lean and rich exhaust correction are shown in these three examples of fuel delivery blocks. (GM)

54 or 55 degrees (full lean) during closed-loop operation. The fixed dwell used during open loop may range between 5 degrees and 55 degrees, depending upon the ECM program.

Testing Electronic Fuel Injection

The duty cycle of electronic fuel injectors cannot be checked as simply as the mixture control solenoid. It can, however, be determined with the use of a "scan" tool, or tester. To do so, you must understand the concept behind the *integrator* and *block learn* functions of the ECM. Integrator and block learn are the terms that GM uses for the adjustment factors of its fuel injection systems. Other carmakers may use different terms, but the principles are the same.

Integrator and block learn

These ECM functions are responsible for minor adjustments to the air-fuel ratio of a fuel-injected engine. They represent injector on-time, or dwell, and are comparable to the mixture control solenoid dwell on a carbureted engine.

The term, *integrator,* applies to a method of temporarily changing the fuel delivery, and it functions only in closed loop. It is displayed through the ALCL or ALDL data line and is monitored by scan tool as a number between 0 and 255. The average integrator number is one-half the maximum, or 128. The integrator function reads the EGO sensor output voltage, adding or subtracting fuel as required to maintain the 14.7:1 ratio. An integrator reading of 128 is neutral, which means that the EGO sensor is telling the ECM that a 14.7 air-fuel ratio has been burned in the cylinders. Thus, a reading of 128 is comparable to a 30-degree dwell

reading on a carbureted engine. Figure 12-23 shows the relationship between EGO voltage, injector dwell, and integrator and block learn commands.

While the integrator can make corrections to the fuel delivery over a wide range, these corrections are only temporary. The *block learn* function is used to make those corrections over a longer period of time. Its name is derived from the fact that an engine's operating range for any given combination of speed and load is divided into 16 cells, or "blocks". Figure 12-24A shows all 16 blocks running at an air-fuel ratio of 14.7 in all speed and load conditions.

A given fuel delivery factor is stored in each block. Every time the engine is started, block learn starts at 128 in every cell and corrects as required to produce a situation in which the EGO sensor reads the results of a 14.7 air-fuel mixture burning in the cylinders. As the operating range changes, the fuel delivery is based on whatever value is stored in the ECM

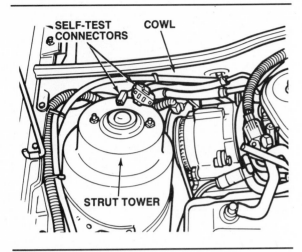

Figure 12-25. Typical Ford EEC-IV self-test connector location. (Ford)

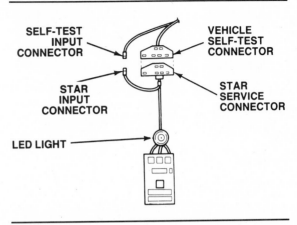

Figure 12-26. Typical connection pattern for the Ford STAR tester. (Ford)

memory for that particular block. Like the integrator, the number represents the injector on-time. While the integrator is functioning, the block learn watches what is going on and makes the same corrections. Figure 12-24B shows examples of what might be seen when the ECM compensates for a slightly lean exhaust. Figure 12-24C shows the ECM compensating for a slightly rich exhaust.

Block learn works with two types of memory:
● Volatile, or memory that is lost when the ignition is turned off.
● Nonvolatile, or memory that keeps its value in the block learn cells when the ignition is turned off.

Integrator and block learn both have limits which vary according to engine design. For example, suppose the air-fuel ratio is so far out of balance that block learn has reached the limit of its control range and cannot correct the condition. If the integrator also is at its limit, the engine will run poorly and driveability will suffer. A *high* integrator or block learn number reading on the scan tool should cause you to look for a vacuum leak or sticking injectors. Block learn should be checked both at idle and at 3,000 rpm, just as mixture control solenoid dwell is checked on carbureted engines.

FORD ELECTRONIC ENGINE CONTROL (EEC) SYSTEM TESTING

Ford has used various engine control systems since 1978. These include feedback carburetor control (FBC), microprocessor control unit (MCU), and four generations of electronic engine controls — EEC-I, EEC-II, EEC-III, and EEC-IV. The FBC and MCU systems are primar-

ily for fuel metering control; the EEC systems are more comprehensive and represent increasing degrees of system integration. The self-diagnostic capabilities built into EEC-III and EEC-IV systems are similar to those we have seen in GM's C-4 and CCC systems.

Since EEC-IV is used on virtually all 1985 and later Ford vehicles, we will deal primarily with this system in our discussion. Remember, however, that the testing principles involved are equally valid for earlier EEC systems.

Ford EEC-IV Systems Diagnostic Test

The area test used by Ford is called a "quick test" and contains self-diagnostic and code displays. Ford's codes are not all trouble codes; they include instruction codes, separator codes, and instructions to the service technician. As with any system, you should test the battery voltage and condition before performing any tests, and check the condition and routing of all vacuum lines and electrical connections. Correct any leaking vacuum lines and loose or corroded connections.

There are three sections to the Ford self-test sequence:
1. Key on, engine off
2. Engine running
3. Continuous (wiggle) testing for intermittent problems.

Any analog voltmeter or Ford's self-test automatic readout (STAR) tester can be used to retrieve the codes from the EEC microprocessor memory. While there is no flashing CHECK ENGINE light with Ford systems, there is a self-test connector in the engine compartment of most late-model Ford vehicles, figure 12-25.

Connect the Ford STAR tester as shown in figure 12-26. It will display codes in its display

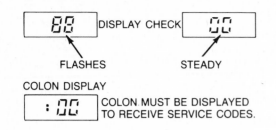

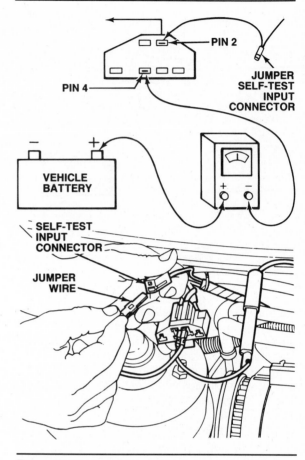

Figure 12-29. A variation of the jumper wire and voltmeter connection on Ford's EEC-IV system. (Ford)

Figure 12-27. Ford's STAR tester readout display. (Ford)

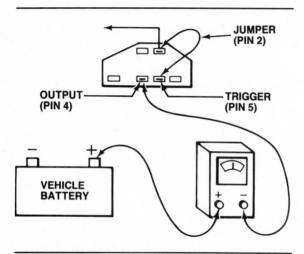

Figure 12-28. Jumper wire and voltmeter connection on Ford's EEC-IV system. (Ford)

window, figure 12-27. When the STAR tester is connected, follow the operational instructions provided with the unit.

If you do not have a STAR tester, connect an analog voltmeter as shown in figures 12-28 or 12-29. The voltmeter needle will pulse to indicate the codes, as shown in figure 12-30.

As an example, code 23 is two quick needle pulses followed by a 2-second pause and then three more quick needle pulses. When more than one code is stored, there will be a 4-second pause between codes.

Key-on, engine-off test
To perform this test, the ignition and air conditioning must be off. The transmission should be in Park or Neutral, with the parking brake set. Connect the voltmeter as shown in figures 12-28 or 12-29 and turn the ignition key on. You can expect the voltmeter to immediately deliver

one rapid pulse. This is a "fast code" used for factory testing. After this, the meter will show service codes.

A code 11 followed by a separator pulse and a second code 11 indicates that the system is functioning properly, figure 12-31, and that you can proceed with the engine-running test. As used by Ford, a code 11 represents a "system-pass" code in the same way that GM's CCC system uses a code 12.

Codes transmitted before a separator pulse are "on-demand" codes that indicate a problem is present during the test (a "hard", or "continuous", problem). These are primarily electronic problems for which Ford has prepared pinpoint test procedures. Codes transmitted after the separator pulse indicate intermittent problems that may or may not be present during testing.

Engine-running test
This test should be performed after the key-on, engine-off test, unless you are directed to a pinpoint test by a specific code.
1. With the ignition off, deactivate the test

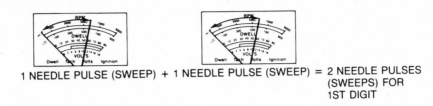

1 NEEDLE PULSE (SWEEP) + 1 NEEDLE PULSE (SWEEP) = 2 NEEDLE PULSES (SWEEPS) FOR 1ST DIGIT

2-SECOND PAUSE BETWEEN DIGITS

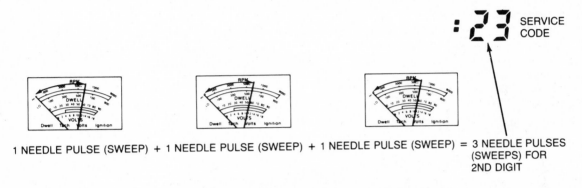

:23 SERVICE CODE

1 NEEDLE PULSE (SWEEP) + 1 NEEDLE PULSE (SWEEP) + 1 NEEDLE PULSE (SWEEP) = 3 NEEDLE PULSES (SWEEPS) FOR 2ND DIGIT

4-SECOND PAUSE BETWEEN SERVICE CODES, WHEN MORE THAN ONE CODE IS GENERATED

Figure 12-30. The analog voltmeter pulsations indicate the Ford EEC service codes. (Ford)

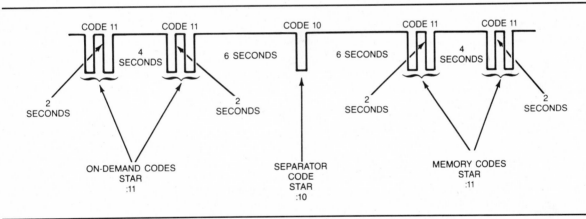

Figure 12-31. Ford EEC-IV key-on, engine-off test code format. (Ford)

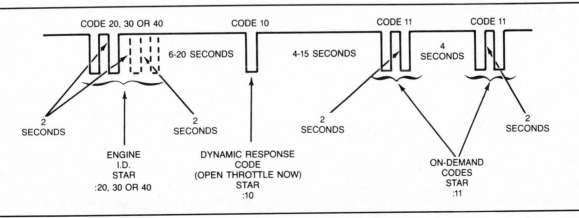

Figure 12-32. Ford EEC-IV key-on, engine-running test code format. (Ford)

TEST STEP	RESULT ▶	ACTION TO TAKE
DA1 SERVICE CODE 24: CHECK AMBIENT TEMPERATURE		
• Ambient temperature must be greater than 50°F for this test.	Yes ▶	GO to DA2 .
	No ▶	RERUN Quick Test.
DA2 CHECK FOR V REF AT THROTTLE POSITION SENSOR		
• Refer to illustration Q. • Key Off, wait 10 seconds. • DVOM on 20V scale. • Disconnect TP sensor. • Key On, Engine Off. • Measure voltage at the TP harness connector between VREF and signal return.	Less than 4.0V or greater than 6.0V ▶	GO to Pinpoint Test Step C1 .
	4.0V to 6.0V ▶	RECONNECT TP sensor, GO to DA3 .

Figure 12-33. An example of Ford's pinpoint test procedures. These are the first two steps for code 24, an air charge temperature sensor fault. (Ford)

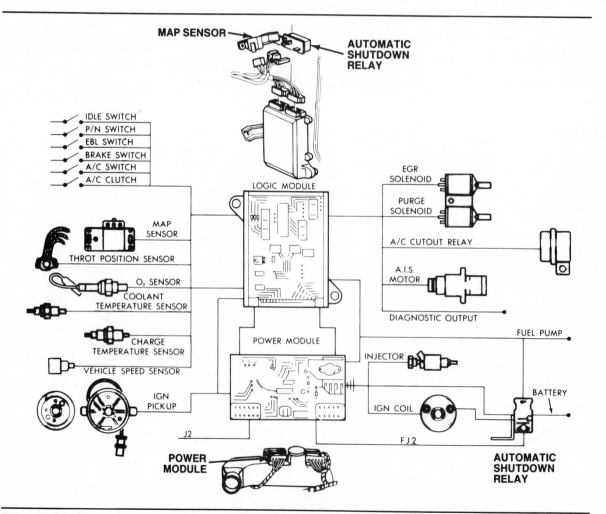

Figure 12-34. Chrysler's modular engine control system uses separate power and logic modules. (Chrysler)

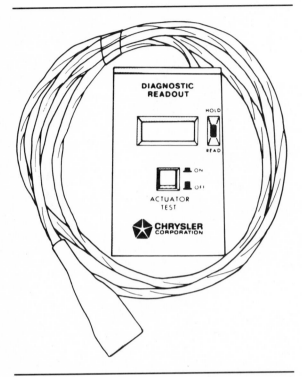

Figure 12-35. The Chrysler readout tool for use with the modular engine control system provides a digital display similar to Ford's STAR tester. (Chrysler)

function by disconnecting the jumper wire from the self-test connector.

2. Start the engine and run it at approximately 2,000 rpm for two minutes to heat up the EGO sensor.

3. Shut off the engine and wait for 10 seconds, then reconnect the jumper wire disconnected in step 1.

4. *Restart the engine* and watch the voltmeter, figure 12-32. When you see an engine ID code (one-half the number of engine cylinders) followed in 6 to 20 seconds by a single pulse response code, the engine is ready for the test.

5. Momentarily open the throttle to its wide-open position and release it, then observe the voltmeter for any additional service codes. If code 11 is transmitted, there are no problems in the system. If problems exist, the appropriate codes will be displayed and you should proceed with the necessary pinpoint tests.

On some EEC-IV applications, the system will activate the throttle position solenoid to start the self-test by itself. This eliminates the need to snap the throttle wide open as described in step 5.

Continuous monitor (wiggle) test
Intermittent open and short circuits can be located in the EEC-IV system with this test.

1. With the ignition off, disconnect the jumper wire from the self-test connector.

2. Turn the ignition on but *do not start* the engine.

3. Wiggle, move, or tap each component and connector in the system. If an intermittent problem is present, a service code will be recorded in the system and displayed on the voltmeter scale in the form of a single pulse. If this happens, you should immediately repeat the key-on, engine-off test to retrieve the code.

4. Reconnect the jumper wire to the self-test connector and start the engine. Allow the system to go through the engine-running self-test and then wait 2 minutes before repeating step 3 to check for intermittent problems with the engine running.

EEC-IV Pinpoint Tests

Ford's pinpoint test procedures are similar to those used by GM, but they are provided in a column format, figure 12-33, instead of the linear chart form. The first column describes the test step, the second column gives possible results, and the third column tells you what to do next according to the results you obtained. When each pinpoint test and service sequence is completed, you should repeat the self-diagnostic tests to ensure that the problem has been solved and that no trouble codes remain in the system.

CHRYSLER MODULAR ENGINE CONTROL SYSTEM TESTING

The Chrysler engine control system was introduced on 1984 front-wheel-drive Chrysler vehicles with fuel injection or a turbocharger. The system uses two separate modules and a variety of sensors and actuators, figure 12-34, to control fuel metering, ignition timing, EGR flow, and canister purge.

The logic module contains the digital microprocessor and is located inside the vehicle behind the right front kickpad. It controls the ignition and fuel systems, memory for onboard diagnostics (OBD) and starts the "limp-in" mode in case of a system failure. It also supplies a reference voltage of 5 volts to the manifold absolute pressure (MAP), throttle position, coolant temperature, and charge temperature sensors. The logic module will set a variety of fault codes.

The power module is located in the left front fenderwell and supplies ground for the ignition coil and fuel injection circuits, as directed by the logic module. The power module supplies 8

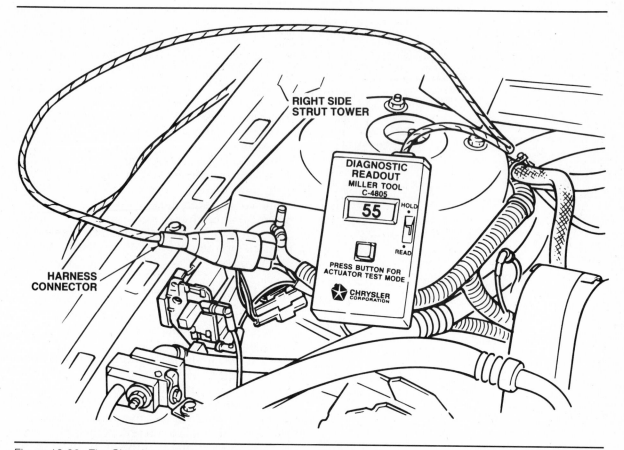

RIGHT SIDE
STRUT TOWER

DIAGNOSTIC
READOUT
MILLER TOOL
C-4805

55

HOLD

READ

PRESS BUTTON FOR
ACTUATOR TEST MODE

CHRYSLER
CORPORATION

HARNESS
CONNECTOR

Figure 12-36. The Chrysler tester connects into the system through a diagnostic connector near the shock tower. (Chrysler)

volts to the logic module and the Hall-effect distributor pickup.

The OBD system is similar in design and function to the GM CCC system and Ford's EEC system. A POWER LOSS or POWER LIMITED lamp on the instrument panel comes on briefly each time the ignition is turned on and remains lighted for several seconds to tell the driver that it is working. If the logic module receives incorrect data or no data from the manifold absolute pressure (MAP), throttle position, or coolant temperature sensors, it will switch to a "limp-in" operating mode. When this happens, the instrument panel lamp comes on and remains lighted until the problem has been corrected.

Fault Codes

A diagnostic readout box (Chrysler tool C-4805) similar to the Ford STAR tester is recommended for retrieving fault codes, figure 12-35. If the readout box is not available, codes can be retrieved through the POWER LOSS lamp.

Fault code retrieval is activated in the same way regardless of whether you see the readout box or the POWER LOSS lamp. To activate the fault code system, turn the ignition key on-off, on-off, on within five seconds.

If you use the readout box, connect it to a diagnostic connector in the wiring harness near the right front shock tower in the engine compartment, figure 12-36. When fault code retrieval is activated, a digital code 88 will appear in the readout box display panel, followed by any fault codes stored in memory. If no code 88 appears and there is not an open in the circuit between the logic module and diagnostic connector, replace the logic module.

The POWER LOSS lamp flashes in the same way as GM's CHECK ENGINE lamp, with a short pause between flashes, a longer pause between digits and a 4-second pause between codes. For example, when the system is accessed, the lamp will come on for two seconds and turn off before flashing stored codes. It will flash again five times, pause and flash once. This is fault code 51. If more codes are stored,

Code	Type	Power Loss/Limit Lamp	Circuit	When Monitored By The Logic Module	When Put Into Memory	ATM Test Code	Sensor Access Code
11	Fault	No	Distributor Signal	During cranking.	If no distributor signal is present since the battery was disconnected.	None	None
12	Indication	No	Battery Feed to the Logic Module	All the time when the ignition switch is on.	If the battery feed to the logic module has been disconnected within the last 20-40 engine starts.	None	None
13	Fault	Yes	M.A.P. Sensor (Vacuum)	When the throttle is closed during cranking and after the engine starts.	If the M.A.P. sensor vacuum level does not change between cranking and when the engine starts.	None	None
14	Fault	Yes	M.A.P. Sensor (Electrical)	All the time when the ignition switch is on.	If the M.A.P. sensor signal is below .02 or above 4.9 volts.	None	08
15	Fault	No	Vehicle Speed Sensor	Over a 7 second period during decel from highway speeds when the throttle is closed.	If the speed sensor signal indicates less than 2 mph when the vehicle is moving.	None	None
16	Fault	Yes	Battery Voltage Sensing (Charging System)	All the time after one minute from when the engine starts.	If the battery sensing voltage drops below 4 or between 7½ and 8½ volts for more than 20 seconds.	None	07
17	Fault	No	Engine Cooling System	During cranking when engine coolant temperature is between −20 and 212°F.	If engine coolant temperature does not reach 160°F within 20 minutes after the engine is started.	None	None
21	Fault	No	Oxygen Sensor	All the time after 12 minutes from when the engine starts.	If there is no oxygen sensor signal for more than 22 seconds when in closed loop.	None	02
22	Fault	Yes	Engine Coolant Sensor	All the time when the ignition switch is on.	If the coolant sensor voltage is above 4.96 volts when the engine is cold or below .51 volts when the engine is warm.	None	04
23	Fault	Yes	Charge Temperature Sensor	All the time when the ignition switch is on.	If the charge temperature sensor voltage is above 4.98 or below .06.	None	03
24	Fault	Yes	Throttle Position	All the time when the ignition switch is	If the throttle position sensor signal is	None	05

Figure 12-37. Part of a typical Chrysler fault code, indicator code, ATM test, and sensor access code table. (Chrysler)

the lamp will pause for four seconds, then flash another code. Any number of codes can be displayed, as long as they are in memory. When all codes have been retrieved, a code 55 is shown, indicating the end of the test sequence.

In addition to fault codes indicating a system problem, Chrysler also uses indicator codes, ATM test codes, and sensor access codes.
• Indicator codes are used to start and end the diagnostic mode, as well as to tell you when certain conditions have taken place.
• ATM test codes identify various circuits to be used during diagnostics. An ATM code also can be a fault code.

• Sensor access codes allow you to access a sensor readout. Like ATM codes, a sensor access code can also be a fault code.

Figure 12-37 shows a sample of the Chrysler OBD fault codes.

Specific (Pinpoint) Tests

Chrysler's pinpoint tests are compiled and published in a "Driveability Test Procedure" booklet. The format, figure 12-38, is similar to the one used by Ford. The first column describes the test step and shows any required equipment connections, the second column gives test indications, and the third column tells you

TEST 15	STEP A	CHECKING FOR FAULT CODE 37 – BARO READ SOLENOID CIRCUIT

PROCEDURE		TEST INDICATION	ACTION REQUIRED
REMINDERS • Diagnostic readout box connected to the engine harness connector.		• Voltmeter reading should be pulsating between 0 and 14 volts.	• Voltmeter is not pulsating but reads within one volt of battery voltage, **Perform STEP B.**
• Connect a voltmeter to the blue wire of the solenoid assembly 4-way connector and ground. • Put the system in the **ATM Test Mode – Code 10.** (Refer to the introduction)	DIAGNOSTIC READOUT BOX VOLTMETER LB PK LG GY WIRE END SOLENOID ASSEMBLY 4-WAY CONNECTOR		• Voltmeter pulsates between 0 and 3 volts, replace the solenoid assembly.
			• Voltmeter is not pulsating but reads 0-1 volt, disconnect the logic module red connector. If voltage is now within one of battery, replace the logic module. If not repair blue wire for a short to ground.

Figure 12-38. An example of Chrysler's pinpoint test procedures. This is step A in checking code 37, the barometric solenoid circuit. (Chrysler)

what action you must take. When each pinpoint test and service sequence is completed, you should repeat the self-diagnostic tests to ensure that the problem has been solved and that no trouble codes remain in the system.

AUTOMATIC SYSTEM TESTERS

We have covered the diagnostic principles involved in area and pinpoint testing for the three major domestic manufacturers' engine control systems. The test procedures generally can be carried out with ordinary test equipment such as a voltmeter, an ohmmeter, and a dwellmeter. There is, however, an increasing variety of automatic system testers available from both the carmakers and independent test equipment manufacturers.

Ford's self-test and automatic readout (STAR) tester and Chrysler's diagnostic readout box are examples of such testers. Both plug into the engine control system's diagnostic connector and show trouble codes on their digital display panels. Independent manufacturers make testers for individual systems, such as the GM CCC or Ford EEC systems. Figures 12-39 and 12-40 show two such testers.

The capabilities of such testers, often called scan testers or "scanners", depend upon the manufacturer's design and price. Some companies even make universal testers that work on all engine control systems. The Alltest Brainmaster II Model 3256 is one such comprehensive tester, and comes with a 1,400-page manual covering its use with GM, Ford, and Chrysler systems. A printer and a data recorder are also available, offering even greater versatility.

Scanners connect into the engine control system through the vehicle diagnostic connector and receive their power from the vehicle's battery. They tap into the computer's serial data transmission line where they can eavesdrop on the microprocessor as it communicates with its sensors and actuators, or even with other microprocessors.

Because a scanner eavesdrops on the computer's main line of communication, it can pick up and can display a good deal of data that is useless to anyone except an engineer, in addition to the information that is necessary to run the particular series of tests for which it is designed.

Figure 12-39. This scan tool, or "scanner" tester, is used to check out GM CCC systems.

Figure 12-40. Another special scanner tester for GM CCC systems.

Scanners are becoming even more sophisticated. Some can be programmed to look for a particular trouble code. Once tied into the engine control circuitry, the scanner monitors the circuit until a "glitch", or intermittent deviation from the norm, occurs, which sets the trouble code for which it was programmed. When this happens, the scanner takes an electronic "picture" of circuit operation. This "picture" can be displayed, but of even more interest is the fact that the scanner can also recall a specified number of increments *before and after* the "picture" to show you what was happening in the circuit. The latest scanners possess far more capabilities than the average service technician can make use of, much less understand, at this time.

Despite their rapidly increasing "intelligence", scanners will not think for you. They will quickly put you on the right track to finding the cause of a problem, but you cannot plug one in and expect it to light up with the exact answer to the problem. You must still use traditional electromechanical troubleshooting methods to identify, locate, and correct the cause of a system problem.

ELECTRONIC CONTROL SYSTEM SERVICE

The basic principles of testing, adjusting, and repairing electrical components that we have learned so far apply equally to electronic engine controls systems. There are, however, some additional system requirements we will deal with

in terms of service. The following paragraphs discuss the components involved.

EGO Sensor Testing and Service

Early engine control systems require periodic replacement of the EGO sensor, either on a specified-mileage or time interval. Late-model systems have EGO sensors warranted for 50,000 miles, and their replacement is not a scheduled maintenance service. You can expect, however, to test EGO sensors when trying to isolate a system problem. If the sensor has failed, you will have to replace it.

EGO sensor test procedures vary somewhat according to the system, as well as the type of sensor (1-wire, 2-wire, or 3-wire). While the methods recommended to test the sensor output voltage signal and the computer's response to the sensor signals may differ slightly, there are common precautions that you should take whenever you are dealing with any EGO sensor. We have covered these previously, but this is a good place to summarize what *not* to do.

● Do not short circuit or ground an EGO sensor output lead. This can permanently damage the sensor.

● Do not check the sensor output with an analog voltmeter. Such testers have low impedance and draw enough current to burn out the sensor.

● Do not check the sensor with an ohmmeter. Any input current can damage it.

● Do not use silicone sprays near an EGO sensor. The silicone compounds will collect and

Figure 12-41. The EGO sensor usually is located in the exhaust manifold, but not all are as easy to reach as on this GM J-car, 4-cylinder engine.

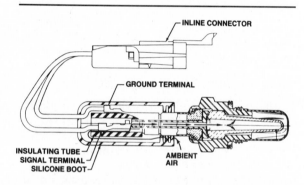

Figure 12-42. Make sure the boot is properly positioned on EGO sensors that use them. It should not block the air vent. (GM)

block off ambient air to the sensor, resulting in an incorrect signal.

• Do not use leaded gas in the vehicle. The lead will collect on the exhaust side of the sensor and cause an incorrect signal.

• Do not incorrectly position the silicone boot, if one is used. The boot position can affect sensor operation and may melt if it contacts the hot manifold surface.

EGO sensor removal and replacement

EGO sensors are similar in appearance to an 18-mm spark plug, but have one, two, or three wires protruding from the top. They generally are installed in the exhaust manifold, figure 12-41. Access to the sensor varies and depends upon the particular engine and control system design. Some may be easily reached, figure 12-41, while access to others is possible only

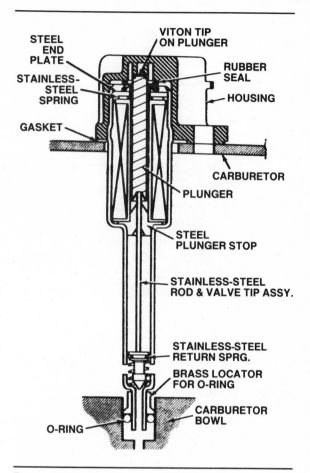

Figure 12-43. The Rochester E2SE mixture control solenoid. (GM)

from underneath the vehicle. If possible, you should use an EGO sensor wrench for removing and installing a sensor. This specially designed slip-on socket accommodates the sensor leads and has an offset drive lug to accept a ½-inch ratchet or breaker bar.

When replacing an EGO sensor, it is a good idea to clean the manifold or exhaust pipe threads with an 18-mm thread chaser to make sure they are well formed and free of dirt and burrs.

All EGO sensors require the use of a special antiseize compound when installed. The compound consists of liquid graphite and glass beads. The graphite burns away, leaving the beads in place on the threads to ease sensor removal. New sensors have this compound already applied but you should clean the threads of a used sensor and apply the specified compound before reinstalling it. Sensor installation without the compound will make it extremely difficult, or even impossible, to remove in the future.

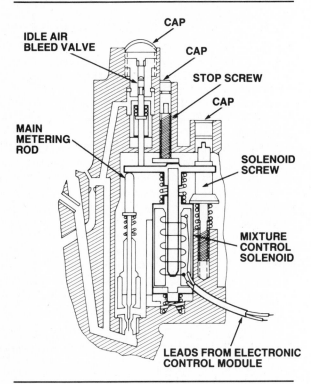

Figure 12-44. The Rochester E2ME and E4ME mixture control solenoid. (GM)

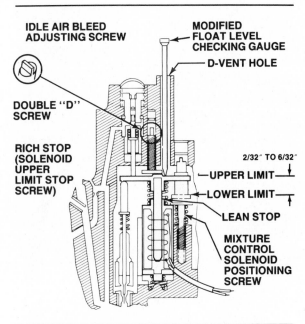

Figure 12-45. Checking and adjusting the travel of the E2ME and E4ME mixture control solenoid. (GM)

EGO sensors should be torqued *exactly* to specifications, which generally are in the 20 to 35 foot-pound (15 to 25 Nm) range. Exposure to the hot exhaust gases will make the sensor more difficult to remove. In some cases, it will require up to two or three times more torque for removal than is required for installation. Be especially careful in positioning any rubber boot used with a sensor. It should be located to protect the sensor without blocking the air vent, figure 12-42.

Mixture Control Solenoid Service

As we have seen, feedback carburetors use a mixture control solenoid to regulate the air-fuel mixture. This solenoid may either regulate a vacuum signal to the carburetor diaphragms used to control the fuel metering rods and air bleeds, or it may control the metering rods and air bleeds as directed by the computer.

GM CCC systems use Rochester carburetors containing mixture control solenoids to control fuel metering and idle air bleeds with factory-set limits. Figure 12-43 shows the mixture control solenoid used in the Rochester E2SE Varajet carburetor. Figure 12-44 shows the mixture control solenoid used with Rochester E2ME and E4ME carburetors. Limit stop screws in both

carburetors are provided to maintain the factory settings and should not be adjusted unless you have the proper service equipment and factory procedures, which must be followed exactly.

Mixture control solenoid travel can be measured with a special float gauge, figure 12-45. After inserting the gauge through the D-shaped vent hole in the carburetor airhorn, you should make sure it moves freely, then record the gauge reading with the solenoid up. Press the gauge lightly until the solenoid bottoms and record the second reading. The difference between the two readings is the total solenoid travel. If travel is out of specifications, either the lean or the rich stop should be adjusted. If travel is within specifications but the driveability problem persists, an idle air bleed valve adjustment may be in order. The adjustments are described in detail in the manufacturer's factory shop manual and should be followed exactly.

The mixture control solenoid can also be removed and tested for sticking, binding, or leaking with the carburetor on the engine:
1. Remove the three screws holding the solenoid. Lift the solenoid from the carburetor airhorn with a twisting motion.
2. Remove and discard the solenoid gasket, stem retainer, and seal.
3. Connect a jumper wire between the battery (+) terminal and one of the solenoid terminals. Connect the other solenoid terminal to a good ground with a second jumper wire.

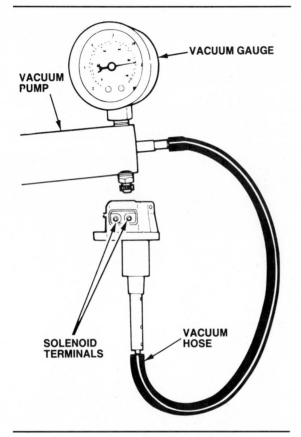

Figure 12-46. Testing the E2SE mixture control solenoid.

4. Connect a hand vacuum pump to the solenoid stem, figure 12-46, and apply a minimum of 25 in. (635 mm) Hg vacuum. Time the leakdown rate from 20 in. (510 mm) Hg vacuum to 15 in. (380 mm) Hg vacuum. If leakage exceeds 5 in. (125 mm) Hg in 5 seconds, replace the solenoid.

5. Disconnect the jumper wire at the battery (+) post while watching the vacuum pump gauge. If the reading does not drop to zero in less than one second, replace the solenoid.

Fuel Injector Solenoid Service

Restricted or otherwise faulty fuel injectors can be located in GM CCC systems with a scan tool by reading the integrator and block learn data. In other systems, volt-ohmmeter tests can determine whether injectors are functioning properly or should be replaced. The injectors must be pulled from the fuel rail or throttle body, however, to check the flow pattern while cranking. If the flow pattern is suspicious, a variety of injector cleaning equipment and cleaners is available. Whenever injectors are cleaned, always follow the equipment manufacturer's instructions and procedures exactly.

Throttle Position Sensor Adjustment

A throttle position sensor (TPS) is used with every engine control system to supply the microprocessor with a signal proportionate to the opening angle of the throttle plate. It may be a simple on-off switch or a variable potentiometer sensor. A TPS that is out of specification can cause incorrect idle speeds or fuel metering. On some control systems, the TPS is adjustable; on others, it is not. To determine whether you can adjust or must replace the sensor, you will have to refer to the carmaker's specifications for the particular vehicle you are servicing.

Most throttle position sensors are externally mounted. Adjustment (if possible) is made by loosening the sensor mounting screws and rotating the sensor housing until a specified voltage reading is obtained. The following procedure, used to check and adjust Ford level C sensors, is typical:
1. Connect the EEC-IV breakout box according to manufacturer's instructions.
2. Connect the (+) lead of a digital volt-ohmmeter (DVOM) to pin 47 and the (−) lead to pin 46.
3. Turn the ignition switch on, but do not start the engine.
4. Loosen the sensor retaining screws and rotate the assembly until the DVOM reading is 0.9 to 1.1 volt, then tighten the retaining screws.
5. Watch the DVOM while opening the throttle to its wide-open position and then back to idle. The DVOM should read 1.0 volt to 4.0 volt and back to 1.0 volt.

GM CCC Solenoids and Relays

The resistance of an engine control system actuator must match the voltage and current capacity of the system in which it is used. We'll use the GM CCC system as an example. All solenoids and relays used in a CCC system are activated by internal electronic switches in the ECM called "drivers". Each driver is part of a group of four called "quad-drivers"; failure of one driver can damage the remaining drivers in the group. The solenoids and relays must have a minimum of 20 ohms resistance. To determine why this is so, let's look at the system. The microprocessor drivers can work with a maximum 0.8 ampere current at a maximum 16 volts system voltage. Ohm's law tells us that 16 volts/0.8 ampere = 20 ohms. Thus, if the solenoid or relay resistance is less than 20 ohms, the high current will destroy the microprocessor drivers.

Figure 12-47. A GM programmable read-only memory (PROM).

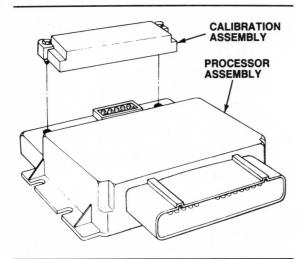

Figure 12-48. The calibration assembly or PROM on Ford EEC-I, II, and III systems attaches to the microprocessor with two screws. (Ford)

CALIBRATION ASSEMBLY

PROCESSOR ASSEMBLY

A solenoid or relay that is shorted or grounded can also damage the microprocessor. They should be checked with an analog ohmmeter on its low-resistance scale. You should check the solenoid resistance in both directions, because some use diodes to protect the microprocessor from reverse current. Use the higher resistance reading to verify solenoid condition.

PROM and CALPAC Replacement

As we have already learned, the calibration data or program for a specific vehicle, engine, and transmission combination is contained within the programmable read only memory (PROM) chip, figure 12-47.

Interchangeable PROM's allow a basic computer to be used in a wide variety of models, cutting down the carmaker's costs and inventory. They also allow the manufacturer to correct certain driveability problems more easily. A revised PROM can be manufactured and installed much less expensively than replacing the entire computer.

Figure 12-49. PROM's are furnished in special carriers.

Replacement computers (called controllers) and PROM's are furnished individually. Whenever a computer has to be replaced, remove the PROM and install it in the replacement computer, since it comes without a PROM. Because the PROM is designed for a given vehicle, the replacement PROM to be installed must always carry the same part number as the one it re-places. Part numbers are stamped on the PROM and can be found in manufacturer's parts catalogs and service bulletins. Using the incorrect PROM in a vehicle will result in false codes and driveability problems at the very least, and possible system damage at the other extreme.

The GM CCC computer, or ECM, used with fuel-injected engines also contains a smaller PROM called a calibration package or CALPAC. Its only purpose is to provide backup logic used to control fuel delivery if the ECM malfunctions. A missing or defective CALPAC, however, can cause a no-start or no-run condition. Like the PROM, a CALPAC must be transferred to a replacement controller.

Ford calls its PROM's "calibration assemblies". They are attached to the outside of the EEC-I, II and III microprocessor assembly, figure 12-48, with screws. EEC-IV calibration assemblies, however, are contained within the microprocessor assembly.

GM PROM's are installed in small plastic housings that have two rows of pins to plug into mating socket openings in the computer. The PROM is held in a small PROM carrier, figure 12-49, and is removed with a special tool, figure 12-50.

To replace a CCC PROM, you should always disconnect the battery ground cable first and remove the ECM from the vehicle's passenger compartment. The ECM generally is located behind the right side kick panel or under the instrument panel. Installing a PROM with the ECM in the vehicle is a tempting timesaver, *but it can be fatal to the PROM*. Static electricity can irreparably damage memory chips. Simply sliding across the seat could create enough static

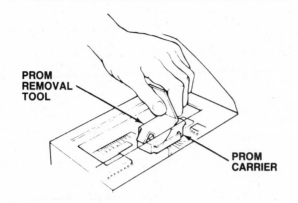

Figure 12-50. A special removal tool is used to extract a GM PROM from the controller assembly. (Chevrolet)

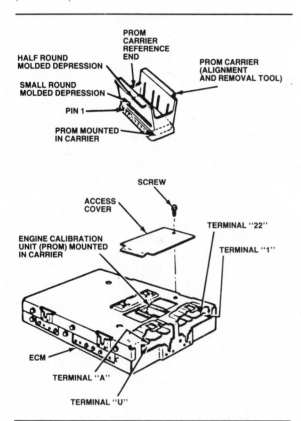

Figure 12-51. Controller and PROM identification. (GM)

electricity to wipe out the PROM when it makes contact with the controller pin sockets. (The same precautions should be taken with any engine control computer when servicing the PROM or calibration assembly.)

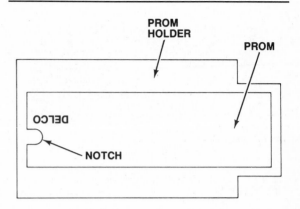

Figure 12-52. The PROM must be properly positioned to install it.

After removing the ECM from the vehicle, remove the access cover screw and cover, figure 12-51. Proceed as follows:

1. Grasp the PROM carrier with the PROM removal tool, figure 12-50. Rock the carrier from side-to-side gently while applying upward pressure.

2. Note the notch on the reference end of the PROM carrier, figures 12-51 and 12-52. CAUTION: Do not install the PROM backwards. If this is done, it will be destroyed as soon as the ignition is turned on.

3. Make sure there is equal space between the ends of the PROM and its carrier. Push the PROM up in the carrier until its pins are above the carrier's inner chamber.

4. Hold the carrier over the PROM socket with its squared-off symmetrical end opposite the notch in the ECM housing.

5. Depress the top of the carrier firmly and use a blunt narrow tool to depress the body of the PROM into its sockets.

6. Reinstall the access cover on the ECM housing and replace the ECM in the vehicle.

7. Reconnect the battery ground cable. Start the engine and ground the diagnostic test lead to check for a code 51. If there is no code 51, the PROM is installed correctly. However, if a code 51 appears, the PROM:
   a. Is not completely seated
   b. Is installed backwards
   c. Has one or more bent pins
   d. Is defective.

This procedure is generalized, since PROM package and controller socket designs differ from year to year or even from vehicle to vehicle. A PROM also is installed in different directions, depending upon whether the engine is

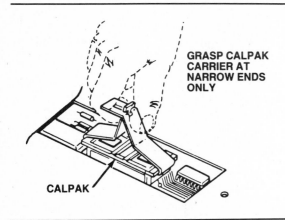

GRASP CALPAK CARRIER AT NARROW ENDS ONLY

CALPAK

Figure 12-53. CALPAC replacement is identical to PROM service, but a different removal tool is used. (Chevrolet)

carbureted or fuel injected. For these reasons, you should always refer to the manufacturer's instructions for a given vehicle before replacing a PROM.

A CALPAC is replaced using the same procedure and precautions, but with a different removal tool, figure 12-53. When performing step 7 of the procedure given above, look for a code 52 if there is a problem with the CALPAC installation. Some 1986 and later ECM's have a single carrier to which the PROM and CALPAC are both permanently attached, and thus must be serviced as a unit.

Adaptive memory and long-term memory recalibration

We have seen that various factors (such as production variations, engine wear, and variable fuel quality) make an engine's real needs different from the design values used to establish the initial control program stored in the microprocessor and PROM.

To compensate for these variables, an "adaptive memory" or "learning ability" feature in late-model engine control systems monitors operation of the engine and its related systems. Whenever a controlled value regularly falls outside design limits, the adaptive memory makes a small modification to the control program, reestablishing proper operation.

Adaptive memory program modifications are stored in RAM and lost when power to the computer is disconnected. When this occurs on an older or high-mileage vehicle, the owner may complain of driveability problems until the car has been driven long enough to allow the adaptive memory to again fine-tune the engine operation. To "teach" the memory, the vehicle should be at operating temperature and driven at part throttle with moderate acceleration and idle conditions until normal performance returns. This usually requires about 20 miles of driving under varied operating conditions.

Some GM CCC systems use a special electronically eraseable programmable read-only memory, or EPROM. The programming of the normal PROM which is generally used is permanent. If defective, it is discarded. An EPROM, however, can be erased with a special procedure and reprogrammed to correct any defects in the original programming or to improve driveability. As you might expect, reprogramming is done by the manufacturer and not in the field by service technicians.

PART FIVE

Lighting, Accessory, and Body Electrical System Service

13

Lighting System Service

Replacing bulbs is probably the most common lighting system service you will do. Other system services include headlamp aiming and circuit troubleshooting. The following paragraphs provide instructions for headlamp replacement and aiming, and for replacing other types of bulbs. The rest of the chapter explains lighting circuit troubleshooting. General procedures are given, as well as steps in locating specific problems in the lighting system.

HEADLAMP REPLACEMENT AND AIMING

Headlamps have a great effect on safe driving. A burned out or misaimed lamp decreases the driver's range of vision. Poorly aimed lamps also can momentarily blind pedestrians and other drivers.

Headlamp Replacement

Because traditional and halogen sealed-beam headlamp designs are all about the same, the procedures for removal and replacement are similar for all cars:

1. If the vehicle has concealed headlamps, activate the system to expose the lamps; then shut the ignition switch off. Make sure the headlamp switch is off.
2. Remove any decorative bezel or part of the radiator grille that hides the headlamp mounting, figure 13-1.
CAUTION: Do not mistake the headlamp aiming screws for the retaining screws.
3. Loosen the several retaining screws and remove the retaining ring:
    a. For round lamps, rotate the ring slightly until the large ends of the screw slots align with the screw heads; then remove the ring, figure 13-2.
    b. For rectangular lamps, remove the retaining screws, figure 13-3.
4. Pull the headlamp out of its housing and unplug the connector from its prongs.
5. Examine the connector for corrosion or damage. Some imported cars use a silicone grease on the bulb prongs. Do not mistake it for corrosion. Clean or replace the connector if necessary.
6. Plug the connector onto the new bulb's prongs. Make sure you are installing the correct type of sealed-beam unit for the system.
7. Place the new lamp in its housing and reinstall the retaining ring:
    a. For round lamps, fit the large ends of the retaining ring screw slots over the screw heads; then rotate the ring until the small ends of the slots rest against the screws.

Figure 13-1. Removing headlamp trim from a rectangular headlamp.

Figure 13-2. Removing the retaining ring from a round headlamp.

Figure 13-3. Removing the retaining ring from a rectangular headlamp.

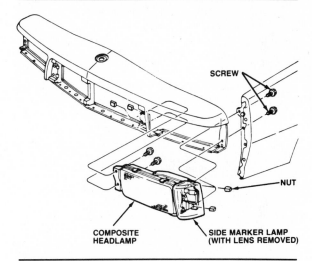

Figure 13-4. A typical composite headlamp. (GM)

b. For rectangular lamps, install the retaining screws.

8. Turn on the headlamps and check the new lamp's operation, then reinstall any trim or grille parts.

9. Check the aim of all the headlamps. Adjust, if necessary, as explained in the paragraphs on headlamp aiming.

Halogen Bulb Replacement

Composite headlamps using replaceable halogen bulbs require a different replacement procedure. If the entire headlamp assembly requires replacement, the procedure is similar to replacing a parking lamp assembly:

1. Make sure the headlamp switch is off.
2. With the hood raised, reach inside the engine compartment and unplug the electrical connector from the bulb.

3. Remove the several screws holding the lamp assembly to the vehicle. On some vehicles, the screws are installed from the rear, figure 13-4.
4. Position the new lamp assembly and reinstall the screws.
5. Reconnect the connector to the bulb.
6. Turn on the headlamp switch and check the new lamp's operation.
7. Check the headlamp aim and adjust as explained in the paragraphs on headlamp aiming.

The halogen bulb can be replaced without removing the headlamp assembly. Do not, however, remove the bulb for any extended length of time before reinstalling the new bulb, because contamination can enter the headlamp assembly and affect reflector performance. NEVER plug the bulb into the connector to see if it is good unless it is within the confines of the headlamp assembly. Bulb replacement by it-

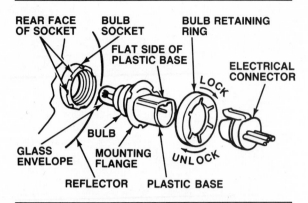

Figure 13-5. Halogen bulb replacement. (Ford)

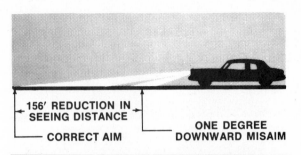

Figure 13-6. A headlamp that is misaimed only one degree downward can reduce the driver's seeing distance by more than 150 feet.

self does not change headlamp alignment, so you should not need to reaim the headlamp.

If only the bulb requires replacement:
1. Make sure the headlamp switch is off.
2. With the hood raised, reach inside the engine compartment and unplug the electrical connector from the bulb.
3. Rotate the plastic retaining ring on the bulb about ⅛-turn counterclockwise, then slide the ring off the plastic base, figure 13-5.
4. Remove the bulb from the reflector socket by carefully pulling it straight to the rear. Do not rotate the bulb during removal.
CAUTION: *The halogen bulb contains gas under pressure and may shatter if scratched or dropped. Handle new bulbs only by their plastic base. Avoid contact with the bulb envelope, which can result in staining and premature failure.*
5. Position the new bulb with the flat on its base facing upward. Carefully align the grooves in the base of the bulb with the socket locating tabs and insert the bulb into the reflector socket until its mounting flange mates with the socket face.
6. Slide the plastic retaining ring removed in step 3 in place against the mounting flange and rotate the ring clockwise until it stops.
7. Reconnect the connector to the bulb.
8. Turn on the headlamp switch and check the new lamp's operation.
9. Check the headlamp aim and adjust as explained in the following paragraphs.

Headlamp Aiming

Three methods can be used to aim headlamps:
1. Aiming screens
2. Mechanical aimers
3. Photoelectric aimers.

Generally, aiming screens are the least accurate method and are rarely used in automotive shops today. Regardless of which method is

used, you should prepare the car as follows before aiming the lamps:
1. Remove any mud or ice from under the fenders.
2. Inflate the tires to their normal operating pressures.
3. Clean lamp lenses and replace any burned-out units.
4. Check the manufacturer's specifications and place the correct weight load in the car, if necessary. For example, the manufacturer may specify a full tank of gas and a driver and passenger in the front seat.
5. Use a darkening cloth to cover Type 2 or 2A lamps when aiming Type 1 or 1A lamps in a 4-lamp system with photoelectric or aiming screen methods.
6. Cover any headlamp photocell controls to prevent their operation.
7. Check the headlamp aim and adjust as explained in the following paragraphs.

Aim limits
Headlamps that are slightly misaimed can greatly reduce a driver's seeing distance, figure 13-6. For this reason, headlamp aiming limits have been established by government regulations. The limits may vary slightly from area to area, but the following limits are generally accepted:
• High-beam — Refer to figure 13-7. The center of the lamp high-intensity zone should be horizontally within 4 inches (100 mm) to the right or 4 inches (100 mm) to the left of the lamp center. The center of the lamp high-intensity zone should be vertically within 4 inches (100 mm) above or 4 inches (100 mm) below the horizontal centerline.
• Low-beam — Refer to figure 13-8. The left edge of the lamp high-intensity zone should be horizontally within 4 inches (100 mm) to the right or 4 inches (100 mm) to the left of the lamp center. The top edges of the lamp high-intensity zone should be vertically within 4

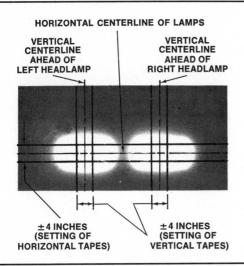

Figure 13-7. The headlamp high beams should show this pattern on the aiming screen.

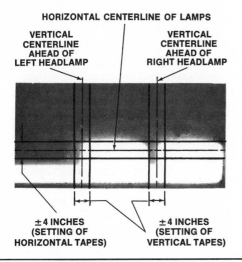

Figure 13-8. The headlamp low beams should show this pattern on the aiming screen.

inches (100 mm) above or 4 inches (100 mm) below the horizontal centerline.

Remember that these are maximum allowable inspection limits. When adjusting lamp aim, be sure to center the high-intensity zones exactly, both horizontally and vertically.

The limits apply to an aiming screen pattern with the car's lamps 25 feet (762 cm) away. When you use mechanical or photoelectric aiming equipment, refer to the manufacturer's instructions for establishing equivalent limits.

Aiming screens

An aiming screen is a fixed screen with guidelines on it. The car's lamp beams are projected on the screen and adjusted according to the guidelines.

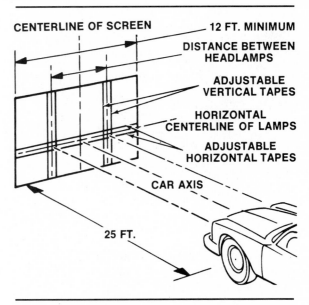

Figure 13-9. Using an aiming screen to adjust headlamps.

The screen should be 5 feet (152 cm) high, 12 feet (366 cm) wide, and have a matte (nongloss) white surface. It should be in a large room that can be darkened. The screen must be mounted so that it is perpendicular to the floor, even if the floor slopes. The screen also must be adjustable so that it can be aligned parallel to the car's rear axle.

The guidelines on the screen, figure 13-9, are:
● An adjustable vertical centerline
● At least two adjustable vertical tapes (two tapes must be in front of each lamp during aiming)
● At least two adjustable horizontal tapes.

In addition, there should be a line on the floor parallel to the screen and 25 feet (762 cm) in front of it.

An aiming screen can be used to check and adjust all types of headlamps. To use the screen:
1. Put the car in the test area so that the headlamps are directly over the 25-foot (762 cm) reference line.
2. Adjust the screen so that it is parallel to the car's rear axle.
3. Adjust the vertical centerline tape so that it is in line with the center of the car:

   a. Measure the width of the car's windshield and rear window; mark the centerlines with narrow tape.

   b. Stand behind the car and sight through the windows at the screen.

   c. Have an assistant move the vertical centerline until it is in line with both window centerlines.

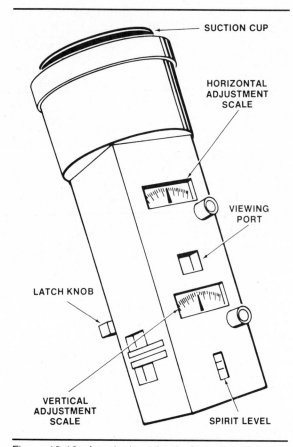

Figure 13-10. A typical mechanical headlamp aimer.

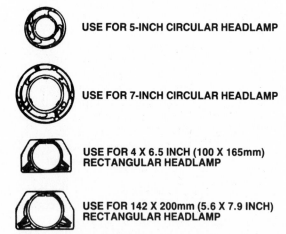

Figure 13-11. Typical mechanical headlamp aimer adapters. (Chrysler)

4. Adjust high-beams first, then low-beams, according to these general procedures.
5. Adjust the two vertical tapes so that they are 4 inches (100 mm) to the left and the right of the vertical centerline of the lamp being checked.

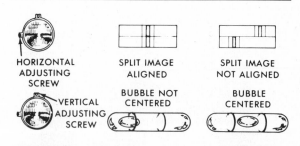

Figure 13-12. The mechanical aimer has adjustments for both horizontal and vertical headlamp aim. (Chrysler)

6. Adjust the horizontal tapes so that they are 4 inches (100 mm) above and below the horizontal centerline of the lamp being checked.
7. Turn on the lamps and check the aim:
   a. For high-beams, refer to figure 13-7.
   b. For low-beams, refer to figure 13-8.
8. Adjust the lamps to obtain beams within the correct areas.
9. Recheck the vertical and horizontal aim of each lamp before replacing any bezels or trim pieces.
10. If any lamp is out of adjustment, aim all lamps.

Mechanical aiming
Mechanical aimers are a pair of portable devices that attach to the headlamp lenses with suction cups, figure 13-10. These aimers can be used on round or rectangular sealed-beams with aiming pads, as well as on composite headlamps. They cannot be used on lamps without aiming pads or lamps covered by a fairing.

A set of mechanical aimers usually includes a set of adapter rings, figure 13-11, for use with various lamp sizes and shapes. Older models have a separate leveling transit to compensate for any slope in the floor; this device is built into newer model aimers. Follow the manufacturer's instructions to make sure that the aimers are properly calibrated.

To check or adjust headlamp aim with mechanical aimers:
1. Put the car in the test area.
2. Make sure the headlamps are turned off.
3. Calibrate the aimers.
4. Clamp the aimers in place on the lamp lenses, using the proper adapter. This may require removing headlamp bezels or trim pieces. Make sure to check 4-lamp systems in matched pairs; that is, both inboard or lower lamps, or both outboard or upper lamps.
5. Check the bubble spirit level or split image on each aimer, figure 13-12. If necessary, use a screwdriver or special tool to turn the head-

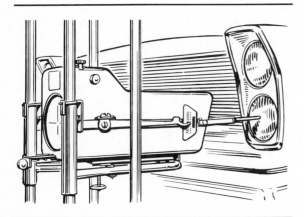

Figure 13-13. A typical photoelectric headlamp aimer.

Figure 13-14. A photoelectric aimer must be properly positioned in front of the headlamp.

lamp adjusting screws until the bubble is centered or the split image is aligned.
6. After adjusting lamp aim, bounce the car fender to settle the aiming screws. Recheck the bubble spirit level. Remember that adjusting the vertical aim may throw off the horizontal aim, and vice versa. Doublecheck both before reinstalling the bezels or trim pieces.
7. If any lamp is out of adjustment, aim all lamps.

Photoelectric aiming
Photoelectric, or optical, aimers are mounted on movable frame-type stands, figure 13-13. The stands may be on rollers or tracks on the floor. Because photoelectric aimers contain photocells, they can be used to measure beam intensity as well as lamp aim. They can be used with all headlamps, because they do not mount on the face of the lamp.

Figure 13-15. Many automotive bulb sockets can be removed from the rear of the lamp assembly.

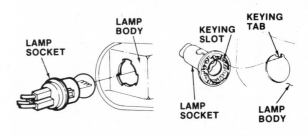

Figure 13-16. The sockets have indexing, or keying, tabs to hold them in the lamp body. (Ford)

To check or adjust headlamp aim with a photoelectric aimer:
1. Position the car in the test area.
2. Turn on the headlamps.
3. Place the aimer in front of the lamps, figure 13-14, as described in the manufacturer's instructions.
4. Check the location of the high-intensity zone on each headlamp. Check Type 1 lamps on high-beam; check Type 2 lamps on low-beam.
5. If necessary, turn the lamp adjusting screws while watching the aiming screen.
6. If any lamp is out of adjustment, aim all lamps.

SMALL BULB REPLACEMENT

Most small bulbs used in exterior lighting systems can be removed and replaced from the rear of the lamp assembly. The lens does not have to be removed. You rotate the socket base and pull it out of the rear of the lamp assembly, figure 13-15. Some sockets are indexed in different ways, figure 13-16. Make sure that you are removing a socket correctly to avoid damaging it. Other sockets simply snap out of the rear of the lamp housing.

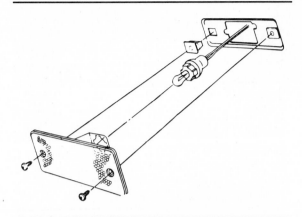

Figure 13-17. This lamp lens is removed by taking screws out from the front of the lamp. (GM)

Figure 13-18. This lamp lens is removed by taking nuts off the back of the lamp. (GM)

Nonindexed and wedge-base bulbs can be pulled from the socket and a replacement bulb pushed in. Indexed bulbs must be pushed into the socket and rotated until the bulb is free. The replacement indexed bulb is pushed into the socket and rotated until it is secure.

If the rear of the lamp assembly cannot be reached, remove the lamp lens to replace the bulb. Lamp lenses also must be removed for cleaning or replacement. Lenses are attached with screws on the outside of the vehicle, figure 13-17, or with nuts on the inside of the vehicle, figure 13-18. You may have to remove other trim parts to reach the screws or nuts. When reinstalling the lens, make sure that all gaskets and washers are correctly positioned. These protect the lamp assembly from dirt and water, which could damage the bulb and socket.

Some interior lamps can be replaced from the rear of the lamp assembly. To do so, however, you may have to remove the instrument cluster because there may not be enough room or clearance to remove the bulb from behind the instrument panel. In other cases, you may

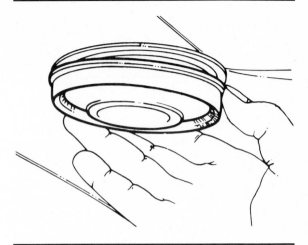

Figure 13-19. Some interior lamp lenses can be pried loose. (AMC)

have to remove the lens or a trim panel to reach the bulb. Dome and courtesy lamp lenses may be retained with screws, or they may be pried loose, figure 13-19.

GENERAL TROUBLESHOOTING PROCEDURES

Some lighting faults can affect all types of circuits. The following paragraphs contain troubleshooting instructions that can be used in many different cases. The problems to be examined are:
● One small bulb does not light
● Circuit protector opens repeatedly (fuse or circuit breaker).
    These tests can be made with:
● A voltmeter or a 12-volt test lamp
● An ohmmeter or a self-powered test lamp
● A jumper wire.
    Meters will provide more accurate results in some tests, such as locating a high-resistance connection that allows enough current to light the test lamp, but not enough to light the normal bulb.
CAUTION: When working with a jumper wire around a lamp socket, be careful not to connect the jumper wire from the insulated (hot) terminal to ground. This would bypass the bulb, which is the circuit load, and can blow a fuse or burn up a socket connection.

In most cases, when only one bulb in a circuit will not light, the bulb is at fault. However, there are other problems that will make a single bulb fail. Here is a guide to troubleshooting these cases:
1. Substitute a known-good bulb of the proper type and base; if it will not light, continue the test.

2. Remove the bulb from the socket and turn on the switch or switches that control current to this bulb.

3. Test for battery voltage at the bulb socket by connecting either the voltmeter or the 12-volt test lamp in series between ground and the insulated terminal on the inside of the bulb socket.

    a. If voltage is present, go to step 6.

    b. If voltage is not present, go to step 4.

4. Turn off the switches that control current.

5. Use the ohmmeter or the self-powered test lamp to check continuity through the socket insulated terminal. If the socket terminals are completely encased in plastic, test from the inside of the socket to the nearest connector.

    a. If there is continuity, trace and repair the wiring between the socket and the next common circuit point.

6. Reinstall the bulb in the socket and connect a jumper wire between the socket base and ground.

7. Turn on the switches that control current to the bulb:

    a. If the bulb lights, go to step 8.

    b. If the bulb does not light, retest the socket's insulated terminal and the bulb condition.

8. Repair the socket ground connection by cleaning and tightening the socket mounting or by checking continuity through the separate ground wire and connection.

A short or a ground in a lighting circuit will bypass all or part of the circuit's resistance (the bulbs). If too much current flows through the circuit, the circuit protector (a fuse or breaker) opens. It is usually easy to recognize this problem, but it can be very difficult to find the damaged part of the circuit.

One way to locate the damage is with a special piece of equipment called a short finder. It consists of a compass and a jumper wire, with a built-in circuit breaker. The circuit breaker is connected into the problem circuit in place of the original circuit protector. Current will flow through the circuit in short spurts as the circuit breaker opens and closes. When the compass is held near the circuit wiring, its needle is affected by the magnetic field of the conductor. The circuit wiring does not have to be exposed — it can be within a harness or under a carpet and the compass will still be affected. The needle will swing back and forth with the spurts of current flow. Move the compass along the circuit wiring until the needle stops swinging. That is the point where the circuit is shorted or grounded to another conductor. The circuit is open beyond the short or ground, and there is no current to affect the compass.

If you do not have a short finder, there is another way to locate the damage:

1. Disconnect all of the connectors in the problem circuit.

2. Install a new fuse or let the circuit breaker cool and close.

3. Close the switch or switches in the circuit.

4. Reconnect the circuit sections one by one, starting at the fuse or breaker and working toward ground.

5. When you reconnect a section and the circuit protector opens, you know that the damage is within that section of wiring.

SPECIFIC CIRCUIT TROUBLESHOOTING

The following instructions cover problems within specific lighting circuits. Because wiring is often hard to reach for testing, you may want to start each test by substituting a known-good bulb for the ones that will not light. If the problem still exists, you must continue with the tests described below.

Headlamp Circuit Troubleshooting

Where it applies, these instructions are divided into those for grounded-lamp circuits, figure 13-20, and those for insulated-lamp circuits, figure 13-21. The instructions apply to 2-lamp and 4-lamp systems.

Some of the tests will be affected by the vehicle design. For example, we will have you test the dimmer switch before testing the main headlamp switch. This is because, in most systems, the dimmer switch is easier to reach for testing. If a floor-mounted dimmer switch is used, it is more likely to fail due to exposure to dirt and rough handling. Refer to your *Classroom Manual* for more information on headlamp circuit designs.

All headlamps do not light — both high and low beams

To test a grounded-lamp system, figure 13-20:

1. Clean and tighten the bulbs' ground connections.

2. Turn on the main headlamp switch.

3. Test for battery voltage at both terminals on the headlamp side of the dimmer switch, moving the dimmer switch from low beam to high beam and back:

    a. If battery voltage is present at both terminals when the dimmer switch is in the appropriate position, test the individual lamp circuit branches as described in the test "One lamp does not light — both high and low beams".

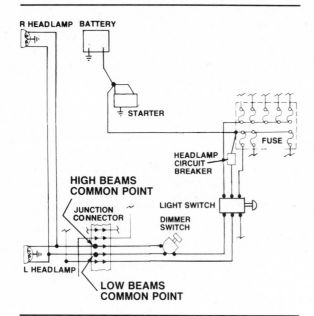

Figure 13-20. A typical grounded-lamp headlamp circuit.

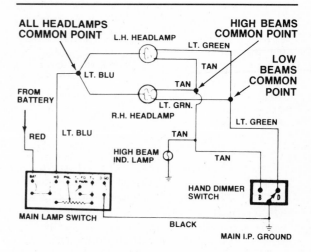

Figure 13-21. A typical insulated-lamp headlamp circuit. (Oldsmobile)

b. If battery voltage is not present, go to step 4.

4. Test for battery voltage at the headlamp switch side of the dimmer switch:

a. If voltage is present, replace the dimmer switch.

b. If voltage is not present, go to step 5.

5. Test for battery voltage at the headlamp terminal on the dimmer switch side of the main headlamp switch:

a. If voltage is present, trace and repair the wiring between the dimmer switch and the main headlamp switch.

b. If voltage is not present, go to step 6.

6. Test for battery voltage at the battery side of the main headlamp switch:

a. If voltage is present, replace the main headlamp switch.

b. If voltage is not present, trace and repair the wiring between the battery and the main headlamp switch.

To test an insulated-lamp system, figure 13-21:

1. Clean and tighten the ground connection at the dimmer switch.

2. Turn on the main headlamp switch.

3. Test for battery voltage at the ground side of the dimmer switch, moving the dimmer switch from low beam to high beam and back:

a. If battery voltage is present at both positions, recheck the dimmer switch ground connection.

b. If voltage is present at one switch position but not at the other, test the faulty circuit

branches as described in the test "All head-lamps do not light — low beam or high beam only".

c. If voltage is not present at either switch position, go to step 4.

4. Test for battery voltage at both terminals on the headlamp side of the dimmer switch:

a. If voltage is present at both terminals, replace the dimmer switch.

b. If voltage is present at one of the terminals but not at the other, test the faulty circuit branches as described in the test "All headlamps do not light — low beam or high beam only".

c. If voltage is not present at either terminal, go to step 5.

5. Test for battery voltage at the last common circuit point between the headlamps and the main headlamp switch:

a. If voltage is present, test the individual circuit branches as described in the test "One headlamp does not light — both high and low beams".

6. Test for battery voltage at the headlamp terminal on the battery side of the bulkhead connector:

a. If voltage is present, trace and repair the wiring between the last common circuit point and the bulkhead connector.

b. If voltage is not present, go to step 7.

7. Test for battery voltage at the headlamp terminal on the headlamp side of the main head-lamp switch:

a. If voltage is present, trace and repair the wiring between the bulkhead connector and the main headlamp switch.

b. If voltage is not present, go to step 8.

8. Test for battery voltage at the battery side of the main headlamp switch:
   a. If voltage is present, replace the main headlamp switch.
   b. If voltage is not present, trace and repair the wiring between the battery and the main headlamp switch.

All headlamps do not light — low beam or high beam only
To test a grounded-lamp system, figure 13-20:
1. Turn on the main headlamp switch.
2. Test for battery voltage at the appropriate terminal on the headlamp side of the dimmer switch, with the dimmer switch in the correct position.
   a. If voltage is present, go to step 3.
   b. If voltage is not present, replace the dimmer switch.
3. Test for battery voltage at the last common point between the appropriate dimmer switch terminal and the headlamps:
   a. If voltage is present, test the individual circuit branches as described in the test "One headlamp does not light — low beam or high beam only".
   b. If voltage is not present, trace and repair the wiring between the dimmer switch and the circuit common point.
To test an insulated-lamp system, figure 13-21:
1. Turn on the main headlamp switch.
2. Test for battery voltage at the appropriate terminal on the headlamp side of the dimmer switch, with the switch in the correct position.
   a. If voltage is present, replace the dimmer switch.
   b. If voltage is not present, go to step 3.
3. Test for battery voltage at the last common circuit point between the dimmer switch terminal and the headlamps:
   a. If voltage is present, trace and repair the wiring between the dimmer switch and the common circuit point.
   b. If voltage is not present, test the individual circuit branches as described in the test "One headlamp does not light — low beam or high beam only".

One headlamp does not light — both high and low beams
To test a grounded-lamp system, figure 13-20:
1. Clean and tighten the faulty lamp's ground connection.
2. Turn on the main headlamp switch.

3. Test for battery voltage at both the high- and low-beam terminals on the headlamp side of the headlamp connector, moving the dimmer switch from low beam to high beam and back:
   a. If voltage is present at both terminals when the dimmer switch is in the correct position, replace the lamp.
   b. If voltage is present at one terminal but not at the other, test the faulty circuit branch as described in the test "One headlamp does not light — low beam or high beam only".
   c. If voltage is not present at either terminal, go to step 4.
4. Test for battery voltage at both the high- and low-beam wires on the battery side of the connector:
   a. If voltage is present at both terminals, replace the connector.
   b. If voltage is not present, go to step 5.
5. Test for battery voltage at the last common circuit point between the lamps in both the high-beam and low-beam circuit branches:
   a. If voltage is present, trace and repair the wiring between the headlamp connector and the common point.
   b. If voltage is not present, test the system as described in the test "All headlamps do not light — both low and high beams".
To test an insulated-lamp circuit, figure 13-21:
1. Turn on the main headlamp switch.
2. Test for battery voltage at the battery terminal on the headlamp side of the headlamp connector:
   a. If voltage is present, go to step 5.
   b. If voltage is not present, go to step 3.
3. Test for voltage at the battery terminal on the battery side of the connector:
   a. If voltage is present, replace the connector.
   b. If voltage is not present, go to step 4.
4. Test for battery voltage at the last common point between the main headlamp switch and the lamps:
   a. If voltage is present, trace and repair the wiring between the common point and the headlamp connector.
   b. If voltage is not present, test the system as described in the test "All headlamps do not light — both low and high beams".
5. Substitute a known-good lamp in the circuit:
   a. If the lamp lights, replace the old lamp.
   b. If the known-good lamp does not light, go to step 6.

6. Test for battery voltage at the high- and low-beam wires on the dimmer switch side of the headlamp connector, moving the dimmer switch from high beam to low beam and back:
  a. If voltage is present, go to step 7.
  b. If voltage is not present, replace the connector.
7. Test for battery voltage at both circuit branch common points between the lamps and the dimmer switch, moving the dimmer switch from low beam to high beam and back:
  a. If voltage is present, trace and repair the wiring between the common points and the dimmer switch.
  b. If voltage is not present, trace and repair the wiring between the common points and the headlamp connectors.

One headlamp does not light — low or high beam only

To test a grounded-lamp system, figure 13-20:
1. Turn on the main headlamp switch.
2. Test for battery voltage at the appropriate terminal on the headlamp side of the headlamp connector, with the dimmer switch in the correct position:
  a. If voltage is present, replace the sealed-beam unit.
  b. If voltage is not present, go to step 3.
3. Test for battery voltage at the appropriate wire on the battery side of the headlamp connector:
  a. If voltage is present, replace the connector.
  b. If voltage is not present, go to step 4.
4. Test for battery voltage at the last common circuit point between the lamps in the appropriate circuit branch:
  a. If voltage is present, trace and repair the wiring between the common point and the headlamp connector.
  b. If voltage is not present, test the system as described in the test "All headlamps do not light — high beam or low beam only"
To test an insulated-lamp system, figure 13-21:
1. Turn on the main headlamp switch.
2. Test for battery voltage at the appropriate wire on the ground side of the headlamp connector:
  a. If voltage is present, go to step 4.
  b. If voltage is not present, go to step 3.
3. Test for continuity through the appropriate terminal of the connector:
  a. If there is continuity, replace the sealed-beam unit.
  b. If there is no continuity, replace the connector.

4. Test for battery voltage just before the first common point in the appropriate circuit between the lamps:
  a. If voltage is present, test the circuit between this point and ground as described in the test "All headlamps do not light — both high and low beams".
  b. If voltage is not present, trace and repair the wiring between the common point and the connector.

All headlamps dim at idle

Some dimming may be normal when many accessories are used at the same time. If only the headlamps are being used and they dim, check the following items:
1. Test the battery state of charge.
2. With the main headlamp switch on, test for full battery voltage at the headlamp connector:
  a. If full battery voltage is present, check for too much resistance in the circuit between the lamps and ground.
  b. If full battery voltage is not present, check for too much resistance in the circuit between the battery and the lamps.
Headlight dimming at idle can also result from low charging system voltage.

Taillamp, License Plate Lamp, Parking Lamp, Side Marker Lamp, and Clearance Lamp Circuit Troubleshooting

All lamps in one circuit do not light
1. Refer to figures 13-22, 13-23, and 13-24.
2. Check the circuit fuse; replace if necessary.
3. Turn on the main headlamp switch.
4. Test for battery voltage at the last common circuit point between the main headlamp switch and the lamps:
  a. If voltage is present, test the individual circuit branches as if only one lamp did not light.
  b. If voltage is not present, go to step 5.
5. Test for battery voltage at the appropriate terminals on the lamp side of the main headlamp switch:
  a. If voltage is present, trace and repair the wiring between the main headlamp switch and the last common circuit point of the lamps.
  b. If voltage is not present but the headlamps light, replace the main headlamp switch.
  c. If voltage is not present and the headlamps do not light, trace and repair the wiring between the battery and the main headlamp switch; replace the switch if necessary.

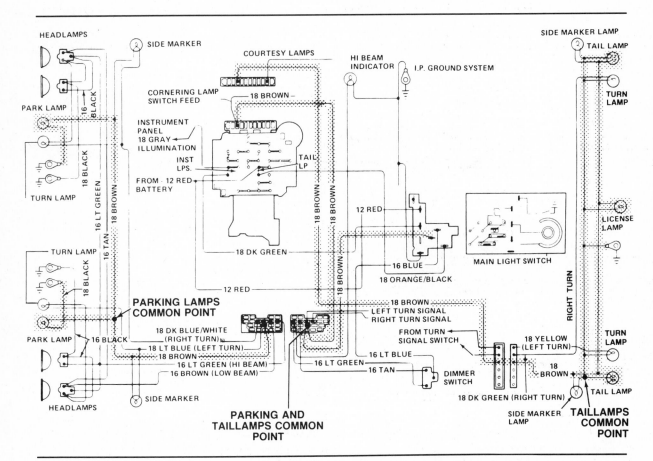

Figure 13-22. A typical parking and taillamp circuit. (Buick)

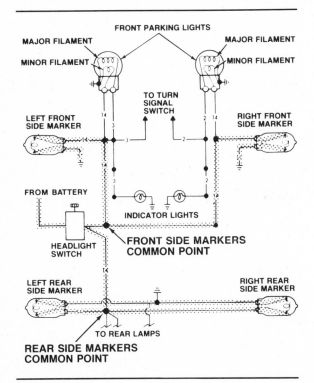

Figure 13-23. A typical side marker circuit, with grounded bulbs. (Ford)

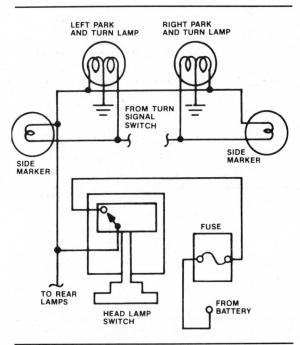

Figure 13-24. A typical side marker circuit, with the bulbs grounded through the turn signal lamps.

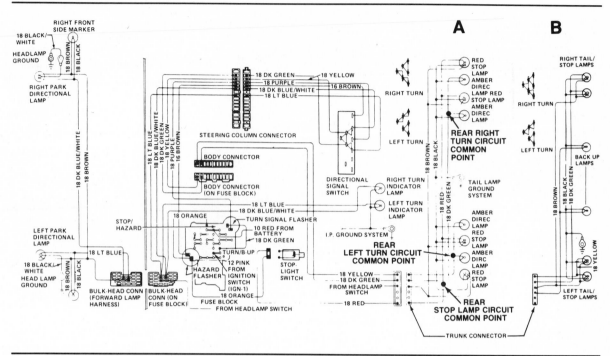

Figure 13-25. Typical stop and turn signal lamp circuits. (Buick)

Stop Lamp Circuit Troubleshooting

All lamps do not light

If the circuit passes stop lamp current through the turn signal switch, use this test procedure:

1. Refer to figure 13-25B.
2. Check the circuit fuse and replace, if necessary.
3. Close the brake switch.
4. Test for battery voltage at the last common circuit point of the lamps:
   a. If voltage is present, test the individual circuit branches as if only one lamp did not light.
   b. If voltage is not present, go to step 5.
5. Test for battery voltage on the lamp side of the switch nearest the lamps (either the turn signal switch or the brake switch):
   a. If voltage is present, trace and repair the wiring between the switch and the last common circuit point of the lamps.
   b. If voltage is not present, go to step 6.
6. Test for battery voltage on the battery side of the switch nearest the lamps:
   a. If voltage is present, replace the switch.
   b. If voltage is not present, go to step 7.
7. Test for battery voltage at the lamp side of the switch farthest from the lamps:
   a. If voltage is present, trace and repair the wiring between the two switches.
   b. If voltage is not present, go to step 8.

8. Test for battery voltage at the battery side of the switch farthest from the lamps:
   a. If voltage is present, replace the switch.
   b. If voltage is not present, trace and repair the wiring between the battery and the switch.

If the circuit does not pass stop lamp current through the turn signal switch, use this test procedure:

1. Refer to figure 13-25A.
2. Check the circuit fuse and replace, if necessary.
3. Close the brake switch.
4. Test for battery voltage at the last common circuit point of the lamps:
   a. If voltage is present, test the individual circuit branches as if only one lamp did not light.
   b. If voltage is not present, go to step 5.
5. Test for battery voltage at the lamp side of the brake switch:
   a. If voltage is present, trace and repair the wiring between the switch and the circuit common point.
   b. If voltage is not present, go to step 6.
6. Test for battery voltage at the battery side of the brake switch:
   a. If voltage is present, replace the switch.
   b. If voltage is not present, trace and repair the wiring between the battery and the switch.

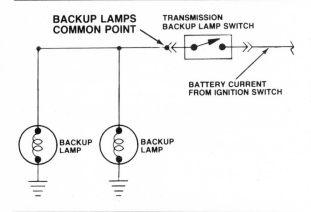

Figure 13-26. A typical backup lamp circuit. (Chrysler)

All lamps stay on with brake pedal released
1. Replace brake switch.

Turn Signal and Hazard Flasher Circuit Troubleshooting

All lamps in one circuit do not light
1. Refer to figure 13-25.
2. For turn signal circuit troubleshooting, make all voltage tests with the ignition switch on.
3. Check the circuit fuse and replace, if required.
4. Test for battery voltage at the last common circuit point between the appropriate switch and the bulbs:
　a. If voltage is present, test the individual circuit branches as if only one lamp did not light.
　b. If voltage is not present, go to step 5.
5. Test for battery voltage at the lamp side of the appropriate switch with the circuit closed. Test the turn signal circuit at the turn signal switch and the hazard flasher circuit at the hazard flasher switch:
　a. If voltage is present, trace and repair the wiring between the switch and the last common circuit point of the lamps.
　b. If voltage is not present, go to step 6.
6. Test for battery voltage at the battery side of the appropriate switch:
　a. If voltage is present, replace the switch.
　b. If voltage is not present, trace and repair the wiring between the battery and the switch.

Flashing rate too fast
1. Check the rating of the flasher unit; replace if necessary.
2. Check the size and type of bulbs in the circuit; replace if necessary.
3. Test the charging system for too much voltage.

No flashing, or flashing rate too slow
1. Check the rating of the flasher unit; replace if necessary.
2. Check the size and type of bulbs in the circuit; replace if necessary.
3. Make voltage drop tests of the circuit wiring to pinpoint any areas of very high resistance; correct as required. Be sure to check for high-resistance ground connections.
4. Test the charging system for low voltage.

Backup Lamp Circuit Troubleshooting

All lamps do not light
1. Refer to figure 13-26.
2. Check the circuit fuse and replace, if necessary.
3. Turn the ignition switch on and shift the transmission or transaxle into Reverse.
4. Test for battery voltage at the last common circuit point of the lamps:
　a. If voltage is present, test the individual circuit branches as if only one lamp did not light.
　b. If voltage is not present, go to step 5.
5. Test for battery voltage at the lamp side of the backup lamp switch:
　a. If voltage is present, trace and repair the wiring between the switch and the last common circuit point.
　b. If voltage is not present, go to step 7.
6. Test for battery voltage at the battery side of the backup lamp switch:
　a. If voltage is present, replace or adjust the switch. Many backup lamp switches are combined with neutral start switches. Adjustment instructions are in Chapter 6.
　b. If voltage is not present, trace and repair the wiring between the backup lamp switch and the ignition switch.

Panel and Interior Lamp Troubleshooting

Panel and interior dome or courtesy lamp circuits that are controlled by contacts within the main headlamp switch can be tested using the procedures given for taillamps. If the circuit is controlled by a separate switch or combination

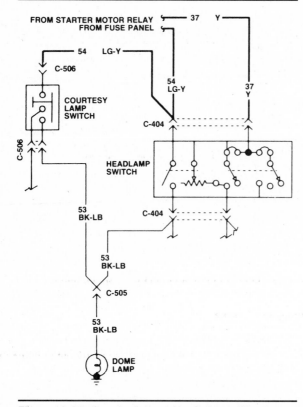

Figure 13-27. A typical dome lamp circuit. (Ford)

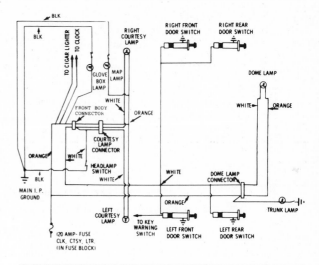

Figure 13-28. A typical interior lamp circuit. (Oldsmobile)

of switches, the procedure will be different. Also, if the bulb is insulated and the switch is grounded, the testing procedure will be different than if the bulb is grounded and the switch is insulated. The printed circuitry used with some panel lamps cannot be repaired, but must be replaced if it is the source of the problem.

To test a typical panel or interior lamp circuit:
1. Refer to figures 13-27 or 13-28.
2. Check the circuit fuse and replace, if necessary.
3. Close the switch or switches in the circuit that should make the lamps light.
4. Clean and tighten the ground connection of whichever part is grounded.
5. Test for battery voltage at the battery side of the grounded component:
   a. If voltage is present, replace the component.
   b. If voltage is not present, go to step 6.
6. Test for battery voltage at the ground side of the insulated component:
   a. If voltage is present, trace and repair the wiring between the insulated component and the grounded part.
   b. If voltage is not present, go to step 7.

7. Check for continuity through the insulated component:
   a. If there is continuity, go to step 8.
   b. If there is no continuity, replace the component.
8. Test for battery voltage at the first common circuit point of the lamp:
   a. If voltage is present, trace and repair the wiring between the insulated component and the common circuit point.
   b. If voltage is not present, trace and repair the wiring between the common circuit point and the ignition switch or fuse panel.

Headlamp Delay System Troubleshooting

Before testing an autolamp system, you should first check the headlamp circuit by turning the autolamp control off and turning the headlamps on with the manual switch. If the headlamps operate properly with the manual switch, check the fuse controlling the autolamp circuit and replace it, if necessary.

To test a typical autolamp circuit:
1. Turn on the manual headlamp switch. Make sure the autolamp switch is off.
2. Test for battery voltage between the autolamp relay connector and the last common point with the taillamp circuit:
   a. If voltage is present, go to step 3.
   b. If voltage is not present, trace and repair the wiring between the autolamp relay and the last common point with the taillamp circuit.

3. Test for battery voltage between the auto-lamp relay connector and the headlamp switch:

   a. If voltage is present, go to step 4.

   b. If voltage is not present, trace and repair the wiring between the autolamp relay and the headlight switch connectors.

4. Turn off the ignition switch and turn on the autolamp control switch. Check for system ground at the photocell connector with an ohmmeter or self-powered test lamp:

   a. If there is continuity, trace and repair the wiring between the potentiometer connector and the autolamp amplifier connector.

   b. If there is no continuity, go to step 5.

5. Check circuit continuity of the autolamp switch potentiometer from the connector wire to the switch bracket with a self-powered test lamp:

   a. If there is continuity, go to step 6.

   b. If there is no continuity, replace the head-lamp switch.

6. Check switch function continuity with a self-powered test lamp or ohmmeter while rotating the autolamp control knob from off to on. There should be no continuity with the switch off, and continuity with the switch on.

   a. If the switch performs as specified, go to step 7.

   b. If the switch does not perform as specified, replace it.

7. Measure resistance of the autolamp switch potentiometer while you rotate the autolamp control from off to its maximum time delay and compare to specifications:

   a. If resistance is within specifications, go to step 8.

   b. If resistance is not within specifications, replace the autolamp switch.

8. With the driver's delay control in maximum-delay position, check for continuity at the photocell connector with an ohmmeter:

   a. If the reading is within specifications, replace the amplifier assembly.

   b. If the reading is not within specifications, trace and repair the circuit between the delay control potentiometer connector and the autolamp amplifier connector.

9. Check the autolamp on-off control switch for continuity with an ohmmeter or self-powered test lamp:

   a. If there is continuity in the off position, go to step 10.

   b. If there is no continuity in the off position, replace the switch.

10. Check potentiometer resistance through its range with an ohmmeter while rotating the thumbwheel from off to maximum:

   a. If resistance is within specifications, the system is satisfactory.

   b. If resistance is not within specifications, replace the autolamp on-off switch.

14

Horn, Wiper and Washer, Cooling Fan, and Instrument Service

These common accessory circuits do not require frequent service. When they do, the following troubleshooting instructions will help you to solve the problem. In many cases, you will need the manufacturer's specifications and circuit diagrams for the system you are servicing.

HORN SYSTEM SERVICE

When a horn sounds but its tone is not right, it can be adjusted. If a horn does not sound at all, or if it cannot be shut off, the circuit must be tested. Testing instructions for different types of horn systems follow the adjustment procedure.

Electromagnetic Horn Tone Adjustment

If the adjuster screw or nut, figure 14-1, can be reached, a horn can be adjusted while it is mounted in the car. If the screw or nut cannot easily be reached, the horn must be removed and adjusted on a test bench. In both cases, make sure the horn's ground connection (usually the horn bracket) is clean and secure.

Electromagnetic horns are adjusted to draw a specified amount of current, usually between 3 and 8 amperes. Do not try to muffle the horn's sound during testing. This affects the current draw and your test will be inaccurate. Adjustment will only clean up the sound; it will not change the horn frequency. In two-horn systems, disconnect the wire from one horn while you adjust the other.

1. Make the following test connections:
   a. If the horn is out of the vehicle, connect an ammeter and remote start switch between the battery and the horn terminal as shown in figure 14-2.
   b. If the horn is in the vehicle, disconnect the wire from the horn to be adjusted. Connect an ammeter between the disconnected wire and horn terminal as shown in figure 14-3.

2. Press the remote start switch (horn out of the car) or the horn button (horn in the car) and observe the ammeter reading. Compare it to the manufacturer's specifications:
   a. If the reading is within specifications but the horn tone is bad, replace the horn.
   b. If the reading is not within specifications, go to step 3.

CAUTION: Do not turn the horn adjustment screw or nut while the horn is sounding, or the horn will be damaged.

3. Turn the horn adjustment screw or nut $\frac{1}{10}$-turn at a time, repeating step 2 between each adjustment until the ammeter reading is

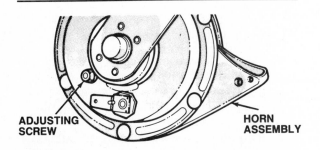

Figure 14-1. If the adjuster screw or nut is within reach, the horn does not have to be removed from the car for adjustment. (Chrysler)

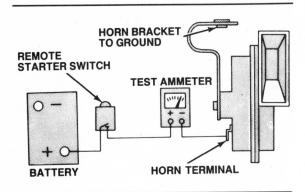

Figure 14-2. Testing and adjusting the horn out of the car. (Chrysler)

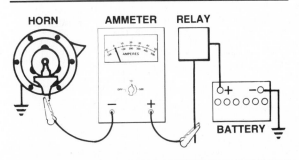

Figure 14-3. Testing and adjusting the horn while it is installed in the car. (AMC)

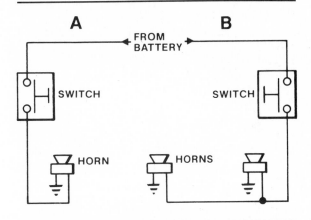

Figure 14-4. Horn systems without relays: position A, one horn: position B, two horns.

within specifications. On most horns, turning the screw or nut counterclockwise increases current; turning it clockwise decreases current.

Air Horn Sound Quality Test

1. Check the circuit fuse, circuit breaker, or fusible link.
2. Disconnect the air horn compressor at the horn. Connect an air source and apply 7 psi (50 kPa) to check the air horn trumpet.
   a. If there is no sound, or if the sound is poor, check for an obstruction in the horn throat.
   b. If there is no obstruction in the horn throat, replace the horn.

Horn Circuit Troubleshooting

If the horn will not sound, or if it cannot be shut off, use these procedures to pinpoint the problem. Where it applies, the tests are divided into those for single- or multiple-horn systems, with and without a horn relay.

Horn will not sound — single-horn system
● Electromagnetic horn system *without* horn relay:
1. Check the circuit fuse or fusible link.

2. Clean and tighten the horn ground connection.
3. Close the horn switch and check for battery voltage at the horn terminal, figure 14-4A:
   a. If voltage is present, replace the horn.
   b. If voltage is not present, go to step 4.
4. Test for battery voltage at the horn side of the horn switch:
   a. If voltage is present, trace and repair the wiring between the switch and the horn.
   b. If voltage is not present, go to step 5.
5. Test for battery voltage at the battery side of the horn switch:
   a. If voltage is present, replace the horn switch.
   b. If voltage is not present, trace and repair the wiring between the battery and the switch.
● Electromagnetic horn system *with* a horn relay:
1. Check the circuit fuse or fusible link.
2. Clean and tighten the horn ground connection.

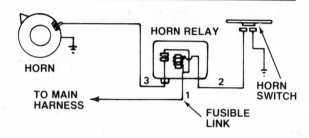

HORN RELAY

HORN

3

TO MAIN
HARNESS

1

2

HORN
SWITCH

FUSIBLE
LINK

Figure 14-5. A single-horn system with a horn relay.
(AMC)

3. Close the horn switch and check for battery voltage at the horn terminal, figure 14-5.
    a. If voltage is present, replace the horn.
    b. If voltage is not present, go to step 4.
4. Test for battery voltage at the armature terminal on the horn side of the horn relay (terminal 3 in figure 14-5):
    a. If voltage is present, trace and repair the wiring between the relay and the horn.
    b. If voltage is not present, go to step 5.
5. Test for battery voltage at the battery feed terminal of the horn relay (terminal 1 in figure 14-5):
    a. If voltage is present, go to step 6.
    b. If voltage is not present, trace and repair the wiring between the battery and the relay.
6. Test for battery voltage at the horn switch terminal on the horn relay (terminal 2 in figure 14-5):
    a. If voltage is present, go to step 7.
    b. If voltage is not present, replace the horn relay.
7. Test for battery voltage on the battery side of the horn switch:
    a. If voltage is present, go to step 8.
    b. If there is no voltage present, trace and repair the wiring between the relay and the horn switch.
8. Test for battery voltage on the ground side of the horn switch:
    a. If there is voltage present go to step 9.
    b. If there is no voltage present, replace the horn switch.
9. Clean and tighten the horn switch ground connection. If the horn still does not sound, replace the horn relay.
• Air horn system:
1. Check the circuit fuse, circuit breaker, or fusible link.
2. Disconnect air horn compressor at the horn. Connect an air source and apply 7 psi (50 kPa) to check the air horn trumpet. If there is no sound, or if the sound is poor, check for an obstruction in the horn throat. If none is found, replace the horn trumpet.

3. If the horn sound is satisfactory in step 2, press the horn button and listen for a whirring noise from the compressor.
4. If there is a whirring noise in step 3, check the air output of the compressor with a gauge.
    a. If air output is within specifications, look for a ruptured or blocked line between the compressor and horn.
    b. If air output is not within specifications, check the wiring polarity at the compressor. If the polarity is reversed, correct and retest. If polarity is satisfactory, replace the compressor.
5. If there is no whirring noise in step 3, make sure the compressor wiring and ground connections are secure, then check the voltage at the compressor.
    a. If the voltage is within specifications, replace the compressor.
    b. If there is no voltage, test the relay and horn switch as described in the "Horn will not sound — single-horn system", for electromagnetic horns with a relay, steps 4 through 9.

Horns will not sound — multiple-horn system
• System without horn relay:
1. Check the circuit fuse or fusible link.
2. Close the horn switch and check for battery voltage at the last common test point between the horns and the horn switch, figure 14-4B.
    a. If voltage is present, test each horn's circuit branch as described in the test "Horn will not sound — single-horn system", steps 1 through 3.
    b. If voltage is not present, go to step 3.
3. Test for battery voltage on the horn side of the horn switch:
    a. If voltage is present, trace and repair the wiring between the horn switch and the common circuit point.
    b. If voltage is not present, go to step 4.
4. Test for battery voltage on the battery side of the horn switch:
    a. If voltage is present, replace the horn switch.
    b. If voltage is not present, trace and repair the wiring between the horn switch and the battery.
• System with horn relay:
1. Check the circuit fuse or fusible link.
2. Close the horn switch and check for battery voltage at the last common circuit point between the horns and the horn relay, figure 14-6.
    a. If voltage is present, test each horn's individual circuit branch as described in the test "Horn will not sound — single-horn system", steps 2 through 4.

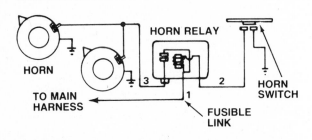

Figure 14-6. A multiple-horn system with a horn relay. (AMC)

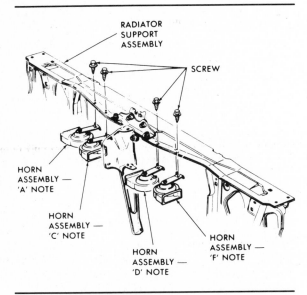

Figure 14-7. A typical horn installation. This automobile has four different horns tuned to F6. (Cadillac)

b. If voltage is not present, test the horn relay and horn switch circuitry as described in the test, "Horn will not sound — single-horn system", steps 5 through 8.

One horn will not sound — multiple-horn system

Test the horn's individual circuit branch as described in the test "Horn will not sound — single-horn system", steps 2 through 4 of the with-relay or without-relay test.

Horn will not shut off — system with no horn relay

In both a single-horn or a multiple-horn system with no relay, a continuously sounding horn must be caused by the horn switch contacts sticking closed. Check for continuity through the horn switch. If there is continuity through the switch when it should be open, replace it.

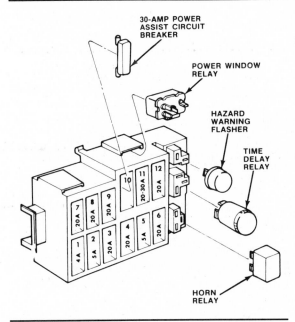

Figure 14-8. The horn relay can plug into the fuse panel. (Chrysler)

Horn will not shut off — system with horn relay

In either a single-horn or a multiple-horn system (electromagnetic or air) with a horn relay, a continuously sounding horn could be caused by either a sticking horn switch contact or by a faulty relay. Check for continuity through the horn switch and the relay armature circuit. If there is continuity where there should be none, replace the component.

Replacing Horn System Parts

To replace a horn, unscrew and remove the old horn from its mounting bracket, figure 14-7. With an air horn, it is necessary to disconnect the compressor hose at the horn. Clean the horn bracket attaching area on the mounting bracket and install the new horn. If a specially plated, corrosion-resistant screw is furnished for the ground connection, be sure to use it.

To replace the compressor on an air horn system, disconnect the hose and wiring connections, then remove the mounting fasteners. Install the new compressor with the mounting fasteners and reconnect the hose and wiring connections.

If the horn relay is mounted in the engine compartment, the new one can be plugged, bolted, or screwed in place of the old one. On late-model GM cars, the horn relay is often located in a "convenience center" under the instrument panel. Chrysler's horn relay plugs into the fuse panel, figure 14-8.

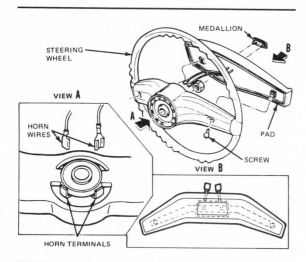

Figure 14-9. This Ford horn switch has two leads and terminals because it is used in a system with no horn relay — all of the current that flows to the horns must pass through this switch. (Ford)

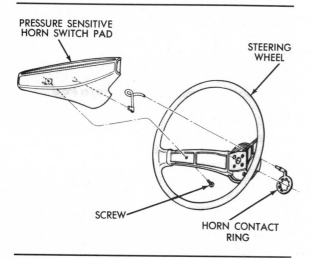

Figure 14-10. This Chrysler horn switch can be closed by pressure on any part of the cental pad. It is a grounding switch, and so has only one lead and terminal. (Chrysler)

Horn switches are generally mounted in the center of the steering column. All or part of the steering wheel may have to be removed to expose the switch. Some typical switch installations are shown in figures 14-9, 14-10, and 14-11.

WINDSHIELD WIPER AND WASHER SERVICE

Windshield wiper and washer systems vary greatly from one manufacturer to another, but some basic troubleshooting procedures can be applied to all electrical parts of the systems. In

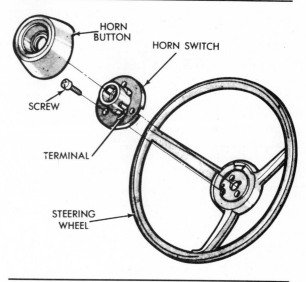

Figure 14-11. A simple horn switch installation. (Chrysler)

some cases, you must have the manufacturer's specifications and diagrams for the system you are testing.

On-Car Windshield Wiper System Testing

The windshield wipers can stop working because of an electrical problem or a mechanical bind in the wiper arm linkage. Generally, if the wipers work at one speed setting but not another, the problem is electrical. One exception: a depressed or a positive park system. If the wipers do not depress or return properly to their correct position at the bottom of the windshield, it could be a mechanical *or* an electrical problem.

To tell the difference between an electrical problem or mechanical bind in such a case, disconnect the wiper arm linkage from the motor. If the motor now works at all speeds, a mechanical bind is causing the problem. If the motor still will not work properly, the problem is electrical.

Make a preliminary check of the system to ensure that:
● The fuse or circuit breaker is not open
● The wiper motor ground connection is clean and tight
● The connectors at the wiper motor, wiper switch, and any system relays or governors are tight.

If the problem is still not evident:
1. Turn on the ignition switch.
2. Turn the wiper switch to its low speed, or to the speed at which the motor will not work.

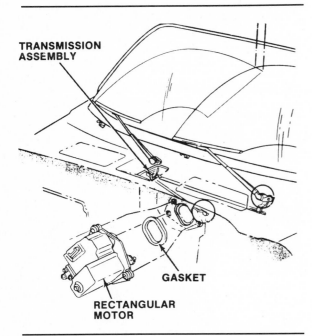

Figure 14-12. A typical GM windshield wiper motor installation. (GM)

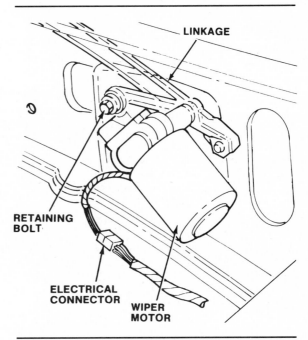

Figure 14-14. A typical Chrysler windshield wiper motor installation. (Chrysler)

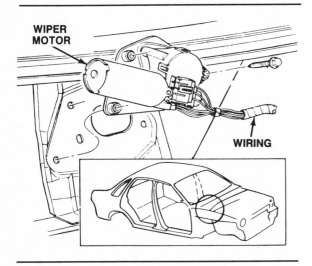

Figure 14-13. A typical Ford windshield wiper motor installation. (Ford)

3. Test for battery voltage at the appropriate wiper motor terminal:
    a. If voltage is present, remove the motor for further testing or replacement.
    b. If voltage is not present, go to step 4.
4. Test for battery voltage at the appropriate terminal on the motor side of the wiper switch:
    a. If voltage is present, trace and repair the wiring between the switch and the motor.
    b. If voltage is not present, go to step 5.
5. Test for battery voltage at the battery side of the wiper switch:
    a. If voltage is present, replace the switch.

    b. If voltage is not present, trace and repair the wiring between the battery and the switch. Be sure to check the ignition switch terminals and the fuse panel.

Windshield Washer System Testing

If no fluid is sprayed when the washer is turned on, the problem could be in the pump or in the delivery system of hoses and nozzles. To tell the difference between these cases, disconnect the main hose from the washer pump. Turn on the washer switch. If the pump sprays fluid, then the problem is in the delivery system. If the pump does not spray, it is defective and must be replaced.

Replacing Windshield Wiper and Washer System Parts

Some parts of windshield wiper motors can be rebuilt, but they often are simply replaced if defective. They are mounted at the base of the windshield, usually on the engine compartment side. Some typical wiper motor installations are shown in figures 14-12, 14-13, and 14-14.

If the vehicle has a rear window wiper, the motor will be located inside the rear door on station wagons or inside the rear hatch panel on hatchback and liftgate models. You will have to remove the inside trim panel to get to the motor for testing or replacement.

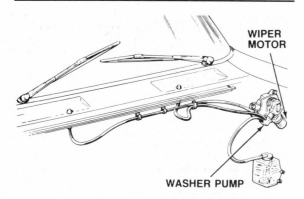

Figure 14-15. Some GM washer pumps are mounted on the windshield wiper motor.

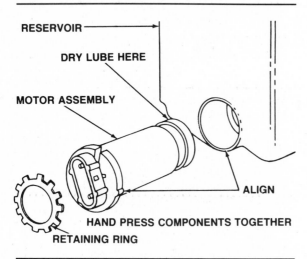

Figure 14-16. The Ford windshield washer pump. (Ford)

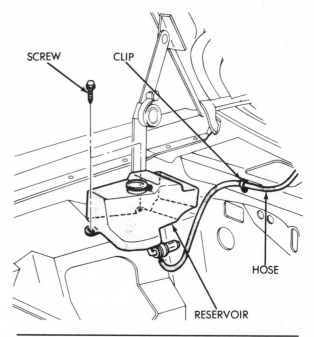

Figure 14-17. The Chrysler windshield washer pump. (Chrysler)

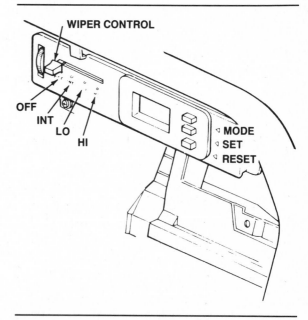

Figure 14-18. Many windshield wiper switches are mounted on the instrument panel. (Ford)

Windshield washer pumps are replaced if faulty. Some GM systems have pumps mounted in the wiper motor, figure 14-15. Most others are mounted in or near the washer fluid reservoir. Typical installations are shown in figures 14-16 and 14-17.

Control switches can be mounted on the instrument panel, figure 14-18, or on the steering column, figure 14-19, where they are operated by a multifunction lever or stalk, figure 14-20.

ELECTRIC COOLING FAN SERVICE

Electric cooling fan systems consist of:
• A fan and electric motor mounted on a fan shroud behind the radiator
• A coolant temperature switch in the cylinder head, thermostat housing, or radiator
• A relay.

If the vehicle has air conditioning (AC), the fan circuit will be interconnected with the AC, because fan operation also is controlled by the AC relay or compressor head pressure. Many late-model fan circuits have some form of computer control which will set a trouble code if a malfunction occurs in the fan circuit (or the AC circuit, if so equipped).

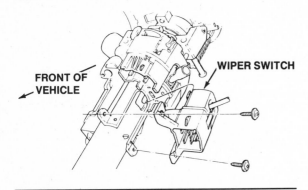

Figure 14-19. Some windshield wiper switches are mounted on the steering column. (Ford)

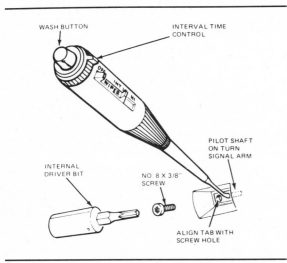

Figure 14-20. Steering column wiper switches are operated by a steering column lever or stalk.

Circuit Troubleshooting

The number and variations of electric fan circuits are almost infinite, as we saw in Chapter 19 of the *Classroom Manual*, with few common features beyond the basic circuit. We will cover basic circuits, provide examples of more complex but typical systems you may have to troubleshoot, and discuss the computer control of late-model systems.

Basic electric cooling fan circuit without air conditioning

When engine coolant reaches a specified temperature, the fan temperature switch provides a path to ground for the fan relay. The relay energizes, sending voltage to the cooling fan. Figure 14-21 shows an example of this basic circuit.

If the fan does not run:
1. Check the circuit fuse and fusible links.
2. Disconnect the fan motor from the wiring

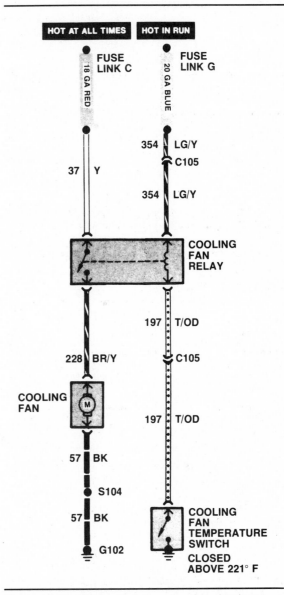

Figure 14-21. Basic electric cooling fan circuits on non-air conditioned vehicles are controlled by a temperature switch and relay. (Ford)

harness and jumper the connector to the battery (+) terminal and ground with No. 14 jumper wires:
   a. If the fan motor runs, go to step 3.
   b. If the fan motor does not run, replace it.
3. Replace the fan relay with a known-good relay, then disconnect the electrical connector at the temperature switch and connect a No. 14 gauge jumper wire between the connector terminals.
4. Turn the ignition switch to the Accessory position:
   a. If the fan motor runs, the original relay is bad.

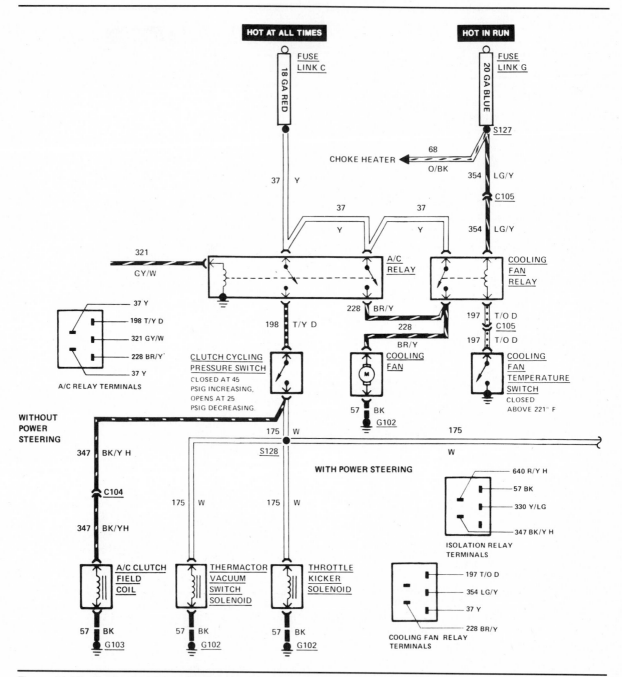

Figure 14-22. Basic electric cooling fan circuits on air conditioned vehicles are interconnected with the A/C relay to permit constant running when the air conditioner is on. (Ford)

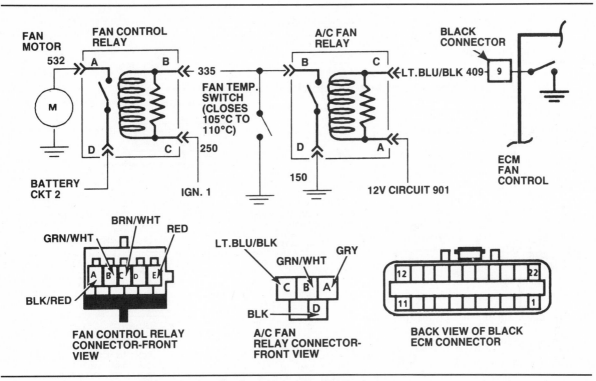

Figure 14-23. GM 1.8-liter TBI engine cooling fan schematic. (Pontiac)

b. If the fan motor still does not run, check the circuit wiring for an open. If none is found, remove and test the temperature switch as described later in this chapter.

If the fan runs continuously:

1. Disconnect the electrical connector at the temperature switch.

a. If the fan stops running, the temperature switch contacts are stuck closed. Replace the switch.

b. If the fan continues running, go to step 2.

2. Replace the relay with one that is known to be good:

a. If the fan stops running, the original relay is bad.

b. If the fan continues running, look for a short to ground in the wiring. If none is found, replace the fan motor.

Basic electric cooling fan circuit with air conditioning

When engine coolant reaches a specified temperature, the fan temperature switch provides a path to ground for the fan relay. The relay energizes, sending voltage to the cooling fan. When the AC compressor is turned on, the AC relay closes an alternate circuit to the cooling fan. This causes the fan to operate regardless of engine temperature. If the AC is turned off while the vehicle is being driven, control of the cool-

ing fan returns to the basic fan circuit. This allows the fan to remain on as long as coolant temperature exceeds the temperature switch calibration. When the engine cools below the switch calibration temperature, the switch opens and the fan stops running. Figure 14-22 shows an example of this basic circuit.

If the fan does not run under any condition, check the fan circuit as described under "Basic electric cooling fan circuit without air conditioning". If the fan operates normally, but does not run when the engine is first started with the AC on, the problem is most likely in the AC relay. A defective clutch cycling switch would cause a noticeable problem in AC operation.

GM front-wheel-drive cooling fan circuits

We will look at three examples of the electric cooling fan circuits used on late-model GM front-wheel-drive vehicles, using circuit diagrams and diagnostic charts. Their complexity, compared to the basic ones we looked at earlier, shows that you *must* refer to the manufacturer's circuit diagrams and trouble shooting procedures when servicing these systems.

1. 1.8-liter Throttle body fuel injection (TBI) system: Figure 14-23 is a diagram of the cooling fan system used with GM 1.8-liter TBI engines in the J-car series. Battery voltage is applied to the fan control relay terminal D; ignition voltage is applied to terminal C. If the AC is off or vehicle

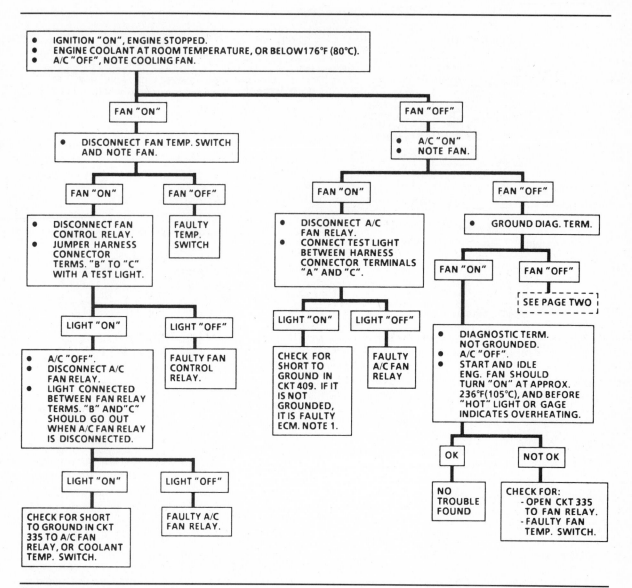

Figure 14-24. Partial GM diagnostic chart for troubleshooting the 1.8-liter TBI engine cooling system. The complete procedure is continued on another chart. (GM)

speed exceeds 30 mph (48 kph), the fan temperature switch controls the circuit. When the switch closes at its calibrated temperature, it completes the relay circuit to ground and the fan runs.

If the AC is on and the compressor high side low-pressure switch is closed, ignition voltage is supplied to the AC fan relay terminal A. At vehicle speeds below 30 mph, terminal 9 of the ECM and circuit 409 between the ECM and terminal C of the AC fan relay are grounded. This energizes the AC fan relay which in turn energizes the fan control relay and supplies battery voltage to the fan.

To troubleshoot this system, refer to figure 14-24.

2. *1.8-liter Port Fuel Injection (PFI) System:*
Figure 14-25 is a diagram of the cooling fan system used with GM 1.8-liter PFI engines in the J-car series. Battery voltage is applied to the fan control relay terminal E and timer relay terminal 7. Ignition voltage is applied to terminal C and timer relay terminal 5. If the AC is off, the fan temperature switch controls the circuit. When the switch closes at its calibrated value, it closes timer relay terminal 3. This activates timer relay terminal 6 and completes the circuit to terminal B of the fan control relay, which turns the fan on.

If the AC is on or if vehicle speed is less than 35 mph (56 kph), the ECM energizes the AC fan relay to complete the circuit to the fan control

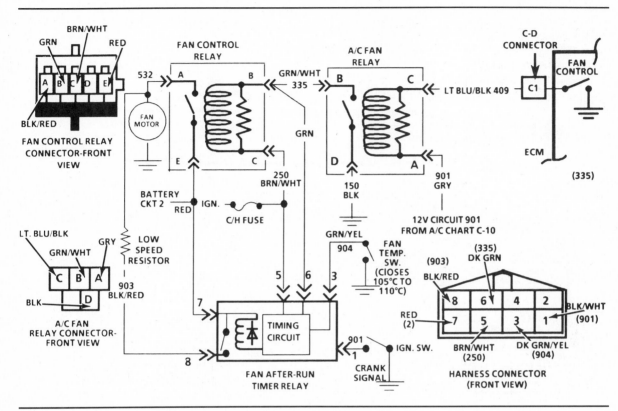

Figure 14-25. GM 1.8-liter PFI engine cooling fan schematic. (Pontiac)

relay terminal B. This energizes the fan control relay, closes its contacts, and supplies battery voltage to the fan motor. At road speeds above 35 mph (56 kph), the ECM opens the ground path on the theory that vehicle speed is high enough to move enough air through the radiator.

When the ignition is turned off with the temperature switch closed, the timer relay will supply battery voltage to the fan motor through terminal 8, running the fan on low speed for about 5 minutes.

To troubleshoot this system, refer to figure 14-26.

3. *Continuously Variable Dual Cooling Fan System:* Figure 14-27 is the circuit diagram of the BCM-controlled, continuously variable dual cooling fan system standard on 1986 Cadillac Eldorado and Seville, and optional on 1986 Buick Riviera and Oldsmobile Toronado models. One fan pushes air through the radiator; the other fan pulls it through.

The cooling fan power is supplied by fusible link A; relay coil power comes from the 5-ampere relay fuse. Ground is provided through ECM terminal D-2 or terminal C of the 3-wire AC pressure switch to operate the low fan speed. The high fan speed is obtained by

grounding through the single-wire temperature switch or terminal C of the 3-wire AC pressure switch.

The ECM turns the standard fan on its low speed when:
● The air conditioning is on.
● Coolant temperature is above 98° C (208° F) with vehicle speed under 45 mph (72 kph).
● The AC pressure switch senses 260 psi (1800 kPa) at the AC high-pressure switch.
The ECM also will cycle the standard fan on and off when the system is in self-diagnostic mode.

The ECM turns the standard fan on its high speed when:
● Coolant temperature reaches 108° C (227° F).
● The AC pressure switch senses 300 psi (2070 kPa) at the AC high-pressure switch.

The pusher fan turns on whenever the standard fan is in its high-speed mode.

One low-speed and two high-speed relays energize the fans. Power from fusible link A is directed to terminal 1 of the relays. When voltage from the 5-ampere fan relay fuse energizes the relay coil between terminals 5 and 2, the relay switch closes and turns the fan on.

Terminal 4 of the low-speed relay furnishes voltage to terminal A of the fan connector for

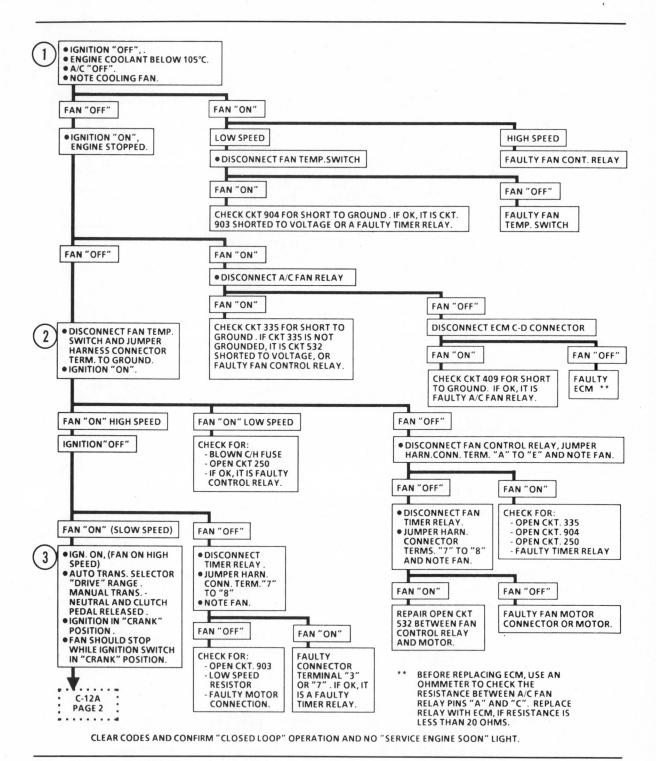

Figure 14-26. Partial GM diagnostic chart for troubleshooting the 1.8-liter PFI engine cooling system.

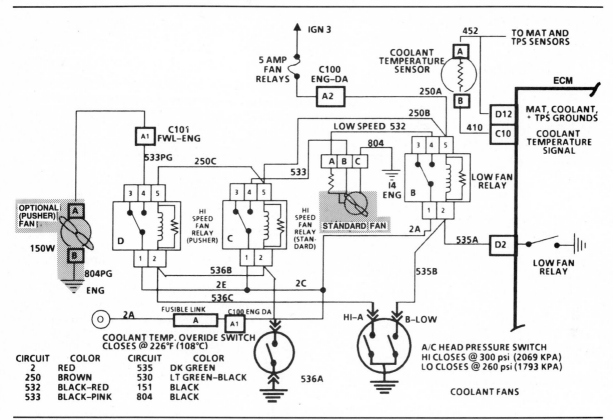

Figure 14-27. GM variable dual fan control circuit diagram. (GM)

CIRCUIT	COLOR	CIRCUIT	COLOR
2	RED	535	DK GREEN
250	BROWN	530	LT GREEN–BLACK
532	BLACK–RED	151	BLACK
533	BLACK–PINK	804	BLACK

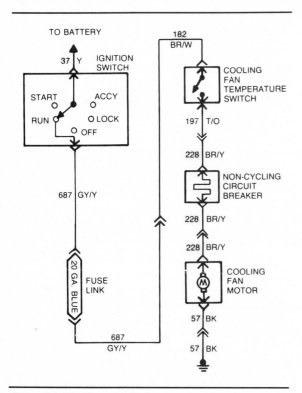

Figure 14-28. The circuit diagram for non-air conditioned Ford Tempo/Topaz vehicles. (Ford)

low-speed operation of the standard fan. Terminal 4 of the high-speed relay furnishes voltage to terminal B of the fan connector for high-speed standard fan operation. Connector terminal C is grounded. The pusher fan is operated by voltage from terminal 4 of the relay to terminal A of the fan connector, with connector terminal B grounded.

The body control module (BCM) switches the control line voltage on and off to provide pulse width modulation to the fan control module. The fan control module in turn switches the fan motor ground to control fan speed. The longer the ground is intact, the longer the fan motors run during the pulse period. A current sensor, or feedback generator, in the fan control module sends a 12-volt signal to the BCM when the fans are off and drops the voltage to zero when the fans are running. This pulsing voltage from the feedback generator tells the BCM that fan operation is correct. Since the system is controlled by the BCM, it will set trouble codes to help you diagnose any malfunction.

Ford front-wheel-drive (FWD) cooling fan circuits

Ford has used the typical fan circuit shown in figure 14-28 on Tempo and Topaz cars without

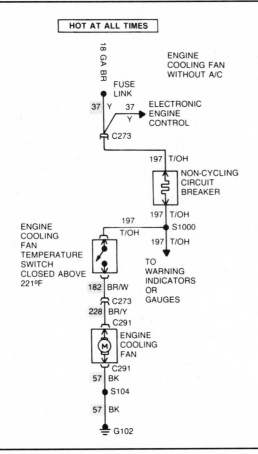

Figure 14-29. The circuit diagram for non-air conditioned Escort/Lynx/EXP/LN7 vehicles from 1983 and later. (Ford)

AC. Early Ford Escort, Lynx, EXP, and LN7 models used the basic fan circuits discussed earlier. Since 1983, models of these vehicles without air conditioning have used the circuit shown in figure 14-29.

To troubleshoot either circuit:

1. Disconnect the fan motor lead. Connect the motor (+) lead to the battery (+) terminal with a jumper wire. Connect the motor (−) lead to a good engine ground:
   a. If the motor runs, go to step 2.
   b. If the motor does not run, replace it.

2. Reconnect the fan motor lead and unplug the temperature switch electrical connector. Check for voltage on circuit 37, figures 14-28 and 14-29:
   a. If battery voltage is shown, go to step 3.
   b. If no voltage is shown, check the fusible link or circuit breaker. If both are good, look for an open or short circuit in circuit 37.

3. Connect a jumper wire across the temperature switch connector pins:
   a. If the motor runs, replace the temperature switch.

b. If the motor does not run, leave the jumper wire in place on the connector pins and go to step 4.

4. Disconnect the fan motor lead. Check for voltage on circuit 228, figures 14-28 and 14-29:
   a. If battery voltage is shown, go to step 5.
   b. If no voltage is shown, look for an open in either circuit 228 or circuit 182.

5. Check for continuity of ground circuit 57:
   a. If there is continuity, replace the fan motor.
   b. If no continuity is shown, look for an open in circuit 57.

6. Remove the jumper wire and reconnect the temperature switch and fan motor. Check cooling fan operation.

Since 1983, the fan circuit on air-conditioned Ford FWD vehicles has been controlled by a solid-state cooling fan controller. Many fan controllers have been used depending on the vehicle powertrain-model-year combination. Proper troubleshooting of the circuit cannot be done without determining the controller used and referring to the specific diagram for that controller. If the cooling fan does not operate properly, Ford recommends that you check the controller first.

To illustrate the typical troubleshooting procedure used on these Ford vehicles, we will look at a 1986 1.9-liter carbureted engine with manual transaxle. Figure 14-30 is the circuit diagram; figure 14-31 shows the three tests to be performed on the controller. If the controller is good, test the rest of the circuit as follows:

1. Check the fuse and fuse link condition, then determine the fan operational condition:
   a. If the fan operates only during AC operation, go to step 2.
   b. If the fan operates only when coolant temperature is high, go to step 6.
   c. If the fan does not operate during AC operation *or* with high engine coolant temperatures, go to step 11.

2. Unplug the temperature switch connector and ground it with a jumper wire (AC off):
   a. If the fan motor runs, go to step 3.
   b. If the fan motor does not run, go to step 4.

3. Check for continuity between the temperature switch body and thermostat housing to make sure the switch is properly grounded. Tighten the switch as required to ensure a good ground:
   a. If the fan motor runs, go to step 4.
   b. If the fan motor does not run, verify that coolant temperature exceeds specifications, then replace the temperature switch.

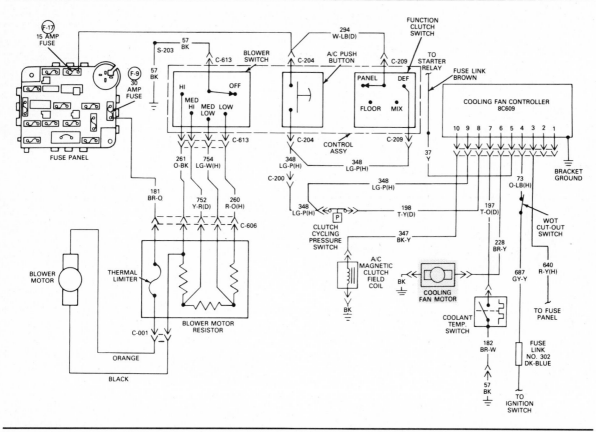

Figure 14-30. Circuit diagram for Ford 1.9-liter engine with manual transaxle and A/C. (Ford)

4. Unplug the fan controller. Check controller connector pin 7 for continuity between controller and temperature switch:
   a. If continuity exists, replace the controller.
   b. If there is no continuity, check the circuit for an open and correct as required.
5. Visually check the wide-open-throttle (WOT) cutout switch to see if it is open or closed:
   a. If the switch is open, either adjust or replace as required.
   b. If the switch is closed, go to step 6.
6. Check controller connector pins 3, 4, 8, and 9 for voltage:
   a. If voltage is shown at each pin, go to step 9.
   b. If voltage is not shown at one or more pins, correct the problem in those circuits and go to step 7.
7. Unplug the compressor clutch cycling switch. Connect a jumper wire across the connector terminals and recheck controller pin 8 for voltage:
   a. If voltage is shown, remove jumper and go to step 8.
   b. If voltage is not shown, remove jumper and go to step 10.

8. Check AC system refrigerant charge pressure:
   a. If pressure is above 50 psi (345 kPa), replace the clutch cycling pressure switch.
   b. If there is less than 50 psi (345 kPa) pressure, leak-test the AC system. Correct any leaks found and recharge the system.
9. Check controller assembly ground (circuit 57):
   a. If the ground is good, replace the fan controller.
   b. If the ground is bad, fix it.
10. Unplug the connector from the controller. Connect a jumper wire between circuits 294 and 348, then check for voltage at pins 8 and 9 of the fan controller:
   a. If both circuits have voltage, replace the AC pushbutton switch.
   b. If there is voltage only at pin 8, service circuit 348.
11. Disconnect the fan motor from the wiring harness and jumper the connector to the battery (+) terminal and ground:
   a. If the fan motor runs, go to step 12.
   b. If the fan motor does not run, replace it.

TEST 1: IGNITION SWITCH OFF

Connector Pin Number	Voltmeter should read
1	0-volts
2	Not used
3	0-volts
4	0-volts
5	Battery voltage
6	0-volts with coolant temperature switch open.
7	0-volts with coolant temperature switch closed.
8	0-volts
9	0-volts
10	0-volts

TEST 2: IGNITION SWITCH IN RUN, ENGINE AND A/C OFF

Connector Pin Number	Voltmeter should read
1	0-volts
2	0-volts
3	0-volts
4	Battery voltage
5	Battery voltage
6	Battery voltage with coolant temperature switch closed.
7	0-volts with coolant temperature switch closed.
8	0-volts
9	0-volts
10	0-volts

TEST 3: IGNITION SWITCH IN RUN, ENGINE RUNNING AND A/C ON

Connector Pin Number	Voltmeter should read
1	0-volts
2	0-volts
3	0-volts
4	Battery voltage
5	Battery voltage
6	Battery voltage with the A/C pressure switch or the coolant temperature switch closed①.
7	Battery voltage with coolant temperature switch open.
8	Battery voltage when A/C clutch cycling pressure switch closed — 0-volts when switch is open.
9	Battery voltage
10	Battery voltage when A/C clutch cycling pressure switch and WOT cut-out switch closed — 0-volts when either switch is open.

NOTE: Indicated voltages in the 50 states and Canada procedures can vary, depending on the type of meter used.

①On fan controllers with prefix E5EZ or later, the fan motor will stay energized when the WOT switch is open.
   The fan motor will stay energized if the A/C cycling pressure switch opens for less than 2-3 minutes.

Figure 14-31. Cooling fan controller troubleshooting charts for use with the Ford 1.9-liter engine with manual transaxle and AC. (Ford)

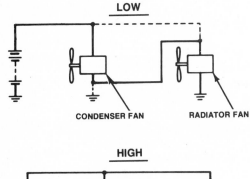

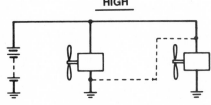

Figure 14-32. Toyota's 3-stage fan system automatically switches from series to parallel connection according to speed. (Toyota)

12. Remove the jumper wires and reconnect the fan motor. Unplug the fan controller, turn the ignition switch to RUN, and check for voltage at circuits 37 and 640:
    a. If voltage is good at both circuits, go to step 13.
    b. If there is no voltage on bracket ground at one or both circuits, locate and correct the problem.
13. Connect fan controller terminals 5 and 6 with a jumper wire:
    a. If fan motor runs, replace the controller.
    b. If fan motor does not run, look for a short or open in the controller-to-fan motor circuit and correct.

Toyota 3-stage electric fan system
Some late-model Toyotas have the dual fan system shown in figure 14-32. Depending upon engine operating conditions, the fans automatically switch back and forth from series connection at low speeds to parallel connection at high speeds. The system is designed to reduce power consumption, vibration, and noise.

Figure 14-33 is a circuit diagram of the dual fan system. Using the principles discussed earlier in dealing with both basic fan circuits, and the GM and Ford fan circuits above, you should be able to trace the circuit operation. To troubleshoot the system, you will need Toyota's specifications and procedures.

Temperature Switch Tests

A simple test will tell you whether a cooling fan temperature switch is good or bad without removing it from the engine. However, the test will not tell you whether the switch is within or outside of manufacturer's specifications. To determine this, you must remove the switch and test it out of the vehicle.

To test a cooling fan temperature switch in the engine:
1. Start and run the engine until it reaches normal operating temperature (upper radiator hose hot), then shut it off.
2. Check continuity between the switch body and the cylinder head, thermostat housing, or radiator to verify switch ground. If it is not grounded, tighten the switch until continuity is shown.
3. Unplug the temperature switch connector and jumper it to a good engine ground.
4. Turn the ignition switch to the RUN position. If the fan runs with the connector grounded but not when the connector is reinstalled, replace the temperature switch.

To test a cooling fan temperature switch out of the engine:
1. Obtain the manufacturer's specifications for the temperature switch.
2. Remove the switch from the cylinder head, thermostat housing, or radiator.
3. Fill a small container with engine coolant and place it on a heating device (a hot plate makes a good, safe heater).
4. Place a thermometer in the container of coolant.
5. Submerge the temperature switch element in the coolant and attach ohmmeter leads, figure 14-34.
6. Watch the ohmmeter scale as you heat the coolant. Compare the ohmmeter readings at specified temperatures with the manufacturer's specifications. If resistance is not within the specified range at the specified temperature, replace the switch.

Some temperature switches are dual-purpose units. One terminal sends a variable return voltage to the engine computer; the other terminal switches on and off at a specified temperature. This switch is tested in the same way, figure 14-35, but separate tests must be made for each function.

Relay Tests

A cooling fan relay or other relay can be tested with a voltmeter or an ohmmeter.

To test a normally open relay with an ohmmeter:
1. Connect an ohmmeter to the relay coil terminals as shown in figure 14-36A. The meter should show no continuity.
2. Connect the ohmmeter leads to the relay contacts as shown in figure 14-36B.

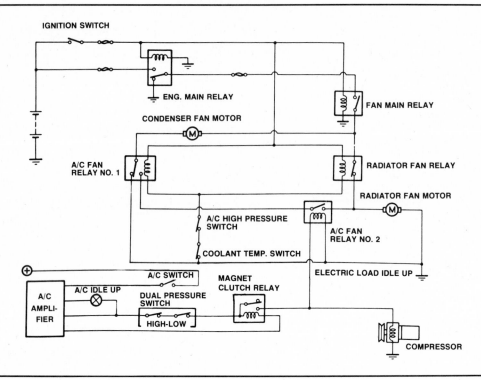

Figure 14-33. Circuit diagram for the Toyota 3-stage fan system. (Toyota)

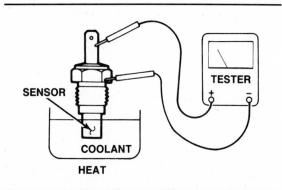

Figure 14-34. Temperature switch test. (Chrysler)

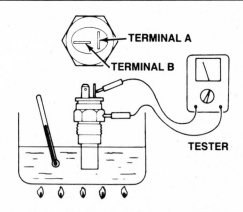

Figure 14-36. Testing a relay with an ohmmeter. (Ford)

3. Connect a 12-volt battery to the relay coil as shown in position B.

4. If the relay is working properly, the contacts should close when battery voltage is applied in step 3 and the ohmmeter should then show continuity.

5. Disconnect the battery from the relay coil. The contacts should open and the ohmmeter should show no continuity.

   To test a normally closed relay with an ohmmeter:

1. Connect an ohmmeter to the relay coil terminals as shown in figure 14-36A. The meter should show continuity.

2. Connect the ohmmeter leads to the relay contacts as shown in 14-36B.

3. Connect a 12-volt battery to the relay coil as shown in position B.

4. If the relay is working properly, the contacts should open when battery voltage is applied in step 3 and the ohmmeter should then show no continuity.

5. Disconnect the battery from the relay coil. The contacts should close and the ohmmeter should show continuity.

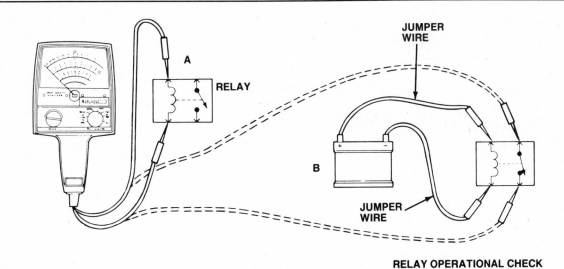

RELAY OPERATIONAL CHECK

Figure 14-36. Testing a relay with an ohmmeter. (Ford)

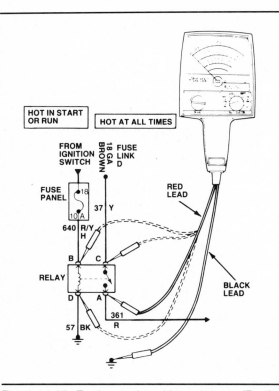

Figure 14-37. Testing a relay with a voltmeter. (Ford)

To test a relay with a voltmeter:
1. Turn the ignition switch on.
2. Connect the voltmeter (−) lead to a good ground. Probe the back of the relay connector where the output wire comes out with the voltmeter (+) lead, figure 14-37A:
   a. If the meter reads approximately 10.5 volts or more, go to step 3.
   b. If the meter reading is less than 10.5 volts, replace the relay.

3. Probe the back of the connector to the control circuit input, figure 14-37B, with the voltmeter (+) lead to check the control circuit supply from the ignition switch:
   a. If the meter reads approximately 10.5 volts or more, go to step 4.
   b. If the meter reading is less than 10.5 volts, check the circuit fuse. If the fuse is good, look for a problem in the wiring or ignition switch.
4. Probe the back of the connector to the power circuit input, figure 14-37C, with the voltmeter (+) lead:
   a. If the meter reads approximately 10.5 volts or more, go to step 5.
   b. If the meter reading is less than 10.5 volts, check the fusible link.
5. Probe the back of the connector to the ground circuit, figure 14-37D, with the voltmeter (+) lead:
   a. If the meter reads less than one volt, the ground circuit is good.
   b. If the meter reading is more than one volt, check and repair the ground circuit.

Fan Motor Test and Replacement

To test the fan motor in the vehicle, disconnect it from the wiring harness. Connect the motor to a 12-volt battery with number 14 jumper wires, observing correct polarity. If the fan motor does not run, it is defective.

Cooling fan motors are attached to a fan shroud, which must be removed to replace the motor. To replace the motor:
1. Unplug the fan motor connector from the

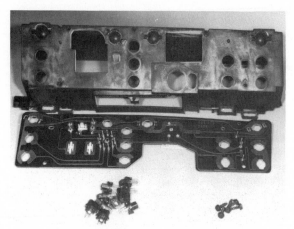

Figure 14-38. A typical printed circuit.

wiring harness. Remove any clips which route the wiring along the shroud.

2. Remove the screws holding the shroud to the radiator support. Remove the shroud and fan motor from the vehicle.

3. Pry the retaining clip off the motor shaft and remove the fan (a few early fans may use retaining nuts instead of a clip).

4. Remove the fasteners holding the fan motor to the fan shroud support. Separate the motor from the support.

5. Install a new motor to the shroud support and tighten the fasteners securely.

6. Fit the fan on the motor shaft and install the retaining clip or nut.

7. Reinstall the shroud and motor assembly to the radiator support and tighten the screws securely.

8. Reconnect the fan motor to the wiring harness and reinstall any routing clips used.

ELECTROMECHANICAL INSTRUMENT SERVICE

The following paragraphs contain trouble-shooting instructions for the most common electromechanical gauges, warning lamps, buzzers, and chimes. Manufacturers now use printed circuitry almost entirely in the instrument panel, figure 14-38. If the printed circuitry opens or shorts, the instrument panel must be removed and the entire printed circuit replaced.

Before testing any instrument that appears to be defective, make sure that the engine condition it monitors is truly normal. For example, if a coolant temperature gauge or warning lamp indicator shows an overheated engine, test the engine cooling system before assuming that the instrument is wrong.

Instrument Voltage Regulator (IVR) Testing and Replacement

An important component in many gauge systems is the instrument voltage regulator (IVR). This unit works like a pulsating circuit breaker to apply an average voltage of about 5 volts to the circuit of each gauge it controls. If it is not working properly, none of the gauges it controls will give accurate readings. The gauges could even be damaged by excessive voltage if the IVR fails. In some systems, the IVR only serves a few of the gauges. The remainder work on unregulated system voltage. Refer to the carmaker's factory shop manual if there is any question about which gauges work on regulated voltage and which do not.

The IVR is often at fault when:
- All regulated-voltage gauges fail at once
- All regulated-voltage gauges give inaccurate readings
- All regulated-voltage gauge needles vibrate by more than the needle's width.

CAUTION: When testing the IVR while it is connected to battery voltage, do not ground or short any of the regulator terminals. This could damage both the IVR and the instrument panel wiring harness.

You should use a voltmeter to test the IVR. A 12-volt test lamp can be used, but it will not show you if the unit is functioning according to the manufacturer's specifications.

If the IVR is difficult to reach for testing, you can make a quick test at one of the gauge sending units in the engine compartment. If the test results show the IVR to be faulty, you must continue to test the unit itself:

- If the regulator can be reached, and if the instrument panel has multistrand wiring, the IVR can be tested at its mounting.
- If the regulator cannot be reached with test leads, or if the instrument panel uses printed circuitry, the IVR must be removed for testing, figure 14-39.

To begin the test in the engine compartment:

1. Check the circuit fuse and replace it if necessary.

2. Disconnect the wire from one of the gauge sending units.

3. Connect the voltmeter (+) lead to the wire and the (−) lead to ground, figure 14-40.

4. Turn on the ignition switch and observe the voltmeter:

    a. If the needle pulsates rapidly from zero to a positive voltage, the regulator is working.

    b. If the needle does not pulsate as described, go to step 5.

Figure 14-39. The IVR must be removed from printed circuit boards for testing.

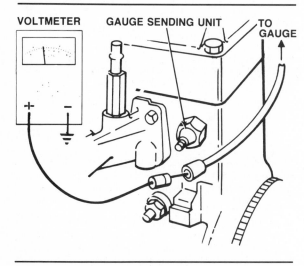

Figure 14-40. Testing the IVR at one of the gauge sending units. (Ford)

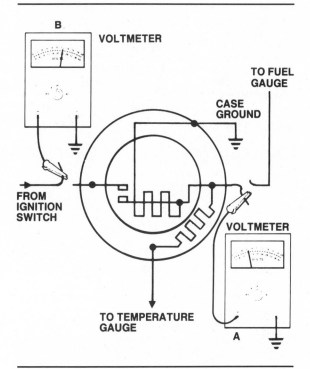

Figure 14-41. Testing the IVR at the instrument panel. (AMC)

5. Turn off the ignition switch, reconnect the sending unit wire, and continue the test:

    a. If the regulator can be tested at its mounting, go to step 7.

    b. If the regulator must be removed for testing, go to step 10.

6. Disconnect the wire from the gauge side of the IVR, figure 14-41. Connect the voltmeter (+) lead to the exposed regulator terminal and the (−) lead to ground.

7. Turn on the ignition switch and observe the voltmeter:

    a. If the needle pulsates as described in step 5a, the IVR is working properly.

    b. If the needle does not pulsate as described, go to step 9.

8. Test for battery voltage at the battery side of the IVR, figure 14-41B:

    a. If voltage is present, replace the regulator.

    b. If voltage is not present, trace and repair the wiring between the battery and the IVR. Repeat steps 7 through 9.

9. Remove the IVR from its mounting. Connect the voltmeter + lead to the terminal on the gauge side of the regulator and connect the (−) lead to ground.

10. Connect a jumper wire between the terminal on the battery side of the regulator and the battery (+) terminal. Observe the voltmeter:

    a. If the needle is pulsating as described in step 5a, the IVR is working properly.

    b. If the needle is not pulsating as described in step 5a, replace the IVR.

Most instrument voltage regulators are separate units held to the back of the instrument panel by screws or nuts, figure 14-42, or plugged into a printed circuit board. You may have to remove some instrument panel trim, part of the panel, or even the entire instrument cluster to reach it. If the IVR is built into a gauge, the entire gauge must be replaced if the regulator is defective.

The pulsing relay of the IVR can be a source of electromagnetic interference that affects electromagnetic gauge operation. Some manufacturers are eliminating the IVR from their clusters by using air core gauges, which require no voltage.

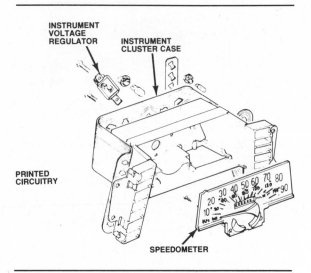

Figure 14-42. A typical IVR mounting. (AMC)

Testing Gauges and Sending Units

Both bimetallic and electromagnetic gauges depend on a variable-resistance sending unit to control the amount of current through the gauge. Ammeters and voltmeters are an exception to this, and will be covered in separate tests later in this chapter.

If a single gauge fails or shows an inaccurate reading, the problem is most likely in that gauge's circuit branch. If all of the gauges fail or show inaccurate readings, the problem is most likely in their shared circuitry.

Air core magnetic gauges like those used in late-model Chrysler FWD vehicles require no IVR control. They can be tested by simply disconnecting and grounding the electrical lead at the sending unit. If the gauge moves to its maximum reading with the ignition switch on, the sending unit is defective. If it does not move to its maximum reading, check the condition of the wiring to the gauge. If the wiring condition is satisfactory, replace the gauge.

Bimetallic and 2-coil or 3-coil electromagnetic gauges can be tested using:
- A voltmeter or 12-volt test lamp
- A field rheostat or a known-good sending unit.

You will need the carmaker's specifications for sending unit resistance if you use a field rheostat. Some manufacturers provide special testers that can be used instead of a known-good sending unit, such as the Ford fuel gauge tester shown in figure 14-43.

Single bimetallic, 2-coil, or 3-coil gauge failure
To test a single faulty gauge:
1. Check the circuit fuse and replace it if necessary.

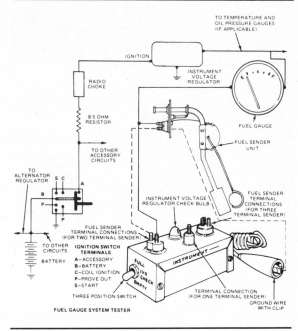

Figure 14-43. Ford's special tester for the fuel gauge system. (Ford)

2. Disconnect the wire from the gauge sending unit.
3. Turn the ignition switch on and use the voltmeter or 12-volt test lamp to check for battery or regulated voltage at the gauge sending unit, figure 14-40:
  a. If the proper voltage is present, go to step 4.
  b. If voltage is present, but it is not properly regulated, test the IVR.
  c. If voltage is not present, go to step 7.
4. Connect the sending unit wire to:
  a. The field rheostat lead; connect the second rheostat lead to ground.
  b. A known-good sending unit; connect a jumper wire between the sending unit and ground. For oil pressure sending units or in cases in which the wire cannot reach the new unit, install the known-good sending unit in the proper mounting.
  c. The manufacturer's special tester.
5. Vary the resistance of the test sender by:
  a. Adjusting the field rheostat to varying resistances as specified by the manufacturer.
  b. Operating the known-good sending unit by moving its float, by heating it, or by running the engine as required.
  c. Following the instructions provided for the manufacturer's special tester.

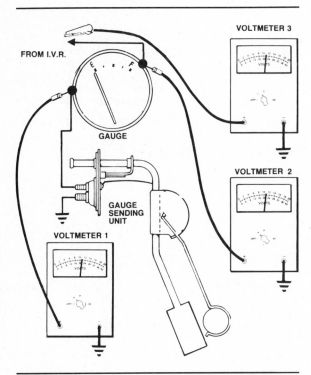

Figure 14-44. Testing an individual gauge's circuit branch. (Ford)

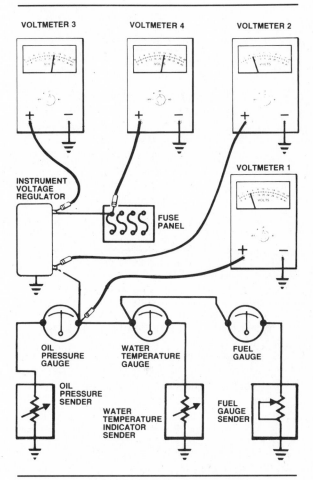

Figure 14-45. Testing the gauge system's shared circuitry.

6. Observe the gauge:
   a. Replace the sending unit if the gauge operates properly.
   b. Replace the gauge if it still does not operate properly.
7. Reconnect the wire to the sending unit and use the voltmeter or the 12-volt test lamp to check for battery or regulated voltage at the sending unit side of the gauge, figure 14-44:
   a. If voltage is not present, go to step 8.
   b. If voltage is present, trace and repair the wiring between the gauge and sending unit.
8. Test for battery or regulated voltage at the battery side of the gauge:
   a. If voltage is present, replace the gauge.
   b. If voltage is not present, go to step 9.
9. Test for battery or regulated voltage at the gauge system common circuit point:
   a. If voltage is present, trace and repair the wiring between the common circuit point and the gauge.
   b. If voltage is not present, trace and repair the gauge system shared circuitry as explained in the following test.

Multiple bimetallic, 2-coil, or 3-coil gauge failure
If all of the gauges in a circuit fail or show inaccurate readings:
1. Check the circuit fuse and replace it if necessary.

2. Turn the ignition switch on and use the voltmeter or the 12-volt test lamp to check for battery or regulated voltage at the gauge system's last common circuit point, figure 14-45, voltmeter 1:
   a. If the proper voltage is present, test the individual gauge circuit branches as explained in the first test.
   b. If voltage is present but it is not properly regulated, test the IVR as described earlier.
   c. If voltage is not present, go to step 3.
3. Test for regulated voltage at the gauge side of the IVR, figure 14-45, voltmeter 2:
   a. If voltage is present, trace and repair the wiring between the IVR and the gauge common circuit point.
   b. If voltage is not present, go to step 4.
4. Test for battery voltage at the battery side of the IVR, figure 14-45, voltmeter 3:
   a. If voltage is present, replace the IVR.
   b. If voltage is not present, go to step 5.

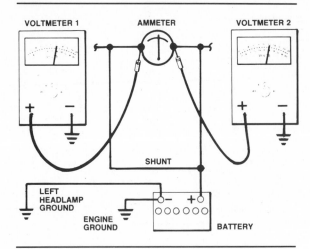

Figure 14-46. Testing the ammeter circuitry. (Chrysler)

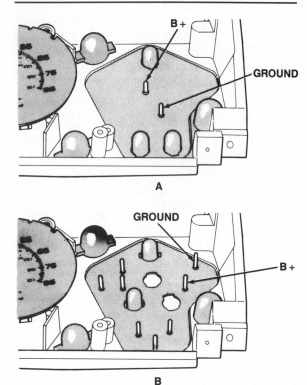

Figure 14-47. Typical voltmeter test points: position A, individual gauge; position B, combination gauge. (Chrysler)

5. Test for battery voltage at the appropriate terminal on the gauge side of the fuse panel, figure 14-45, voltmeter 4:

a. If voltage is present, trace and repair the wiring between the fuse panel and the IVR, if present, or the last common gauge circuit point.

b. If voltage is not present, recheck the fuse. Trace and repair the wiring between the fuse panel and the battery.

Ammeter testing

To test an ammeter's circuit branch:

1. Turn on the ignition switch, but do not start the engine.

2. Turn on the headlamps and other accessories.

3. Observe the ammeter needle:

a. If the needle moves to the discharge side of the scale, the gauge is working correctly.

b. If the needle moves to the charge side of the scale, the ammeter connections are reversed.

c. If the needle does not move, go to step 4.

4. Use a voltmeter or a 12-volt test lamp to check for battery voltage at the alternator side of the ammeter. See voltmeter 1, figure 14-46:

a. If voltage is present, trace and repair the wiring between the ammeter and the alternator.

b. If voltage is not present, go to step 5.

5. Check for battery voltage at the battery side of the ammeter. See voltmeter 2, figure 14-46:

a. If voltage is present, replace the ammeter.

b. If voltage is not present, trace and repair the wiring between the ammeter and the battery.

Voltmeter testing

To test a voltmeter circuit branch:

1. Remove the instrument panel voltmeter from the cluster.

2. Turn on the ignition switch, but do not start the engine.

3. Connect a test voltmeter between the voltmeter battery + and ground pins in the cluster. See figure 14-47A. If the voltmeter is combined with other instruments, you must refer to the carmaker's factory shop manual to determine which terminals control the voltmeter function. See figure 14-47B. The test voltmeter should read battery voltage.

4. If battery voltage is not shown in step 3, start the engine and note the test voltmeter's scale. If the vehicle's charging system is in good condition, the meter reading should increase slightly, as the voltmeter is now showing regulated alternator output.

5. If battery voltage is not present at the pins in step 3 or if the meter reading does not increase as specified in step 4, replace the instrument panel voltmeter.

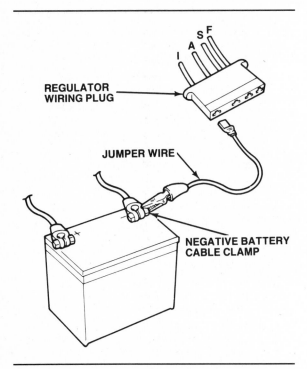

Figure 14-48. Warning lamp test for Ford EVR charging system. (Ford)

Testing Warning Lamps, Buzzers, and Chimes

Warning lamps, buzzers, and chimes are controlled by one or more switches. The exception to this is the charging system warning lamp, which is controlled by current flow into and out of the battery. Tests of the charging system warning lamps are covered separately, manufacturer by manufacturer.

The remaining warning lamps, buzzers, and chimes are either grounded units controlled by insulated switches or insulated units controlled by grounded switches. Seatbelt warning systems often include a timed circuit breaker so that the lamp and buzzer work for a brief period of time and then shut off.

You may want to start each test by substituting a known-good component in the circuit, especially if only that one unit has failed. Buzzers and chimes can be tested by removing them from the vehicle and applying 12-volts. If this does not solve the problem, the circuit can be tested in the same way as the interior lamp circuits you tested in Chapter 13.

Testing alternator warning lamps

Always test the battery and charging system as explained in Chapters 3 and 4 to be sure they are in proper operating condition before troubleshooting the warning lamp circuit.

- Delco-Remy CS charging system:
1. Turn on the ignition switch, but do not start the engine. The warning lamp should be on:
    a. If the lamp is on, go to step 3.
    b. If the lamp is not on, go to step 2.
2. Disconnect the wiring harness at the alternator and ground the L terminal lead:
    a. If the lamp comes on, repair or replace the alternator.
    b. If the lamp does not come on, trace and repair the open circuit between the grounded lead and the ignition switch.
3. Start the engine and run it at idle. The light should go off. If it does not, disconnect the wiring harness at the alternator:
    a. If the lamp goes off, repair or replace the alternator.
    b. If the lamp does not go off, trace and repair the grounded L terminal wire in the harness.
- Delco-Remy SI charging system:
1. If the lamp stays on with the ignition switch off, disconnect the leads from the number 1 and number 2 terminals at the alternator:
    a. If the lamp goes out, the alternator diode bridge is faulty.
    b. If the lamp stays on, there is a short between the leads to the number 1 and number 2 terminals.
2. If the lamp is off when the ignition switch is on and the engine is stopped, repeat the previous test and then check for an open in the warning lamp circuit, such as:
    a. A blown fuse
    b. A burned-out bulb
    c. A defective bulb socket
    d. An open in the number 1 lead between the alternator and the ignition switch.
3. If the lamp stays on when the engine is running:
    a. Check for a blown 20-ampere air conditioning fuse between the warning lamp and ignition switch.
    b. Some GM circuits use a diode in the warning lamp circuit. If the diode is defective, the lamp will remain on when the engine is running, with its brightness increasing as engine speed increases.
- Delco-Remy DN charging system:
1. If the warning lamp will not go out when the engine is running, check for:
    a. A charging system problem
    b. A defective bulb socket
    c. An open in the regulator, the field, or the charging system wiring.

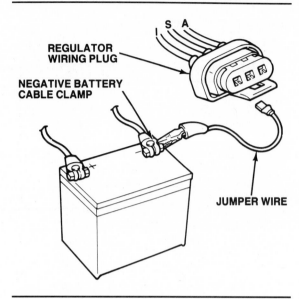

Figure 14-49. Warning lamp test for Ford IAR charging system. (Ford)

- Ford electronic voltage regulator (EVR) system:
1. If the warning lamp does not light, disconnect the wiring plug at the regulator (ignition off). Connect the I terminal of the plug to the battery (−) cable with a jumper wire, figure 14-48.
2. Turn the ignition switch to the Run position. The lamp should light. If it does not, substitute a known-good bulb. If the lamp still does not light, there is an open in either the bulb-to-ignition switch circuit, or in the resistor that is connected in parallel with the lamp.
- Ford internal alternator-regulator (IAR) system:
1. If the warning lamp does not light, disconnect the wiring plug at the regulator (ignition off). Connect the I terminal of the plug to the battery (−) cable with a jumper wire, figure 14-49.
2. Turn the ignition switch to the Run position:
    a. If the lamp lights, go to step 3.
    b. If the lamp does not light, substitute a known-good bulb. If the lamp still does not light, perform a regulator I circuit test as described in Chapter 4.
3. Shut off the ignition. Remove the jumper wire from the connector plug and reattach the plug to the regulator.
4. Connect the voltmeter (−) lead to the battery (−) terminal cable clamp and the (+) lead to

the A terminal screw on the back of the regulator housing:
    a. If battery voltage is indicated, clean and tighten the ground connections at the engine, the alternator, and the regulator. Tighten the regulator mounting screws from 15 to 26 inch-pounds (0.9 to 1.6 Nm), if loose.
    b. If battery voltage is not indicated, trace and repair the A circuit wiring.
5. Turn the ignition on but do not start the engine. If the lamp still does not light, replace the regulator.
- Chrysler ammeter warning LED:
1. If the battery is in good condition and the charging system is working properly but the LED remains on, replace the gauge.
2. If the LED does not light, turn the ignition switch on, but do not start the engine. Turn on the headlamps and other accessories, then watch the LED:
    a. If it does not light within one minute, replace the gauge.
    b. If it lights, go to step 3.
3. Start and run the engine at a fast idle. If the LED does not go off, replace the gauge.
- Motorola charging system:
1. Check all system fuses.
2. If the bulb lights when the engine is running, check for:
    a. An open in the instrument panel printed circuitry.
    b. A short in the wiring between the bulb and the regulator.
3. If the bulb flashes while the engine is running, check for battery voltage at the yellow feed wire to the printed circuitry.
4. If the bulb does not light when the ignition switch is on and the engine is stopped, check for:
    a. A defective bulb
    b. An open in the printed circuitry
    c. An open between the regulator and the printed circuitry.

Instrument Replacement

On some vehicles, you will have to disassemble all or part of the instrument panel to replace a gauge, lamp, or buzzer. Figures 14-50 and 14-51 show typical instrument panel assemblies. On other vehicles, all that is necessary is to remove the instrument cluster. Once the cluster is out of the instrument panel, remove the screws holding the defective instrument and remove it from the cluster, figure 14-52.

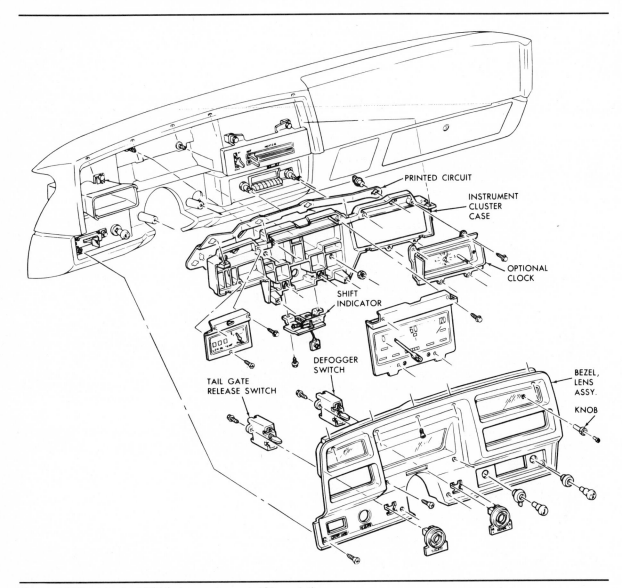

PRINTED CIRCUIT

INSTRUMENT
CLUSTER
CASE

OPTIONAL
CLOCK

SHIFT
INDICATOR

DEFOGGER
SWITCH

TAIL GATE
RELEASE SWITCH

BEZEL,
LENS
ASSY.

KNOB

Figure 14-50. A typical GM instrument panel. (Chevrolet)

ELECTRONIC INSTRUMENT SERVICE

Regardless of its level of sophistication, an electronic instrument panel combines conventional sending units, such as a coolant temperature switch or the variable resistor of a fuel tank float, with the solid-state equivalent of the electromagnetic display devices (analog gauges). A microprocessor installed between the sending units and the display devices "reads" the sending units' signals and uses them to compute actuator signals to be transmitted to the display devices. As we saw in Chapter 19 of the *Classroom Manual*, the display device may be a light-emitting diode (LED), a liquid crystal display (LCD), a vacuum fluorescent display (VFD) or cathode ray tube (CRT). The actuator signals from the microprocessor are voltage pulses that activate the displays according to their design.

As with electromagnetic instruments, you should make sure that the engine condition monitored by any electronic instrument that appears to be defective is truly normal. Test the engine condition before assuming that the instrument is wrong.

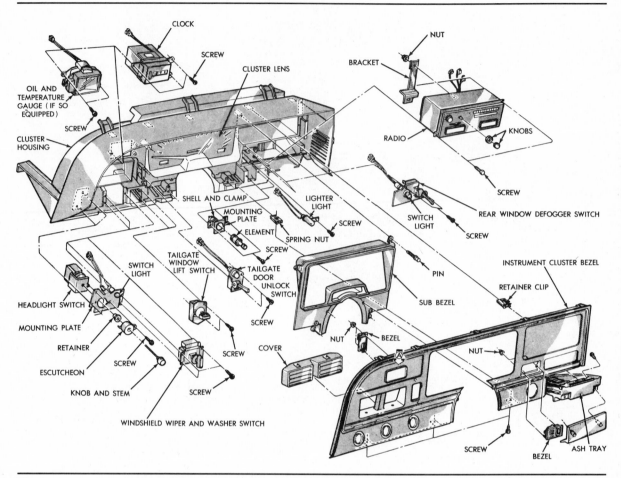

Figure 14-51. A typical Chrysler instrument panel. (Chrysler)

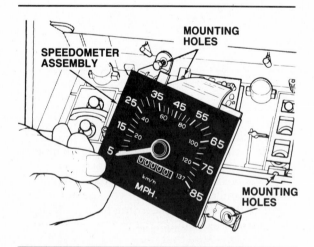

Figure 14-52. Some gauges can be removed from the cluster by removing their mounting screws. (Chrysler)

General System Tests

The electronic system of which the cluster is a part contains a self-diagnostic program or test sequence to isolate problems within the cluster. In most cases, if the system microprocessor successfully completes its self-diagnostic test, the problem will be found in the wiring, the connectors, or the sensors outside the cluster. Once you have determined that the cluster is good, you can check the wiring, connectors, or sensors just as you would for any other electrical system.

Each instrument cluster display is either unique to certain models in a carmaker's line, or may be combined with various other electronic functions for use in higher-line models. Furthermore, the field of automotive instrumentation has been moving so rapidly that display functions and operational sequences:
● Change from one model year to another
● Occur as running changes during a model year, with different systems used in a given vehicle

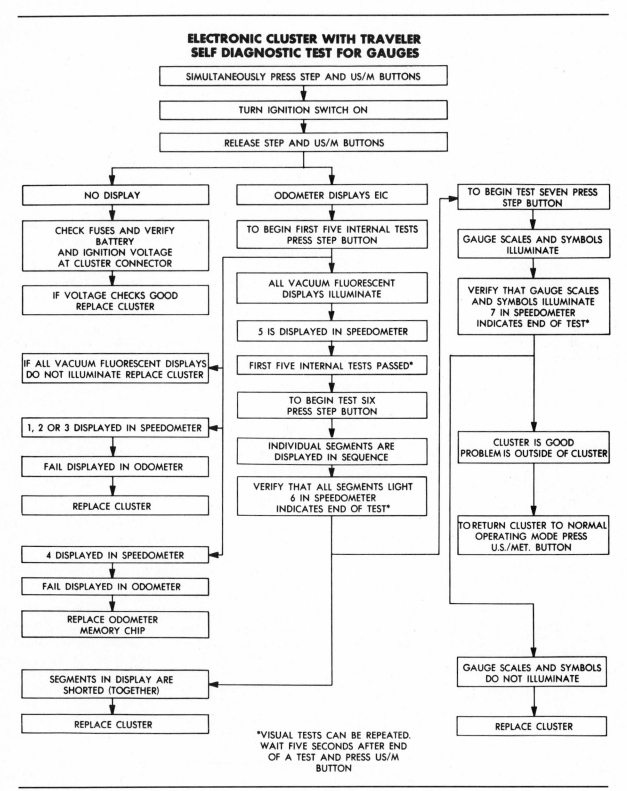

Figure 14-53. Self-diagnostic test sequence for Chrysler electronic cluster equipped with Traveler function. (Chrysler)

● May be manufactured by more than one vendor and thus use different circuitry with the same cluster display (Chrysler uses displays built by its own Huntsville electronics division and by Motorola).

For these reasons, you will need the carmaker's diagnostic charts to troubleshoot an electronic instrument cluster problem. To demonstrate this, we will use the 1986 Chrysler displays as representative.

For 1986, Chrysler offered an electronic instrument cluster by itself. The cluster could also be combined with one of the following:
● An elapsed timer
● A trip computer called, "Traveler"
● A more complex trip computer called, "Electronic Navigator".

In addition to these combinations, the vehicle also could be equipped with:
● "Electronic Voice Alert" (11 different audible warnings and messages)
● "Electronic monitor" (up to 24 different audible and visual warnings, depending on vehicle equipment).

Each of these systems uses different circuitry and different diagnostic procedures.

Figure 14-53 provides the self-diagnostic sequence required to check the gauge displays on the 1986 Chrysler electronic cluster equipped with the Traveler function. By following this sequence as the self-diagnostic program runs, you can determine whether the cause of the problem is in the system circuitry or outside the cluster.

Testing Electronic Displays

If the cluster passes the self-test, you should look outside the system for the cause of the problem. In the case of the Chrysler cluster with Traveler function:

1. If the fuel, oil, and temperature gauges show a maximum reading and remain there after the engine is started, look for a poor connection or a disconnected module connector at the rear of the electronic module.

2. If a fuel, oil, or temperature gauge does not work, check for a defective sensor by grounding the sensor leads at the sending unit with the ignition on (engine off). If the gauge reads maximum with the lead grounded, replace the sensor.

3. If the speedometer and odometer do not operate, or operate erratically, check the distance sensor circuit. If the circuit is good:
   a. Remove the sensor from the vehicle and connect it to an ohmmeter set on its lowest scale (do not use a 12-volt test lamp, because it can damage the sensor).
   b. Slowly rotate the sensor shaft one full turn, noting the needle deflections. There should be eight pulses, each with a value of ½ ohm or less. If the reading is higher, or if there are not eight pulses in one shaft rotation, replace the sensor.

4. If the cluster display does not dim when the headlamp switch is turned on or when the rheostat is rotated:
   a. Check the headlamp circuit fuses.
   b. Check the headlamp switch-to-cluster for loose connections or faulty wiring.
   c. Test the headlamp switch.

5. If the tachometer does not work, check the wiring connections between the cluster and the tach sensor. If the engine has electronic fuel injection, also check the connections between the cluster and the EFI power module.

Replacing Displays

In almost all cases, an electronic instrument cluster is serviced as an assembly by replacing it, using the same procedures as with a conventional cluster. If one instrument is defective, the entire cluster must be replaced. Trip computers and other electronic display devices are also serviced by replacement.

If an electronic cluster uses an odometer memory chip, the chip must be removed from the defective cluster and installed in the new one, much like switching a PROM from a defective ECM to the new controller.

State laws vary regarding the installation of new odometer memory chips to replace a defective one. Some require that the original mileage be posted on a door jamb label. Others require the chip to be programmed to display the mileage of the previous chip. In areas where the law requires the display of original mileage in the odometer, you should contact the carmaker.

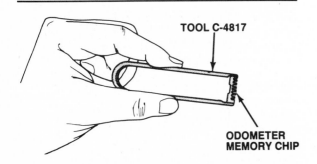

Figure 14-54. Chrysler's electronic odometer is removed with a special tool. (Chrysler)

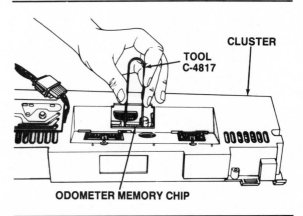

Figure 14-55. Replacing the electronic odometer in a cluster. (Chrysler)

Odometer memory chip replacement differs, but the Chrysler procedure is typical. A special Chrysler tool is provided to grasp and remove the chip, figure 14-54, with a rocking motion from end to end while pulling upward gently.
1. Remove the instrument cluster and place it front side down on a clean shop cloth with the bottom of the cluster facing you.
2. Gently press the latch ears on the odometer chip access door toward the center of the door and swing the door open.
3. Note that the distinctive notch on the IC chip installed under the door faces to the left (with the bottom of the cluster facing you). The chip must be reinstalled in the same position.
4. Grasp the chip with the special tool, figure 14-55, and remove it from the cluster. If the chip is not to be reinstalled in the new cluster

immediately, write the vehicle VIN number and mileage on an envelope and place the chip inside for protection.
5. Before installing the chip in the new cluster, check the chip pins to make sure they are perpendicular to the chip body and straight. If not, gently align them before reinstalling the chip.
6. Fit the chip in the jaws of the special tool and position it over the cluster socket. Make sure all of the 14 pins start in their sockets at the same time and press the chip into place with the special tool.
7. Make sure that the notch on the chip faces to the left (with the bottom of the cluster facing you). Close the access door and reinstall the cluster.

15

Electrical Accessory Service

These common accessory circuits seldom require service. When they do, however, the following troubleshooting instructions can help you solve the problem. In many cases, you will need the manufacturer's specifications and circuit diagrams for the system you are testing.

AIR CONDITIONING AND HEATER ELECTRICAL TESTING

The primary job of all air conditioning (AC) and heater systems is to control the temperature inside the passenger compartment. How they do this determines the amount of electrical circuitry you may have to troubleshoot and the methods to be used.

When troubleshooting any temperature control system, the first step is to make sure that the problem is really in the system. Before you test the AC and heater electrical system, you should check:

- Coolant level
- Refrigerant charge
- Drive belt tension
- Vacuum line routing and connections
- Radiator airflow
- Electric cooling fan operation (if used)
- In-car sensor air intake suction (if used).

Basic Control Circuits

The blower motor circuit is common to all heater and air conditioning systems, figure 15-1. The compressor clutch control system is common to all air conditioning systems, figure 15-1. If the AC system has a semi- or full-automatic temperature control, various other switches or relays may be included in control circuits.

State-of-the-art temperature control systems are computer controlled, either by a single microprocessor or by a central computer which uses inputs from other computer-controlled systems to determine its mode of operation. These temperature control systems have self-diagnostic capability and provide the technician with trouble or fault codes to aid troubleshooting.

All heater and AC systems control the engine electric cooling fan circuit on vehicles so equipped. Troubleshooting of this circuit is covered in Chapter 14. Remember that if you are dealing with a circuit containing solid-state components, or where computer control is involved, use a digital volt-ohmmeter (DVOM) to prevent damage to the circuit or components.

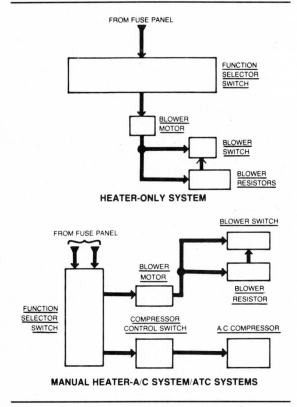

Figure 15-1. Typical climate control electrical circuits. (Ford)

Blower motor circuit

The blower motor circuit includes the heater-AC function control assembly on the instrument panel, the blower switch, the resistor block, and the blower motor. Setting the function control to the Heat or Defrost mode allows current to flow to the blower motor when the ignition switch is on.

Some blower control circuits use ground-side switching to control blower speeds, figure 15-2A. Other circuits use positive-side switching, figure 15-2B. While basic operation of the blower motor is identical, the power for a ground-side switching circuit comes from the fuse panel, through the function selector switch, to the blower motor, figure 15-2A. The blower motor switch is the ground side of the circuit. The opposite occurs in positive-side switching, as power reaches the switch first, figure 15-2B.

All blower control circuits use a resistor block. The resistor block has one less resistor than the number of blower switch positions. That is, a 4-speed blower uses three resistors; a 3-speed blower has only two resistors. The resistors are used to reduce blower speed by dropping the voltage to the motor. When the blower switch is set to its lowest speed, all of

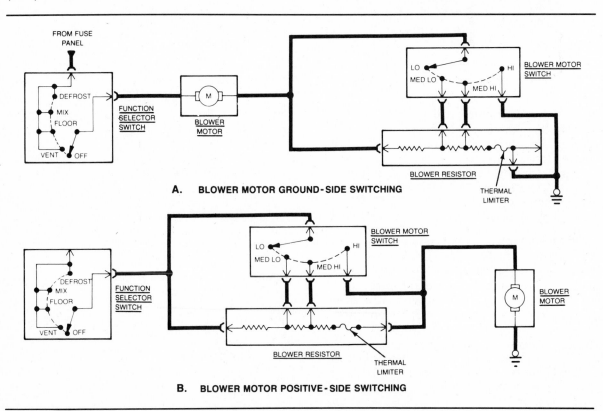

Figure 15-2. Blower motor circuits may use ground side or positive side switching. (Ford)

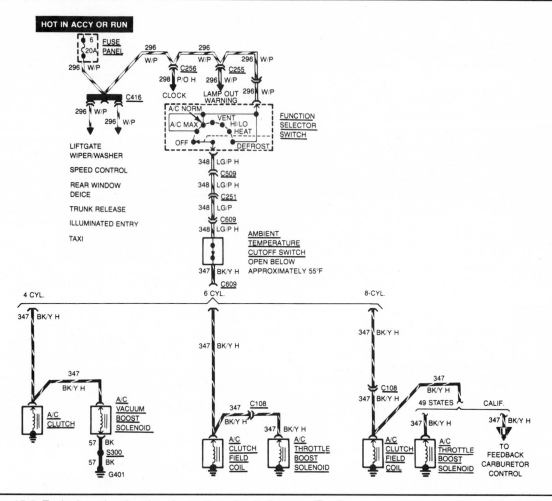

Figure 15-3. Typical suction throttle valve system circuit diagram. (Ford)

the resistors are in the circuit. When the switch is set to its highest speed, voltage is routed around the resistor block and applied directly to the blower motor.

Some systems use a thermal limiter on the resistor block as a protective device. The thermal limiter opens when the circuit current exceeds a safe level.

Compressor clutch control circuit

The amount of cooling that occurs in any air conditioning system depends upon the flow of refrigerant through the evaporator core. All AC compressors have electromagnetic clutches in their drive pulleys. When the clutch engages it locks the compressor shaft to the pulley and pumps refrigerant through the system. Compressor-control circuits vary on different systems but all operate on similar principles. The examples in the following paragraphs will help you understand typical systems and how to trace circuit operation using the trouble-

shooting methods you have learned throughout this *Shop Manual*.

In the circuit shown in figure 15-3, setting the function control to the AC or Defrost mode allows current to flow to the ambient temperature cutoff switch when the ignition switch is on. If the temperature is above the switch's calibrated value, the current continues to the compressor clutch coil. A throttle boost solenoid (or vacuum boost solenoid) is used to maintain engine speed and compensate for the increased load of the compressor. If the temperature falls below a specified value, the ambient temperature switch opens, cutting off current to the compressor clutch coil. A pressure relief valve is used to protect the system from excessive refrigerant pressures.

Figure 15-4 is a compressor clutch circuit using other temperature and pressure-cycling devices. Setting the function control to the AC or Defrost mode allows current to flow to the low-pressure switch when the ignition switch is on.

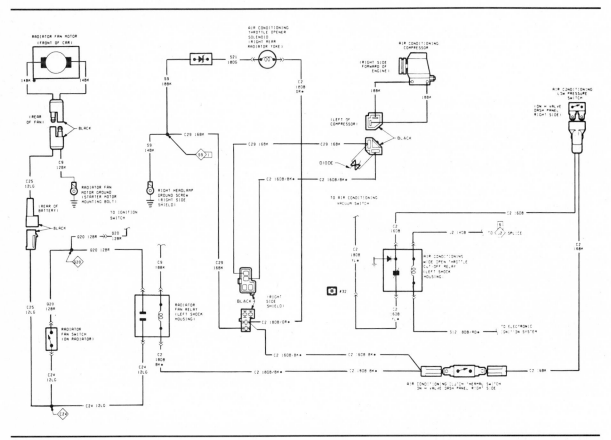

Figure 15-4. Typical temperature cycling expansion valve system circuit diagram. (Chrysler)

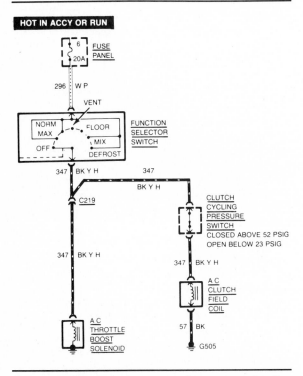

Figure 15-5. Typical pressure cycling system circuit diagram. (Ford)

If the system pressure is above the switch's calibrated value, the current continues to the clutch thermal switch. The thermal switch cycles the compressor clutch according to the evaporator coil temperature. Depending upon the temperature, the switch contacts are closed (allowing current to flow) or open (preventing current flow). When the switch is closed, current may flow directly to the compressor clutch coil in some systems. In others, it continues to the wide-open throttle (WOT) switch or relay. The WOT switch or relay opens the AC clutch circuit whenever it senses a wide-open throttle. If the throttle is not wide open, current will flow to the compressor clutch coil. From the coil, it goes to ground, completing the circuit and making the compressor run.

Figure 15-5 is a typical compressor clutch circuit using a low-pressure-cycling switch. When the ignition is on, setting the function control to the AC or Defrost mode allows current to flow to the pressure cycling switch in the low-pressure side of the system. If refrigerant pressure is above the switch's calibrated value, the current continues to the compressor clutch coil. If refrigerant pressure drops below the pressure cycling switch's value, it opens and shuts off current to the clutch coil, breaking the circuit to the compressor clutch. A high-pressure cut-off switch located in the high-pressure side of the system opens if refrigerant pressure exceeds the switch's specified value.

Late-model systems of this design also may depend on the engine control computer for operational signals. For example, a compressor-control relay may be grounded through the computer. When the computer wishes to reduce engine load, it breaks the ground to the relay and turns off the compressor clutch. The computer also may receive a signal from the AC control assembly, indicating that the system has been turned on. The computer then delays its ground signal to the relay coil long enough for the engine's idle speed to increase enough to handle the compressor load.

In systems without computer control, a throttle boost solenoid is activated to maintain engine idle speed when the compressor is on.

Blower Motors, Switches, and Compressor Clutches

Although the components used in heater and air conditioning circuits vary according to system design, the basic principles of locating and testing to determine the cause of the problem remain the same. You will need a circuit diagram of the system you are troubleshooting. This will show you how the components fit into the circuit and provide you with the correct sequence of testing. The following procedures will help you isolate the problem and locate the defective component.

Blower motor

If the blower motor will not run at any speed:
1. Check the condition of the circuit fuse:
    a. If the fuse is blown, replace it and go to step 2 if the motor still does not run.
    b. If the fuse looks good, check for battery voltage at both ends of the fuse with a 12-volt test lamp. Replace the fuse if voltage is shown only at the battery side.
2. Check for a stalled motor by rotating it by hand:
    a. If the motor is stalled, replace the motor and fuse.
    b. If the motor is good, go to step 3.
3. Unplug the blower-to-wiring harness connector and connect a jumper wire between the blower connector plug (−) terminal and a good body or engine ground. Reconnect the connector plug to the wiring harness and turn on the ignition:
    a. If the motor runs, trace and repair the open in the ground circuit.
    b. If the motor does not run, go to step 4.

4. Repeat step 3 to jumper the blower connector plug (+) terminal to the battery (+) post:
    a. If the motor runs, go to step 5.
    b. If the motor does not run, replace it.
5. Disconnect the resistor terminal connectors. With the ignition on, check the terminal connectors for battery voltage in every fan switch position with a voltmeter:
    a. If there is voltage at all switch positions, replace the resistor block.
    b. If there is no voltage at one or more switch positions, go to step 6.
6. Unplug the blower switch connector. Refer to the manufacturer's continuity diagram and check the blower switch for continuity in each switch position with an ohmmeter:
    a. If switch continuity is not as specified, replace the switch.
    b. If switch continuity is correct, go to step 7.
7. With the ignition on, check the blower switch connector battery terminal for voltage.
    a. Replace the switch if voltage is shown.
    b. If the switch is burned or charred, test the blower motor current draw and compare to manufacturer's specifications.

If the blower motor operates at some but not all speeds:
1. Visually check the resistor block for signs of overheating or other damage.
2. Unplug the wiring connections at the resistor block. Test the resistor block for an open circuit with a self-powered test lamp:
    a. If any resistor is open, replace the resistor block.
    b. If the resistor block is satisfactory, go to step 3.
3. Unplug the blower switch connector. Refer to the manufacturer's continuity diagram and check the blower switch for continuity in every switch position with an ohmmeter:
    a. If switch continuity is not as specified, replace the switch.
    b. If switch continuity is correct, trace and repair the wiring between the resistor block and the blower switch.

Switches

As we have seen, switches perform two functions: they control current by turning it on and off, and they direct the flow of current within a circuit. Heating and air conditioning systems use many electrical, pressure, or temperature-actuated switches for system control.

The basic test for any switch is to check its continuity with an ohmmeter or self-powered test lamp. The ohmmeter is the best choice, because it indicates the internal resistance of the switch and shows the actual resistance between terminals that should have continuity. When

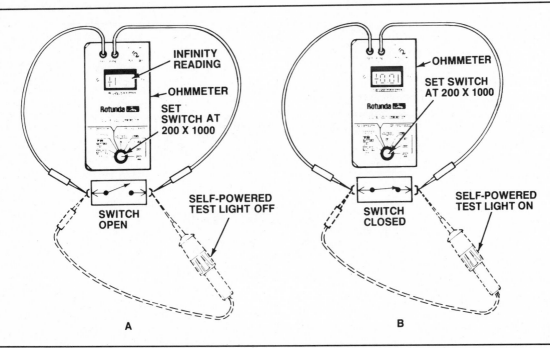

Figure 15-6. Testing switch operation with an ohmmeter or self-powered test lamp. (Ford)

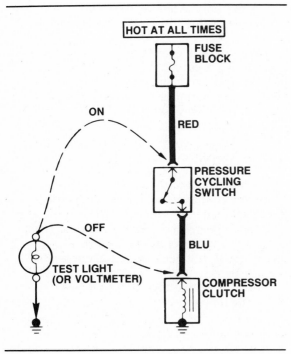

Figure 15-7. Voltage test of pressure cycling switch. (Chevrolet)

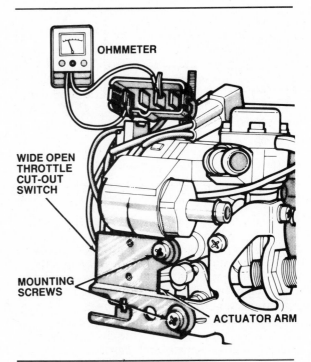

Figure 15-8. Testing the wide-open throttle (WOT) switch operation on the carburetor. (Chrysler)

resistance is not zero but close to it, the internal resistance may be too high and the switch should be replaced. Since a self-powered test lamp cannot make this fine a distinction, it may lead you to believe the switch is satisfactory when it actually should be replaced.

Simple switches, such as clutch-cycling switches or damped pressure-cycling switches, can be tested quite easily. Connect an ohmmeter as shown in figure 15-6. The meter should show an infinite reading when the

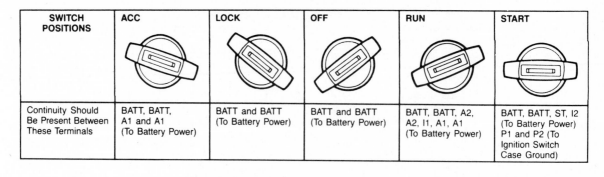

SWITCH POSITIONS	ACC	LOCK	OFF	RUN	START
Continuity Should Be Present Between These Terminals	BATT, BATT, A1 and A1 (To Battery Power)	BATT and BATT (To Battery Power)	BATT and BATT (To Battery Power)	BATT, BATT, A2, A2, I1, A1, A1 (To Battery Power)	BATT, BATT, ST, I2 (To Battery Power) P1 and P2 (To Ignition Switch Case Ground)

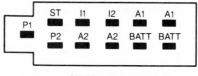

SWITCH TERMINALS

Figure 15-9. A continuity chart is required to test complex switch operation. (Ford)

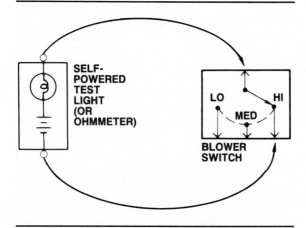

Figure 15-10. Continuity test of blower switch. (Chevrolet)

switch is open, figure 15-6A, and zero or nearly zero when the switch is closed, figure 15-6B.

Test the continuity of these switches without removing them from the vehicle (engine off) by disconnecting the electrical connector from the switch. Connect the ohmmeter across the switch terminals and compare the reading to specifications. If the switch passes the continuity test, check switch operation as follows:
1. Reconnect the switch connector to its terminals.
2. Start the engine and run it for approximately 5 minutes with the air conditioning turned on to stabilize the system:
   a. If the compressor clutch cycles on and off two or three times a minute during this time, switch operation is normal.

b. If the clutch does not engage, trace and repair the open in the circuit.
c. Once engine temperature climbs above a specified value, the clutch should remain engaged.

If the switch is good, you can do a voltage check to make sure that current is reaching or passing through the switch, figure 15-7. The voltmeter should read within one volt of battery voltage. A lower reading indicates a problem.

The continuity of a wide-open-throttle (WOT) switch can also be tested with the engine off. Disconnect the electrical connector from the switch and connect the ohmmeter across the switch terminals, figure 15-8. There should be continuity with a closed throttle. Watch the meter as you rotate the throttle to the wide-open position. Continuity should break about 10 degrees before the throttle is completely open. If it does not, adjust or replace the switch as required.

Blower motor and ignition switches have more than one switch position and multiple terminals. Such switches require the use of a continuity diagram, figure 15-9. Continuity diagrams may be provided by the carmaker, or you may have to construct one from the switch's electrical schematic.

Once you have a continuity diagram, disconnect the switch connector and test the terminals involved in each switch position, figure 15-10. When several terminals are involved in one switch position, hold an ohmmeter lead on one terminal. Use the other lead to probe each of the remaining terminals used in that position, one at a time, noting the ohmmeter reading at

Start car, allow engine to warm up. Turn off instrument panel lights. Select panel mode operation by momentarily pushing the panel button.

Does the ATC Control light up?

NO

Are the fuses and wiring OK? Refer to Electrical.

YES

YES

Replace the ATC Control.

NO

Repair the wiring or replace fuse.

Momentarily push the DEF., FLOOR and BI-LEV buttons together to start the self diagnostics test.

The control will flash an:

This means the computer is busy testing.

1) The blower will stop and the control will flash an error code number from 1 to 15. Record this number and push the PANEL button to resume test.

3) Check the following items when the display is flashing.

QUESTIONS

A) Do **all** the symbols flash as above?
B) Is the blower motor running at its highest speed?
C) Does the air blow out of the panel outlets?
D) Does discharge air become hot then cold?

The Control will do one of two things

2) Display

This display means the test is over. If no error codes occurred and the answers to questions A, B, C and D were yes, then the system is OK. Refer to the Fault Code Page if the display indicated any error code or if the answer to any of the questions was no.

A NO ANSWER

See the chart on the following page.

Figure 15-11. Chryser ATC diagnostic flow chart. (Chrysler)

each terminal. The reading should be zero or nearly zero for each test point requiring continuity in the switch position tested. Before moving to the next switch position, you should also check all the other terminals to make sure they read infinite resistance (no continuity). Repeat this procedure for all remaining switch positions. If the switch fails any part of the test, replace it.

Compressor clutch

You can tell if the clutch is engaging by moving the mode selector between the OFF and MAX AC position with the engine running. You should hear a click and momentary change in engine speed every time the selector lever is moved. This indicates that the clutch is engaging or disengaging.

If the clutch is not engaging and refrigerant pressure is satisfactory (low-pressure switch closed):
1. Shut off the engine, but leave the ignition switch on with the AC control engaged.
2. Connect a voltmeter between the battery side terminal of the compressor clutch and ground:
   a. If battery voltage is shown, momentarily ground the battery side terminal of the clutch with a fused jumper wire. If the clutch does not engage, check for an open in the wiring from the clutch to ground. If the wiring is good, replace the clutch.
   b. If battery voltage is not shown, there is an open in the circuit between the control assembly and compressor clutch.

ATC System Testing Overview

You should realize that the electrical components and circuitry of semi- and full-automatic (or "Climate Control" systems, as they are called) vary significantly from one model to another, as well as from model year to model year. You *cannot* satisfactorily troubleshoot these systems without the carmaker's circuit diagrams, component schematics, and diagnostic procedures. However, much of what you learned in Chapter 12 regarding engine control systems also applies to troubleshooting ATC systems, as we will see.

Semiautomatic temperature control systems usually can be diagnosed by running an electrical wiring harness continuity test using an ohmmeter or test light and then testing suspect components as described earlier. Remember that high-resistance components of the system, such as the in-car and ambient temperature sensors, can only be checked satisfactorily with

an ohmmeter. As mentioned earlier, a digital volt-ohmmeter (DVOM) should be used with solid-state components or in circuits where computer control is involved.

Fully automatic temperature control systems have some form of self-diagnostic program that will display trouble or fault codes. Depending upon the ATC system design, fault codes may be displayed digitally on the control assembly or as pulsations of an analog voltmeter.

The Chrysler electronic ATC system is an example of fully automatic temperature control systems. Figure 15-11 shows the self-diagnostic procedure. Note that the questions in box 3 deal with problems the computer cannot find by itself, and thus require the participation of the service technician while the self-diagnostic test is running. Figure 15-12 directs you to the probable cause and action to be taken when a *No* answer is given to any of the questions.

After recording the system fault codes, figure 15-13, you must go to a specific diagnostic chart for each code. These charts are used in the same way as the engine control system diagnostic charts you learned to use in Chapter 12. For example, in the Chrysler ATC system, fault codes 01, 02, 03, and 04 involve the blend-air door, feed wiring, and control computer, figure 15-14. The diagnostic charts direct you to the proper wire connector, terminal pins, and sequence in which they should be checked.

By running through its self-diagnostic procedure, the ATC microprocessor performs an area test for you. Any fault codes obtained direct you to make one or more pinpoint tests. Once the necessary adjustments or repairs have been made, you should rerun the self-diagnostic program. This is your system operational check to make sure that you have corrected the problem, and that the system is again functioning properly.

RADIO AND SOUND SYSTEMS

Troubleshooting the internal circuitry of radios and sound systems is beyond the scope of this text. However, a service person should be able to troubleshoot the external circuitry.

The most common complaint with radios and sound systems is noise which interferes with reception. Electronically tuned radios are especially sensitive to this problem. Since different late-model radio systems are susceptible to different types of interference, it is important to use the manufacturer's diagnostic charts when troubleshooting these systems. It is also important that you determine the type of noise.

"NO" ANSWERS	PROBABLE CAUSE	PROCEDURE
A	1) Control	a) Replace the Control Module
B	1) Wiring problem 2) Power/Vacuum Module	a) CAUTION: STAY CLEAR OF THE BLOWER MOTOR WHEEL. POWER/VACUUM HEAT SINK IS HOT (12 VOLTS), DO NOT RUN THE POWER/VACUUM MODULE EXCESSIVELY (10 MINUTES) WITH THE UNIT REMOVED FROM THE A/C HEATER HOUSING. b) Check to see if connections are made at the blower motor and at Power/Vacuum Module. c) Did the diagnostic test give an error code of 8 or 12? If yes, refer to Fault Code Page. If no error code then check 30 AMP fuse for blower motor (fuse #4). d) Disconnect blower motor, check voltage at connector (green is +, black is --). Reading should be 3 to 12 volts for 1 to 8 bar segment on the display. If correct then problem is the motor. e) If blower voltage is not correct, then measure volts at green wire to vehicle ground (not blower ground) should be 12 volts (key on). If the voltage is OK, then replace the P/V Module.
C	1) Vacuum Leakage 2) Power/Vacuum Leakage	a) Service, if any codes are found. b) Check all connectors. c) Disconnect 7 port vacuum connector and connect it to a "manual control" and test each mode. Test Check Valve selecting the Panel Mode and disconnecting engine vacuum to see if mode changes quickly. d) Try a new Power/Vacuum Mod.
D	1) Refrigeration System 2) Heater System 3) Blend-Air Door	a) Complete diagnostics test, refer to Fault Code Page if error occurs. b) If a temperature difference of at least 40 Fahrenheit degrees is felt during the diagnostic test, then the Blend-Air door is engaged in the Servo Motor Actuator. If temp difference is less than 40 degrees, then a possible problem is the Blend-Air Door operation. c) Check heater system. 85 temp setting is full heat and 65 is full cool. d) Check refrigeration system. NOTE: Panel, A/C and holding down the bottom of the TEMP button for 4 seconds once 65 is obtained will cause Max A/C.

Figure 15-12. Chrysler ATC diagnostic chart. (Chrysler)

FAULT CODE	RECOMMENDED ACTION
01 02 03 04	a. Substitute a Blend-Air Door Servo b. Substitute a Control Module c. Check pin-outs (see Fault Code Section, Blend-Air door pages)
05	a. Replace Control Module
06 07 08 09 10, 11, 12, & 13	a. Substitute a Vac-Power/Module b. Substitute a Control Module c. Check pin-outs (see Fault Code Section, Vac-Power/Module pages)
14	a. Substitute an In-Car Sensor b. Substitute a Control Module c. Check pin-outs (see Fault Code Section, In-Car Sensor pages)
15	a. Substitute an Ambient Sensor b. Substitute a Control Module c. Check pin-outs (see Fault Code Section, Ambient Sensor pages)
MULTIPLE CODES 6, 7, 9, 10, 11 12, 13 maybe 14	a. Check connectors on Vac-Power/Module b. Check ign. to Vac-Power/Module (1 may or may not occur) c. Substitute a Control Module
01, 06, 07, 08, 09, 10, 11, 12 13, 14, 15	a. Check 21-way at Control Module for connection

Note: Fault code 14 can occur with other codes and may not be a problem. Fix other error codes first and retest.

Figure 15-13. Chrysler ATC fault code chart. (Chrysler)

Two kinds of noise can affect a radio:
1. Radiated
2. Conducted.

Radiated noise results from an accessory which gives off a signal that is picked up along with the desired radio signal by the antenna. This extraneous signal is then amplified with the desired signal and fed to the speakers. It is loudest outside, when the vehicle is away from large power lines, or on weak AM/FM stations at a normal volume. Radiated noise is generally controlled by the use of capacitors or ground straps. It can be caused by:
- Defective ignition components
- Heater blower, wiper, cooling fan, or ATC system motors
- The electronics in ATC systems, trip computers, engine control computers, or instrument clusters
- Electric fuel pumps
- An overhead compass
- Loose ground straps or a loose antenna mount.

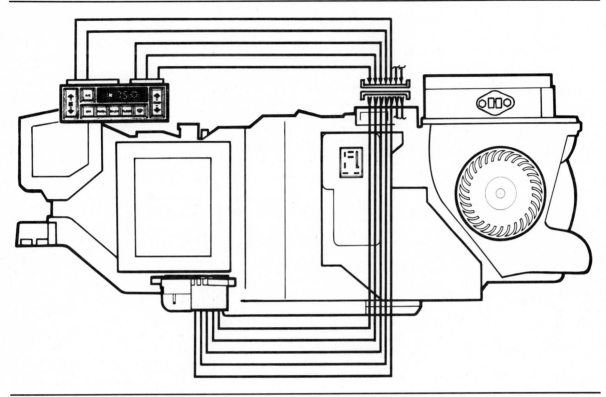

Figure 15-14. Problems with the ATC blend-air door, feed wiring, or control computer are indicated by fault codes 01, 02, 03, and 04. (Chrysler)

Conducted noise is audible only at a very low volume setting. This noise reaches the radio power feeds through component power feeds. An inline filter choke installed in the ignition power feed to the radio generally controls conducted noise. It can be caused by:
- The alternator
- Power modules
- Trim, interior, or "opera" lamps.

Some noises behave in a similar manner. If a noise increases with engine speed, it may either be a conducted alternator whine or radiated ignition noise. However, a conducted alternator whine will be louder when the electrical load is heavy, as when the headlights or a rear window defogger are on.

To distinguish between radiated and conducted noise, disconnect the antenna lead at the radio. If this eliminates the noise, you have determined that it is radiated, *not* conducted.

One way to isolate a radio noise is to pull the accessory circuit fuses one at a time to see if the noise disappears. If it does, the cause of the noise will be found within that particular circuit.

A loose antenna will result in poor FM reception. It can also cause noisy or no AM reception. Check the antenna mount to make sure it

is tight. If a known-good, or test, antenna is not available, disconnect the antenna plug from the radio and use an ohmmeter to check continuity between:
  a. The tip of the antenna mast and the pin plug on the end of the antenna cable. There should be continuity.
  b. The antenna connector plug ground shell and the plug pin. There should be no continuity.
  c. The connector ground shell and the mounting hardware on the car's fender.
To check for a nonfunctioning speaker or stereo channel, connect a known-good speaker. If the problem remains, check for an open or ground in the speaker to radio wiring. If none is found, the radio is defective.

WINDOW DEFOGGERS AND DEFROSTERS

You can troubleshoot the rear-mounted, motor-driven fan used as a window defroster in older vehicles in the same way you would a blower motor fan circuit.

Rear window defoggers using a horizontal grid of electrically conductive lines are sometimes called a heated backlight or backlight

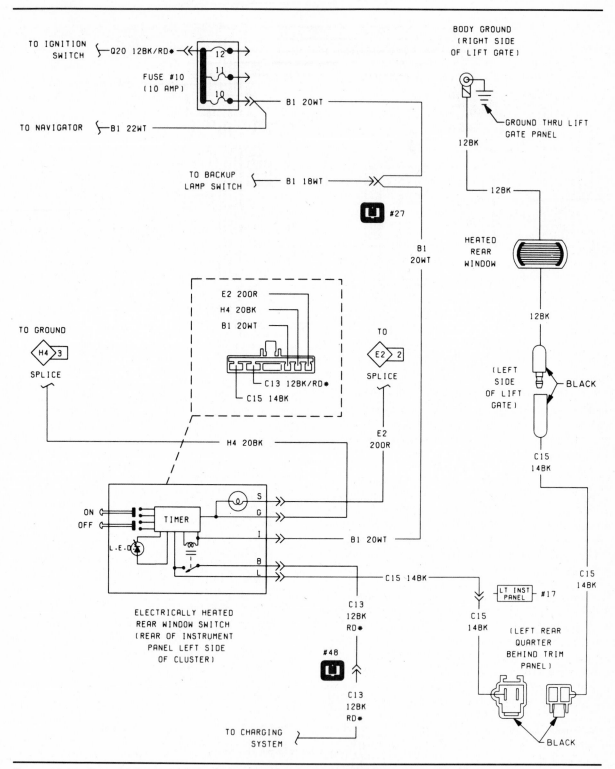

Figure 15-15. Circuit diagram for a typical Chrysler rear window defroster system. (Chrysler)

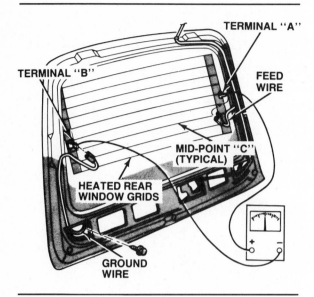

Figure 15-16. Typical test points for a backlight grid. (Chrysler)

grid. The system consists of a control switch with indicator lamp, timer relay, and an electrical grid with vertical buss bars. The grid in these systems generally is protected with a fusible link, while the relay control circuit is fused. Figure 15-15 is a typical circuit diagram.

To check the operation of a backlight grid:
1. Turn the ignition switch on.
2. Watch the vehicle ammeter or voltmeter, if so equipped, and turn on the backlight grid switch. There should be a distinct deflection of the meter needle when the switch is turned on. If the vehicle has an alternator warning lamp instead of an ammeter or voltmeter, you should be able to feel a temperature difference on the window surface within 2 to 4 minutes.
3. Connect a voltmeter as shown in figure 15-16. It should read 10 to 14 volts.

If the backlight grid does not operate, isolate the problem as follows:
1. Make sure the ignition switch is on.
2. Check the backlight grid feed wire for a loose or corroded connection. Correct as required.
3. Check the backlight grid ground wire for a proper ground. Correct as required.
4. Check the fusible link and fuse. Correct as required.
5. If the system check is satisfactory to this point, either the control switch or the relay timer is defective, or there is an open in the feed wire. A break in one grid wire will cause only the broken wire to malfunction. All of the grid wires would have to be broken to render the entire backlight grid inoperative.

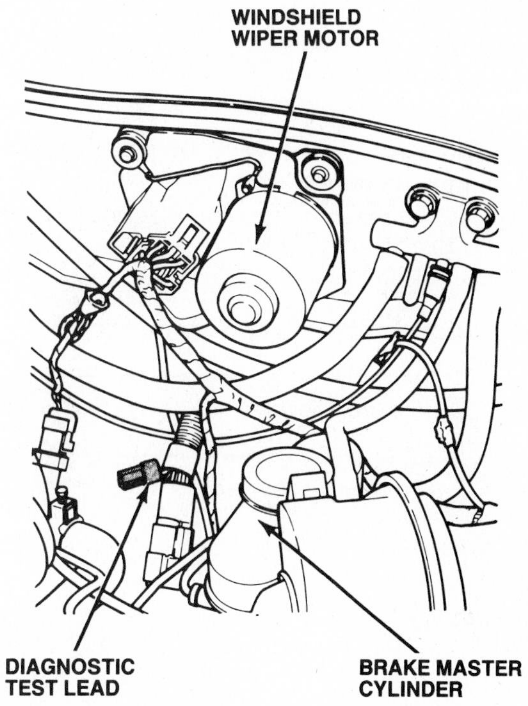

Figure 15-17. Grounding this diagnostic connector in the engine compartment of Fords with a heated windshield system overrides the control module's temperature control. (Ford)

The control switch and relay can be tested with an ohmmeter and voltmeter using a circuit diagram and the procedures you have learned. To test the backlight grid lines:
1. Turn the ignition and control switch on.
2. Connect a voltmeter (−) lead to the ground terminal of the grid (terminal B, figure 15-16) and the (+) lead to the feed terminal of the grid (terminal A, figure 15-16):
   a. If the voltage is 10 to 14 volts, move the voltmeter (−) lead to a good ground. The voltage should not change.
   b. If the voltage is less than 10 volts, there is a bad ground connection.
3. Reconnect the voltmeter (−) lead to the ground terminal of the grid. Touch each grid line at its midpoint, figure 15-16, with the (+) lead:
   a. If the voltage is approximately 6 volts, the line is good.
   b. If no voltage is shown, there is a break in the line between the midpoint and the feed terminal.
   c. If the voltage is 10 to 14 volts, there is a break in the line between the midpoint and the ground terminal.
4. If a break in the line is indicated, move the voltmeter (+) lead in the direction of the break.

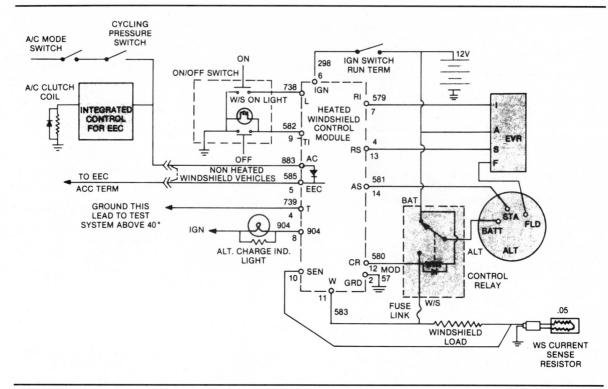

Figure 15-18. The circuit diagram for Ford's heated windshield system. (Ford)

As soon as the (+) lead crosses the break, the voltmeter reading will change.

If the backlight grid operates, but it does not heat up enough, there may be too much resistance in the system. Disconnect the feed and ground wires from their terminals. Connect an ohmmeter between the terminals and compare the reading to the carmaker's specifications.

HEATED WINDSHIELD

Since the Ford heated windshield uses alternator voltage to power the system, make sure that the charging system is in good operating condition before attempting to troubleshoot a nonfunctional windshield. To override the control module's ambient temperature control, ground the black diagnostic test lead in the engine compartment, figure 15-17.

Figure 15-18 is a circuit diagram of the Ford heated windshield system. To troubleshoot a window that will not heat, check the battery, drive belt tension, and all system wiring connections, making any repairs or corrections required, then perform the following procedure:
1. Ground the test connector, figure 15-17, with a jumper wire to an engine ground. Connect a voltmeter between the alternator BAT terminal and ground. Set the voltmeter to the 100-volt scale.

2. Start the engine and run at 1,000 to 1,500 rpm with all accessories off.
3. Turn the windshield heater control switch on. Wait 10 seconds and read the voltmeter:
   a. If the voltage exceeds 30 volts, go to step 8.
   b. If the voltage is 13 to 15 volts, go to step 4.
   c. If no voltage is shown, replace the control module.
4. Remove the alternator output control relay cover from behind the right front fender splash shield. Turn on the ignition and windshield heat switches, but do not start the engine. Connect the voltmeter between the relay MOD terminal push-on connector and ground:
   a. If the voltage is approximately 1 volt, the system is functioning properly. Go to step 6.
   b. If no voltage is shown, go to step 5.
   c. If the voltage exceeds 2 volts, go to step 10.
5. Remove the alternator relay MOD terminal push-on connector. Connect the voltmeter directly to the MOD terminal and ground:
   a. If the voltage is approximately 9 volts, go to step 10.
   b. If no voltage is shown, replace the output control relay.

A7 WINDSHIELD RESISTANCE TEST

| Disconnect windshield connector and measure resistance across windshield. | Less than 1 ohm or greater than 4 ohms. | Replace or service windshield. |
| | Resistance is 1–4 ohms. | System is operating properly. Go to A8. |

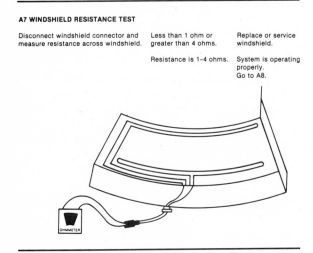

Figure 15-19. Ohmmeter test of windshield resistance. (Ford)

6. Repeat step 5 with the voltmeter connected between the alternator relay W/S terminal and ground:
  a. If the voltage exceeds 30 volts, go to step 7.
  b. If no voltage is shown, replace the output control relay.
7. Unplug the windshield connector. Connect the voltmeter between the connector and ground. Start the engine and run at 1,000 to 1,500 rpm with all accessories off. Turn on the windshield heater control switch. Wait 10 seconds and read the voltmeter:
  a. If the voltage exceeds 30 volts, go to step 8.
  b. If no voltage is shown, trace and repair the wiring between the windshield connector and the alternator output relay.
8. Connect an ohmmeter across the windshield connector terminals, figure 15-19:
  a. If the resistance is 1 to 4 ohms, go to step 9.
  b. If the resistance is outside the 1 to 4 ohms specified, replace the windshield.
9. Disconnect the current-sense resistor connector and connect an ohmmeter between the connector terminals:
  a. If the resistance exceeds 0.1 ohm, replace the sense resistor.
  b. If the resistance is less than 0.1 ohm, go to step 10.
10. Connect the voltmeter between the windshield control module connector terminal 6 and ground. Turn on the ignition switch, but do not start the engine:
  a. If battery voltage is shown, go to step 11.
  b. If no voltage is shown, trace and repair the wiring between the connector and ignition switch.

11. Move the voltmeter (+) lead to the connector terminal 12 and turn off the ignition switch:
  a. If battery voltage is shown, go to step 12.
  b. If voltage is 1 to 10 volts, replace the control module.
  c. If no voltage is shown, trace and repair the wiring between the alternator output control relay coil and the control module.
12. With the voltmeter connected as in step 11, start the engine and run at 1,000 to 1,500 rpm with all accessories off. Turn on the windshield heater control switch. Wait 10 seconds and read the voltmeter:
  a. If voltage at terminal 12 drops from battery voltage to about 1 volt shortly after the switch is turned on, the system is functioning properly.
  b. If voltage at terminal 12 remains above 3 volts or under 1.5 volts, replace the control module.

POWER WINDOWS AND SEATS

The control switch, wiring, and any relays used in these circuits can be tested with an ohmmeter and voltmeter using a circuit diagram and the procedures you have learned. The next section provides a review of the proper technique.

Depending upon the system you are troubleshooting, the motor may be a single-, dual- or three-armature design. The circuit diagram will tell you which one you are testing. To test motor operation:
1. Disconnect the electrical connections at the motor terminals. Connect the motor terminals to the battery with number 14 jumper wires. Replace the motor if it does not run.
2. Reverse the jumper wire connections at the motor terminals. Replace the motor if it does not operate in the opposite direction.
3. Repeat steps 1 and 2 to test the remaining armatures of dual- and three-armature motors. Replace the motor if it fails to run at any step.

POWER DOOR LOCKS, TRUNK LATCHES, AND SEAT BACK RELEASES

Just as with other electrical accessory systems, you will need the carmaker's electrical schematic to test the locking systems on a particular vehicle. As you learned in Chapter 1, the ability to read wiring diagrams and analyze the problem with a circuit schematic can be applied to any electrical problem. The schematic is used to narrow down the possibilities and reduce the amount of troubleshooting required.

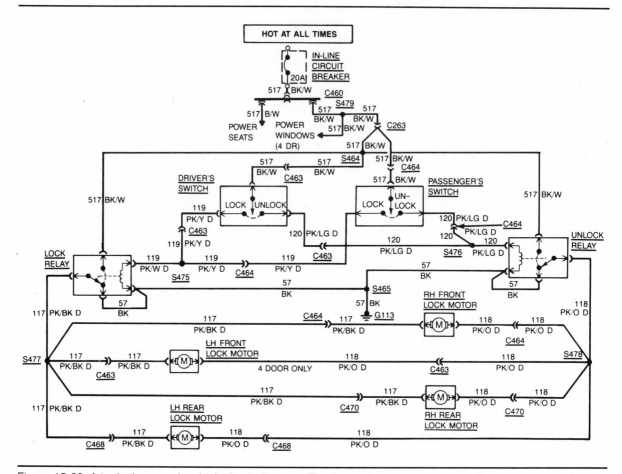

Figure 15-20. A typical power door lock circuit diagram. (Ford)

As an example, suppose that the power door lock system shown in figure 15-20 can be locked with the power switch, but not unlocked. Applying the symptom to the circuit diagram, you can deduce the following:
- The inline breaker is good.
- Since both switches lock the door, both switches are probably good.
- Circuit 119 energizes the lock relay, so it is good. This means that the ground circuit 57 is good.
- Circuit 517 provides power to the switches and lock relay, so it is good.
- Circuit 117 transmits power from the relay to the motors in the lock position, so it is good.
- Circuit 118 is the ground path in the lock position for all of the motors to the unlock relay, so it is good.
- The ground path through the unlock relay and circuit 57 is good.
- The motors are good.

You have now eliminated much of the overall circuit without using any test equipment or running any tests.

Since the following circuits and components must work in order to unlock the doors, you have isolated the problem to:
- Circuit 120 and circuit 517 to the unlock relay.
- The unlock relay itself.
- The ground circuit 57 between the lock relay coil and contacts.

You now have identified the components and wires that are most likely causing the problem. Since the unlock relay is the only component in your analysis, it is a good point to begin testing:

1. Use the carmaker's component location chart (if you do not already know its location) to find the unlock relay.

2. Have an assistant hold the door lock switch in the unlocked position while you probe circuit 118 connector on the relay with a 12-volt test lamp as shown in figure 15-21:

   a. If the test lamp lights, the relay is working properly. Trace and repair the ground wiring between the relay coil and contacts (circuit 57).

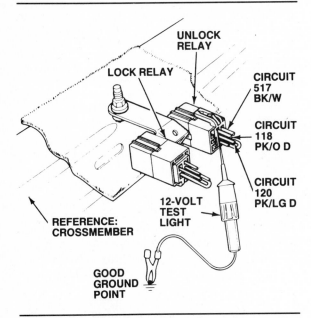

Figure 15-21. Testing a power door lock system unlock relay with a test lamp. (Ford)

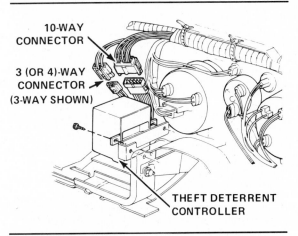

Figure 15-22. Delco's UTD system controller contains the electronics and power relays that operate the system. (GM)

b. If the test lamp does not light, the voltage signal is not passing through the relay to the door lock motors. Go to step 3.

3. Repeat step 2 to probe circuit 120 on the relay:

a. If the test lamp lights, the problem is in circuit 517 or the relay. Go to step 4.

b. If the test lamp does not light, locate and repair the open in circuit 120.

4. Repeat step 2 to probe circuit 517 on the relay:

a. If the test lamp lights, replace the unlock relay.

b. If the test lamp does not light, locate and repair the open in circuit 517 between the unlock relay and splice S464.

THEFT DETERRENT SYSTEMS

When you are troubleshooting a factory-installed antitheft system, the carmaker's circuit diagrams will provide you with a road map to isolate the problem. Troubleshooting an after-market installation may prove more difficult, because it is unlikely that you will have a circuit diagram of the system. We will cover the Delco UTD system in this section; however, you should be able to apply the principles to other systems.

Before making any diagnostic tests, you should be sure that the following components and circuits work properly:
- Parking and low beam headlights
- Dome and courtesy lights
- Horn
- Wipers
- Clock
- Electric door locks (if so equipped).

Correct any problems and then do the following operational sequence, leaving a door window open to let you open the door without a key. The operational check should confirm the driver's complaint.

1. Check the condition of the various components. When the system activates for no apparent reason, it may be caused by a loose lock cylinder or corrosion on one or more of the tamper switches installed in the door jambs.

2. Check the condition of the 10-way and 3- or 4-way connectors at the controller, figure 15-22, and make sure they are securely plugged in.

3. Check the inline fuse in the horn feed line that controls power to the controller. Replace as required (you should have already checked the fuses to subsystems such as lighting, the horns, and the wipers).

4. With the driver's door open, the security light should start flashing. Lock the doors with the manual door lock button or electric switch and note whether the security light changes to a steady glow. If so, get out of the car and close the door. Watch the security light. It should go off after several seconds, arming the system.

5. Reach through the open window and unlock the door with the manual door lock button or

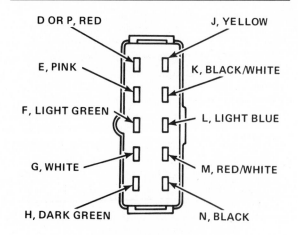

WIRING HARNESS

Figure 15-23. The UTD wiring harness 10-way controller connector terminals. (GM)

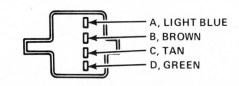

Figure 15-24. The UTD wiring harness 4-way controller connector is used with starter interlock-equipped (E-type) system. (GM)

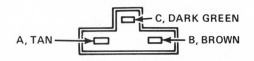

Figure 15-25. The UTD wiring harness on vehicles without a starter interlock feature uses a 3-way controller connector. (GM)

1. Connect a test lamp between ground and the D or P wire. The lamp should light if there is power to the horns.
2. Move the test lamp to the E wire. The lamp should light only when the electric door switch is tripped to unlock the doors.
3. Connect the test lamp between a 12-volt battery and the F wire. The test lamp should light brightly once the outside door key is turned to the unlock position.
4. Reconnect the test lamp to ground and probe the G wire. The lamp should remain off until the ignition switch is turned on.
5. Jumper the H wire to a good ground. The security warning lamp should come on.
6. Move the test lamp to the J wire. The lamp should light if there is power to the electrical door lock switches.
7. Connect the test lamp to a 12-volt battery and the K wire. Open a door and the lamp should light. If a door or the trunk lock cylinder has been tampered with, the lamp will light with the doors closed. Repeat this step with the L wire. The result should be the same.
8. Reconnect the test lamp to ground and probe the M wire. The lamp should light if there is power to the exterior lights.
9. Connect the test lamp to a 12-volt battery and the N wire. If the lamp lights, the system is properly grounded.
  To test the 3- or 4-way connector circuits, refer to figures 15-24 and 15-25:
1. Momentarily jumper the A wire to a 12-volt battery. The horns should sound if the circuit is complete.
2. Repeat step 1 with the B wire. The low-beam headlights should come on.
3. Repeat step 1 with the C wire. The parking, taillamp and side-marker lights should all come on.
4. Ground the D wire with a jumper. If the starter interlock relay is good, you should be able to start the engine.
  These tests will indicate if any of the circuits are incomplete. If so, you should check and repair or replace the individual components, wiring, fuses, or circuit breakers involved. If all circuits check out good and the UTD system does not work properly, replace the controller.

electric switch. Open the door; the horn should sound and the lights should flash. This should continue for 3 to 7 minutes before the system automatically shuts down. After assuring yourself that the horn system works properly, it is a good idea to disconnect the horn system while you wait for the time interval to pass. This will be easier on your ears and those around you.
6. Repeat the arming procedure, but remain in the vehicle and close the door. When the security light goes out (system armed), turn the ignition switch on, then off. Open the door and the alarm should not activate; it should remain in a standby mode with the security light flashing.
  Once you have completed these operational checks, you should next check all of the circuits leading into the controller. Make sure that all switches are in their normal, or off, positions, and unplug the 10-way and 3- or 4-way connectors at the controller, figure 15-22. Figure 15-23 shows the location of the terminals in a typical 10-way connector. Use a test lamp of no greater than 1 candlepower and leave it connected to ground unless otherwise specified:

16

Testing Electronic Motion Control Systems

Electronic motion control systems are relatively new and will undergo considerable modification and refinement in the coming years. For this reason, it is important that you have the manufacturer's specifications and circuit diagrams for the exact system you are testing. These control circuits do not require frequent troubleshooting. When they do, however, the following general procedures, based on common principles of operation, will help you solve the problem.

Some manufacturers provide special testers for their systems, figure 16-1. If these are available to you, follow the test procedure instructions provided with them. If a special tester is not available, you can troubleshoot most circuits with ordinary test equipment. Remember, however, that you should use a digital volt-ohmmeter (DVOM) in all circuits leading to the electronic control module. A test lamp or low-impedance meter may draw too much current and damage the circuit or its components.

SPEED CONTROL TROUBLESHOOTING

As with all electrical systems, you should thoroughly inspect the system before beginning any troubleshooting procedure. Check for bare, broken, or disconnected wires and damaged or deteriorated vacuum lines. Make sure that all vacuum line connections are good and correct any problems with loose or corroded electrical connections. Figure 16-2 shows a typical electronic speed control circuit diagram.

System Does Not Work At All

If the speed control system does not work:
1. Press the brake pedal and note whether the brake warning light works:
   a. If the warning light works, go to step 2 (manual transmission or transaxle) or step 3 (automatic transmission or transaxle).
   b. If the warning light does not work, trace and service the brake lamp circuit wiring before testing the speed control system any further.

Some carmakers provide voltage specifications for the circuit with the pedal released and with it pressed. If these are given, you can determine correct circuit operation using the procedure specified by the carmaker.
2. Disconnect the clutch switch pigtail to the speed control harness and connect an ohmmeter across the switch terminals to measure resistance with the pedal released and pressed. There should be continuity with the pedal released and no continuity when the pedal is

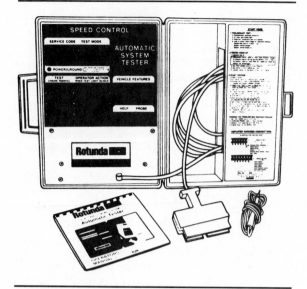

Figure 16-1. Ford's Speed Control System automatic tester is typical of the special testers offered by carmakers to check their electronic motion control systems. (Ford)

pressed. If the carmaker provides a voltage specification for switch testing, probe the specified cavity of the module connector with the voltmeter (+) lead (connect the (−) lead to ground) and obtain a voltage reading with the pedal released and pressed.

3. Verify that manifold vacuum reaches the servo, then check servo vacuum action with a hand vacuum pump and compare to manufacturer's specifications. On diesel engines, you also should check vacuum pump operation to make sure there is enough vacuum to operate the system.

If servo vacuum operation is correct, check the servo apply and release valves as follows:

a. With the ignition and speed control switches on (engine off), disconnect the servo electrical connector and check for battery voltage at the connector battery terminal with a voltmeter. If there is no voltage, trace and repair the harness wiring as required.

b. Connect the male and female connector plug battery terminals with a jumper wire and check the other terminals on the servo unit connector plug for battery voltage.

c. Connect a hand vacuum pump to the servo and apply 10 to 15 in. (25 to 38 mm) Hg vacuum; then ground the servo unit connector plug terminals to the solenoids with jumper wires. You should hear a click as each connection is made.

d. If the servo unit does not perform as specified, replace it.

4. Disconnect the speed sensor at the transmission or transaxle and connect an ohmmeter across the sensor connector terminals, figure 16-3. Replace the sensor if the resistance reading is outside the manufacturer's specifications. Some carmakers may specify an additional step. This requires sensor removal so that it can be rotated one full turn while connected to the ohmmeter. If you do this, the ohmmeter should pulse eight times during one full rotation; if not, replace the sensor.

5. If the system checks out satisfactorily to this point, you should check the control switch and circuits for opens, shorts, and continuity. You can do this with the circuit diagram and a DVOM, using the tests and procedures you have learned.

6. To check the module, connect a voltmeter (−) lead to ground and probe the module harness connector with the (+) lead, figure 16-4. Use the manufacturer's procedure and circuit diagram to determine the specific terminals to probe when the switch is in a given position.

7. Other tests may be required, depending upon the system configuration and components used. These will be found in the manufacturer's troubleshooting procedures.

Intermittent System Operation

If speed control system operation is intermittent:

1. Drive the vehicle and carefully note when the intermittent action occurs.

2. Visually inspect the components, electrical wiring, and vacuum connections. Look for loose or corroded electrical connections, poor vacuum line connections, damaged wiring, and deteriorated vacuum lines. Correct as required.

3. Check that manifold vacuum is reaching the servo, then check servo action as described under step 3 of "System Does Not Work At All" procedure above.

4. If the system checks out okay to this point, you should check the control switch and circuits for opens, shorts, and continuity. You can do this with the circuit diagram and a DVOM using the tests and procedures you have learned.

You can troubleshoot other system malfunctions by combining these basic tests according to the symptom, as shown in the table in figure 16-5.

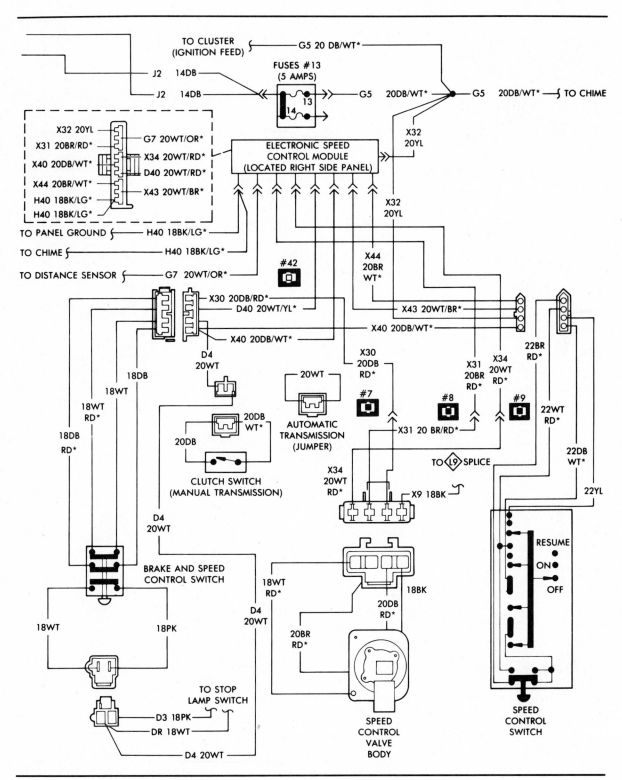

Figure 16-2. Typical electronic speed control circuit diagram. (Chrysler)

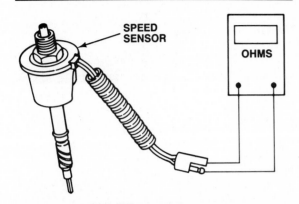

Figure 16-3. Ohmmeter test of a vehicle speed sensor. (Chrysler)

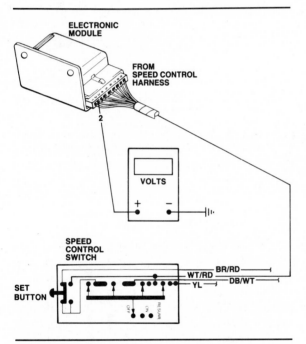

Figure 16-4. Voltage test of a speed control module. (Chrysler)

ANTILOCK BRAKE SYSTEM (ABS) TROUBLESHOOTING

Most malfunctions of an antilock brake system will light the CHECK ABS lamp or brake warning indicator lamp. These lamps may light individually, together, or in sequence. The sequence in which the warning lamps light, combined with the problem symptoms, will determine the exact diagnostic tests you must

ELECTRONIC SPEED CONTROL TROUBLESHOOTING

PROBLEM	CHECK
Speed control operates, but does not accelerate or coast down properly	Control switch and circuit servo assembly
Speed changes up or down constantly	1. Throttle linkage adjustment 2. Servo assembly 3. Speedometer cable and sensor 4. Vacuum dump valve 5. Amplifier or reservoir
Does not disengage when brakes are applied	1. Brake switch and circuit 2. Vacuum dump valve 3. Servo assembly 4. Amplifier or reservoir
Does not disengage when clutch pedal is depressed	Clutch switch and circuit
Speed does not set in system	1. Throttle linkage adjustment 2. Control switch and circuit 3. Vacuum dump valve 4. Clutch or brake switch 5. Servo assembly 6. Speed sensor
Speed wanders up or down after it is set	1. Actuator cable adjustment 2. Vacuum dump valve 3. Servo assembly
System operates but does not resume properly	1. Control switch and circuit 2. Servo assembly 3. Amplifier or reservoir
Speed will resume below 20 mph	Control module
Speed engages without operating set button	Control switch and circuit

Figure 16-5. Basic tests of a speed control system are recombined according to symptom.

perform to pinpoint the defective component. Figure 16-6 shows the symptom chart used to troubleshoot the GM TEVES system.

Since these systems are relatively new, their evolution has been, and will continue to be, quite rapid. Figures 16-7 and 16-8 show the 1986 and 1987 TEVES system schematic as used on GM cars. These illustrate the fact that you will absolutely have to have the circuit diagram and procedures relating to the specific vehicle you are troubleshooting.

Troubleshooting the Ford system requires the use of the EEC-IV breakout box. After disconnecting the 35-pin controller plug from the controller and plugging it into the breakout box, you can use an ohmmeter to perform the pinpoint diagnostic tests.

The GM TEVES system requires the use of a pin-out box, pressure gauge, and DVOM. Figure 16-9 shows the 1986-87 diagnostic procedures to be used with the symptom chart, figure 16-6, in troubleshooting this system.

SYMPTOM	ACTION
ANTILOCK light on solid, BRAKE light normal	Do Tests 1, 2, 3, 4, 5, 6. Start with Test 1, the Pin-Out Box Tests. If all Tests are good, replace the EBCM.
ANTILOCK light comes on while moving or BRAKE pedal pulses during non-antilock stops, BRAKE light normal	Measure the Wheel Speed Sensor resistances and voltage in Test 1, the Pin-Out Box Tests. If a Speed Sensor voltage is missing or low, check the gap at the toothed wheel. Also check wheel bearing end play and runout.
ANTILOCK light on solid, BRAKE light on solid	Check brake fluid level and Test 3, the Fluid Level Switches Test. Do Tests 5 and 6, the Pump Motor Test and the Pump Motor Relay Test. Do Test 2, the Pressure Switches Test. If condition persists, do the Hydraulic System Pressure Test.
Intermittent ANTILOCK light, BRAKE light normal	Do Tests 2 and 3, the Pressure Switches Test and the Fluid Level Switches Test. Check the connectors and contacts at the Wheel Speed Sensors.
ANTILOCK light normal, BRAKE light on solid	Check circuit 33 (TAN/WHT), the Park Brake Switch, and the Ignition Switch for a short to ground. Disconnect the Timer/Flasher Module. If light goes out, replace the module. Do Tests 2 and 3, the Pressure Switches Test and the Fluid Level Switches Test.
No ANTILOCK light during startup, BRAKE light normal	Check for battery voltage at terminal 27 of the Pin-Out Box. Repair open in circuit 852 (GRY/WHT) if no voltage. Check diode, terminal 27 and 3. Do Test 1.
ANTILOCK and BRAKE lights on while braking	Do Test 10, the Hydraulic System Test to check the Accumulator.
Poor tracking during ANTILOCK braking	Do Test 9, the Wheel Valve Functional Test.
Spongy brake pedal	Bleed brakes, check mounting of hydraulic unit. Check condition of calipers and rotors.
Pump motor runs longer than one minute, ANTILOCK light normal, flashing BRAKE light	Check the brake fluid level. Do Test 10, the Hydraulic System Pressure Test. Do Tests 2 and 5, the Pressure Switches Test and the Pump Relay Test. If the BRAKE light flashes but the Pump Motor turns off OK, in less than one minute, do Test 7, the Timer/Flasher Module Test. (Buick, Oldsmobile and Cadillac models only.)

Figure 16-6. The symptom chart used to troubleshoot the GM TEVES antilock braking system. (GM)

A microprocessor-based ABS tester is required to troubleshoot the Bosch ABS used by GM. This is used in conjunction with the same pin-out box and DVOM required by the TEVES system. As in the Ford system, the controller plug is plugged into the ABS tester. After the tester is powered up by turning the ignition on, it goes into a status test of input lines and checks the wheel speed sensors for continuity. System problems are displayed on a 16-character vacuum fluorescent display (VFD), figure 16-10. The fault message is used to select the appropriate diagnostic chart provided by the carmaker, which will direct you to the component to be tested.

For example, suppose the tester reads "CHK LF SPD SENS". This fault message directs you to the wheel sensor chart, which tells you that there may be an open circuit in the left front speed sensor. You would then connect the pin-out box to the module connector with the ignition switch off and check the left front sensor resistance, as well as checking the sensor wires for an open circuit.

To preserve system integrity and prevent possible problems, all manufacturers caution that the pin-out or breakout box be used instead of directly probing the ABS harness connector.

RIDE CONTROL TROUBLESHOOTING

As we saw in Chapter 21 of the *Classroom Manual*, the automatic leveling suspension systems used by domestic manufacturers rely on microprocessor control of an air compressor and air adjustable shocks. Foreign manufacturers have taken a slightly different approach to suspension control, preferring to control the shock absorber dampening rate according to driver preference or microprocessor control.

Automatic Load Level Rear Suspension

The Ford automatic leveling system used on some Ford, Lincoln, and Mercury models provides microprocessor control of the rear suspension through input data from a height sensor. The height sensor controls two basic circuits:
1. The compressor relay coil ground
2. The exhaust solenoid coil ground.

The microprocessor, or control module, can be used to perform a self-diagnostic area test with a test lamp. Do this by grounding a diagnostic pigtail located in the wiring harness near the module connector on the compressor

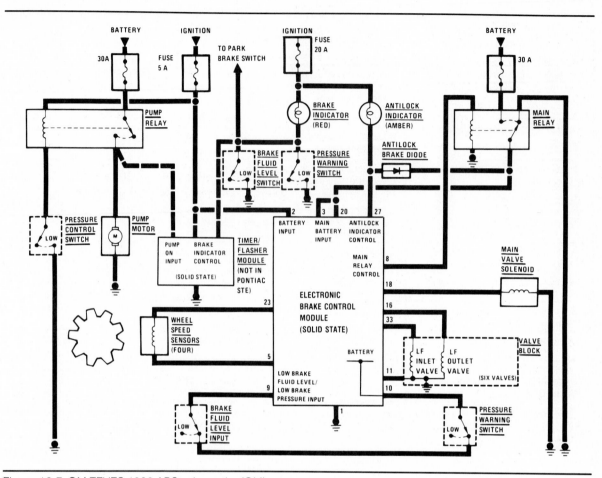

Figure 16-7. GM TEVES 1986 ABS schematic. (GM)

bracket, figure 16-11. The information provided by the area test directs you to the appropriate diagnostic chart or pinpoint test to locate the circuit problem or malfunctioning part. You then check for voltage at the component or trace and repair any open, short, or ground in the circuitry.

Before performing any electrical tests, however, you should check the air line system to make sure that the problem is not caused by a pressure loss. If you find a damaged or leaking nylon air line, fix it before starting the diagnostic procedure.

Since the module memory is lost when the ignition is turned off, you must test drive the vehicle and leave the ignition on while retrieving the failure code information from the memory.

Figure 16-12 is a circuit diagram of the system. It tells you that electrical power to operate the system is distributed from the main body wiring harness through the following circuits:

● Circuit 14A435 connects directly to circuit 12614 and supplies battery power to the system.

● Circuit 12614 transmits the battery voltage directly to the height sensor, compressor motor, relay, vent solenoid and control module.

● Circuit 14401 provides an extension of ignition switch circuit 298 (sends the ignition Run position input to the control module).

If it is necessary to connect a charger to the battery while performing the necessary diagnostic tests to maintain sufficient battery power, be careful to observe correct polarity, since internal diodes are installed in the compressor relay and vent solenoid to eliminate RFI. Reversing the battery feed and ground cables will destroy the diodes.

Electronic Height Control

The Chrysler system is less sophisticated electronically, figure 16-13, and incorporates the logic function (module) in the height sensor. An operational test is required to determine if the system is working properly. The vehicle should be tested on a flat surface with no load over the rear suspension. After turning the ignition key on, there should be a delay of 28 to

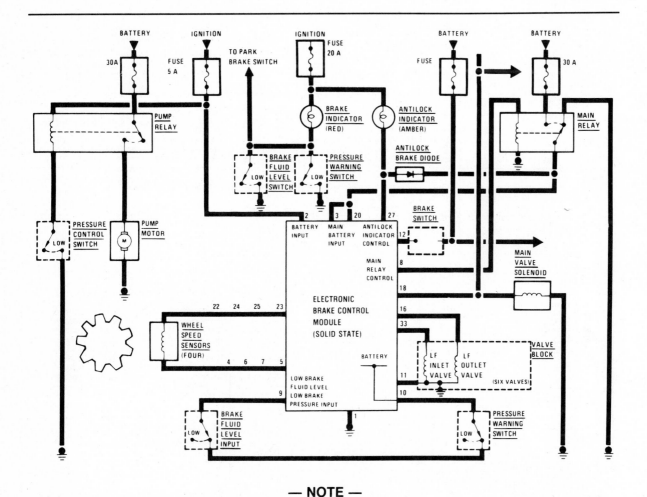

— NOTE —

A brake switch input has been added to 1987 Buick, Oldsmobile and Cadillac models. Pontiac models will have the wiring to the control module, but the input is not used for 1987 start of production.

Figure 16-8. GM TEVES 1987 ABS schematic. Notice the differences between the 1986 and 1987 systems. (GM)

56 seconds before the compressor operates for 3 to 5 seconds. As soon as this occurs, place a load of approximately 300 pounds (136 kg) over the rear suspension and note the time delay before the compressor readjusts vehicle height. It should be between 13 and 27 seconds. Once the readjustment has taken place, measure the vehicle curb height. It should be within ½ inch (13 mm) of the specified curb height. Remove the weight from the rear suspension and within 13 to 27 seconds, the compressor should make another height adjustment.

If the system does not function as specified, refer to figure 16-13 and check the circuit voltage at the height sensor pin-outs. If the sensor pin voltages are within specifications, refer to the appropriate diagnostic chart to locate the problem. Figure 16-14 shows a typical diagnostic chart to be used with the circuit diagram, figure 16-13.

Automatic Shock Dampening and Electronically Modulated Suspension

The Nissan adjustable shock absorber system relies on the three control switch lamps to indicate system problems. Diagnostic charts are used according to the sequence and combination in which the lamps come on and go off. As figure 16-15 shows, the system consists of a control switch, four sensors and control motors, and the control module. Depending upon the symptom, you may be directed to:
● Check portions of the wiring harness for opens, shorts, or grounds

COMPONENT TEST	IGN MODE	MEASURE BETWEEN PINS	SCALE	SPEC	IF NOT IN SPECS
1. Battery (EBCM pin 2)	ON	1,2	20 Volts	10V Min	Check antilock fuse and circuit 650
2. EBCM ground (EBCM pins 1, 11)	OFF	1,11	200 Ohms	Continuity	Repair circuit 450 or circuit 155
3. Wheel speed sensors A. Right rear	OFF	4,22	2K Ohms	800-1400 Ohms	Check resistance at sensor connector – if not in Specs, replace sensor. If OK, repair circuit 882 and 883
B. Left rear C. Right front D. Left front	OFF OFF OFF	6,24 7,25 5,23	2K Ohms 2K Ohms 2K Ohms	800-1400 Ohms 800-1400 Ohms 800-1400 Ohms	Same check as above – if OK, repair circuit 884, 885 Same – if OK, repair circuit 833, 872 Same – if OK, repair circuit 873, 830
4. Main relay A. Terminal 3 to relay ground B. Terminal 20 to relay ground	OFF OFF	1,3 1,20	200 Ohms 200 Ohms	Continuity Continuity	Go to Main Relay Test
5. Main relay A. Remove fuse. Use a jumper wire between breakout box pins 2, 8.	ON	1,20 1,3	20V 20V	10V Min 10V Min	Replace main relay or repair circuit 855, 640, 852, 850, diode or module harness connector
6. Main valve	OFF	11,18	200 Ohms	2-5 Ohms	Go to Main Valve Test (8)
7. Inlet valves A. Right front B. Left front C. Rear	OFF OFF OFF	11,15 11,35 11,17	200 Ohms 200 Ohms 200 Ohms	5-8 Ohms 5-8 Ohms 5-8 Ohms	Check circuit 857 – if OK, replace hydraulic unit Check circuit 858 – if OK, replace hydraulic unit Check circuit 859 – if OK, replace hydraulic unit
8. Outlet valves A. Right front B. Left front C. Rear	OFF OFF OFF	11,34 11,16 11,33	200 Ohms 200 Ohms 200 Ohms	3-5 Ohms 3-5 Ohms 3-5 Ohms	Check circuit 861 – if OK, replace hydraulic unit Check circuit 862 – if OK, replace hydraulic unit Check circuit 863 – if OK, replace hydraulic unit
9. Sensor output voltage* – Raise vehicle, turn wheel by hand. A. Right rear B. Left rear C. Right front D. Left front	OFF OFF OFF OFF	4,22 6,24 7,25 5,23	2-AC Volts 2-AC Volts 2-AC Volts 2-AC Volts	.05-.7V .05-.7V .05-.7V .05-.7V	Check air gap, toothed sensor runout, visually inspect for damage, toothed sensor, sensor face
10. Reservoir warning/pressure warning switch circuit check NOTE: Depressurize accumulator and make sure reservoir is full. A. Pressure switch (circuit 853-865 only) Turn key ON. Recharge accumulator, turn key OFF. B. Pressure switch	OFF OFF	9,10 9,10	200 Ohms 200 Ohms	Infinite Continuity	See Pressure Switch Test (2) See Fluid Level Switch Test 3 See Pressure Switch Test (2) See Fluid Level Switch Test 3
11. Antilock brake diode (Remove main relay connector)	OFF	27,20 (Reverse Meter Leads)	Diode Test	Different readings with meter leads reversed	If test is uncertain, remove diode and test it out of the circuit.
12. **Brake switch input. Ignition off, depress brake pedal.	OFF	1,12	20 Volts	10V Min	Check brake switch, brake switch input and fuse.

*Wheel Speed Sensor test must be done first.

**1987 Buick, Oldsmobile, Cadillac ONLY.

Figure 16-9. Typical diagnostic procedures used with the symptom chart shown in figure 16-6. (GM)

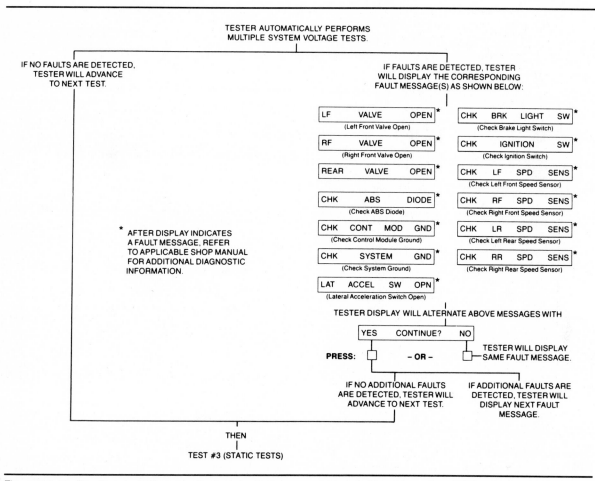

Figure 16-10. The Bosch ABS tester displays fault messages instead of trouble codes. (GM)

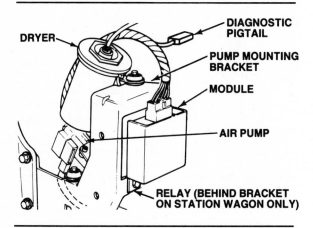

Figure 16-11. A diagnostic pigtail located near the control module must be grounded to put Ford's automatic load level system into a self-diagnostic mode. (Ford)

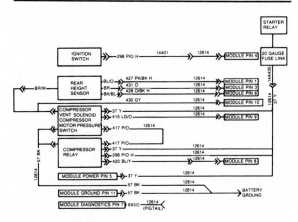

Figure 16-12. Ford's automatic load level system circuit diagram is necessary to troubleshoot electrical problems. (Ford)

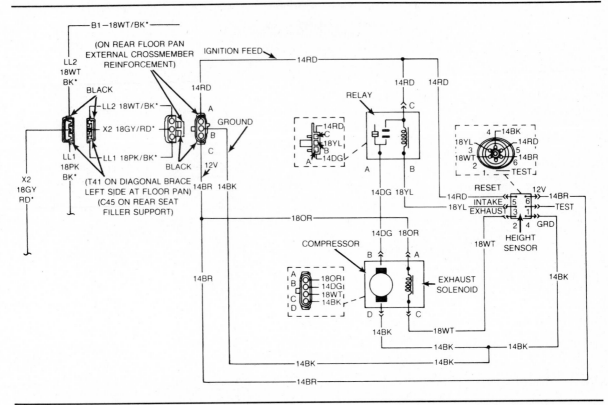

Figure 16-13. Since Chrysler's Electronic Height Control system logic is stored in the height sensor instead of a separate module, voltage checks are made at the sensor connector. (Chrysler)

- Check control module voltage as shown in figure 16-15
- Check the continuity of the sensors at the wiring harness connector, figure 16-16.

Toyota's TEMS system also uses the control switch lamps to indicate problems. However, a diagnostic connector in the engine compartment is grounded to check the steering sensor operation. With the ignition on (engine off) and the switch in the Normal position, both lights will come on for about two seconds, then start flashing. Turning the steering wheel at least a quarter turn in one direction should turn off the opposite side lamp while the other lamp continues to flash. That is, if the wheel is turned to the right, the left lamp should go out and the right lamp continue to flash. The sequence is reversed if the wheel is turned to the left. If the lamps do not light as specified according to direction of steering wheel movement, the steering sensor is defective.

The control switch lamps also are used to check automatic damping operation by bouncing the fender with the switch in different positions and noting the sequence of lamp illumination. The shock absorber actuators can be tested by:
- Listening for a click as the control switch is operated

- Bounce testing while disconnecting and connecting individual actuator connectors
- Checking for voltage at the actuator connector terminals.

Air Suspension System

Troubleshooting Ford's air suspension system is similar to diagnosing its automatic leveling system. However, the system is more complex, since it controls all four wheels. Three sensors are required — one at each front wheel and one for the rear axle.

The microprocessor, or module, provides power and ground for the three digital height sensors, continuously monitoring their input as well as the ignition Run, Brake-on, and Door-open circuits.

The microprocessor will perform a series of self-diagnostic tests (area tests) by flashing the CHECK SUSPENSION light on the overhead console. To activate the self-test:
1. Turn the air suspension switch on.
2. Connect a battery charger to prevent battery drain. Be careful to observe correct polarity, since internal diodes are installed in the compressor relay, vent solenoid, and all air spring

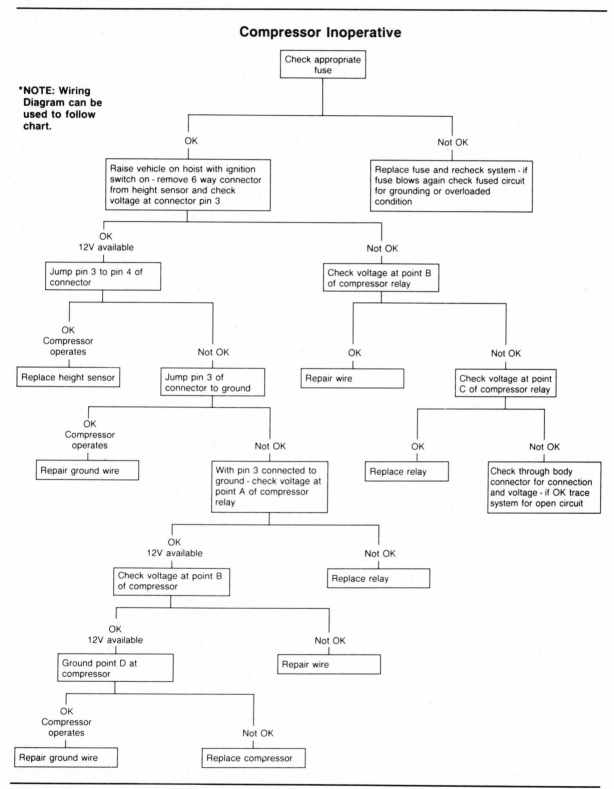

Compressor Inoperative

*NOTE: Wiring Diagram can be used to follow chart.

Figure 16-14. This diagnostic chart is used with the circuit diagram in figure 16-13 to troubleshoot Chrysler's Electronic Height Control system. (Chrysler)

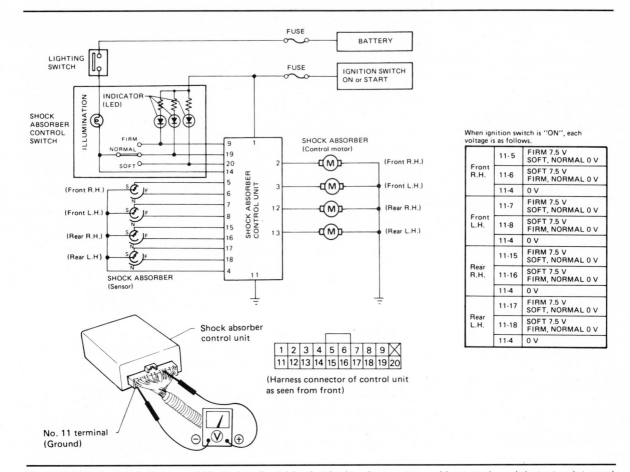

Figure 16-15. A circuit diagram of Nissan's adjustable shock absorber system, with control module test points and specifications. (Nissan)

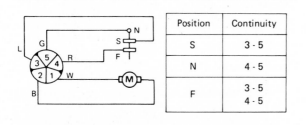

Position	Continuity
S	3 - 5
N	4 - 5
F	3 - 5 4 - 5

Figure 16-16. Adjustable shock absorber system sensors are checked for continuity at the wiring harness connector. (Nissan)

solenoids to eliminate RFI. Reversing the battery feed and ground cables will destroy the diodes.

3. With the driver's door open (all others closed), turn the ignition switch on and hold in the Run position for at least five seconds, then shut it off.

4. Ground the diagnostic pigtail in the wiring near the module connector.

5. Turn the ignition switch back on, but do not start the engine. The CHECK SUSPENSION warning lamp on the overhead console will blink continuously, indicating that the diagnostics mode has been activated.

At this point, you must refer to Ford's diagnostic procedure to perform nine tests, opening and closing the driver's door between each phase of the sequence. With some tests, the module will pass or fail the system; other tests require the service technician to make a judgment based on observing the component's operation. As with the automatic leveling system, completion of the area test will direct you to the appropriate diagnostic chart or pinpoint test to locate the circuit problem or bad part. You must then check for voltage at the component or trace and repair any open, short, or ground in the circuitry.

Before performing any electrical tests, however, you should check the air line system to make sure that the problem is not caused by a pressure leak. If you find a damaged or leaking air line, fix it before starting the diagnostic procedure.

The complexity of the system is shown in its circuit diagram, figure 16-17. This tells you that

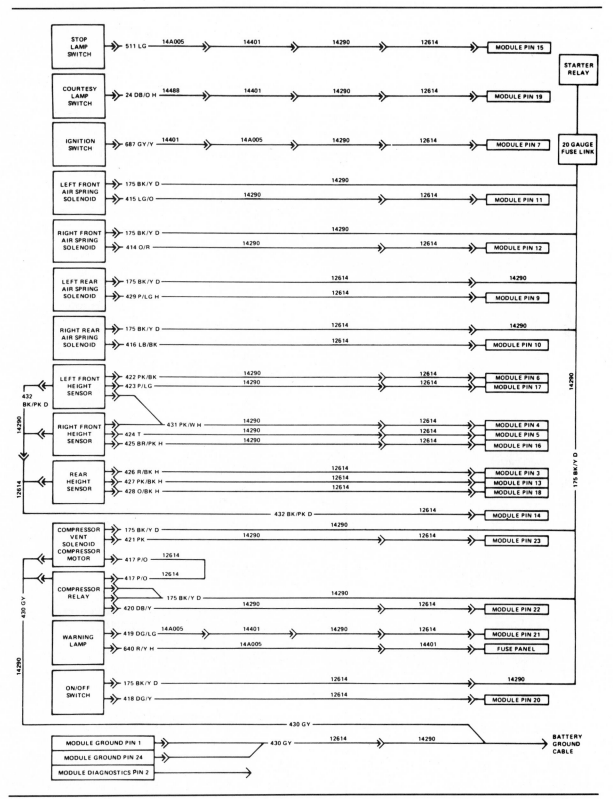

Figure 16-17. Ford's Air Suspension system circuit diagram is more complex than its automatic load level system. (Ford)

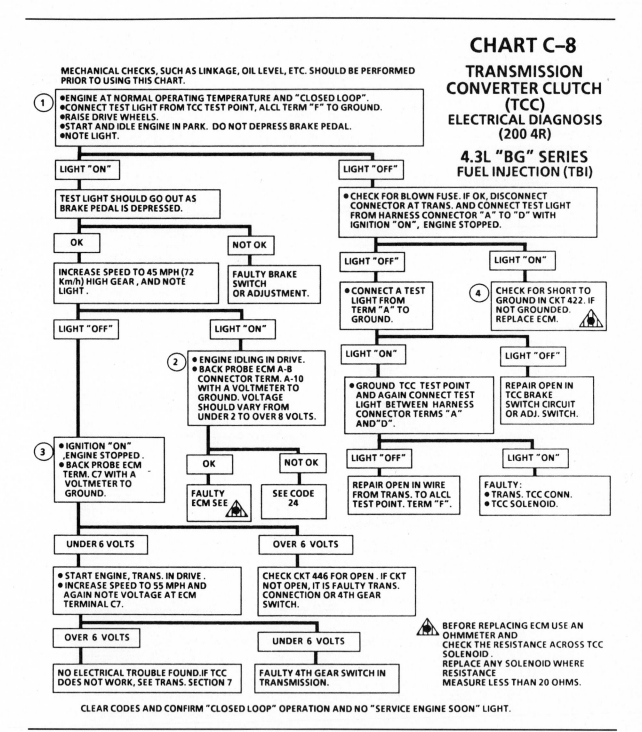

CHART C-8
TRANSMISSION CONVERTER CLUTCH (TCC)
ELECTRICAL DIAGNOSIS (200 4R)

4.3L "BG" SERIES
FUEL INJECTION (TBI)

MECHANICAL CHECKS, SUCH AS LINKAGE, OIL LEVEL, ETC. SHOULD BE PERFORMED PRIOR TO USING THIS CHART.

① ●ENGINE AT NORMAL OPERATING TEMPERATURE AND "CLOSED LOOP".
●CONNECT TEST LIGHT FROM TCC TEST POINT, ALCL TERM "F" TO GROUND.
●RAISE DRIVE WHEELS.
●START AND IDLE ENGINE IN PARK. DO NOT DEPRESS BRAKE PEDAL.
●NOTE LIGHT.

LIGHT "ON"

LIGHT "OFF"

TEST LIGHT SHOULD GO OUT AS BRAKE PEDAL IS DEPRESSED.

●CHECK FOR BLOWN FUSE. IF OK, DISCONNECT CONNECTOR AT TRANS. AND CONNECT TEST LIGHT FROM HARNESS CONNECTOR "A" TO "D" WITH IGNITION "ON", ENGINE STOPPED.

OK

NOT OK

LIGHT "OFF"

LIGHT "ON"

INCREASE SPEED TO 45 MPH (72 Km/h) HIGH GEAR, AND NOTE LIGHT.

FAULTY BRAKE SWITCH OR ADJUSTMENT.

●CONNECT A TEST LIGHT FROM TERM "A" TO GROUND.

④ CHECK FOR SHORT TO GROUND IN CKT 422. IF NOT GROUNDED. REPLACE ECM.

LIGHT "OFF"

LIGHT "ON"

LIGHT "ON"

LIGHT "OFF"

② ●ENGINE IDLING IN DRIVE.
●BACK PROBE ECM A-B CONNECTOR TERM. A-10 WITH A VOLTMETER TO GROUND. VOLTAGE SHOULD VARY FROM UNDER 2 TO OVER 8 VOLTS.

●GROUND TCC TEST POINT AND AGAIN CONNECT TEST LIGHT BETWEEN HARNESS CONNECTOR TERMS "A" AND "D".

REPAIR OPEN IN TCC BRAKE SWITCH CIRCUIT OR ADJ. SWITCH.

③ ●IGNITION "ON",ENGINE STOPPED.
●BACK PROBE ECM TERM. C7 WITH A VOLTMETER TO GROUND.

OK

NOT OK

LIGHT "OFF"

LIGHT "ON"

FAULTY ECM SEE

SEE CODE 24

REPAIR OPEN IN WIRE FROM TRANS. TO ALCL TEST POINT. TERM "F".

FAULTY:
●TRANS. TCC CONN.
●TCC SOLENOID.

UNDER 6 VOLTS

OVER 6 VOLTS

●START ENGINE, TRANS. IN DRIVE.
●INCREASE SPEED TO 55 MPH AND AGAIN NOTE VOLTAGE AT ECM TERMINAL C7.

CHECK CKT 446 FOR OPEN. IF CKT NOT OPEN, IT IS FAULTY TRANS. CONNECTION OR 4TH GEAR SWITCH.

OVER 6 VOLTS

UNDER 6 VOLTS

NO ELECTRICAL TROUBLE FOUND. IF TCC DOES NOT WORK, SEE TRANS. SECTION 7.

FAULTY 4TH GEAR SWITCH IN TRANSMISSION.

BEFORE REPLACING ECM USE AN OHMMETER AND CHECK THE RESISTANCE ACROSS TCC SOLENOID. REPLACE ANY SOLENOID WHERE RESISTANCE MEASURE LESS THAN 20 OHMS.

CLEAR CODES AND CONFIRM "CLOSED LOOP" OPERATION AND NO "SERVICE ENGINE SOON" LIGHT.

Figure 16-18. A typical GM transmission converter clutch diagnostic chart. (GM)

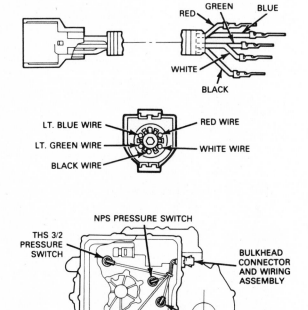

Figure 16-19. Ford AXOD transaxle converter clutch test points. (Ford)

electrical power to operate the system is distributed from the main body wiring harness through the following circuits:

• Circuit 14290 supplies battery power and ground to the system. It connects directly to the air compressor and relay, and both front air spring solenoids and height sensors.

• Circuit 12614 transmits the battery voltage directly to the rear height sensor, rear air spring solenoids, air suspension switch, and control module.

• Circuit 14401 provides an extension of ignition switch circuit 687 and sends the ignition Run position input to the control module.

• Circuit 14A005 connects to the CHECK SUSPENSION warning lamp in the overhead console and provides an extension of stoplamp switch circuit 511 (sending a brake-on input to the control module).

• Circuit 14488 provides an extension of the courtesy lamp door switch circuit 24 to send a door-open input to the control module.

AUTOMATIC TRANSMISSION OR TRANSAXLE CONTROL TROUBLESHOOTING

Electronically controlled, lockup torque converters depend on correct hydraulic line pressure and a solenoid controlled by the engine control computer, or ECM, to properly engage and disengage. All such systems will set one or more trouble codes in the ECM memory and can be retrieved following the procedures you learned in Chapter 12.

To refresh your memory and demonstrate the troubleshooting procedure used with GM transmission converter clutch systems, refer to figure 16-18 and work your way through the diagnostic procedure for a late-model Chevrolet Caprice with a Turbo Hydra-matic 200 4R automatic transmission and throttle body fuel injection. Since procedures differ according to vehicle, transmission, and model year, each diagnostic chart will be clearly identified with its proper application.

The car should be on a hoist with its rear wheels off the ground, running at normal operating temperature and in closed loop with the ALCL diagnostic terminal grounded. Note that the procedure is broken into four stages or sections:

1. Section 1 — If the test lamp is on, battery voltage is indicated and there is continuity through the TCC solenoids.

2. Section 2 — Vehicle speed sensor voltage should vary from less than 2 volts to more than 8 volts.

3. Section 3 — The lack of a signal from the 4th gear switch will not prevent the converter from locking up, but it will cause the engagement and disengagement speed points to change.

4. Section 4 — Solenoid coil resistance less than 20 ohms can result in damage to the ECM driver or internal electronic switch.

The reference to Code 24 tells you to check the vehicle speed sensor circuit.

Ford uses a different approach to troubleshooting its AXOD automatic transaxle. If a converter clutch problem is detected by the EEC-IV microprocessor, it will set one or more service codes. When these are retrieved during a self-test sequence, Ford recommends that an AXOD drive cycle test be performed:

1. Record and erase the service codes.

2. Start the engine and warm to normal operating temperature.

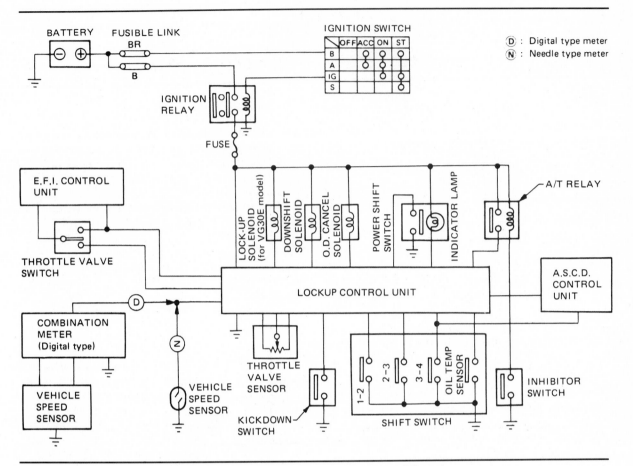

Figure 16-20. The Nissan E4N71B automatic transmission circuit diagram. (Nissan)

| 1 | 2 | 3 | | 4 | 5 | 13 | (14) | 15 | 16 | 17 |
| 6 | 7 | 8 | 9 | 10 | 11 | 12 | 18 | 19 | (20) | 21 | 22 |

(A/T control unit harness connector as seen from front)
Note: (14) and (20) is not used.

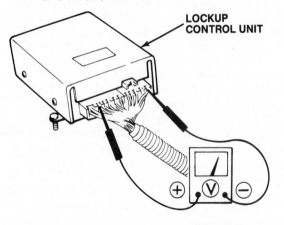

Figure 16-21. Voltage checks of the E4N71B transmission are made at the control module connector. (Nissan)

3. Place the transaxle in Drive and start off, lightly accelerating to 40 mph (65 kph). The transaxle should shift into 3rd gear. Maintain a 40-mph (65-kph) speed with a constant throttle opening for at least 15 seconds (30 seconds above 4,000 feet or 1,220 meters).

4. Move the transaxle selector to the overdrive range and accelerate from 40 mph (65 kph) to 50 mph (80 kph). The transaxle should shift into 4th gear. Maintain 50 mph (80 kph) with a constant throttle opening for at least 15 seconds.

5. Lightly apply and then release the brakes, then maintain speed and throttle opening again for at least 15 seconds.

6. Brake the vehicle to a stop and leave the transaxle in overdrive for at least 20 seconds.

7. Run the EEC-IV self-test and record any continuous codes that are retrieved.

8. Refer to the proper diagnosis charts and run pinpoint tests to determine the cause of the problem. Figure 16-19 shows the location of the AXOD bulkhead connector and wiring. It also identifies the connector terminals and wires by color code to be used for ohmmeter testing.

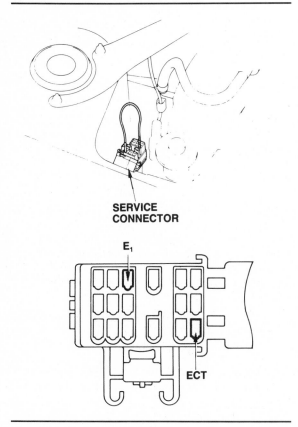

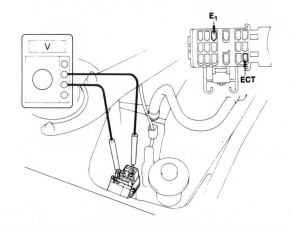

Figure 16-24. Voltmeter testing of the Toyota A14OE transaxle at the service connector. (Toyota)

Figure 16-22. Toyota's A14OE transaxle has a service connector that must be grounded to obtain fault codes. (Toyota)

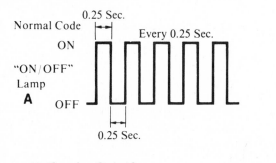

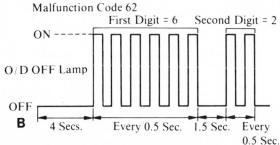

Figure 16-23. The Toyota A14OE transaxle fault code pattern. (Toyota)

Some service codes will appear which are not directly related to transaxle operation, but can affect converter clutch bypass operation. These include a malfunctioning speed sensor or a brake switch that is not operating properly. Any non-transaxle service codes that show up should be serviced first, since they may affect electrical operation of the converter clutch.

Troubleshooting the Nissan E4N718 transmission circuit, figure 16-20, involves the use of a voltmeter at the control unit, figure 16-21. A diagnostic chart identifies the terminals (No.22 is the ground). It tells the service technician what signal is being checked and how to do it, as well as providing the necessary specifications.

Toyota uses various trouble code display methods. To troubleshoot the A14OE automatic transaxle in a 1986 Celica, you must connect the ECT and E1 terminals in the service connector with a jumper wire as shown in figure 16-22. Codes are displayed by flashing of the OVER-DRIVE OFF indicator lamp, in much the same way that the GM CHECK ENGINE light works. If there is no malfunction, the lamp will flash every ¼ second, figure 16-23A. When the system has registered a code, the lamp will pause for four seconds, then flash every half second to display the first number, pause another 1.5 seconds and then flash every half second to display the second number, figure 16-23B. To check the system operation, replace the jumper wire with a voltmeter as shown in figure 16-24 and check the results against specifications.

Index

88 89 90 91 92 6 5 4 3 2